Strategic Supply Management

'Cousins et al. have drawn from their extensive experience in industry, and crafted a book that provides deep contextual insights into why supply chains are the foundation for competitive strategy, the dynamics that drive economic change, and most importantly, the importance of relationships as the glue that keeps supply chains functioning properly. Executives and students will benefit from the frameworks, examples, and discussions in this book, which should be on the bookshelves of everyone who has an interest in global competitiveness.'

Rob Handfield
Bank of America University Distinguished Professor of Supply Chain Management
North Carolina State University
Consulting Editor, *Journal of Operations Management*
Director, Supply Chain Resource Cooperative

Strategic Supply Management
Principles, Theories and Practice

Professor Paul Cousins
Professor of Operations Management
CIPS Professor of Supply Chain Management
The University of Manchester, Manchester Business School

Professor Richard Lamming
Director
School of Management, University of Southampton

Dr Benn Lawson
Senior Lecturer in Operations Management
CIPS Research Fellow
School of Management and Economics, Queen's University Belfast

Dr Brian Squire
Lecturer in Operations and Supply Chain Management
The University of Manchester, Manchester Business School

 Prentice Hall
FINANCIAL TIMES

An imprint of **Pearson Education**
Harlow, England • London • New York • Boston • San Francisco • Toronto • Sydney • Singapore • Hong Kong
Tokyo • Seoul • Taipei • New Delhi • Cape Town • Madrid • Mexico City • Amsterdam • Munich • Paris • Milan

Pearson Education Limited

Edinburgh Gate
Harlow
Essex CM20 2JE
England

and Associated Companies throughout the world

Visit us on the World Wide Web at:
www.pearsoned.co.uk

First published 2008

ISBN: 978-0-273-65100-0

British Library Cataloguing-in-Publication Data
A catalogue record for this book is available from the British Library

10 9 8 7 6 5 4 3 2 1
12 11 10 09 08 07

Typeset in 10/12.5pt Sabon by 35
Printed by Ashford Colour Press Ltd., Gosport

The publisher's policy is to use paper manufactured from sustainable forests.

The authors would like to express their thanks to their families for help throughout the years.

Joan and David Cousins, Julia, Tony, Ash and Elly
PDC

Leigh, Louise and Rosie Lamming
RCL

Norman and Dawn Lawson, Karen, Lauren, Kate and Corey
BRL

Cliff and Jill Squire
BCS

Contents

Part 2
DEVELOPING SUPPLY STRATEGY 89

Chapter 7
Supply strategy: the development of the strategic supply wheel 91

Chapter 8
Aligning supply with corporate strategy 99

Chapter 9
Competency and skills development for strategic supply   111

Chapter 10
Organisational structures for supply management   126

Part 3
STRATEGIC ISSUES IN SUPPLY CHAIN MANAGEMENT   193

Chapter 14
Environmental and ethical issues in supply management   195

Chapter 15
Involving suppliers in new product development   216

List of figures

List of tables

List of boxes

Preface

The original idea for this book emerged in 2002: four years ago, as we write this page. It began with Paul Cousins and Richard Lamming discussing the lack of a structured strategically focused text for teaching supply management. Instead of bemoaning it, we decided to write the text ourselves. Having embarked on the exercise we realised why such a text did not exist! The subject area is vast, wide ranging and still developing. During the first few years of the project, Richard took up the Directorship of the School of Management at the University of Southampton and Paul spent time working in Melbourne, Australia, at Queen's University Belfast and eventually settled at Manchester Business School, The University of Manchester. In 2005 we decided that this book would not be completed without further authors. It was at this point that we recruited Dr Benn Lawson (Queen's University Belfast) and Dr Brian Squire (Manchester Business School) to help with the writing. This proved to be an excellent choice and both Benn and Brian have worked extremely hard to make the book into what it is today.

Acknowledgements

Authors' acknowledgements

Creating a book of this size and time scale involves a large number of people in addition to those listed on the front cover. This section affords us the opportunity to formally thank those people that have supported us and enabled this book to come to fruition.

First, we should like to thank those people who have had a direct involvement in the production of the book. One of the most important people in helping us to get organised and deliver this text on time was Lesley Gilchrist. Lesley has worked tirelessly with us: she has helped to typeset the entire text, kept us focused and made sure everything was presented in a coherent and uniform manner. We are very grateful to Lesley for her help and professional attitude: thank you, Lesley. Secondly, we would like to thank our Research Assistant Craig Artley. Craig has provided background research for every chapter. He has also helped in the management process. Craig leaves us in September 2006 to pursue a postgraduate degree and we wish him well with his future endeavours. Third, we should like to acknowledge the important contribution to Chapter 16 made by Mr Fred Harvey, one of the UK's leading experts on European Procurement regulation. Finally, we would like to thank Sam Alford who took over the management of the book and through her perseverance and tenacity made sure that the authors delivered a timely and quality product – thanks very much, Sam.

Next, we should like to thank our anonymous reviewers for their helpful and encouraging comments. We would also like to thank our publishers, commissioning editor and editorial adviser Matthew Oxenham and in the latter stages Matthew Smith for his management of this book project.

Finally, we should like to thank our families, friends and partners for supporting us during the writing of this text. Anyone who has taken on a large project will know how time consuming and draining such a project is. Whilst work colleagues can offer professional support, it is families and friends that take most of the strain. We would like to thank them for their help and support. Specifically we would like to thank Leigh Lamming, Jennifer Cassels and Karen Coyle.

Publisher's acknowledgements

We are grateful to the following for permission to reproduce copyright material:

Figure 1.2, Figure 7.2, Figure 8.1, Figure 9.1, Figure 9.6, Figure 10.1, Figure 11.1, Figure 12.1, Figure 13.1 and Figure 13.3 reprinted from *European Journal of*

Purchasing and Supply Management, 8 (2), Cousins, P. D., A conceptual model for managing long-term inter-organisational relationships, 71–82, Copyright (2002), with permission from Elsevier; Figure 2.4 from Developing the concept of supply strategy in *International Journal of Operations & Production Management*, Emerald Group Publishing Limited (Harland, C. M., Lamming, R. C. and Cousins, P. D. 1999); Table 2.1 this article was published in *Journal of Purchasing and Materials Management*, **24**, Reck, R. F. and Long, B. G., Purchasing: a competitive weapon, pp. 2–8, Copyright Elsevier (1988); Box 2.1 from *www.clearspeed.com*, ClearSpeed Technology plc (note that information published on the ClearSpeed Website may be subject to change); Figure 2.3 from An empirical taxonomy of purchasing functions, in *International Journal of Operations and Production Management*, Emerald Group Publishing Limited, (Cousins, P. D., Lawson, B. and Squire, B. 2006); Figure 3.3 reprinted from Comparative Economic Organization: The Analysis of Discrete Structural Alternatives by Oliver E. Williamson published in *Administrative Science Quarterly*, Volume 36, June by permission of *Administrative Science Quarterly*, Volume 36. © Johnson Graduate School of Management, Cornell University; Box 3.3 from Twenty five years of contact lenses: the impact on the cornea and ophthalmic practice in *Cornea: The Journal of Cornea and External Diseases* 19 (5), pp. 730–40, Lippincott, Williams & Wilkins (McMahon, T. O. D. and Zadnik, K. 2000); Figures 4.2 and 9.4 from Purchasing must become supply management in *Harvard Business Review*, Harvard Business School Publishing (Kraljic, P. 1983); Figure 4.3 adapted with the permission of The Free Press, a Division of Simon & Schuster Adult Publishing Group, from COMPETITIVE ADVANTAGE: Creating and Sustaining Superior Performance by Michael E. Porter. Copyright © 1985, 1998 by Michael E. Porter. All rights reserved; Figure 6.3 from Sako, M., Supplier development at Honda, Nissan and Toyota: comparative case studies of organizational capability enhancement, *Industrial and Corporate Change*, (2004), 13 (2), pp. 281–308, by permission of Oxford University Press; Box 6.2 from *www.unctad.org*, United Nations; Figure 6.4 from Avoid the pitfalls in supplier development in *MIT Sloan Management Review* (Handfield, R. B. et al. 2000). Copyright 2000 by Massachusetts Institute of Technology. All rights reserved. Distributed by Tribune Media Services; Box 8.2 from *Strategies for Change: Logical Incrementalism*, © The McGraw-Hill Companies, Inc., (Quinn, J. B. 1980); Figure 8.3 from What is the right supply chain for your product? in *Harvard Business Review*, Harvard Business School Publishing (Fisher, M. 1997); Box 8.1 from Align buying and corporate strategies, chairman urges in *The Journal of Supply Chain Management*, Blackwell Publishing (Arminas, D. 2002); Figure 11.6 Copyright © 1996, by The Regents of the University of California, Reprinted from the *California Management Review*, Vol. 39, No. 1. By permission of the Regents; Table 12.1 from A smarter way to buy in *Harvard Business Review*, Harvard Business School Publishing (Degraeve, Z. and Roodhooft, F. 2001); Box 12.1 from Achieving world-class supplier quality by Trent, Robert J. and Monczka, Robert M., *Total Quality Management & Business Excellence*, (1999), reprinted by permission of the publisher (Taylor & Francis Ltd, http://www.informaworld.com); Figure 12.3 from Purchasing: the cornerstone of the total cost of ownership concept in *Journal of Business Logistics*, Council of Supply Chain Management Professionals (Ellram, L. M. and Perrott-Siferd, S. 1993);

Figure 13.4 from The alignment of appropriate firm and supply strategies for competitive advantage in *International Journal of Operations and Production Management*, Emerald Group Publishing Limited (Cousins, P. D. 2005); Figure 13.8 from Mari Sako, *Price, Quality and Trust*, (1992) Cambridge University Press; Figure 14.1 from Environmental soundness: a pragmatic alternative to expectations of sustainable development in business strategy in *Business Strategy and the Environment* (Lamming, R. C., Faruk, A. C. and Cousins, P. D. 1999); Figures 14.2, 14.3, 14.4, 14.5 and 14.6 from The environment: issue and implications for purchasing in *The Environment and Purchasing: Problem or Opportunity*, The Chartered Institute of Purchasing and Supply (Lamming, R. C. and Hampson, J. 1996); Tables 16.1 and 16.2 © Crown copyright, 2007. Reproduced under the terms of the Click-Use licence; Box 19.2 from New computer system for NHS to improve patient care in *Telecomworldwire*, M2 Communications Ltd, (5 September 2005); Box 19.5 from Medical News Today, *www.medicalnewstoday.com*.

p14 from A structural analysis of the effectiveness of buying firms' strategies to improve supplier performance in *Decision Sciences*, Decision Sciences Institute (Krause, D. R., Scannell, T. V. and Calantone, R. J. 2000).

In some instances we have been unable to trace the owners of copyright material, and we would appreciate any information that would enable us to do so.

Abbreviations

3PL	Third party logistics	NGO	Non-governmental organisations
ABC	Activity-based costing	NPD	New product development
AHP	Analytical hierarchical processing	NVQ	National Vocational Qualification
ASP	Application Software Provisions	ODM	Original design manufacturers
B2B	Business to business	OEM	Original equipment manufacturers
B2C	Business to consumer	OGC	Office of Government Commerce
CCT	Compulsory competitive tendering	*OJEU*	*Official Journal of the European Union*
CIPS	Chartered Institute of Purchasing and Supply	OLA	Operating level agreement
CKD	Completely knocked down	OSI	Open systems integration
CPD	Collaborative product development	PC	Personal computer
CSR	Corporate social responsibility	PCDM	Purchasing Competency Development Model
DOU	Discrete operating units	PEST	Political, Economic, Social and Technological
DPS	Dynamic purchasing system		
DRAM	Dynamic random access memory	PFI	Private Finance Initiative
EDI	Electronic data interchange	PIN	Prior Indicative Notices
ERP	Enterprise resource planning	PQQ	Pre-qualification questionnaire
ESI	Early supplier involvement	RBV	Resource-based view
FM	Facilities management	RFI	Request for information
GATT	General Agreement on Tariffs and Trade	RFP	Request for proposal
		RFQ	Request for quotation
GDP	Gross domestic product	ROP	Return on partnership
GPA	Government Purchasing Agreement	SBR	Strategic supply-base reduction
GSM	Global supply management	SCM	Supply chain management
ICT	Information and communications technology	SDR	Special Drawing Rights
		SDS	Service delivery system
IPT	Integrated project teams	SFOM	Strategic Focused Outcomes Model
ISP	Internet service provider	SINPD	Supplier integration in new product development
ITP	Invitation to participate		
ITT	Invitation to tender	SLA	Service level agreement
JIT	Just-in-time	SMART	Specific, Measurable, Actionable, Relevant, and Timely
MCDM	Multi-criteria decision-making		
MEAT	Most Economically Advantageous Tender	SME	Small and medium-sized enterprises
		SoW	Statement of work
MRO	Maintenance, repairs and overhaul	SRPM	Strategic Relationship Positioning Model
MRP	Materials requirement planning		
MRP II	Material resource planning	TCA	Total cost of acquisition
NAFTA	North American Free Trade Agreement	TCE	Transaction cost economics

TCO	Total cost of ownership	TQM	Total quality management
TQEM	Total quality environmental management	WCM	World-class manufacturing
		WTO	World Trade Organization

Part 1

THE FUNDAMENTALS OF SUPPLY

Chapter 1

The supply challenge

Aim of chapter

The aim of this chapter is to set out the structure of our book and provide a brief overview and scene setting of the development of purchasing and supply management, from its origins as a tactically based, commercial function to a strategic process, which is how it is viewed or aspires to be seen today – a key element for business success.

Introduction

In this book we integrate conceptual models with practical examples in order to focus on theory and application. Our perspective begins with developing a philosophical and theoretical understanding of the subject area. We shall then build on concepts and models that help to explain and expand on these philosophies. Finally, through the use of boxed case examples we illustrate techniques that can be used to implement the philosophies and concepts discussed in this book. It is important for the reader to realise that it is essential to have an understanding of all three dimensions of the subject area, illustrated in Figure 1.1. Understanding philosophy, concepts and techniques is necessary if successful change is to be facilitated within organisations. Our pedagogical approach is designed to permit the reader to understand how the various theories, concepts and models discussed in this book can be applied to business organisations in the private and public sectors and in manufacturing and service businesses.

We shall explain the traditional, conventional concepts of purchasing and supply management but also introduce new ideas, radical concepts, and examples of interesting practice. In presenting these, we draw on extensive research and experience in this field over 25 years, in several countries around the world.

Structure of the book

The book is designed to provide a comprehensive course structure for the teaching and studying of this wide and constantly developing topic area; in other words, the book aims to take the reader through a logical development of knowledge

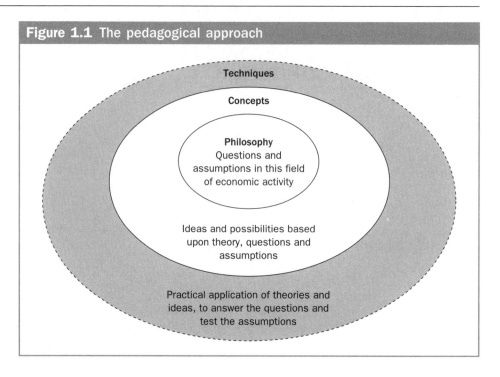

Figure 1.1 The pedagogical approach

providing extensive coverage of this complex topic area. However, students and practitioners can also use this book in two other ways. Firstly, the book can be read on a section-by-section basis. Whilst the sections build on each other, they can also be read in a 'stand-alone' context. Secondly, the book can be used by students and practitioners as a reference work providing a comprehensive overview of each area. Whilst writing and editing this book we have tried to ensure that the explanation is clear in a practical sense, but the reader must be prepared to think conceptually to make the best use of the text. Finally, we have also tried to ensure that at the time of going to print the most up-to-date references and websites have been referenced.

This book is divided into four sections; we will now briefly discuss each of these to give the reader a flavour of the content and focus.

Part 1: The fundamentals of supply

This section develops a discussion on the development of purchasing and supply. We open with the supply challenge, which examines the question 'why is supply important?' Chapter 2 discusses the evolution of purchasing and supply by examining the historical development of manufacturing paradigms, from craft, mass production, lean and eventually to agile. Chapter 3 introduces some of the underlying economic theories of transaction cost economics (TCE) and the resource-based view (RBV) as theoretical 'lenses' through which we can explain, understand and predict the role of supply management. Chapter 4 begins by discussing the concept of sourcing configurations. This chapter examines how supply strategists might structure their supply markets and which relationships are appropriate within each structure. Chapter 5 discusses supplier selection and evaluation mechanisms, using a technique called analytical hierarchical processing (AHP). Finally Chapter 6 discusses supplier development, by examining how buyers can work effectively with suppliers to improve overall levels of firm performance.

Part 2: Developing supply strategy

This section introduces a model known as the strategic supply wheel (Figure 1.2) as developed by Cousins (2002).

We use the supply wheel as a framework to discuss the main issues relating to supply management. The model brings together the key areas for consideration in strategic supply management, introducing theories, concepts and techniques.

The supply wheel was developed to explain and teach the main principles and concepts of supply management. The model was born out of a three-year research project which examined 750 firms across both the private and public sectors. In addition, a further 25 best practice interviews were conducted to confirm the model's validity. The supply wheel illustrates that managers and academics should not consider any one element in isolation, for example focusing on relationship manage-

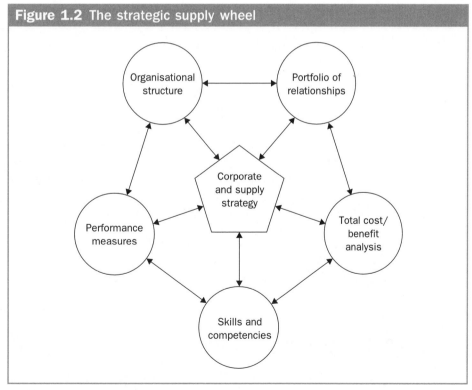

Figure 1.2 The strategic supply wheel

Source: Cousins (2002)

ment and ignoring measurement, improving skills and ignoring the structure of the supply process and so on. Each of these elements is interrelated. At the centre of the model is the development of supply policy and strategy. It is this policy and strategy development that holds the wheel together – without this it would fall apart. The model shows that the level of alignment and strategic thinking from the firm will affect all elements of the model and vice versa. For example, the firm could have a great strategy, but if it does not have the people or the infrastructure to deliver it then the policies and strategies are worthless.

The model goes on to review the key elements of supply management: performance measurement, skills and competences, organisational structure, relationship portfolios, and cost–benefit modelling. Whilst it is acknowledged that these are not the only elements and cases could be made for variations on this theme, the research clearly showed that these five main elements significantly affected the management of supply. We have used this approach as the basis of our book (Part 2). Each element of the model is discussed and within each chapter cross-referencing is made to other chapters that have an effect on the discussion.

Part 3: Strategic issues in supply chain management

Each of the last six chapters explores a strategic issue affecting the management of supply. We explore issues such as the need for environmental policies, the implications of electronic commerce, developments in public procurement, commodity purchasing, and involving suppliers in new product development. We have also added in this section a chapter on the purchasing of services. We felt that other books in the market have not given this area enough attention and hope this book redresses that balance.

Part 4: Future directions

The final part of the book serves two purposes: it is both a conclusion and a challenge. The conclusion section takes us through the main points raised in this book and reminds the reader of the implications for theory and practice. The challenge section of this chapter is couched as an 'allegory'. An allegory is defined by the OED as a story (or it could also be a play, poem or picture) in which the meaning or message is represented symbolically. We present in this allegory a view of the future and we challenge the reader to think long and hard about the picture that we paint, as we believe it holds important and profound messages for scholars and practitioners of supply management.

A note on terminology

This is an area of microeconomic activity that is beset by problems of terminology. The basic term 'buying' has become outdated, implying, as it does, the simple matter of spending money in acquiring an item. It is actually a perfectly good term and describes exactly what is going on. Its connotations let it down, however, and whilst many people involved in the activity still have the title of 'Buyer', the terms purchasing and procurement have been more popular for the function (i.e. both the practice of buying and the office in an organisation responsible for doing it). Differentiation between these two has been made without general agreement; some say that procurement is the more strategic of the two while purchasing is the day-to-day activity; others say exactly the reverse. We consider such wordplay is specious. The term 'supply' has long been linked to 'purchasing', indicating the integral nature of buying something and having it provided or supplied. Other terms include: 'materials management' (not only for manufacturing – many service operations use large quantities of materials); 'logistics' (a term of military origins, generally accepted to refer to the management of physical distribution, including warehousing and transportation); 'materiel' (one of the few examples of a French word being used in the lexicon of management, but never widely popular); and 'supply chain management' (invented by management consultants in the 1980s: oversimplistic in its metaphor but popular in the 1990s). Supply management appears to have survived and has perhaps the fewest connotations: ensuring that the enterprise is supplied with what it needs so that it can provide what it sells to its market would appear to be a simple and clear description of the economic activity on which we are focusing. The need to acknowledge the context is often expressed and business networks are brought into the terminology; the current focus is on supply networks (as opposed to chains).

We shall use several of these terms. Where we refer to the department in an enterprise, or the individual job title, the terms will have capital initials: Purchasing (department) and Buyer. This is to differentiate them from non-specific reference to purchasing as an activity or buyers in general. The same applies to supply management. Since much of this book focuses on strategic supply management, we shall frequently address the needs and responsibilities of Supply Strategists.

Overview

The importance of purchasing to an organisation cannot be overstated. Traditionally it has been considered as the area of the business that manages the inputs into the organisation. Standard textbooks[1] in the early days would generally refer to good 'purchasing practice' as buying the correct goods and services for the organisation, at the right price, right quality and on time, i.e. price, delivery and quality were seen as the key drivers for successful purchasing. This approach would seem to be common sense and follows from most traditional operations management texts, which generally devote a small amount of their book's content to discussing this area of management. The concept is usually discussed as part of the input, transformation, output model, where it is purchasing's role to manage the inputs into the firm after being told what to purchase from the various planning systems (e.g. materials requirement planning) contained within the firm. This leads us to pose the following crucial question.

Why should purchasing be seen as important to an organisation?

There are several possible answers to this question. The importance of purchasing to the firm has actually been debated in academic circles for some considerable time. There are numerous articles by the first and foremost writer in the UK field, David Farmer, in the early 1970s, which focused on the importance of linking purchasing into the main strategic decision-making process of the firm. Parallel research was also being conducted in the USA in the 1960s by David Burt and Hal Fearon who were investigating the role that purchasing played in the organisation and the opportunities that it could afford to business success (usually in the form of price savings). In the 1980s phrases such as 'a 1 per cent saving in purchasing is equal to a 10 per cent increase in sales' were also used to uplift the profile and importance of purchasing. When analysing the reasons for purchasing's importance to the firm two distinct arguments emerge: economics and strategic congruence (see Box 1.1).

By the early 1980s, Western firms had begun to focus on their supply structures (the activities of their suppliers, grouped conceptually into an imaginary 'supply chain' in the search for opportunities to achieve quick savings via price reduction strategies). These might bring into play traditional negotiation tactics, or call for different approaches, such as collaborative relationships (or Partnership arrangements as they were then known) with suppliers to explore ways of creating mutual value for both parties (see Box 1.2). This focused approach on the supply chain began in the mid-1980s and gained momentum throughout the 1990s.

Development of supply chain strategies has become a major growth industry in its own right; most organisations now see managing their supply chain (or 'base'), perhaps coupled with developing relationships, as a key strategic issue. As a variety of supply strategies are followed (such as outsourcing, supply base restructuring and partnership development), supply management is being seen as the facilitator of this success.

Box 1.1 Traditional view of the impact of purchasing

A traditional textbook might use a hypothetical example such as the following.

An organisation with annual sales of £100m spends £50m on materials and £10m on employment costs and makes £5m profit. How can it double its profit? It could reduce its employment costs by 50 per cent, but this is probably unachievable. It could double its sales – equally implausible. It could reduce its materials costs by 10 per cent – through better purchasing. The saving goes straight to the 'bottom line'.

Examples of organisations taking 10 per cent out of their material costs (or the costs of other purchases such as travel, IT or stationery) are not hard to find; however, few would claim to have doubled profits as a result. In practice, such savings rarely reach the 'bottom line' (operating profit) but become lost in the complexities and politics of managing budgets.

Box 1.2 Growth in supply chain consultancy

The popularity of the supply chain focus can be illustrated by simply examining the number of North American and European management consultancy organisations that developed supply chain practices. In the late 1980s only two of the major consultancies had skills in this area. By the end of the 1990s all of the major 'strategy houses' and mainstream consultancies clearly considered supply chain management as a key growth area. In 2000 one major strategy house, A. T. Kearney, earned consultancy fees of $900 million from its work in strategic supply management.

Summary

The main tenet of this book is that supply needs to be thought about as a dynamic strategic process and not as a bureaucratic business function. Through the efficient use of this process firms can achieve significant value added. The process of supply coordinates the method of input and supports transformation through the organisation's value system. In order to be able to achieve this, each part of the strategic supply wheel should be understood and also the effect that each element has on each other within the supply wheel; we refer to this as the integration of the supply wheel.

References

Cousins, P. D. (2002) 'A Conceptual Model for Managing Long-Term Inter-Organisational Relationships', *European Journal of Purchasing and Supply Management*, Vol. 8 (2), pp. 71–82.

Endnotes

1. See Farmer, D. (1985) *The Purchasing Manager's Handbook*, Gower Publications, London.

Chapter 2

The evolution of purchasing and supply management

Aim of chapter

The purpose of this chapter is to discuss the evolution of the purchasing function from basic procurement through to strategic supply management. Students will gain an understanding of the key drivers of this evolution and of the strategic roles played by the purchasing and supply management function.

Learning outcomes

At the end of this chapter, readers will:

■ appreciate how the purchasing function has evolved;

■ have an understanding of the key drivers of the evolution from purchasing to supply management;

■ have a clear understanding of the various roles that purchasing and supply management can play in achieving strategic success;

■ understand the different levels of analysis in supply chain management.

Introduction

We can ask many questions about the role of purchasing, and lately, supply management. Does purchasing have a role in business strategy? Is purchasing really strategic? What contribution can the purchasing function make to overall business performance? We define strategy as 'an integrated set of choices positioning a firm in an industry to earn superior financial returns over the long run'. The ability of purchasing to contribute to firm strategy and impact on performance has long been recognised. Various studies and authors have recognised that 'poor' purchasing decisions may be detrimental to business performance, while 'good' purchasing decisions might result in superior performance. In this chapter we discuss the evolution of the purchasing function from a clerical activity to one that makes a strategic contribution to firm performance, in the process highlighting the different roles the function can play in achieving strategic success.

The evolution of purchasing

The 1940s–1960s: logistics

With its origins in military practice, 'logistics' is well over a century old. Battles and wars have been won and lost based on the ability of the supply lines to deliver reliably and on time. Alexander the Great paid considerable attention to his army's supply lines. During the Second World War the Atlantic run was shadowed by German U-boats seeking to disrupt the Allies' supply lines supporting the war in Europe. The US Chief of Naval Operations at the time reportedly said that although he did not know what logistics was, he certainly wanted it to be used.

As a business discipline, logistics really only began to receive attention in the 1950s. Initially focused on improving productivity within the four walls of the factory, logistics over time was able to expand its scope and became the forerunner to formal purchasing departments. The emergence of a specialised logistics function challenged traditional conceptions of departmental boundaries, receiving a good deal of opposition from other functions who saw it as 'encroaching on their turf'. Up to this point, production and manufacturing received the attention of senior management, finished goods inventory was the responsibility of marketing, and order processing was an accounting or sales responsibility. This fragmented approach to purchasing led to a great deal of friction: accounting wanted to minimise inventory, production wanted large stores of work-in-process inventory 'just in case', while marketing wanted finished goods inventories to respond quickly to customers.

Today, we use the term *logistics* to describe the entire process of material and products moving into, through, and out of the firm. Initially, however, purchasing was conceptualised as the management of the firm's inputs (i.e. raw materials, services and sub-assemblies) as they are acquired or 'enter' the enterprise. For physical goods and materials, this is sometimes known as *inbound logistics*, a term that covers the movement of material, components and products received from suppliers. *Materials management*, on the other hand, describes the movement of components and materials within the factory or firm. *Physical distribution* (or outbound logistics) is the movement of finished goods outward from the end of the assembly line, and through the shipping department to the end customer. As logistics evolved, we also saw the advent of materials requirement planning (MRP) and material resource planning (MRP II), which enabled organisations for the first time to look at material inflows and outflows as part of a broader system. These various sets of relationships are described in Figure 2.1 on p. 12.

The 1970s: purchasing as an administrative function

A general level of recognition of the importance of purchasing dates back to the mid-1970s. Indeed, despite the 1973–4 oil crisis and related raw materials shortages drawing attention to the importance of purchasing, top management and purchasing professionals did not react to improve the role of purchasing in corporate strategy (Farmer, 1978). Throughout the 1970s the purchasing function continued to be seen as more administrative than strategic. Purchasing played a passive role

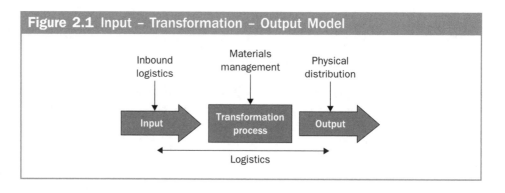

Figure 2.1 Input – Transformation – Output Model

in the organisation. The function operated in an isolated environment, trying to optimise the 'silo', rather than optimising the enterprise-wide supply chain. Firms typically adopted multiple sourcing strategies through competitive bids, and maintained arm's-length relationships with suppliers. Purchasing's role was to be a service provider to other functions within the enterprise, with the primary task of buying the required goods and services from approved sources of supply, making sure that they conformed to the required levels of quality and performance, delivery schedules and the most competitive price. This view of purchasing, as simply a service department performing predominantly a clerical role, has been profoundly challenged by the pressures of the economic environment.[1]

The 1980s: purchasing as supply chain management

In the 1980s firms began to appreciate the potential contribution of purchasing to the bottom line. Porter (1980) emphasised the importance of purchasing in his five forces model of competitive advantage. We also began to see the term 'supply chain management' emerge, first by consultants in the late 1980s and subsequently adopted by the academic community in the 1990s. Within the profession, the thinking of supply managers moved from one of efficiency towards effectiveness. Purchasing strategy began to align consciously with the overall corporate and business strategies of the firm. Advances in technology also saw the increased application of enterprise resource planning (ERP) systems, which made supply chain optimisation feasible. Organisations were now able to share long-term demand schedules and inventory levels throughout their entire supply chain (at least in theory), with the aim of having inventory moving continuously through a 'pipeline' and never in storage.

The intense Japanese competition of the 1980s also saw manufacturing firms shift from emphasising internal operations towards supply chain optimisation. World-class manufacturing (WCM) required that the entire supply chain be world-class, necessitating a focus on just-in-time (JIT) production and supply, supported by total quality management (TQM) programmes. Today, continuous improvement of internal operations remains an imperative, but will no longer lead to success if the external linkages are not up to par. Thus, a supply chain focus is vital for the long-term well-being of any manufacturing firm. A well-known example of such integrated supply chains is Wal-Mart. In 1996, Moore and Curry wrote that:

Part of the genius of Wal-Mart's ecosystem was also its unprecedented involvement and entanglement in the affairs of its suppliers. By 1984, Wal-Mart, which had become a very powerful channel to customers, began exerting heavy pressure on their suppliers like P&G to keep their prices down. Moreover, Wal-Mart compelled its suppliers to set up cross-company information systems to attain maximum manufacturing and distribution efficiency. For example, Wal-Mart and P&G reached an unprecedented partnership that involved extensive electronic ordering and information between companies.

The 1990s: supply management and strategic decision making

By the 1990s, supply chain management (SCM) had moved away from disparate functions of logistics, transportation, purchasing and physical distribution. Today's supply chain management goes by many terms, including: supply network management, demand chain management, pipeline management and value-net integration. Supply chain management has drastically changed the way purchasing deals with suppliers. Buyers have moved towards long-term, collaborative relationships with fewer suppliers. Terms such as supplier development, strategic cost management, collaborative relationships, shared databases, product lifecycle sourcing and total cost of ownership (TCO) have become commonplace. These focused strategic sourcing initiatives and sourcing projects have often generated savings in the region of 10–20 per cent of total purchase costs. The realisation that the strategic management of supply could save substantial money (as we saw in Chapter 1) has led firms to invest in it as a management discipline, and created dedicated strategic purchasing departments.

Part of the redefinition of purchasing as an important and strategic process has been to differentiate between purchasing operations, purchasing strategy and purchasing as a strategic function. *Purchasing operations* deal with the day-to-day buying activities of the firm, while *purchasing strategy* refers to the specific actions of the function to achieve its goals. This might include standardisation of parts and services, supplier tiering, and e-business sourcing. While this is advantageous to the purchasing function, it does not necessarily mean it is viewed as a strategic function by the rest of the firm. Only when the activities and strategies of the purchasing function are aligned with the overall strategies of the firm can *purchasing be a strategic function*.

As a strategic function, purchasing can contribute to shaping firm strategy and firm boundaries. For example, a supply manager might be tasked with assessing strategic options in outsourcing elements of the firm's activities.[2] This might include examining the best way to organise the supply structure. For example, should the firm buy from multiple suppliers, or should it identify a small number of key suppliers who take responsibility for larger parts of the firm's transformation process? The second approach is very popular within the manufacturing industry, where a number of product assemblers tend to identify roles for their suppliers within a *supply base*. Roles include being *mega*, *first-tier* or *tier-half*'[3] suppliers who assemble entire subsystems – even the complete, assembled product. This modular approach is easy to picture in the case of an aircraft, personal computer or car (e.g. an entire aircraft wing, a computer 'motherboard' or car 'cockpit'). It is also

---

Box 2.1 Supply strategy as the delivery of corporate strategy

ClearSpeed, an innovative, hi-tech British company, has developed a high-speed microchip that will revolutionise data processing in computers. Of the 38 people in the company, all but four are scientists. One of the non-scientists is the *Operations Director*. She is responsible for supply strategy – for getting the new chip made and to market. This includes all the production activities, which will be entirely outsourced. She has arranged for the chips to be made by a foundry partner in Burlington, Vermont, and then tested by another large firm in California. While the chip design will be done in Bristol, the VP Operations says she will 'keep the supply chain in North America', which is also the location of the initial prime sales market. ClearSpeed is an example of the supply strategy determining key aspects of strategic implementation as the firm grows.

Source: www.clearspeed.com

---

the way a designer of a new high-speed microchip might choose to have its product brought to market, such is the scale of investment necessary to produce, test and deliver such 'hi-tech' products.

Further, once the organisation accurately identifies what is core to their business, supply strategy could then focus on these non-core areas. The firm's strategic vision, for example, may not include assembly, but identify design as core to its business. The firm's supply strategy would therefore be to outsource assembly to other organisations. Supply management must translate the firm's corporate strategy into an appropriate supply strategy which is then manifested in the supply base activities of the firm. See Box 2.1 for an example of this. However, it is important to note that what may be considered core may change, and within high-clockspeed industries this may occur rapidly. Some strategists would now say that nothing is core and thus, logically, anything (but perhaps not everything!) could be outsourced. We discuss the 'make–buy' decision in further detail in Chapter 3.

Supply management permeates the entire enterprise. In deciding which activities should be done in-house and which to outsource, however, the Supply Strategist will usually be considered as having a vested interest (i.e. the more there is outsourced, the more important or secure the Supply Strategist's role). Genuinely strategic make-or-buy decisions, therefore, are rarely made by Supply Strategists; they are political rather than economic, and require a general strategic management perspective. Nevertheless, supply strategy is increasingly a factor in identifying the organisation's boundaries. Supply management assumes responsibility for developing and implementing supply structures that will sustain the competitive position of the firm. When an organisation decides it is no longer an assembler of products but a design house, for example, the supply structure will have to change to facilitate this strategic move.

Supply management is thus concerned not only with the input but also the transition and management process of goods and services through the enterprise. Its aim is to make the enterprise more competitive, involving not only purchasing goods and services at competitive prices but also focusing on cost reduction techniques, improving cycle times, reducing time-to-market, and constantly seeking to exploit actual and potential innovations from within the supply market. See Box 2.2 for an example.

Box 2.2 Palm Computing

Palm, a company known for its personal digital assistants (PDAs), describes itself as a virtual manufacturer. Palm does not manufacture or assemble its products nor deal with logistics. Instead, original design manufacturers (ODMs) are used to help make and design certain products. So what precisely does Palm do? The answer is strategic sourcing. Critical components such as semiconductor chips, displays, batteries and speciality plastics are sourced by Palm, who then establish pricing and contractual relationships with suppliers. Palm's contract manufacturers then buy directly from these contracts, allowing Palm control of their manufacturers' material costs. In the rare cases where Palm does not control the contract for a component, they still control the costing and supplier selection.

Palm takes this core competency seriously. It does not consider itself to have buyers; instead it has 'Commodity Managers', experienced sales staff with a plethora of responsibilities. These responsibilities include negotiation of contracts, sourcing and supplier evaluation, and working with marketing, engineering and new product introduction teams. This approach has allowed Palm to introduce new products at rock-bottom prices, such as the Zire PDA. The Zire entered the market at a price of $99 when most PDAs retailed at four or five times this price. Angel Mendez, the Senior Vice-President of Global Operations and Accessory Solutions, credits this directly to strategic sourcing which allowed them to produce the Zire at '. . . as good or better gross margins than any of our other products'. The benefits of strategic sourcing also go beyond price. Palm has increased inventory turns from 3 to 22 in two years and improved gross margins by 30 per cent on top of reducing material costs by 20–30 per cent. Virtual manufacturing has a lot to offer.

Source: based on Carbone (2003)

Drivers of purchasing evolution

The prime reason for purchasing assuming a more strategic focus stems from the many pressures placed upon it from the competitive environment. A simple PEST (political, economic, social and technological) model illustrates this point (see Figure 2.2).[4]

Political pressures

Political pressures have forced changes in both the focus of supply (e.g. the need to source materials in countries to which a firm wishes to export) and the structure of industries (e.g. privatisation of formerly public services). For example, the introduction of the Private Finance Initiative (PFI) in the UK during the 1990s had a major impact on how public sector organisations now fund major projects.[5] Previously, the government would disburse money directly to projects, such as new schools or hospitals, or public bodies (such as local or central government departments, or the National Health Service). Instead they now contract with private sector organisations and finance providers to fund projects, linked to the business prospects, and requiring very long-term relationships and responsibilities. These major policy shifts have forced changes in the focus of organisations, particularly

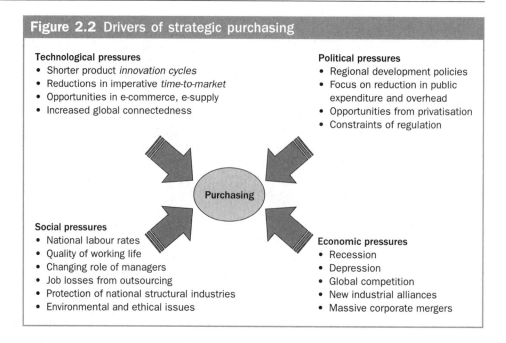

Figure 2.2 Drivers of strategic purchasing

Technological pressures
- Shorter product *innovation cycles*
- Reductions in imperative *time-to-market*
- Opportunities in e-commerce, e-supply
- Increased global connectedness

Political pressures
- Regional development policies
- Focus on reduction in public expenditure and overhead
- Opportunities from privatisation
- Constraints of regulation

Purchasing

Social pressures
- National labour rates
- Quality of working life
- Changing role of managers
- Job losses from outsourcing
- Protection of national structural industries
- Environmental and ethical issues

Economic pressures
- Recession
- Depression
- Global competition
- New industrial alliances
- Massive corporate mergers

industrial economic sectors, which have moved away from defining the 'best' specification possible, and towards seeking the lowest total cost solution – the best *value for money*[6] or *most economically advantageous tender* (MEAT). For example, in defence spending public bodies have abandoned a traditional 'cost-plus' focus and adopted 'value for money' as their new dictum.[7] They now focus on understanding the entire cost of their product (including their transformation processes) and then work jointly with suppliers to reduce total cost. Policy changes such as privatisation moved public sector services into the private sector, where the pressures of competition and cost competitiveness were much greater.[8]

Economic pressures

Economic pressures force organisations to examine the ways in which they manage their supply chains. The current low-inflation environment, at least partially fuelled by low-cost Chinese manufacturing, has prevented firms in many industries from shifting increased costs onto the consumer. Firms can respond to these cost pressures in a variety of ways. They might accept lower profits, attempt to pass costs forward onto the immediate customer (difficult, since the customer would be trying to reduce its input costs), or shift them onto other stakeholders (by demanding lower wages, reducing social contributions, etc.). They might also shift price pressure backwards onto suppliers in the form of lower prices. Paradoxically, the challenges posed by the rise of low-cost Chinese and Far East manufacturing also represent an opportunity for Western manufacturers to reduce costs. Outsourcing production to Chinese suppliers can yield massive gains. Around 80 per cent of

Wal-Mart's global suppliers are located in China, enabling the company not just to control supply costs, but to pass these savings on to their customers. For Wal-Mart at least, low price trumps brand loyalties. In combination with one or all of the above approaches, firms also strive for *kaizen*, or continuous improvement in internal processes. Using concepts such as lean manufacturing and lean supply, firms attempt to eliminate costs by innovating to improve efficiency and reduce waste within their own enterprises and across their entire business system.[9]

Social pressures

Social pressures have driven change in purchasing. In order for Purchasing to develop as a profession, well-qualified personnel are required. In order to attract these individuals, Purchasing's professional profile has been raised so that careers within it are as attractive, say, as those in Finance or Marketing. Purchasing has acquired higher status within the enterprise, implying a direct contribution to competitive strategy. Professional bodies in the UK (The Chartered Institute of Purchasing and Supply) and the USA (Institute for Supply Management)[10] have sought to change Purchasing's traditional image as a support function. Meanwhile, consumer awareness of social issues remote from their own has grown; conditions for people in foreign countries making the products bought in domestic shops have become significant in the purchase decision. Issues associated with the rise of ethical sourcing organisations such as FairTrade are discussed in Chapter 14.

Technological pressures

Advances in information technology have raised the visibility of the supply process in the enterprise. Purchasing now communicates and interacts with a much wider range of individuals in the organisation. For example, authorised budget holders across the firm are now able to purchase via the Internet using electronic catalogues, online auctions and internet portals (see Chapter 17). Purchase cards (credit cards for managers) have also enabled many firms for the first time to identify and analyse their overall spending. Customers have improved time-to-market for their own products by moving the order penetration points and value offering points in their supply chains.[11]

During the 1980s, Porter (1980) proposed the concept of the value chain, which was a systems model involving the purchasing (input) function. Strategists began to realise that concepts such as lean production, just in time, and total quality were only feasible if their supply processes were also closely managed. In the UK, this led to the development of a government initiative leading to the formation of a special company called Partnership Sourcing Limited (PSL). PSL aim to promote the principles of partnership sourcing throughout UK industry.[12] Many organisations – private and public sector – see partnership sourcing approaches as a key strategy to gain competitive advantage in the marketplace and increase the effectiveness of their supply processes.

The role of the purchasing function

When we talk about the role of the purchasing function we mean the part it plays within the organisation – the reason the function exists. As Ellram and Carr (1994) remind us, however, 'It is critical to understand that there is a difference between purchasing strategy and purchasing performing as a strategic function. When purchasing is viewed as a strategic function, it is included as a key decision maker and participant in the firm's strategic planning process.' Three distinct types of 'purchasing strategy' are proposed:

■ Purchasing function *implements competitive strategy.*

■ Purchasing function *supports strategy* of other functions and those of the firm as a whole.

■ Purchasing function *drives* strategy of the firm.

Implementing strategy

At the most basic level, purchasing can implement strategy. If the organisation has developed a new product, the supply function needs to manage requisition and logistics issues to ensure the required parts arrive on time, at the lowest price and of acceptable quality. In this role purchasing was not involved in the formulation of strategy, simply the implementation of strategies determined elsewhere in the firm.

Supporting strategy

Purchasing can play a role in supporting the strategic goals and objectives of the firm. This is achieved by aligning purchasing's functional strategies and activities with the firm's overall strategy. For example, a local manufacturer competes on the basis of innovation, and thus seeks to be first-to-market with new products and to lead the industry in new technologies. Pursuing lowest-cost suppliers would not be a supportive strategy in this situation! Instead, the purchasing function needs to be able to understand these technologies and develop an agile and responsive supply base that can cope with the stream of constant innovations. The better the purchasing function is at doing these things, the more support it is providing to the firm's innovation strategy.

Driving strategy

The third, and most challenging, role of purchasing and supply management is to drive strategy by providing the firm with a long-term competitive advantage. In this situation, supply is the key driver of the firm's strategy. For example, the ability of Wal-Mart's managers to select, evaluate and develop suppliers throughout their global supply chain is a key to the success of their lowest-price strategy. The combination of excellent supplier relationships and lean supply practices makes it extremely difficult for competitors to imitate.

Judging purchasing's contribution to strategy

The priorities of the purchasing function, as with any function, must be derived from the firm's competitive strategy. Thus, we can evaluate the growth of purchasing development via the role they play in enabling and implementing the firm's strategy. One of the earliest typologies of purchasing function development was a four-stage model developed by Reck and Long (1988), which evaluates the competitive role and contribution of purchasing to any type of company. It begins with a contribution in Stage 1 which is largely passive, through to purchasing becoming a competitive weapon of the organisation in Stage 4 (see Table 2.1). The stages help managers assess their current position and identify the type of changes

Table 2.1 Strategic stages in the development of a purchasing function

Stage	Definition and characteristics
Stage 1 PASSIVE	**Definition:** Purchasing function has no strategic direction and primarily reacts to requests from other functions **Characteristics:** ■ High proportion of time spent on quick-fix routine operations ■ Purchasing function and individual performance based efficiency measures ■ Little inter-functional communication due to purchasing's low visibility in the organisation ■ Supplier selection based on price and availability
Stage 2 INDEPENDENT	**Definition:** Purchasing function adopts the latest purchasing techniques and practices, but its strategic direction is independent of the firm's competitive strategy **Characteristics:** ■ Performance primarily based on cost reduction and efficiency measures ■ Coordination links between purchasing and technical disciplines are established ■ Top management recognises the importance of professional development ■ Top management recognises the opportunities in purchasing for contributing to profitability
Stage 3 SUPPORTIVE	**Definition:** Purchasing function supports the firm's competitive strategy by adopting purchasing techniques and products, which strengthen the firm's competitive position **Characteristics:** ■ Purchasers are included in sales proposal teams ■ Suppliers are considered a resource, which is carefully selected and motivated ■ People are considered a resource, with emphasis on experience, motivation and attitude ■ Markets, products and suppliers are continuously monitored and analysed
Stage 4 INTEGRATIVE	**Definition:** Purchasing's strategy is fully integrated into the firm's competitive strategy and constitutes part of an integrated effort among functional peers to formulate and implement a strategic plan **Characteristics:** ■ Cross-functional training of purchasing professionals and executives is made available ■ Permanent lines of communication with other functional areas are established ■ Professional development focuses on strategic elements of the competitive strategy ■ Purchasing performance is measured in terms of contributions to the firm's success

Source: Reck and Long (1988)

in attitudes, practices and procedures needed to shift purchasing from a clerically oriented function to a strategic contributor.

Stage 1: Passive

This is the poorest level of contribution by the purchasing function. The function has no strategic direction and reacts to requests from other departments. Purchasing perceive their main role to be one of filling requisitions, expediting shipments and auditing invoices. There is little opportunity to add value to the organisation as the Purchasing Manager (if there is one) is kept busy with more immediate supply problems.

Stage 2: Independent

The first step in breaking out of Stage 1 is for purchasing to continuously embrace the latest purchasing techniques and tools (e.g. value analysis, information technology links, and supplier partnerships) used in the outside market. Purchasing may not necessarily contribute to advantage, but by benchmarking with competitors it ensures the firm maintains parity with the competition. By this stage, purchasing is usually seen as 'professional', though the primary focus remains efficiency.

Stage 3: Supportive

Stage 3 purchasing functions have probably reached 'top division' in their market. They may not be better than competitors on every aspect of purchasing, but they are broadly up with the best. Purchasing is thus 'supportive' of the firm's strategy, and emphasises consistency with this strategy when making purchasing and departmental decisions. Top management also view the Purchasing department as an essential business function. Purchasing is expected to support and strengthen the firm's competitive advantage by providing timely information to all departments in the firm about potential changes in the price and availability of materials, which may impact the firm's strategic goals.

Stage 4: Integrative

For many firms Stage 3 would be the limit of the purchasing function's contribution. Reck and Long, however, suggest that the function can still increase in importance by forming the basis of the firm's competitive success, enabled by the skills and capabilities built up over the previous three stages. Purchasing is an integral part of the firm's competitive strategy. It looks to the long term, attends strategic planning sessions and looks to likely changes in supply markets. Essentially, they are trying to be 'one step ahead' of competitors to take advantage of opportunities and minimise potential threats before they become a problem.

Empirical taxonomies of purchasing

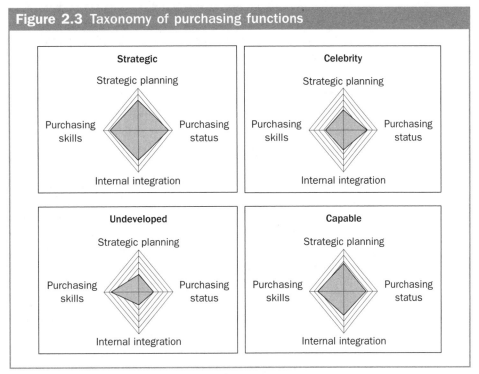

Figure 2.3 Taxonomy of purchasing functions

Source: Cousins et al. (2006)

A recent study of UK organisations by three of the authors (Cousins, Lawson and Squire, 2006[13]) provided empirical evidence of firms' progression along the Reck and Long (1988) phases. Their study examined different configurations of purchasing functions based on purchasing status, internal integration, purchasing skills and involvement in strategic planning. The results highlighted four distinct types of purchasing functions within firms, which they called Strategic, Celebrity, Undeveloped and Capable. These characteristics are shown in Figure 2.3.

Strategic purchasers

Strategic purchasers parallel Reck and Long's 'integrative' group where the purchasing function is highly regarded, tightly integrated with the business and heavily involved in strategic decision making. They are heavily involved in planning about strategic issues affecting the firm, such as make-or-buy decisions, and strategic sourcing. Strategic purchasers are closely aligned with the internal business needs, highly regarded by top management and possess high skill levels and knowledge. Strategic purchasers are focused more on supply chain management issues rather than in managing contracts, as shown by high levels of integration with suppliers in communication channels and information technology.

Capable purchasers

Capable purchasers reflect the 'supportive' phase where the function is contributing to strategy, though not as integrated internally nor held in the same esteem as strategic purchasers. The function is highly skilled, but has not fully been able to translate these skills into the rest of the business. Capable purchasers have moderate levels of status, internal integration and involvement in strategic matters. The group are making progress toward actualising their potential contribution to the organisation, and over time, are likely to build on their skills to evolve towards strategic purchasers.

Undeveloped purchasers

Undeveloped purchasers are akin to the 'independent' phase where they are a professional function as shown by high levels of purchasing skills and knowledge, but reactive and responding to the needs of the business. Undeveloped purchasers are the laggards of purchasing functions. Despite high skill and knowledge levels, the group have low levels of organisational status, less integration with other functions and little involvement in strategic planning. Although purchasing possesses the skills to contribute to the success of the firm, the function is of little concern to top management, does not engage with other areas of the business and has only limited involvement in strategic planning. Undeveloped purchasers appear to represent the nascent form of purchasing – it possesses a solid base, but has not yet been able to project its influence into the firm's strategic dialogue or engage with other functions of the business to any substantive extent, and perhaps consequently, is not recognised by top management as being important to the firm.

Celebrity purchasers

Celebrity purchasers represent an interesting group, outside of current classification systems. The group has high levels of status in the eyes of top managers, yet lower skill levels, involvement in strategic planning and internal integration than any other group. Celebrity purchasers may have come about through the presence of a charismatic leader who is able to sell the purchasing function to top management, but is an 'emperor without clothes'. Alternatively, the configuration may reflect a purchasing function that concentrates on hard negotiations with many suppliers and is assessed based on the price savings achieved. The low skill level of buyers is due to a focus on 'hands-on' operational issues, rather than higher-level strategic thinking. Thus, the function may be seen as valuable, though within a role limited to cost-saving activities.

Moving between phases

The results of the Cousins et al. (2006) study provide initial evidence of how firms might evolve between stages. With the exception of the special case of celebrity purchasers, the study shows that undeveloped purchasers can build on their base of high skills by engaging with the rest of the organisation, gaining respect and status, and in the process become a capable purchaser. Finally, a strategic purchaser is developed initially by building skills, then engaging with the rest of the organisation, and ultimately integrating both these aspects. Only a strategic purchaser is able to gain full benefit for the organisation from its supplier relationships.

The scope of strategic supply management

The evolution of purchasing from a clerical function to a strategic process is well documented in the literature. The way we think about the management of supply has developed during this period and the unit of analysis has changed in its complexity and its strategic nature. The supply structure model (Figure 2.4) illustrates these differing units of analysis.

Initially, academics and practitioners concentrated on 'dyadic' linkages. That is, the relationship between a single supplier and a single buyer. This thinking was extended in the late 1980s to conceptualise supply as a chain (see New and Westbrook, 2004) or pipeline (Farmer and Van Amstel, 1991). The complexity of supply management has increased and now spans the triad of relationships between supplier, buyer and customer. In the next stage in the evolution of supply thinking, the supply structure was conceptualised as a network. This involved examining the interrelationships across an entire industry sector where frequently buyer and supplier roles are reversed multiple times throughout the network structure.

It is possible to go further and observe that the systems with which Supply Strategists are trying to cope are a mess – full of broken lines of communications, 'dark' areas where it is not clear what is going on, corruption, bad faith, feedback loops, and so on. The power of management science, which might be able to help strategists make sense of this mess, has yet to be applied in this context.

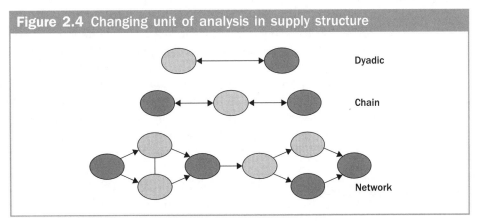

Figure 2.4 Changing unit of analysis in supply structure

Dyadic

Chain

Network

Source: Harland, Lamming and Cousins (1999)

Box 2.3 Integration of supply chain activities

R. S. Components is an example of an organisation coordinating its entire supply chain activities. R. S. Components provide a catalogue service to industrial and service firms. The catalogue covers all manner of items, ranging from transistors and resistors through to large-scale transformers and other heavy-duty equipment. This firm viewed itself primarily as a logistics and marketing operation, with purchasing performing the service role of providing the goods at the right time, right price and right quality. R. S. Components competes in a market with two other major firms, all using the same type of marketing channel (catalogue). In the mid-1990s, they found their sales were declining and experienced difficulty in differentiating themselves within the marketplace. The company could not overcome this problem, nor understand how the purchasing function could add value, other than logistical and inventory management. The key to their problem was that of strategic focus: i.e. where was value being added in the business?

The company decided to form a 'supply chain management' team consisting of purchasing, marketing and logistics. After close analysis of their business they discovered that while they could not offer suppliers joint risk sharing and value engineering work (as per traditional partnership thinking), they could offer market intelligence. Essentially, RS were the link between the customers' future requirements and their suppliers (manufacturers). If this communication flow could be optimised by clear and efficient communication, RS would be able to place new items in its catalogue almost six months before its competitors. This new approach had the effect of increasing customer loyalty and differentiating RS as a supplier responsive to market demands.

Source: www.rsww.com

Managing in the supply network is a complex task requiring cross-functional cooperation. As previously suggested, the customer firm will often not consider the ramifications of trying to manage the entire supply chain and its interfaces, i.e. the supplier/buyer, buyer/customer and internal buyer/buyer linkages. Box 2.3 provides an example of how this integrated network approach can operate.

Summary

Purchasing and supply management is of growing importance to organisations. With the pressures of increased competition, improved time-to-market and cost reduction, organisations have to respond by re-engineering their supply structures to match the strategic pressures and priorities that are being placed on the firm. Firms can do this in a variety of ways but they must consider the appropriateness of each of these approaches. In turn, the approaches must be balanced with the other enabling elements in the strategic supply wheel.

Seminar questions

1. Discuss the evolution or the purchasing function from logistics, through administration, supply chain management to supply management and strategic decision making.

2. Using a PEST model, discuss the key drivers of the evolution of the supply management function in an organisation with which you are familiar.

3. Examine three case study companies and analyse what role their Purchasing department fulfils. In each case discuss whether the role that the Purchasing department fulfils has had an impact on the overall success of the business.

References

Carbone, J. (2003) 'Strategic Sourcing', *Purchasing*, 17 April, pp. 32–6.

Cousins, P. D., Lawson, B. and Squire, B. (2006) 'An Empirical Taxonomy of Purchasing Functions', *International Journal of Operations and Production Management*, Vol. 26 (7), pp. 775–94.

Ellram, L. M. and Carr, A. (1994) 'Strategic Purchasing: A History and Review of the Literature', *International Journal of Purchasing and Materials Management*, Spring, pp. 10–18.

Farmer, D. (1978) 'Developing Purchasing Strategies', *Journal of Purchasing and Materials Management*, Vol. 14, pp. 6–11.

Farmer, D. and van Amstel, R. (1991) *Effective Pipeline Management*, Gower, Aldershot.

Harland, C. M., Lamming, R. C. and Cousins, P. D. (1999) 'Developing the Concept of Supply Strategy', *International Journal of Operations & Production Management*, Vol. 19 (7), pp. 650–73.

Hoover, W. E., Eloranta, E., Holmström, J. and Huttunen, K. (2001) *Managing the Demand-Supply Chain – Value Innovations for Customer Satisfaction*, John Wiley & Sons, New York.

Lamming, R. (1993) *Beyond Partnership: Strategies for Innovation and Lean Supply*, Prentice Hall, New York.

Moore, J. F. and Curry, S. R. (1996) 'The Death of Competition', *Fortune*, 15 April, p. 144.

New, S. J. and Westbrook, R. (eds) (2004) *Understanding Supply Chains: Concepts, Critiques and Futures*, Oxford University Press, Oxford.

Porter, M. E. (1980) *Competitive Strategy*, The Free Press, New York.

Reck, R. F. and Long, B. G. (1988) 'Purchasing: A Competitive Weapon', *Journal of Purchasing and Materials Management*, Vol. 24 (3), pp. 2–8.

Womack, J. P., Jones, D. T. and Roos, D. (1990) *The Machine that Changed the World*, Rawlinson Associates, New York.

Womack, J. P. and Jones D. T. (2003) *Lean Thinking*, The Free Press, New York.

Endnotes

1. In 2004, for example, the UK government was challenged by the Director of the Office of Government Commerce, John Oughton, to reduce spending in administrative departments by £7bn per annum for three years, not simply as a way of saving public money but as the catalyst for significant strategic change within central civil service. The *Financial Times* reported that 'About £2bn is to be saved under the heading of "policy, funding and regulation" – reducing red tape and the burden of inspection and regulation on both the

public and private sectors, and providing easier to administer block grants rather than earmarked funds to local government, the police, schools and other parts of the public sector.' (22.11.04)

2. We shall refer to outsourcing at several stages in the discussion. For interesting perspectives on the subject, see the National Outsourcing Association at www.noa.co.uk.

3. This rather odd term is used simply to describe a firm that is strategically closer to the customer firm than its *first-tier suppliers*.

4. The PEST analysis is a well-established way of understanding the environmental pressures that an organisation faces. It has sometimes been extended to PESTLE (or even PESTEL), the extra letters denoting legal (regulatory) and environmental pressures. Here, we include these pressures within the main four categories.

5. See www.hm-treasury.gov.uk/documents/public_private_partnerships/ppp_index.cfm.

6. See Chapter 16 for an in-depth discussion of public and regulated procurement.

7. *Cost-plus* contracts were those where the supplier was paid a margin (the 'plus') above the costs it incurred in carrying out the work. This did not encourage them to reduce or even control input costs – especially where the margin was agreed as a percentage of costs! Cost-plus contracts were common in the 1980s in defence and other large-scale strategic industries. By the 1990s, they had largely been replaced by fixed price contracts, where the supplier had to bid a firm price and then keep to it. This encouraged the supplier to control costs in order to make the desired profit margin.

8. In the late 1990s a research initiative known at the 'Lean Aerospace Initiative' was started; its aim was to find ways to help aerospace become more competitive. See www.sbac.co.uk (search for UK-Lean Aerospace Initiative). A presentation on LAI can be downloaded from http://www.bestpracticecentre.com/community/dms/docdetails.asp?txtDocPK=379&m=1& hidedetails=1.

9. For a discussion on lean production and supply, see Womack et al., 1990, 2003 and Lamming 1993. See also www.lean.org.

10. See www.ism.ws for the Institute for Supply Management (USA), and www.cips.org for the Chartered Institute of Purchasing and Supply (UK).

11. Hoover et al. (2001) define the order penetration point as 'the point in the supply chain at which the customer demand (an order) is allocated to the [supplier's] product' (p. 74). They define the value offering point (VOP) as 'the point in the customer's demand chain where the supplier fulfils demand. Moving the VOP largely benefits the customer, and required the supplier to do more work' (p. 76). The goal is to change how demand is linked to supply, thereby improving supply chain synchronisation, and to change how supply is linked to demand, thereby increasing value-added to the customer.

12. See www.pslcbi.com.

13. An executive summary of this study can be found at www.scmrg.com.

Chapter 3

The make–buy decision: a theoretical perspective

Aim of chapter

The purpose of this chapter is to provide an understanding of the theories that underpin the make–buy decision within organisations. This will be achieved through an exploration of the theoretical perspectives that inform the make–buy decision.

Learning outcomes

At the end of this chapter, readers will:

- understand the fundamental significance of the make–buy decision to organisations in general and supply chain management in particular;
- have a clear understanding of transaction cost approaches and be able to apply the theory to practical dilemmas;
- have a clear understanding of competency approaches and be able to apply the theory to practical dilemmas.

Introduction

The link between the make–buy decision, corporate strategy and supply strategy is clear: the decision determines the areas where the firm will compete and those it will leave to others. Firms must decide where to participate in the overall value-adding process of the supply chain, both in terms of their network position and how far they wish to extend their boundaries upstream and downstream.

We tackle this problem from a theoretical perspective but also show the process of applying the theory to practical situations. We begin with a description of the make–buy decision and underline its importance to strategic supply management. We shall then briefly explore and critique neoclassical theory of the firm to set up the development of the two main theories. The two theories, transaction cost economics and the resource-based view, then comprise the majority of the discussion. We conclude with implications for managers.

The make–buy decision

The make–buy decision is fundamental to the field of supply management. Very few organisations possess all of the skills and resources required to design and manufacture entire products in-house. Instead, managers must choose which items will be produced internally and which items will be purchased externally from a supplier. This decision is among the most important facing managers because it defines the areas in which the organisation will operate and those areas that it will leave to others. Even individual make–buy decisions can have a critical bearing on areas such as employment, working capital and industry positioning.

The aggregation of these individual make–buy decisions defines the boundaries of the firm. The boundaries of the firm[1] are the combined activities that an organisation performs in-house rather than using external suppliers. Boundaries are therefore concerned with both the scale of production (how many widgets are we going to produce?) and the scope of production (what widgets are we going to produce?). This can be explained with reference to Figure 3.1.

Figure 3.1 shows a simplified four-stage supply chain, from raw materials, through assembly and manufacture, to retail. In Scenario 1 the focal firm completes the manufacturing portion of the transformation process, while buying raw materials from an external supplier. Here the boundaries of the firm are limited to a single stage in the supply chain. However, in Scenario 2 the focal firm takes the strategic

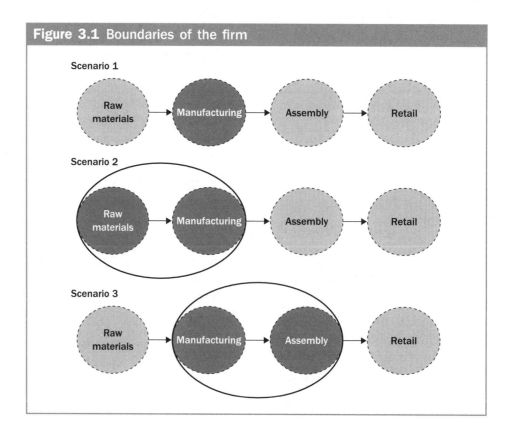

Figure 3.1 Boundaries of the firm

Box 3.1 Supply in action: Vertical integration in the oil and gas industry

Although not as fashionable as 20–30 years ago, some industries retain high levels of vertical integration. A good example of this is in the oil and gas industry where single organisations control the entire supply chain, from exploration and production of crude oil, refining and manufacturing of petrochemicals, to the transportation, marketing and sales of end productions, such as petrol, diesel and lubricants. In the context of the make–buy decision, companies such as BP, Texaco and Shell choose to 'make' along the length of the supply chain, from raw material production through to retail. Gazprom, the Russian gas behemoth, is also engaged in building a vertically integrated gas company with designs on 'downstream' European and UK gas distributors.

---

decision to continue manufacturing but also to integrate raw materials production. In other words, the firm has chosen to make (as opposed to buy) the raw materials and in doing so has extended the scope of its boundaries one stage upstream within the supply chain. Scenario 3 represents the reverse situation where the focal firm makes the decision to continue manufacturing but also to integrate into the assembly stage. The firm now buys raw materials but performs the manufacturing and assembly in-house. Of course, the firm could equally choose to make at all stages in the supply chain, a situation known as vertical integration. An illustration of vertical integration in the oil industry is described in Box 3.1.

The position of these boundaries has clear implications for supply management. It informs managers when the firm will have to interact with external suppliers and is the starting point of the sourcing process. In the remainder of this chapter we examine the challenge of making this decision from a theoretical perspective. We first consider why orthodox economics does not provide an adequate basis for this decision and then move on to discuss two contrasting approaches that have become prevalent within the field of supply management.

The inadequacy of neoclassical economic theory

Before we review transaction cost and competency approaches, it is important to consider the application of neoclassical economic theory to the make–buy decision. The neoclassical view of the firm is one of a production set, transforming inputs into outputs. The neoclassical manager enjoys complete rationality and full information to maximise the owner's profits (Hart, 1989; Chandler, 1992). The profit-maximising level of output determines production levels. The firm will continue to increase production until marginal revenue equals marginal cost, thus maximising profit.

The sole reason for the existence of firms in the neoclassical view is to make a profit. Firms are homogeneous entities because of perfect information (about cost and demand conditions) and have equal access to production technology (Conner, 1991). Thus, while the neoclassical firm's *raison d'être* is to maximise profits, the perfect competition model necessitates that any super normal profits are temporary and will return to a normal level.

Neoclassical firms exist to maximise profits. However, profit maximisation does not provide any clear motivation for the formation of firms in a market. Since it is assumed that there is no cost to economic exchange, there would appear to be no reason for the existence of firms in the first place. Given that contracts are less costly than hierarchies and that the objective of firms is to maximise profits, Barney and Ouchi (1986) argue that all transactions should be conducted in the marketplace. Put simply, neoclassical economics requires a theory of producers, not a theory of firms (Kay, 2000).

Most importantly to this discussion, neoclassical theory tells us little about the make–buy decision. Although it is argued that firms increase output until the last (marginal) unit does not add to profit, this offers little practical relevance to the 'make–buy' decision, the decision dictating the boundaries of the firm. The internal workings of the firm remain a 'black box' and managers are offered little guidance or assistance in making decisions. What is required is a more prescriptive theory that examines the characteristics of a given situation and helps to derive a well-informed and rational choice. We examine two approaches that may assist managers in this process: transaction cost economics and the resource-based view.

The transaction cost approach

Transaction cost economics (TCE) emerged as an economic explanation for the existence and scope of the firm. Nobel Prize winner Ronald Coase (1937) asserted that firms exist due to what he termed 'marketing costs' (now transaction costs),

Table 3.1 Summary of the assumptions of Transaction Cost Economics

Assumption	Description
Bounded rationality	'Human behaviour is intendedly rational but only limitedly so' (Simon, 1957). Bounded rationality takes forms of neurophysiological and language limits. In uncertain or complex environments bounded rationality is predicted to cause a shift to hierarchy.
Opportunism	'Self-interest seeking with guile' (Williamson, 1975). Argued that not all actors will behave opportunistically but due to the constraints of bounded rationality and uncertainty it is difficult if not impossible to distinguish between those who will cooperate and those who will behave opportunistically.
Asset specificity	Asset specificity considers how specialised a particular asset is to a relationship. Specialised assets are risky in that the full production value of the asset cannot be transferred if a contract or relationship is prematurely terminated. Williamson categorised four types of specific assets: site specificity, physical asset specificity, human asset specificity, and dedicated assets. A relationship with high asset specificity is theorised to increase the possibility of opportunism. As such, firms may choose to integrate the process rather than run the risk of the open market.
Uncertainty	Uncertainty costs consist of *ex ante*, environmental costs, and *ex poste*, behavioural costs. A firm facing a highly uncertain environment will face highly complex *a priori* contractual agreements or may face high renegotiation costs as the relationship develops. Firms face *ex poste* costs when the behaviour of the partner firm is uncertain. TCE logic holds that when uncertainty is high firms should resort to hierarchy.

or the price of using the open market price mechanism. TCE logic is based on the interaction of two behavioural assumptions, bounded rationality and opportunism, and two transaction assumptions, asset specificity and uncertainty. These assumptions are explained in Table 3.1.

The application of TCE to the 'make–buy' decision can be seen with reference to Figure 3.2. Starting in the middle box, we can define transaction costs as the costs of planning, adapting, coordinating and safeguarding exchange. For instance, supply managers will be involved in searching for suitable suppliers, selecting among a shortlist, negotiating and drawing up contracts with the winning company and ensuring that the supplier's goods are delivered on time and to the correct specification. These are the transaction costs to an exchange. As we will see, the higher the level of these transaction costs, the more likely the firm is to 'make' rather than 'buy'. The benefit of TCE is that it provides a clear and structured framework to assist in the decision-making process. Figure 3.2 shows that the level of transaction costs will be dictated by the exchange characteristics in terms of behavioural characteristics and transaction characteristics.

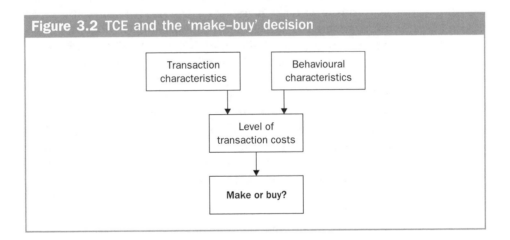

Figure 3.2 TCE and the 'make–buy' decision

Behavioural characteristics

Behavioural characteristics include two key assumptions: opportunism and bounded rationality. The first behavioural characteristic considers that people are opportunistic and driven by self-interest. Opportunism is defined as achieving one's goals through calculated efforts of guile, lying, stealing, cheating, passing false information, distorting or disguising information, and generally misleading the other party. The second behavioural characteristic moves away from neoclassical economics and suggest that individuals are boundedly rational, that managers satisfy objectives or muddle through in a way that does not optimise/maximise profits. For example, how do managers know the optimal network configuration or set the exact percentages to allocate among suppliers that will minimise total costs?

Transaction characteristics

Transaction characteristics also focus on two key assumptions: asset specificity and uncertainty. Asset specificity refers to the transferability of an asset within an exchange relationship. Specialised assets are risky because the full value cannot be transferred to a different supplier if the contract is prematurely terminated. For example, a buyer that invests in training a supplier would lose the value of that investment should they choose to switch to a different supplier. The second transaction characteristic suggests that future states are uncertain. Williamson (1985) develops two types of uncertainty: behavioural uncertainties, such as not being able to predict the behaviour of the exchange partner, and environmental uncertainties, such as not being able to predict the future states of technology, demand or supply.

TCE and the make–buy decision

Having defined the primary characteristics of TCE we can now examine how their interaction determines the make–buy decision. The basic understanding of TCE is that firms must make investments to transact with each other. These investments are relationship specific; their value in another relationship is appreciably lower (perhaps even zero) (Klein, Crawford and Alchian, 1978). Where the transaction demands investment in relationship-specific assets parties may be liable to opportunistic behaviour. Not all actors will behave opportunistically but due to the effects of bounded rationality and uncertainty it is not possible *ex ante* to distinguish those who will cooperate from those who will be opportunistic.

This is known as the 'hold-up problem' (Holmstrom and Roberts, 1998, p. 74). For example, a buyer firm that has to make significant, unilateral investments is liable to hold-up from the supplier firm, where the supplier feels that the buyer is locked into the relationship. In this case TCE predicts that the buyer firm would choose to 'make' rather than 'buy'. Integration is argued to be preferable because the firm may control opportunistic behaviour through the use of distinctive governance mechanisms unavailable to markets[2] (Williamson, 1985). On the other hand, exchange involving low asset specificity will take place in the marketplace, the risk of opportunistic behaviour is low and thus the market is more efficient (Williamson, 1985; Powell, 1990). The decision to make or buy is thus one of efficiency: the optimal choice is the one that minimises the transaction costs (the costs of planning, adapting, coordinating and safeguarding) of the exchange. This can be shown by way of a simple cost curve as illustrated in Figure 3.3.

Figure 3.3 shows when make or buy is most efficient. At low levels of asset specificity and uncertainty the market (or 'buy') is more efficient and therefore preferable. However, as asset specificity becomes significant the risk of hold-up increases, reaching a point of equilibrium where both choices are equally efficient. From this point, one further arbitrary unit of asset specificity pushes the transaction costs of exchange to the point the buyer firm would choose to integrate (or 'make') rather than rely on the market.

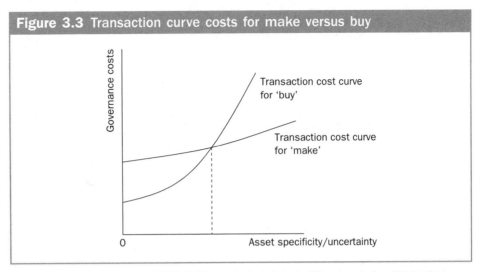

Figure 3.3 Transaction curve costs for make versus buy

Source: reprinted from Williamson (1991). © Johnson Graduate School of Management, Cornell University

TCE criticisms

TCE provides a clear and logical answer to the make–buy decision; however, it is not without critics. Two critiques are especially relevant here. First, TCE does not address the limitations of firms. By equating production functions across firms (Hodgson, 1998), TCE assumes that the capabilities required for production pre-exist or can be developed equally in all firms (Madhok, 1996). However, capabilities have been shown to be both heterogeneous and path dependent (Nelson and Winter, 1982; Barney, 1991). In other words, capabilities are not spread evenly among firms and are dependent on the unique trajectories of individual firms. TCE thus offers a somewhat static and limited view of the production capabilities of the firm. Madhok (1996) suggests that accounting for both transaction costs and the costs of external production may mean that the market is preferable even in the face of high asset specificity. This may be the case where it is not efficient, or even possible, to develop the required internal production capabilities.

Second, TCE is a theory of cost minimisation, not of value maximisation. Zajac and Olsen (1993) suggest that the value created in a transaction may be greatest under circumstances that may, from a TCE perspective, appear inefficient. Firms do not exist simply because of market failure, but have positive, value-creating attributes not found in markets (Lazonick, 1991; Ghoshal and Moran, 1996).

These two critiques lead us into the next approach, which specifically addresses the differences between firm-level capabilities and considers the firm in a more positive light.

The capability approach

The capability approach is associated primarily, but not exclusively,[3] with the resource-based view of the firm. The resource-based view of the firm is founded on the seminal contribution of Penrose (1959). Of special importance is the manner in which she conceptualised the firm. Whereas the prevailing neoclassical view of the firm is one of a production set, transforming inputs into outputs, Penrose argues for the firm as a bundle of productive resources under the direct control of the administrative unit. Resources are tangible things such as plant, equipment, land, raw materials, and inventory, and also human resources such as skilled and unskilled labour, clerical, administrative, technical, financial and managerial staff. The combination of these resources yields a diverse range of services, thus accounting for the unique character of individual firms.

The RBV of the firm adopts this notion of the firm as a bundle of resources and capabilities to explain long-term performance differentials within and across industries. The terms resources and capabilities are used here interchangeably to describe intangible and tangible assets firms use to conceive of and implement strategies that improve performance (Barney, 1991). A basic assumption of the RBV is that resources are heterogeneous (limited in supply) and endowed with differential levels of 'efficiency' (Peteraf, 1993). Superior resources (those that are more 'efficient') enable firms to produce at lower cost or better satisfy customer demand and are considered to be the primary source of supernormal profits in the form of rents[4] (Ricardo, 1911; Rumelt, 1987).

The primary contribution of the RBV lies in the identification of the conditions under which the returns from superior resources are sustained over the long term. If resource heterogeneity is transient, rents will be quickly eroded and only normal returns will be earned. The conditions under which competitive advantage can be sustained are therefore of particular interest. Three criteria are identified: imperfect imitability, imperfect substitutability and imperfect mobility (Barney, 1991).

Inimitability

Resources are only imperfectly imitable if firms that do not have them cannot obtain them. Resources can be inimitable for one or a combination of the following: unique historical conditions, causal ambiguity and/or social complexity (Lippman and Rumelt, 1982; Dierickx and Cool, 1989). First, temporal opportunities can mean that firms accumulate or develop resources in a way that is no longer available. For example, Caterpillar was able to create a worldwide service and support network at low cost because they were subsidised by the Allies during the Second World War (Barney, 1999). This opportunity is obviously no longer available to potential competitors. Second, the link between resources controlled by the firm and its competitive advantage may not be understood when supported by causally ambiguous resources (Reed and De Fillippi, 1990). Where the link is not fully understood it is difficult for rival firms to imitate the specific combination of resources used to derive competitive advantage. Lastly, resources may be inimitable if they are socially complex. For example, resources such as reputation or culture may be understood by competitors but are difficult to replicate and may require substantial investments over time (by which time competitive advantage may have moved elsewhere).

Non-substitutable

Resources should also be resistant to substitution. Substitutability can be of two forms. First, a firm may be able to substitute a similar resource that enables it to develop the same strategy as its rival. Alternatively, a firm can substitute a very different resource that has the same effect over the long term. Either way, the point is that resources that can be substituted cannot sustain competitive advantage over the long term.

Immobile

Lastly, resources should not be mobile between firms. Assets such as a reputation for quality, loyalty or innovation cannot be traded freely on factor markets but must be accumulated over a sustained period of time. Such resources closely resemble the concept of externalities in economics (Arrow, 1974), those commodities that cannot be appropriately priced or traded on the open market. Resources may also be immobile in the sense that their value is significantly lower, perhaps even zero, outside of their current use or that the transaction costs of transferring that resource are prohibitively high (Williamson, 1985). It is thus apparent that only superior resources that are non-tradeable or significantly less valuable to others will be capable of generating sustained competitive advantage.

Resource-based view and the make–buy decision

The resource-based view is an attempt to advance a reason for the existence and boundaries of the firm independent of the effects of opportunism. Authors in this field see their work as distinct from the foregoing transaction cost approach; firms are not the form of last resort. Rather, they share a belief that firms are positive entities that exist because the combination of specific resources garners advantage that is not available in market forms of transactions. Comparing transaction cost and capability perspectives, Madhok (1996) suggests that the market (buy) may be preferable to hierarchy (make) even in situations where the potential costs of hold-up are higher than the potential costs of employee shirking. This holds if the costs of creating or acquiring the necessary capabilities are significant. Thus the make–buy decision depends on the extent to which the new undertakings are specific to current capabilities (Conner, 1991), and the costs of developing the necessary capabilities.

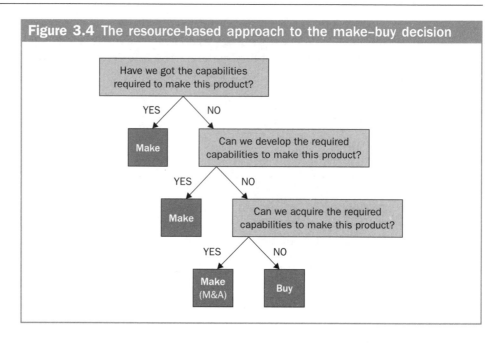

Figure 3.4 The resource-based approach to the make–buy decision

The resource-based approach to the make–buy decision can be found in Figure 3.4. The process begins with the question 'Do we have the capabilities to make this product in-house?' It is worth pointing out a distinction here between transaction cost economics and the resource-based view. Unlike TCE, firms are not seen as the form of last resort (Williamson, 1999), but in a far more positive light, as entities that can combine resources to produce efficiencies unavailable in the market (Hodgson, 1998). The preferred option is therefore to look inside the firm and ask whether they have the existing capabilities required to produce the item.

A firm may, however, not possess all of the capabilities it requires to produce all the desired items and to capitalise on existing opportunities. In this instance three options are presented, as shown in Figure 3.4. First, the firm can try to develop the capabilities internally; second, the firm can choose to acquire a firm that already possess the capabilities; third, the firm can choose to buy from an external supplier. The choice between these various options is predicated on the costs of developing and acquiring the capabilities. There are several reasons why it may be costly to develop resources internally (taken from Barney, 1999):

- **Historical context.** The 'right place–right time' syndrome, where the cost of developing particular capabilities was undertaken at a time when certain advantages that were available are no longer available to your competitors. This is often the case where governments are trying to stimulate growth in a region and offer start-up grants to companies for a given period.

- **Path dependence.** Some capabilities can only be developed through a long learning process. For example, it is not possible to 'short circuit' the process of moving from Stage 1 (passive) to Stage 4 (integrative) of the Reck and Long (1988) typology of purchasing function development (see Figure 2.1, p. 12).

- **Social complexity.** Some capabilities are costly to develop because they are socially complex, such as a company's culture or reputation. These types of capabilities are problematic to develop in the short term and need a long-term strategic effort.

- **Causal ambiguity.** Some capabilities are difficult to develop because the link between the capability and the development process is unclear. For example, even though much has been written on the Toyota Production System few firms really understand the process sufficiently to secure the full benefits.

Where the costs of developing the required resources are prohibitively high (for one or a combination of the above reasons), managers must look outside the boundaries of the firm. Resources can either be acquired from another firm, through either a merger or an acquisition, or they may simply choose to source from an external supplier. Again several costs (this time acquisition costs) may help inform managers during the decision-making process:

- **Legal constraints.** Some firms are prevented from acquiring others on the basis of, for example, acquiring monopoly market positions. For example, in 2001 General Electric wanted to merge with Honeywell to take advantage of their capabilities within aviation electronics. However, the EU rejected the proposal, arguing that it would stifle competition.

- **Knock-on effects on value.** Several studies have indicated that the value of companies, and therefore their capabilities, can rise and fall post merger or acquisition.

- **Technology tie-in.** Firms may find that the capability that they desired at the time of the proposed merger or acquisition becomes redundant over the long term as technologies and fashions change.

- **Unwanted 'baggage'.** Firms may also have difficulty separating the desired capabilities from the company as a whole. It may make more economic sense to partner in cases where the desired capabilities are only a small proportion of the overall business. The issues of RBV and TCE are further discussed in Box 3.2.

Where these costs are seen as prohibitively high, the firm is likely to buy from an external supplier and is therefore the start of the sourcing process. In summary, the RBV is concerned with the role and nature of capabilities within the make–buy

Box 3.2 Discussion: Is RBV a complete theory?

The RBV has also faced criticisms, primarily from those aligned with TCE. A number of these critiques are centred on the exclusion of opportunism. Williamson (1999) contends that absent opportunism, the ideal forms of organisation would be peer groups or ideal merit assignment; firms and markets would simply not exist. Similarly, Foss (1996) suggests that without opportunism actors could meet under the same roof and enjoy the same learning benefits as anticipated in the firm. Essentially, these analyses highlight the need for further formalisation of the RBV, especially concerning its predictive content. For example, it is not clear what limits the size of the firm (Williamson, 1999), apart from perhaps dissimilarity with current capabilities. At present, neither TCE nor RBV offers complete theories, but instead they offer differing perspectives on this fundamental question within supply chain management.

Box 3.3 Supply in action: Developing contact lens capabilities at Johnson and Johnson

In the late 1970s the contact lens industry was undergoing a revolution. Previously contact lenses had been made individually by small independently owned firms and supplied directly to doctors. The development of soft contact lenses, which increased comfort for wearers, looked set to change this, bringing contact lenses to the attention of large firms as a growth market. Johnson and Johnson (J&J), a company with a history of successful acquisitions and mergers dating back to 1905, wished to expand into this market but lacked the requisite skills within the company. Development of these skills internally was hindered by copyright, as much of the development of materials for soft lenses had taken place behind the Iron Curtain and the rights had been sold to rival Bausch and Lomb.

Instead J&J started looking at potential acquisition targets. Frontier Contact Lenses had done well in the hard contact lens market, and had begun to diversify into the soft lens market in the late 1970s as new polymers and changes in distribution rights made this feasible. Frontier was by no means a market leader in the soft lens industry; it did, however, have a reputation for innovation and was one of the first companies in the USA to utilise advanced lens-making technology such as lathes for production of soft lenses. In 1981 J&J acquired Frontier, and in June of 1982 renamed the firm Vistakon. J&J then added to this acquisition by buying the rights to a soft moulding process that allowed the mass production of soft contact lenses. This process of acquisition had enabled J&J to quickly develop capabilities in an emerging market where internal development was troublesome. Since then Vistakon (as a member of the J&J family) has been a story of success, launching ACUVUE®, the first disposable contact lens, nationally (US) in 1988. In 2006 ACUVUE® soft disposable contact lenses remain the number one brand in the world and, more importantly, a highly profitable part of J&J's portfolio.

Sources: http://www.jnj.com/; McMahon and Zadnik (2000)

decision. Figure 3.4 serves as a checklist for managers, who can work their way through the process to derive a capability-contingent make–buy decision. This is further illustrated in Box 3.3.

Summary

This chapter demonstrated the importance of the make–buy decision to organisations. The chapter introduced and described the make–buy decision with particular reference to the effect on firm boundaries. It outlined why neoclassical economics was an inadequate basis for analysis. It further discussed two theoretical perspectives, transaction cost economics and the resource-based view, which tackle this important issue.

With rising levels of outsourcing and many firms seeking to focus on fewer core capabilities, the make–buy decision is increasingly important to competitive advantage. Firms must ensure that individual decisions make sense at both the operational and strategic levels. The theoretical perspectives provide purchasing and supply managers with a framework to help identify a number of the critical factors bearing upon these decisions. Where the outcome of the decision is to 'buy' the product or service it serves as the trigger for the sourcing process that will be discussed in Part 2.

Seminar questions

1 An outsourcing dilemma!

Your roles:
An in-house, cross-functional team developed to assess the viability of outsourcing production of components to Hungary.

Your firm:
A multinational furniture manufacturer specialising in the design, manufacture and fitting of stadium and auditorium seating.

The problem:
Your firm has enjoyed a great deal of success over the past 20 years and has become a market leader, known for high-quality, innovative solutions. However, owing to the global economic slowdown, fewer stadiums and theatres are being commissioned and financed. Competition is also increasing as several of your key staff have left over the past few years to set up rival firms. These pressures have made your firm examine its costs and you have taken the decision to outsource production to lower-wage economies whenever it is viable.

One component that you are asked to assess is the chair legs. Legs are a fairly standard product that do not vary a great deal in specification between orders and are currently used in 80 per cent of the overall product range. A number of possible suppliers have been assessed but only one in Hungary was considered to have the capability to deliver to the required quality levels and at a reasonable price. The supplier already manufactures legs for one of your competitors and a facilities management (FM) capability means minimal up-front investment.

Please apply the principles of transaction cost economics to this situation and reach a decision as to whether the legs should be outsourced to Hungary.

2 A resource gap!

Your roles:
A team of strategic consultants from a small strategy boutique tasked with examining whether a medium-sized biotechnology company should develop an in-house manufacturing capability.

Your client:

A biotechnology firm that has just developed and received approval for a potential new blockbuster drug that can reduce male-pattern balding.

The problem:

Given the potential success of the drug, the company is considering whether it should manufacture and distribute in-house, rather than license the drug to a major pharmaceutical company. In the past your client has always sold the technology or licensed the intellectual property to larger pharma companies in the knowledge that it did not have the capabilities required to bring the drug to market. However, it has noticed that one of its major competitors has recently acquired a medium-sized pharma company and is flourishing under this change of strategy.

The biotechnology firm has little experience in the mass manufacture, distribution and marketing of products. As you may expect, its strategic resources and capabilities currently rest in the R&D function, an area that the firm believes directly contributes to its current success. It would, however, like to explore the potential options for delivering this new drug to market.

Please apply the principles of the resource-based view of the firm to this problem. You should state your assumptions and justify any decision that you reach.

References

Arrow, K. (1974) *The Limits of Organization*, Norton, New York.

Barney, J. B. (1991) 'Firm Resources and Sustained Competitive Advantage', *Journal of Management*, Vol. 17, pp. 99–120.

Barney, J. B. (1999) 'How a Firm's Capabilities Affect Boundary Decisions', *Sloan Management Review*, Vol. 40, pp. 137–45.

Barney, J. B. and Ouchi, W. G. (1986) *Organizational Economics*, Jossey-Bass, San Francisco, CA.

Chandler, A. D. (1992) 'Organizational Capabilities and the Economic History of the Industrial Enterprise', *Journal of Economic Perspectives*, Vol. 6, pp. 79–100.

Coase, R. H. (1937) 'The Nature of the Firm', *Economica N. S.*, Vol. 4, pp. 386–405.

Conner, K. R. (1991) 'A Historical Comparison of Resource-based Theory and Five Schools of Thought within Industrial Organization Economics: Do we Have a New Theory of the Firm?', *Journal of Management*, Vol. 17, pp. 121–54.

Dierickx, I. and Cool, K. (1989) 'Asset Stock Accumulation and Sustainability of Competitive Advantage', *Management Science*, Vol. 35, pp. 1504–14.

Foss, N. J. (1996) 'Knowledge-based Approaches to the Theory of the Firm: Some Critical Comments', *Organization Science*, Vol. 7, pp. 470–6.

Ghoshal, S. and Moran, P. (1996) 'Bad for Practice: A Critique of the Transaction Cost Theory', *Academy of Management Journal*, Vol. 21, pp. 13–47.

Hart, O. (1989) 'An Economist's Perspective on the Theory of the Firm', *Columbia Law Review*, Vol. 89, p. 1757.

Hodgson, G. M. (1998) 'Evolutionary and Competence Theories of the Firm', *Journal of Economic Studies*, Vol. 25, pp. 25–56.

Holmstrom, B. and Roberts, J. (1998) 'The Boundaries of the Firm Revisited', *Journal of Economic Perspectives*, Vol. 12, pp. 73–94.

Kay, N. (2000) 'Searching for the Firm: The Role of Decision in the Economics of Organizations', *Industrial and Corporate Change*, Vol. 9, pp. 683–707.

Klein, B., Crawford, R. G. and Alchian, A. A. (1978) 'Vertical Integration, Appropriable Rents, and the Competitive Contracting Process', *The Journal of Law and Economics*, Vol. 21, pp. 297–326.

Lazonick, W. (1991) *The Myth of the Market Economy*, Cambridge University Press, Cambridge.

Lippman, S. A. and Rumelt, R. P. (1982) 'Uncertain Imitability: An Analysis of Interfirm Differences in Efficiency Under Competition', *The Bell Journal of Economics*, Vol. 13, pp. 418–38.

Madhok, A. (1996) 'The Organization of Economic Activity: Transaction Costs, Firms Capabilities, and the Nature of Governance', *Organization Science*, Vol. 7, pp. 577–90.

McMahon, T. O. D. and Zadnik, K. (2000) 'Twenty Five Years of Contact Lenses: The Impact on the Cornea and Ophthalmic Practice', *Cornea: The Journal of Cornea and External Diseases*, Vol. 19 (5), September, pp. 730–40.

Nelson, R. R. and Winter, S. G. (1982) *An Evolutionary Theory of Economic Change*, Harvard University Press, Cambridge, MA.

Penrose, E. T. (1959) *The Theory of the Growth of the Firm*, Wiley, New York.

Peteraf, M. A. (1993) 'The Cornerstones of Competitive Advantage: A Resource-based View', *Strategic Management Journal*, Vol. 14, p. 191.

Powell, W. W. (1990) 'Neither Market nor Hierarchy: Network Forms of Organization', *Research in Organizational Behavior*, Vol. 12, pp. 295–336.

Reck, R. F. and Long, B. G. (1988) 'Purchasing: A Competitive Weapon', *Journal of Purchasing and Materials Management*, Vol. 24, pp. 2–8.

Reed, R. and De Fillippi, R. J. (1990) 'Causal Ambiguity, Barriers to Imitation, and Sustainable Competitive Advantage', *Academy of Management Review*, Vol. 15, pp. 88–102.

Ricardo, D. (1911) *The Principles of Political Economy and Taxation*, Dent, London.

Rumelt, R. P. (1987) *Theory, Strategy and Entrepreneurship*, Ballinger, Cambridge, MA.

Simon, H. A. (1957) *Models of Man, Social and Rational*, Wiley, New York.

Williamson, O. E. (1975) *Markets and Hierarchies*, The Free Press, New York.

Williamson, O. E. (1985) *The Economic Institutions of Capitalism*, The Free Press, New York.

Williamson, O. E. (1991) 'Comparative Economic Organization: The Analysis of Discrete Structural Alternatives', *Administrative Science Quarterly*, Vol. 36, pp. 269–96.

Williamson, O. E. (1999) 'Strategy Research: Governance and Competence Perspectives', *Strategic Management Journal*, Vol. 20, pp. 1087–108.

Zajac, E. J. and Olsen, C. P. (1993) 'From Transaction Cost to Transactional Value Analysis: Implications for the Study of Interorganizational Strategies', *Journal of Management Studies*, Vol. 30, pp. 131–45.

Endnotes

1. Here we are primarily concerned with vertical firm boundaries.
2. Specifically, firms may control opportunism through the use of fiat, unavailable to markets, and additional incentive instruments, such as promotion or profit sharing (Williamson, 1991).
3. Other competency approaches include evolutionary economics and the knowledge-based view of the firm.
4. Economic rent is the surplus earning a firm receives due to differential factors of production that are limited in supply (Peteraf, 1993). In the classical Ricardian argument (Ricardo, 1911), land is considered to represent a prime example of a factor of production that varies in levels of productivity and is limited in supply. For example, where the price of corn is set at equilibrium, those landowners at the margin (i.e. where the value of output equals the costs of capital and labour) do not earn rents. On the other hand, landowners away from the margin (where the land is more fertile) will earn rents because they can produce the same yield at lower average cost.

Chapter 4

Sourcing strategies and supply chain configurations

Aim of chapter

The aim of this chapter is to examine various sourcing strategies and supply chain configurations available to firms.

Learning outcomes

At the end of this chapter, readers will understand:

■ the concept of supply strategy as it relates to supply chain configurations;

■ the implications of Kraljic's positioning matrix;

■ the four key sourcing configurations;

■ the implications for choosing and applying appropriate sourcing strategies to commodity, product and service groups.

Introduction

In previous chapters we discussed how purchasing is developing into supply management, moving from a clerical function towards a strategic business process. This chapter builds on those arguments and develops two principal ideas. Firstly, the concept of supply strategy is discussed, with models and definitions provided to help you think about this rather broad term and what it might mean for firms. Secondly, we also need to consider how firms structure their supply activity in a 'strategic' sense. We present a range of sourcing strategies and approaches that firms use to manage their complex supply activity. Naturally the choice of sourcing configuration will depend on a range of organisational and environmental objectives.

Supply base reduction

The move towards increased supplier integration in the 1990s also spawned another strategy which became known as supply base rationalisation,[1] or supply base reduction. The underlying rationale of this approach is relatively simple; it involves working more closely with fewer suppliers. The concept builds on the idea that a firm has only a limited amount of resources and that by reducing the number of suppliers that a firm has to manage it can focus its resources. This strategy was very popular in the early 1990s and was used by a wide range of consultancies to enable a leveraging strategy, i.e. consolidating business with a few major suppliers as opposed to spreading the business over a larger number of suppliers. This strategy allows the firm to realize significant cost savings. Some examples of this are shown in Box 4.1.

While this strategy may realise short-term cost savings, and is supported by manufacturing systems such as lean manufacturing, SBR is not without its problems. For example, by reducing the supply base firms change the market and power dynamics of their inter-firm relationships. When a supply base is reduced, by definition, the nature of the inter-firm relationship changes from being relatively independent

---

Box 4.1 Examples of strategic supply base reduction

Strategic supply-base reduction (SBR) has become a major tool used by leading firms to reduce costs and improve quality, responsiveness, flexibility, and other key dimensions of performance. Here are some examples of SBR in action.

AlliedSignal: AlliedSignal's first step in its sourcing strategy was to prune the supply base from 10,000 in 1992 to fewer than 2000 in 1997. Plans called for its supply base to shrink further to 1500 over the next few years. AlliedSignal's automotive sector saved $28 million in 1993, which came primarily from winnowing the supply base and negotiating new contracts (Minahan, 1997).

Boeing: 'Boeing will cut 13,000 of its 31,000 suppliers over the next four years, mostly smaller companies that duplicate equipment' (Rae-Dupree, 1999).

Chrysler: From 1989 to 1993, Chrysler reduced its production supplier base from 2500 companies to 1114 and fundamentally changed the way it works with those that remain. The time to develop a new vehicle is approaching 160 weeks, down from an average of 234 weeks during the 1980s. The cost of developing a new vehicle has decreased by an estimated 20 to 40 per cent. Since 1988, Chrysler has reduced its number of buyers by 30 per cent and has increased the dollar value of goods procured by each buyer. Profit per vehicle has increased from approximately $250 in the 1980s (taking the average from 1985 through 1989) to $2110 in 1994 (Dyer, 1996). 'Now about 90 per cent of Chrysler's purchasing volume is with 150 suppliers' (Lewis, 1995).

GEC Marconi Electronics: GEC Marconi replaced the multiple systems it used to manage and order parts with a single system. As a result, it was able to reduce its supply base from 97,000 to 28,000 and generate a yearly savings in its component costs of 15 per cent (Bylinsky, 1999).

Intel: 'Since the mid '80s, Intel has made a serious effort to consolidate its supply base, adopting an n + 1 rule-of-thumb in determining the maximum number of suppliers ('n') needed in each commodity area to satisfy production requirements.' That is, Intel will not have more than one extra supplier above the minimum number needed to satisfy its production requirements. For example, the number of suppliers of lead frames has been trimmed from 12 to 3, ceramic packages from 6 to 3, and wire and moulding compound from 3 to 1 (Morgan, 1995).

Kraft Foods: 'Recent initiatives to consolidate activity [copier equipment and records retention] with a single vendor for each function are generating annual cost savings of 30 to 40 per cent' (Westfall, 1999).

(when there are multiple sources of supply) to becoming relatively dependent (when there are fewer sources of supply). Naturally this requires different measurement and management systems to enable the relationship to work effectively.

Very often firms do not make these changes and find themselves working in highly dependent relationships, utilising the same methods that they used when these relationships were independent. This can cause many problems, e.g. over-reliance on suppliers that are not capable of working in a more collaborative manner. Figure 4.1 illustrates conceptually what can happen when this strategy is followed, based on research work by Cousins (2005). Remember that the main motivation for following this strategy is to attain cost reduction. While this is certainly possible, it also creates a host of additional issues. Firstly, firms tend to not be aware of the true costs of procurement. Indeed, in the experience of the authors very few firms have a clear understanding of their cost structure. Therefore, when firms are asked the question, 'Has the strategy of supply base reduction been successful?', most firms would agree that it has. However, the more important question to ask is: What was the cost of doing business before you reduced your supply base? And what are the costs of doing business after the supply base has been reduced? Figure 4.1 attempts to provide some answers to these questions, assuming we accept that there are three main types of cost:

1 **Operational costs.** These are the costs of running the day-to-day relationship, e.g. costs of producing the purchase order, invoicing and so on.

2 **Managerial costs.** These are the costs of managing the relationship, e.g. problem solving, travelling to visit the supplier, quality workshops, supplier conferences etc.

3 **Strategic costs.** These can be thought of as strategic risk, i.e. the ability for a supplier to act opportunistically. When there are a large number of suppliers the strategic risk/costs are relatively low and when there are fewer suppliers the strategic costs are relatively high.

Figure 4.1 demonstrates that these costs range from objective (easily measurable) to subjective (much more difficult to measure). The other axis examines the impact of these costs on the business, ranging from low to high.

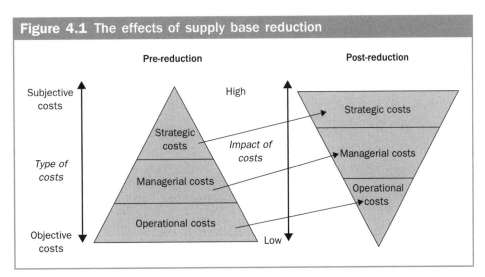

Figure 4.1 The effects of supply base reduction

There are several interesting issues about this model. Firstly, when we consider the 'types of cost' axis and ask firms which of these costs they measure, the answer is invariably 'operational costs'. When asked why, they often respond 'because we can'. In other words, the more subjective the costs, the more difficult they are to measure and therefore the less likely they are to be considered by the firm. If we then consider the impact of these costs on the firm we see that operational costs have a relatively low impact on the business; however, as the costs increase in subjectivity and sophistication they have a much larger impact on the business.

The second point is what happens when firms move from a large supply base to a reduced supply base. Figure 4.1 illustrates this effect; the pyramid effectively turns upside down. Strategic costs post reduction increase by a large amount as the buyer firm becomes more dependent on a smaller number of suppliers, whereas operational costs decrease by a given proportion because the number of transactions has decreased in proportion to the reduction of supplier numbers, e.g. moving from five suppliers to one means four times fewer purchase orders, invoices and so on.

The key point here is not the effect on the costs *per se*, but the way these costs are captured. Again, referring to Figure 4.1, it is the operational costs that the firm tends to capture and not the more subjective strategic costs, which results in a misleading interpretation of the strategy's success. In other words, in the short term this strategy appears to be very successful as it has achieved cost reductions and taken out transaction costs. However, in the medium to long term it has changed the nature of the buyer–supplier relationship, from independent to dependent, which means that the buyer needs to consider carefully how this should be managed. Managing this relationship as though there are many suppliers is no longer appropriate. If the relationship is managed with a short-term outlook the buyer firm could be placed in an extremely vulnerable position. For example, an interview with the purchasing director of a large automotive firm revealed an interesting point. When asked what he thought of the success of supply base reduction strategies, he replied 'if I knew then what I know now I would never have gone through with this approach . . .' Further conversations revealed that the problem was that whilst the buyer was willing and able to work in this manner, the supplier did not have the capabilities. Indeed, there are other examples where this situation is reversed, i.e. the supplier is capable of working in this close, cooperative manner, but the buyer firm is not.

The term 'supply base reduction' is to an extent a misnomer. While firms have indeed reduced the number of direct suppliers, in a majority of cases the actual number of suppliers within the overall supply network has hardly varied. This is because they have become indirect as opposed to direct suppliers. In fact, there has been a two-pronged strategy in the market. One strategy (known as leverage) focuses on reducing suppliers by having a key dominant supplier – this strategy tends to be favoured by consultants as it can generally achieve significant short-term savings. The other strategy is commonly known as supplier tiering. This involves restructuring the supply base into direct and indirect suppliers. In actual fact the number of suppliers is not necessarily reduced but simply reorganised into layers of suppliers. The following section will discuss these strategies within the context of sourcing strategies.

Sourcing strategies

A firm can organise its supply process using a variety of sourcing strategies. The choice of these different approaches is contingent upon a variety of factors, such as the importance of a good or service to the firm and the competitiveness of the supply marketplace. Firms must also consider the technical complexity of the product. To help Buyers formulate appropriate sourcing and competitive strategies, Kraljic (1983) developed a simple positioning matrix based on these factors. Virtually every Purchasing department and consultancy firm uses this matrix today and it is the main strategic positioning tool for thinking about supply management decisions. While this model is widely used it is not without its problems; we shall discuss these later in the chapter. The matrix's simplicity belies its power and usefulness to supply professionals when formulating optimal procurement approaches. Kraljic identified four key purchasing approaches or strategies (see Figure 4.2). He suggested that selecting the best supply strategy is a function of the level of supply exposure, technical risk and the strategic nature of the product or service (i.e. its value or cost to the buying firm). Figure 4.2 also maps the type of products and services supplied (also known as 'sourcing groups'[2]) to particular sourcing strategies. Despite its age, Kraljic's matrix remains central to many purchasing and supply strategies, testament to the foresight shown by its author. The article was similarly foresighted, entitled 'Purchasing Must Become Supply Management', and published in the *Harvard Business Review* in 1983. While this article is over

Figure 4.2 Kraljic product and service positioning matrix

Classification of purchase items

High	**Leverage: Best deal** (High profit impact, low supply risk) • Unit cost management important because of volume usage • Substitution possible • Competitive supply market with several capable suppliers	**Critical: Cooperation** (High profit impact, high supply risk) • Custom design or unique specification • Supplier technology important • Changing source of supply difficult or costly • Substitution difficult
Impact on business (internal issues)	**Routine: Efficiency** (Low profit impact, low supply risk) • Standard specification or 'Commodity'-type items • Substitute products readily available • Competitive supply market with many suppliers	**Bottleneck: Supply continuity** (Low profit impact, high supply risk) • Unique specification • Supplier's technology important • Production-based scarcity due to low demand and/or few sources of supply • Usage fluctuation not routinely predictable • Potential storage risk
Low	Low	High

Supply risk/supply market complexity (external issues)

Source: adapted from Kraljic, 1983

20 years old it is still used and quoted on a regular basis by academics and practitioners alike.

Supply market complexity

The horizontal axis is concerned with the supply-side risk that occurs due to external supply market issues and the complexity of the market.[3] Supply Strategists should consider factors such as power relations, the availability of supply and substitution possibilities that will have a fundamental effect on risk. Porter's (1980) five forces model gives a good indication of the factors causing rivalry (or competition) in an industry, as can be seen from Figure 4.3.

The key elements of Porter's model all have an influence on the amount of supply-side risk and complexity in a given marketplace.

'Barriers to new entrants' is concerned with the costs of investment of entering a marketplace. This might be because market channels are expensive, logistics networks are required or there is a substantial amount of investment in tooling,

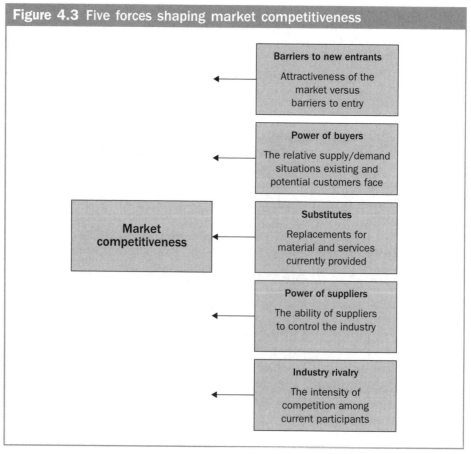

Figure 4.3 Five forces shaping market competitiveness

Source: adapted from Porter (1985)

machinery and processes that needs to be made. This will restrict suppliers (if the barriers are high) or allow them to enter the marketplace and will therefore have an impact on the level of risk of trading in this supply market.

'Power of buyers' is influenced by the relative concentration of buyer firms in a market. If there is a high concentration of buyers relative to the number of suppliers, then buyer power is likely to be low; if there are only a few major buyers in the marketplace and a large amount of supply, then buyer power is likely to be high. Naturally there are also equilibrium and a range of other points on the concentration scale. The point is that buyer (and indeed supplier) firms should consider the market structure when thinking about managing their sourcing (or customer) relationships.

'Substitutes' refers to replacement goods or services. These can be created by new or disruptive technologies, e.g. a new material could be developed which means that buyers will switch from one type of production method to another. New products or services entering the market and replacing existing technologies and services will tend have a major effect on the competitive structure of that industry and in turn will affect the supply-side risk of the buyer firm.

'Power of suppliers' is inversely related to the 'Power of buyers', i.e. when one is high the other tends to be low. If either party can maintain a dominant power position in the marketplace, they can extract competitive advantage from that market, usually in the form of higher prices.

'Industrial rivalry' refers to the level of competition within an industry. Internal competition can be considered in terms of industry growth and exit barriers from the market. Where industry growth is low and exit barriers are high the market is stable and therefore complexity is low.

Impact on business

The vertical axis of Kraljic's matrix is fundamentally concerned with the impact on profit or the value obtained from the sourcing group. Whereas the horizontal axis shows market exposure risks that are 'external' to the firm, the impact on business factors can be thought of as 'internal' to the firm. Determining what product and service categories fall into this group is reasonably difficult, owing to the contradictory nature of the terms on this axis; for example, a product could be low cost, but high value. An example would be specialised bolts which are used in the aircraft industry to secure the gearbox housing on military and commercial helicopters. Compared to the total cost of the aircraft these are relatively cheap, but if they were to come off in-flight the results would be disastrous. Therefore their relative *value* is high. Most consultancy firms, when conducting the initial positioning of products and services, would tend to use the cost category first and then sort by relative value and risk.

The cost approach to product and service positioning tends to use Pareto analysis. Pareto was an economist and sociologist who died in 1923. He discovered a phenomenon which exists in much of the natural environment. It became known as the 80/20 rule. This rule can be applied to a wide range of business situations,

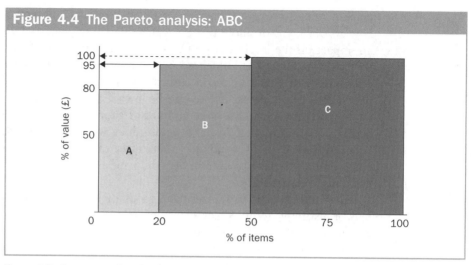

Figure 4.4 The Pareto analysis: ABC

Source: Author's representation of the Pareto Equilibrium. See also Bannock et al. (2003)

for example 20 per cent of the products used to build a car will make up 80 per cent of the costs. In other words, there are a small number of high-cost items and a large number of low-cost items. This is known as ABC analysis. 'A' items account for 80 per cent of cost and 20 per cent of volume, 'C' items represent low cost and high volume and B items are in the middle. Figure 4.4 shows an example of this. This analysis tells us that we must pay careful attention to the 'A' items, with ascending priority down to 'C' items.

Pareto's method allows firms to classify their products and services into A, B and C class items. Naturally an 'A' item would be placed in the high area of the spectrum, a 'B' class item somewhere in the middle, and a 'C' item at the low end. The second stage of analysis is to decide on the level of sourcing risk (external), which then gives the coordinates to place it in the positioning matrix.

Calculating risk, and indeed value, is much more difficult. In practice, the firm generally positions based on the ABC analysis described above. It would then go back through these items and decide what level of (internal) risk they might represent. Internal risk needs to be defined by the firm and may vary depending on what type of firm it is and what it sees as important to its business. For example, an automotive firm may decide that something is high risk if it is going to have an adverse impact on the production schedule. An aerospace firm might consider something to be high risk if its failure would cause a catastrophic effect in the aircraft, e.g. the earlier bolt example.

Strategic directions for managing category spends

The matrix itself forces firms to consider categories of spend based on their level of supply market exposure and internal risk and cost. It is worth emphasising at this point that the matrix does *not* allow for the positioning of companies, but rather spend categories. These categories may well be spread across a range of suppliers. The model offers buyer firms four distinct strategies that they can follow:

■ **Strategy 1: Routine.** This strategy is aimed at a spend category known as *routine* items. The recommended approach here is to follow a strategy based on *efficiency*. This quadrant contains products or services of low value or cost and low technical or supply risk. The recommendation is that these should be sourced from the most efficient suppliers. Examples of low-level parts or commodity products include nuts, bolts or rivets in manufacturing or an administrative item such as stationery or low-level temporary labour. The objective is to pay the most competitive price for the product, whilst maintaining delivery and quality standards. As switching costs are low and the market is highly competitive, buyers would negotiate on price.

■ **Strategy 2: Bottleneck.** This strategy is aimed at the spend category known as *bottleneck* items. These are items that can seriously affect the delivery of the buyer firm's product or service. They tend to be relatively low value but are relatively rare in terms of the supply market. A good example of this may be computer chips. These don't cost a great deal compared to the total unit price, but they are essential to the running of the product. Here the strategy is to maintain supply continuity by, for example, establishing long-term contracts containing liquidated damages clauses. The buyer will tend to focus on total cost rather than simply on purchase price.

■ **Strategy 3: Leverage.** This strategy is aimed at the spend category known as *leverage*. The focus of this strategy is to obtain the best deal possible. This strategy occurs when the buyer perceives market exposure to be low yet the cost or value of the item is high (e.g. foam for car seats at an automotive assembler). The buyer can obtain the best deal by using 'leverage' strategies (Porter, 1980) where the buyer power is high and the supplier power is low. Leveraging involves pulling together a range of similar products – sometimes the same product bought at different locations throughout the firm – to increase contract size and therefore buyer bargaining power. An automotive manufacturer might source two models of car seat using a single supplier rather than multiple suppliers. This may achieve economies of scale for the buyer, providing a stronger negotiation position. Firms pursuing a cost reduction strategy consistently follow this strategy. A development of this is to split a requirement three ways – giving each of two suppliers one-third of the business on a long-term contract, the remaining third being available to the more competitive of them on a shorter-term basis. This approach to purchasing can, and often does, change the nature of supply market exposure. Supply market exposure increases as a buyer moves from several suppliers to one major source. A dependency relationship may result from the leverage strategy, often without the buying company knowing. Companies pursuing cost minimisation programmes in the late 1990s sometimes hastened large-scale consolidation of their supply markets (discussed earlier in this chapter), ultimately requiring transition to the final 'critical' box of Kraljic's matrix.

■ **Strategy 4: Critical.** This strategy is aimed at the spending category known as *critical*. The suggested strategy for buyers in this quadrant is 'cooperation', because these suppliers are both high risk and can have a high impact on the buyer firm's profitability. Suppliers that fall into this segment of the model provide products or services which are characterised by high supply risk and having a high impact on the business in terms of value or cost. These suppliers tend to fall into the top end of the Pareto curve discussed earlier; that is, the top 20 per cent of suppliers account for 80 per cent of the cost. These are firms' strategic suppliers. Examples include modular assembly suppliers (e.g. first-tier suppliers), key technology suppliers and major outsourcing providers (e.g. mega providers of information technology services). These relationships tend to be single or sole sourced due to the large amount of investment required; switching costs are generally very high, with mutual dependencies.[4] They need to be managed very carefully since they are often long-term and the focus tends to be on collaboration and mutual development, as opposed to price reduction and short-term aggressive strategies.

Supply structure and design

Each quadrant of the Kraljic matrix suggests a sourcing *strategy* which in turn dictates a related sourcing or supply *structure*. It is important to choose the structure that is suitable for the strategy and the sourcing category. There are four primary sourcing structures that can be used (with some amount of variation): single, multiple, delegated and parallel.

The complexity of the various sourcing approaches ranges from the simplest structure, single or sole sourcing, to the more complex structures of delegated and parallel sourcing. It is the role of the Supply Strategist to decide when and where to apply each of these structures. This decision will be dependent upon the needs and wants of the firm, the type of relationship desired, the acceptable level of dependency for both buyer and supplier and the nature of market-based competition. Note that the most dependent relationship is found in the simplest structure, i.e. the sole or single sourced arrangement. Each of these sourcing configurations will be discussed in turn.

Single sourcing

This structure characterises a buyer with only one source of supply for a particular good or service, as can be seen in Figure 4.5. It may be the result of a deliberate choice by the Buyer, perhaps because of the high cost of the item or its strategic importance to the end product. Alternatively it may occur because the final customer has explicitly required the firm to work with a particular sub-supplier's product in the completed product. For example, many customers of personal computers demand the Windows Operating System, thereby forcing manufacturers to source exclusively from Microsoft.

There may also be only one source of supply. According to the Kraljic strategic positioning model, this sourcing strategy is likely to be prevalent in either the critical or bottleneck quadrants of the model. While single sourcing may appear to have negative connotations, there are advantages to managing this type of rela-

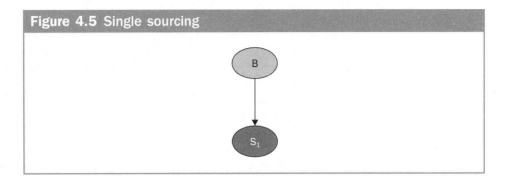

Figure 4.5 Single sourcing

tionship. For example, buyers and suppliers working in a single-sourced scenario often report that it is easier to exchange ideas (knowledge exchange for new product development), have a clear understanding of cost structures (move towards cost transparency) and look for ways to redesign or enhance the product and processes. By definition these relationships tend to be much more long term in focus, allowing firms to spend time focusing on the development of the relationship, i.e. a feeling that they are both committed.

The disadvantages of this sourcing configuration is that firstly there is only one source of supply, which could put the buyer in a position of weakness if the relationship is not managed properly, i.e. the buyer becomes overly reliant/dependent on the supplier. Alternatively, if the supply source were to cease doing business suddenly, the customer would be highly exposed in the marketplace. Secondly, if the buyer is 'locked' into a sole sourcing relationship with the supplier, this may restrict the buyer's flexibility to acquire new technologies or innovations that exist within the wider network. This could mean that the buyer's market position and therefore the firm's competitiveness is jeopardised. It is important to remember that the market dynamics (i.e. competitive-dynamic or uncompetitive-stable) will influence the optimal buying sourcing configuration.

Multiple sourcing

Multiple sourcing describes securing multiple supply sources to supply the product or service, as illustrated in Figure 4.6. In this model competition is based on price,

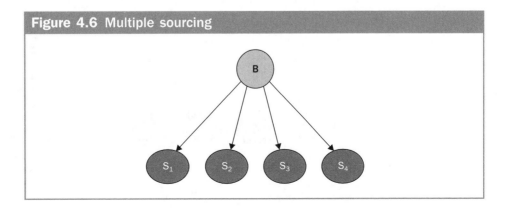

Figure 4.6 Multiple sourcing

with many suppliers guaranteeing a market price for the good or service. The structure is often used to maintain competition in a given supply market.

The Buyer will have a range of suppliers to choose from, and will carefully balance capacity constraints with individual supplier performance when placing orders. The old adage, 'don't put all your eggs in one basket', is often used to describe this supply structure. Buyers will also frequently use so-called 'Dutch auctions' to play suppliers off against each other to achieve the best price.[5] This is often viewed as an adversarial approach and prevails in marketplaces where there are a high degree of competition, low switching costs and low levels of technological competence. This structure would tend to appear in the 'Routine' quadrant of the strategic positioning matrix and applies to the low-level type of purchase. Buyers using this structure will tend to focus on purchase price rather than total cost. This approach maintains continuity of supply in the short term, whilst enabling the buyer to achieve price reductions. Sometimes, however, the market suffers from collusion and prices rise on average. There is unfortunately little opportunity for the buyer to use strategic tools. Although this model has traditionally been the mainstay of procurement strategy, it is being replaced by more sophisticated and value-adding approaches such as delegated and parallel sourcing.

Delegated sourcing strategy

Delegated sourcing strategies have grown in popularity since the mid-1990s, across a wide range of industries. The structure (which can be seen in Figure 4.7) was first pioneered in the aerospace and automotive industries (see Womack, Jones and Roos, 1990; Lamming, 1993) as a way of more efficiently managing supply.

This sourcing configuration involves making one supplier responsible for the delivery of an entire sub-assembly as opposed to an individual part. The customer delegates authority to a key supplier who becomes known as a first-tier supplier. The customer's objective is to work with one supplier; the supplier in turn works with all other suppliers that provide parts to complete the product. Box 4.2 describes one buying firm's use of this structure.

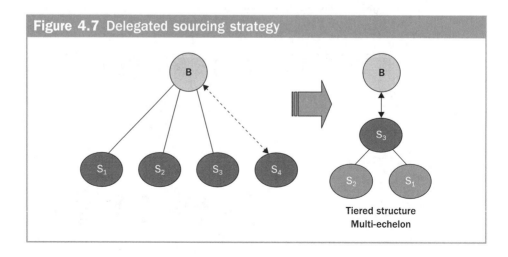

Figure 4.7 Delegated sourcing strategy

Tiered structure
Multi-echelon

Box 4.2 Automotive industry supply delegation

A major car manufacturer was investigating how they could reduce the number of suppliers to their business while maintaining quality, cost and delivery requirements. They decided to implement a 'tiered structure' approach to supply management. Since they would then be able to work closely with one key or first-tier supplier, they expected to exchange learning and develop a clear, integrated cost structure. The buyer firm would also not have to assemble the part itself since it would arrive complete to be inserted directly into the vehicle.

The buyer chose a major product area: the wheel assembly. They looked closely at all the suppliers of parts to the assembly and decided that the bearing manufacturer should be the prime or first-tier supplier. It became the bearing manufacturer's responsibility to provide the buyer with a completed wheel assembly. The buyer thus migrated from a multiple sourcing to a delegated sourcing strategy.

The move significantly reduced the number of suppliers to the customer (95 per cent reduction). It also enabled the manufacturer to focus its resources on the relationship with the first-tier supplier.

Delegated sourcing has a number of advantages for customer and supplier. Focusing on one supplier enables the Buyer to work closely with that one supply source to reduce day-to-day transaction costs. The increased dependence on one supplier results in the buyer and supplier exchanging more detailed information, particularly around cost issues. The buyer tends to transfer capabilities and technologies that enable that supplier to produce the required sub-assembly. The buyer thus becomes a major player for the supplier, increasing the supplier's dependence on the buyer, whilst simultaneously giving the supplier more authority and control over the delivery and production of the sub-assembly.

The process of delegated sourcing tends to create 'mega' suppliers that may evolve into a potential threat. Suppliers can become very powerful and exert their power over the buyer, usually in the form of price increases. It is vitally important for the buyer to understand and manage all the dependencies when these arrangements are put in place. This strategy is often found initially in the 'leverage' quadrant of the matrix, moving to 'critical' quadrant in the medium term due to the high dependency and high switching costs. This strategy tends also to be followed by firms that are trying to optimise and/or reduce their supply base. As we discussed earlier in this chapter, delegated sourcing allows a firm to reduce the number of 'direct' suppliers without necessarily reducing the total amount of supply. In effect, it is a different way of coordinating the supply network.

Parallel sourcing

The concept of parallel sourcing is a little more complex (see Figure 4.8). Richardson (1993) developed the concept using game theory to optimise supply for the buyer (see also Axelrod 1984, 1987). Richardson suggests that the supply structure provides the buyer with the advantages of sole and multiple sourcing whilst excluding the disadvantages of these strategies. Parallel sourcing allows the buying firm to work on a single or sole-sourced basis with each component supplier within a

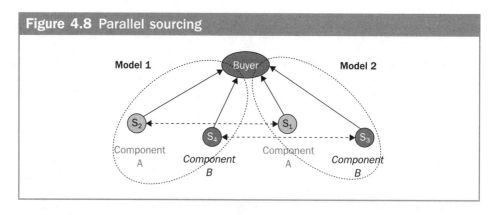

Figure 4.8 Parallel sourcing

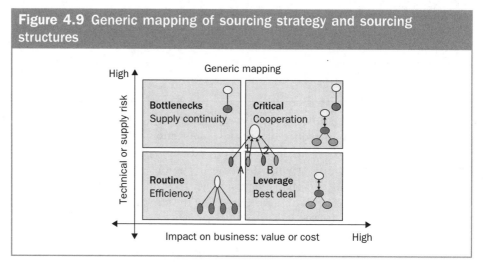

Figure 4.9 Generic mapping of sourcing strategy and sourcing structures

product group while maintaining a multiple-sourced relationship across product groups. This allows the firm to maintain price competition, reduce complacency, and protect against capacity constraint issues while at the same time working more closely with suppliers within the model groups. This may involve sharing cost information and design specifications and embarking on process improvement initiatives.

Although the model looks complicated at first glance, the principle is quite simple. Assume that the buyer (the customer) is making two products: product 1 and product 2. For example, it might be a vehicle manufacturer making two models of car. Each product (model of car) requires two components, A (the gearbox) and B (the braking system). For product 1, the customer sources the gearbox from supplier A1 and the braking system from supplier B1. For product 2, the buyer sources the gearbox from another supplier A2 and the braking system from yet another supplier B2. Therefore there are two suppliers of brakes and two suppliers of gearboxes. While each supplier supplies into a separate product group (sole sourced), the buyer has alternative sources of supply if necessary (multiple sourced). Furthermore, the buyer can compare the price, delivery and quality of goods across different suppliers but for similar components. This makes comparison easier and more meaningful than for completely different products.

Sourcing structures provide the means for implementing supply strategy. As such, they must be aligned to the requirements of the organisation. For these strategies to work effectively they need to sit within an appropriate organisational structure and be measured in the correct manner. The various sourcing structures can be mapped to the Kraljic matrix to portray those strategies most appropriate to a particular commodity grouping (see Figure 4.9).

Mapping the sourcing configurations to the various supply strategies allows us to understand the most appropriate configurations for managing within each of the quadrants within Kraljic's matrix.

Summary

This chapter has set out to show how supply strategy and sourcing configurations are combined to create sourcing strategies for the various commodities, products and services that a firm needs to purchase. We have discussed in detail Kraljic's positioning matrix and shown how the four generic sourcing configurations can be positioned within this matrix. This positioning allows the buyer (and supplier) to choose appropriate sourcing strategies for market conditions whilst minimising risk and cost exposure to the business. The next chapter examines how you can select between suppliers to fit into these various configurations.

Seminar questions

- Discuss how the concept of supply strategy relates to supply chain configurations.
- Apply Kraljic's positioning matrix to a company of your choice, identifying suppliers that fall into each category within the matrix.
- Using case studies give examples of the four key sourcing configurations.
- Discuss examples (good and bad) of the application of different sourcing strategies to commodity, product and service groups.

References

Axelrod, R. (1984) *The Evolution of Cooperation*, Penguin, Harmondsworth.

Axelrod, R. (1997) *The Complexity of Co-Operation: Agent-based models of conflict and cooperation*, Princeton University Press, Princeton, NJ.

Bylinsky, G. (1999) 'Challengers are Moving In on ERP', *Fortune*, 6 December, pp. 250B–250D.

Cousins, P. D. (1999) 'Supply Base Rationalisation: Myth or Reality?', *European Journal of Purchasing and Supply Management*, Vol. 5 (3), pp. 143–55.

Cousins, P. D. (2005) 'The Alignment of Appropriate Firm and Supply Strategies for Competitive Advantage', *International Journal of Operations and Production Management*, Vol. 25 (5), pp. 403–28.

Dyer, J. H. (1996) 'Specialized Supplier Networks as a Source of Competitive Advantage: Evidence from the Auto Industry', *Strategic Management Journal*, Vol. 17 (4), pp. 271–91.

Kraljic, P. (1983) 'Purchasing Must Become Supply Management', *Harvard Business Review*, September–October, pp. 109–17.

Lamming, R. (1993) *Beyond Partnership: Strategies for Innovation and Lean Supply*, Prentice Hall, New York.

Lewis, J. D. (1995) *The Connected Corporation: How Leading Companies Win through Customer-Supplier Alliances*, The Free Press, New York.

Minahan, T. (1997) 'Allied Signal Soars by Building up Suppliers', *Information Access Company*, Vol. 123 (4), p. 38.

Morgan, J. P. (ed.) (1995) 'Purchasing's Book of Winners', *Purchasing.com*.

Porter, M. E. (1980) *Competitive Strategy*, The Free Press, New York.

Porter, P. D. (1985) *Competitive Advantage*, The Free Press, New York.

Rae-Dupree, J. (1999) 'Can Boeing Get Lean Enough?', *Business Week*, 30 August, p. 182.

Richardson, J. (1993) 'Parallel Sourcing and Supplier Performance in the Japanese Automobile Industry', *Strategic Management Journal*, Vol. 14 (5), pp. 339–50.

Westfall, S. (1999) 'Benchmarking at Kraft Foods Gets Results', *FM Data Monthly*, April.

Womack, J., Jones, D. T. and Roos, D. (1990) *The Machine That Changed the World*, Rawson Associates, New York.

Further reading

Bannock, G., Baxter, R. E. and Davis, E. (2003) *The Penguin Dictionary of Economics*, 7th Edn, Penguin, London.

Endnotes

1. See Cousins (1999).
2. The term 'sourcing group' refers to a range of products or services that might be purchased. For example, nuts, bolts and rivets are often referred to as max–min sourcing group. This is because the buyer will order to maximum and minimum stock levels.
3. Buyers must calibrate the model using their interpretation of high versus low. This is an inherent weakness of this type of conceptual model as interpretation/definition of these terms may differ between users of the model.
4. See discussion of asset specificity in Chapter 3.
5. In a 'Dutch auction' the Buyer acts opportunistically by telling one supplier the other's bid price, encouraging them to reduce their own bid in order to win the business. The practice often degenerates (and hence the title) with the Buyer distorting the bids and repeating the process until one supplier drops out. The degeneration is possible because the suppliers do not really know what each is bidding. See the discussion on e-auctions in Chapter 17.

Chapter 5

Strategic supplier selection

Aim of chapter

The aim of this chapter is to provide readers with an understanding of the challenges, techniques and process of supplier selection.

Learning outcomes

At the end of this chapter, readers will be able to:

- identify the stages of supplier selection;
- identify some of the primary criteria used to select suppliers;
- understand different sources of information used to evaluate and distinguish between suppliers;
- understand and be able to apply the analytic hierarchy process to the selection of suppliers.

Introduction

The previous two chapters have considered the make–buy decision and sourcing strategies. Chapter 3 explored two contrasting theoretical perspectives that inform the make–buy decision, helping decision makers to set the boundaries of the firm. Chapter 4 considered various sourcing strategies, including supply base rationalisation and sourcing configurations. Having made the decisions contained within Chapters 3 and 4, the next problem facing the Supply Strategist is to select potential suppliers. This chapter looks at the major steps in making this choice and some of the criteria and models that may help guide efficient and effective decision making.

Twenty to thirty years ago, the problem of selecting among potential suppliers would have been of little interest at the strategic level of the organisation. Buyers traditionally sent out for three bids for each required component and simply selected the supplier with the lowest bid price. Although some firms still operate in this manner, recent business trends make this approach increasingly untenable.

Box 5.1 Supply in action: Fire at Ericsson

Through the 1990s Ericsson, like many firms, went through a process of supply base rationalisation. This involved simplifying the supply chain and evaluating and selecting suppliers based on performance and the importance of the product they supplied. This process had served to cut costs and Ericsson, giving the matter little thought, was pleased with the results. One of the items Ericsson sourced in this manner was radio frequency chips for its mobile phone handsets, produced by Phillips at a plant in Albuquerque, New Mexico. As the semi-conductor industry is highly concentrated and securing alternative suppliers may be difficult, Ericsson opted for a single supplier sourcing strategy.

In March 2000 storms hit New Mexico and a lightning bolt caused power fluctuations throughout the state. This was not the only by-product of the storm; it also caused a fire in a production room at Phillips' New Mexico plant. This resulted in water damage and smoke contamination of a sterile room, ruining millions of radio frequency chips. Ericsson, as one executive put it, 'had no plan B', having focused on cost cutting and neglected to construct a detailed risk management plan. This lack of a contingency plan resulted in Ericsson losing months of production costing US$400 million dollars and seriously impacting its competitiveness with rivals such as Nokia. Ericsson learnt its lesson and now has a proactive risk management strategy, but this came too late. Ericsson has now pulled out of mobile phone production, choosing instead to outsource production of its handsets.

Sources: Agarwal (n.d.); Reese (2004); Schmid (2000)

Practices such as outsourcing, supply base rationalisation, long-term collaborative relationships and supplier involvement in new product development not only improve business performance but also raise the buyer firm's dependence on its suppliers. In particular, the ability (or at least threat) of switching between suppliers is often reduced as relationship-specific assets increase. More than ever, Supply Strategists are under pressure to select the 'right' supplier first time to maximise value creation. The potential pitfalls of using supply base rationalisation as a mechanism for cost cutting are discussed in Box 5.1.

Main stages of supplier selection

Strategic supplier selection involves four main stages:

1 initial supplier qualification;
2 agree measurement criteria;
3 obtain relevant information;
4 make selection.

The remainder of this chapter follows the process model shown in Figure 5.1.

Step 1: Initial supplier qualification

Supplier qualification is the first step towards supplier selection. The goal is to identify suppliers who meet the requisite product and process standards and are

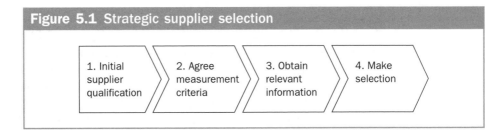

Figure 5.1 Strategic supplier selection

1. Initial supplier qualification

2. Agree measurement criteria

3. Obtain relevant information

4. Make selection

capable of supporting the buyer's long-term objectives. Because organisations are resource constrained, qualification helps to reduce the pool of potential suppliers to a more manageable number for detailed evaluation and selection.

Supplier qualification is concerned with the supplier's capabilities as a whole. It is therefore a 'sorting' rather than a 'ranking' exercise (de Boer, Labro and Morlacchi, 2001), where suppliers must meet a minimum standard to be eligible for later selection. Information for qualification is usually obtained using surveys (often online) or requests for information. The three main types of request and when they may be used are shown in Table 5.1.

Table 5.1 Requests for proposals, information and quotations

Type of request	Definition	When will you use this?
Request for Quotation (RFQ)*	An RFQ is a document issued when an organisation wishes to procure an item, product or service and makes the specifications available to other firms for competitive bids. This does not constitute an offer on the part of the buyer, merely a request for price and availability. If these are satisfactory then negotiations will begin.	If the monetary value of the item is high and the firm has no existing supplier then the buyer will issue an RFQ. This allows the supplier to give a quotation based on the information the buying firm provides. Standard practice is to request at least three quotations for comparison.
Request for Proposal (RFP)*	An RFP is a document issued when an organisation wishes to procure an item, product or service, but requires complete or partial design input from the supplier. As with RFQs this does not constitute an offer on the part of the buyer, merely a request for designs, price and availability. If these are satisfactory negotiations will begin.	If the contract requires negotiation rather than competitive bidding an RFP maybe used rather than an RFQ. This is often related to the item's complexity, when issues besides price are important in the supplier's response. This will often include factors such as capability to innovate and strength of R&D within the supplier firm.
Request for Information (RFI)	An RFI is a document issued when an organisation wishes to collect more information regarding a product or supplier. This can include information such as the supplier's capacity or capability to supply an item, product or service. An RFI may lead to the issuing of an RFQ or RFP.	An RFI may be used if the buyer has insufficient knowledge relating to a market or product to issue an RFP or RFQ.

* RFQ and RFP are sometimes used as synonyms within a firm. This usage is incorrect. RFPs are utilised in different circumstances to RFQs and this use neglects the more complex nature of RFPs

The precise criteria used for qualification will vary between firms and industries. However, buyer firms will usually wish to assess two categories:

1 **Manufacturing capabilities.** Manufacturing capabilities are best conceived as stocks of strategic assets that are accumulated through a pattern of investments over time and cannot be easily imitated, acquired by trade, or substituted (Dierickx and Cool, 1989). Thus, capabilities such as low cost, quality, flexibility and delivery performance are stocks of strategic assets that the supplier has accumulated over time.

   Of course, it is difficult to directly measure overarching concepts such as cost, quality, flexibility and delivery. Instead, buyer firms ask the supplier questions about their use of standards (such as ISO 9000 and 14000), techniques (such as continuous improvement, statistical process control and vendor managed inventory), and systems (such as electronic data interchange (EDI) or MRP).

2 **Financial viability.** Buyer firms also need to assess the long-term financial health of the suppliers. This is especially important for strategic items where the development of long-term relationships and investment in relationship-specific assets can make switching suppliers problematic. A useful resource for buyers is the Dun and Bradstreet Supplier Qualifier Report (see http://www.dnb.com). This third-party report evaluates suppliers across a number of categories to produce ratings for risk, financial stability and business performance.

Suppliers that meet the minimum standards set by the buyer firm for each of these measures may then be included within the detailed selection procedure explained in the next three steps.

Step 2: Agree measurement criteria

The strategic selection process continues with identifying relevant and appropriate selection criteria. We use the words relevant and appropriate deliberately to emphasise the need for criteria that are specific to the particular product purchased and that do not create unnecessary effort within a resource-constrained organisation. Unfortunately, far too many businesses throw measures at supplier selection and evaluation without considering why the measures are necessary and what value they will add. Recent research by two of the authors demonstrates that high-performing firms are likely to have a smaller number of measures than low performers but that these measures will be more relevant to the context (see Cousins and Lawson, 2007).

The most significant trend within selection criteria has been the move away from price and towards a total cost approach. Figure 5.2 shows an 'iceberg' model with price immediately visible above the waterline but also several costs, for example delivery, quality, training, environmental and so on, that are hidden below the surface. Price is immediately visible because it will be the bottom line of any supplier bid or quote. However, price rarely reflects the total costs of doing business. Buyers should also factor in the costs of poor quality, late delivery, environmental penalties and poor innovation to develop a more complete picture of total unit cost.

Figure 5.2 Price versus total costs

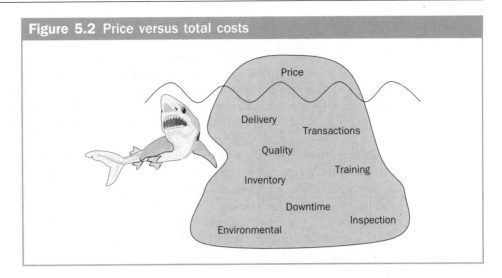

Furthermore, buyers may have to handle criteria that are in trade-off. For example, a common situation is the need to decide between a high-quality, expensive supplier and an inconsistent, cheaper supplier. Which supplier should the buyer select? If we were only to look at price the second supplier appears to be the best choice; however, working with the total costs it may be that the first supplier is cheaper over the long term.

As shown in Figure 5.2, price is only one of the criteria that affect the supplier selection decision. Supply Strategists should also consider other factors, such as those shown in Table 5.2, when making tier supplier selection decisions.

Table 5.2 groups the various criteria into five main competitive priorities: cost, quality, delivery, flexibility and others. Although it is unlikely that all 21 criteria will be used in any one sourcing decision, all will certainly have an impact on the total costs of using a particular supplier. In the following sections we describe the criteria within each of the five priorities and show their impact on total cost.

Table 5.2 Criteria for supplier selection

Cost	Quality	Delivery	Flexibility	Others
Unit price	Quality system certification	On-time performance	Supplier flexibility	Financial risk analysis
Pricing terms	Quality circles	Lead-time		Ethical analysis
Exchange rates, taxes and duties	Continuous improvement	Delivery frequency		Environmental analysis
	ISO 9000 series	Minimum lot size		E-commerce capability
		Inbound delivery cost		Reputation
		Location		Diversity of ownership
				Innovation capability

Cost criteria

The most obvious cost criterion is **unit price**. The unit price is simply the price of one unit and will be clearly specified on a supplier's response to an RFQ (see Table 5.1). It is easy to compare the unit price across various supplier firms because the data are objective and comparable. However, as shown in the iceberg model (Figure 5.2), price is only one component of the total cost and is also affected by pricing terms and exchange rates.

Pricing terms include quantity discounts, promotions and payment terms. *Quantity discounts* can be an important factor in the timing of purchases, but it is important that any discounts are considered against the cost of holding additional inventory, depreciation of that inventory and reduced flexibility. *Payment terms* refer to the length of time before payment is due. Longer payment terms have a positive effect on working capital and therefore are an important factor when comparing suppliers. Buyer firms may also seek discounts for quick or early payment.

Exchange rates will vary according to the location of each supplier. Buyers operating global supply chains will find that fluctuating exchange rates can have an enormous impact on profits. Although financial hedges can be put in place (see Chapter 18), Supply Strategists may wish to consider the volatility of currencies as part of the supplier selection decision.

Quality criteria

Apart from price and delivery, quality is probably the most common criterion used in the supplier selection decision and in some circumstances is given primary importance. For example, the Ministry of Defence spends around £15 billion every year across about 32,000 suppliers on a range of goods and services, from tanks and helicopters to paper and window cleaning. This represents the largest spend by any single organisation within the United Kingdom. The MoD clearly states that quality is the major concern during supplier selection, and given the risks to troops on the frontline it is not hard to see why.

Measuring supplier quality *ex ante* presents an interesting management conundrum: how do you measure supplier quality before delivery? In lieu of actual measurement, organisations have adopted a range of proxy criteria that provide information about the level of quality management within the supplier firm. Foremost among these criteria is the use of **quality system certification** (González-Benito and Dale, 2001), such as **ISO 9000 certification**. By following a series of guidelines produced by the International Standards Organization, companies can apply for ISO 9000 certification that officially reports conformance to quality standards. Criticisms of over-reliance on quality certification are listed in Box 5.2.

Furthermore, buyer firms may also visit supplier plants to ascertain the general attitude of management and workers to quality. Criteria used here may range from the use of **quality circles** and **continuous improvement** techniques through to very simple checks of the state of the plant floor and the amount of rework.

Box 5.2 Critique of quality certification

Despite many benefits of quality certification (see Dale, 2003) there are also some criticisms that readers should be aware of. These include:

■ the cost (fees and resources) of registration and maintenance;

■ the perceived lack of relevance, especially within small and service-based organisations;

■ lack of flexibility in the process may stifle management innovation and creativity.

Delivery criteria

JIT production places increasing pressure on the delivery performance of suppliers. As discussed in Chapter 2, JIT is concerned with reducing safety stock and lot sizes. This will impact significantly on how delivery from suppliers is structured. Buyer firms using JIT will require suppliers to deliver exactly to their build schedule and more frequently with smaller lot sizes. This should be reflected in the original supplier selection criteria, creating the need to measure on-time delivery performance and minimum lot size.

On-time delivery considers the variability of a supplier's delivery compared to the time agreed by the buyer. Buyers aim to select suppliers with low variability to help reduce the need for high quantities of safety stock. Typically, on-time delivery is measured as a percentage, with figures approaching 100 per cent now common within first-tier suppliers in the automotive industry.

Lot size refers to the quantity that is ordered (or produced) at any stage in the supply network. For example, a supermarket that sells an average of 50 packets of biscuits every day may place orders of 350 packets from the supplier every week. The lot size in this example is 350 units. **Minimum lot size** simply refers to the minimum order quantity the buyer firm can place with the supplier. Suppliers maintain minimum order quantities because they can gain economies of scale by manufacturing long runs of the same product. Firms implementing JIT will seek to reduce the minimum lot size with their suppliers, as they will want smaller, more frequent deliveries.

Delivery criteria are further highlighted in this age of global sourcing. The trade-off between delivery characteristics and unit price escalates as buyer firms seek to balance production in low-wage economies with the need to be flexible and responsive to their customers. The **location of the supplier, lead-time** and **inbound delivery costs** must all be considered against any savings a low cost manufacturer may offer. In an era of agile manufacturing and mass customisation, shipping delays from distant supplier locations can significantly stymie efforts to pull components through the supply chain. Even in low-variety mass production environments, distant suppliers can delay responses to variations in demand and create the need for expensive expediting. We do not mean to argue against the use of outsourcing but to highlight the importance of building total cost models during supplier selection. Reliance on any one criterion may disguise the true costs of the sourcing process.

Flexibility criteria

Flexibility is the ability of the supplier to manage variation from the buyer firm without significant trade-offs with other competitive priorities. Two types of flexibility are important when selecting suppliers: volume flexibility and mix flexibility.

Volume flexibility refers to the ability and willingness of the supplier firm to change order volumes without significant penalties. Volume flexibility is important when firms face progressively uncertain environments, global competition and technological acceleration (Gerwin, 1993). Flexible suppliers are of particular benefit where demand is uncertain by reducing the need to hold high levels of safety stock.

Mix flexibility refers to the ability and willingness of the supplier to change the mix of ordered products without significant penalties. Increased product variety can increase customer perceived value by offering greater choice with little or no trade-off with price or time. Mix flexibility within suppliers is especially important within agile or mass customisation environments.

Other criteria

A number of other criteria may also be integrated into the supplier selection decision, many of which are shown in Table 5.2. Here, we discuss the growing importance of environmental analysis, diversity of ownership and innovation capability.

Environmental measures are growing in importance as new legislation and consumer pressures hold end manufacturers (or OEMs) increasingly responsible for the impact of their products across the product life cycle. However, perhaps more important is the potential impact on competitive advantage. Studies have shown that firms that proactively engage with environmental issues can reduce costs and increase customer value. For example, firms have found that simple processes such as restricting access to computer printers, employing double-sided photocopying and working on electronic documents have had a major cost-saving effect as well as improving process efficiencies. We discuss some of the criteria that can be used to assess environmental performance in Chapter 14.

Diversity of ownership criteria are gaining prominence as Western governments (particularly in North America) seek to promote the use of firms owned or managed by minority groups. Multinational buyer firms are starting to give preference to minorities who meet other selection criteria. Minority-owned suppliers refers to firms that are at least 51 per cent owned by minority, women and disabled groups, but may also be applied to small businesses. For example, Visa USA has integrated diversity selection criteria within their existing framework. Visa states that it is seeking to grow the amount of products and services from diverse suppliers and to engage indirectly with firms that also engaged in supplier diversity programmes.[1] However, it is important to remember that diverse suppliers must also meet standards for the other criteria; diversity is not a substitute for quality.

Innovation capabilities are becoming an important consideration for supplier selection. Involving suppliers in product development allows the Buyer to focus on core capabilities and tap into suppliers' expertise, resulting in reduced time-to-market,

Table 5.3 Selection criteria for functional versus innovative products

Functional		Innovative	
Cost		Flexibility	
Delivery	On time	Innovation capability	
	Cost	Delivery	Location
	Minimum lot size		Lead-time
	Quality		
	Environmental		
	Diversity of ownership		

better product design and quality, and a lower product cost. From an innovation perspective, the Buyer needs to ensure a technological and cultural 'fit' between the two organisations. The Buyer may consider the rate of innovation (the number of new products or patents) and the type of innovation (continuous versus discontinuous).

This section has reviewed key criteria that may be used in the supplier selection decision. It is important to remember that not all criteria should be used for any one decision. Instead, Supply Strategists should use only those criteria relevant to a particular product. A useful distinction can be made between 'functional' and 'innovative' products (Fisher, 1997). Fisher argues that these two types of products require very different supply management practices, including supplier selection procedures. Functional products, such as office stationery or grocery staples, have relatively stable, predictable demand with long product life cycles. On the other hand, innovative goods, such as fashion goods and laptop computers, are characterised by lumpy, unpredictable demand with much shorter product life cycles.

This distinction can help identify relevant criteria for the supplier selection decision. Table 5.3 identifies those criteria that should be applied depending on the type of product. Functional products require suppliers that are as physically efficient as possible, therefore criteria concerned with cost and reliable delivery characteristics are most relevant. In contrast, innovative products require suppliers that are responsive to changes in the marketplace and therefore criteria concerned with flexibility, innovation and the speed of delivery characteristics are more relevant. Quality, environmental and diversity criteria are shown across both categories because they are equally applicable to functional and innovative products.

This section has reviewed a range of criteria and discussed their applicability in different contexts. The next stage in the process is to obtain information to measure these criteria.

Step 3: Obtain relevant information

The third stage in the process is obtaining the information used to compare suppliers across criteria. It is important that the information is comparable across suppliers so that, for example, information on quality from supplier A can be compared to information on quality from supplier B. Information should also be timely and accurate. The supplier selection procedure relies on having up-to-date information that provides an accurate representation of suppliers. Supply Strategists can obtain information from a variety of sources, including information from suppliers, supplier visits and supplier performance measures.

- **Information from suppliers.** Table 5.1 describes three sources of information commonly provided by suppliers. For selection purposes both RFP and RFQ may be used.

- **Supplier visits.** A team (possibly cross-functional) from the buyer may visit potential supplier(s). The visits may be used to evaluate specific areas, for example the amount of rework on the factory floor, but also to get a feel for the culture of the workplace and staff. Site visits are especially useful if there have been few historical dealings with the supplier. They allow the buyer to see the level of technological expertise and also gauge levels of capacity utilisation. Furthermore, visiting the supplier's facilities provides a good forum for information exchange, sharing cultures and approaches (the way we do things around here), and allows both parties to understand more about each other's businesses. This process is often referred to in the academic literature as 'socialisation', helping to build and enhance understanding and inter-firm relationships (see Cousins and Menguc, 2005 for a discussion on this).

- **Supplier performance measures.** Existing or incumbent suppliers can be evaluated against current performance. Chapter 11 covers the subject of supplier performance measurement in detail.

Step 4: Make selection

A range of models has been developed to assist the Supply Strategist in making the final selection between potential suppliers. Selection models range from the highly quantitative (such as fuzzy set theory) to the highly qualitative (such as categorical methods), and from the very simple (such as eyeballing RFQ data) to the much more complex (such as artificial intelligence based models).[2]

The model and the amount of effort put into the final selection should reflect the impact on the business and market complexities:[3]

- **Impact on the business**
  - For low-value products, selection may involve little more than a comparison of the information contained within the responses to the RFQ or RFP.
  - For high-value, strategic products, selection should be more complex and will often involve the use of multi-criteria decision-making models.
- **Market complexity**
  - For products with few alternative sources of supply, selection should be comprehensive because the possibility of substitution is low.
  - For products with many alternative sources of supply, selection can be less comprehensive.

Box 5.3 What are multi-criteria decision-making models?

We constantly face situations that force us to make a decision, or to choose one alternative over another. But how do we choose between alternatives? *Most of us will either explicitly or implicitly compare, rank and order preferences against a 'criterion of choice'.*

However, only in very simple dilemmas can we apply a single criterion of choice. For example, if you are choosing between several job opportunities you may consider salary as one criterion but you may also wish to consider the location of the jobs, opportunities for promotion, job satisfaction and so on. In other words, choosing between jobs will involve multiple criteria.

Because people have limited information-processing capacity, simple human judgement may not be sufficient for complex tasks. The theory of bounded rationality (Simon, 1957) posits that humans do not necessarily make optimal decisions, but instead seek to satisfy conflicting objectives (see Chapter 13). Multi-criteria decision-making (MCDM) models aid decision making by reducing complexity and organising thinking into a systematic process. MCDM models can help us to determine the importance of the criteria and then compare the alternatives across these criteria in an efficient process.

Here we are primarily interested in the selection of suppliers for products of high value where there are limited alternative sources of supply, in other words, the organisation's 'strategic' items. In this situation we recommend the use of multi-criteria decision-making (MCDM) models and in particular the analytic hierarchy process (AHP) technique. These models are described in Box 5.3.

AHP has been used to select suppliers since the early 1990s.[4] AHP is an MCDM model that enables decision makers to weight criteria according to their importance to the decision and the extent to which each alternative meets the criteria. The process requires decision makers to develop a hierarchical structure to the problem, first providing judgements about the relative importance of each criterion and then specifying a preference for each alternative with respect to each criterion. The model then provides a prioritised ranking indicating the overall preference for each of the alternatives. An example of the hierarchy for three criteria (innovation, quality and price) and three alternative suppliers (S1–3) is shown in Figure 5.3.

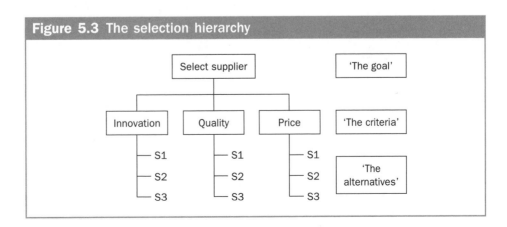

Figure 5.3 The selection hierarchy

Table 5.4 Measurement scale for pairwise comparisons

Preference	Numerical rating
Equally preferred	1
Moderately preferred	3
Strongly preferred	5
Very strongly preferred	7
Extremely preferred	9
2, 4, 6, 8 represent intermediate preferences	

AHP uses pairwise comparisons to express the relative importance of one criterion versus another. Each comparison is made on a measurement scale that represents a ratio between two criteria. Table 5.4 shows a typical scale used for AHP.

AHP is a useful technique for supplier selection because it is designed to handle tangible as well as intangible criteria, especially those in which the subjective decisions of individuals constitute an important part of the decision making. The process also forces Supply Strategists to think seriously about the criteria used to select suppliers and the weights they consciously or unconsciously ascribe to those criteria. Figure 5.4 presents the process of using AHP to select between suppliers. It should be stressed that it is the *process of thinking* and choosing the criteria that is most interesting and not the mathematical *mechanism*, which is relatively straightforward. Firms who use this process can focus on their cross-functional teams as a way of bringing together the disparate views of individuals within the team. The following simplified example will help to illustrate this process.

This example assumes that the buyer firm has chosen three criteria: innovation, quality and price, and has qualified three suppliers to participate in the final selection.

Assign weights to criteria

The first step is to develop a set of pairwise comparisons for the selected criteria. In this example the buyer would compare innovation against quality, innovation against price, and quality against price. Following the scale developed in

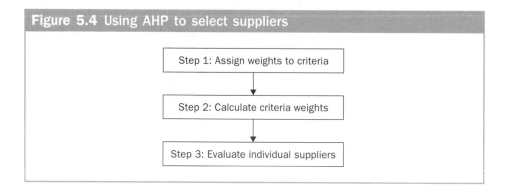

Figure 5.4 Using AHP to select suppliers

Step 1: Assign weights to criteria

Step 2: Calculate criteria weights

Step 3: Evaluate individual suppliers

Table 5.5 Pairwise comparison matrix (original matrix)

	Innovation	Quality	Price
Innovation	1	3	5
Quality	1/3	1	4
Price	1/5	1/4	1
Column total	1.533	4.250	10.000

Table 5.4, if the buyer considers that innovation is moderately more important than quality then a value of 3 is recorded. This continues until all comparisons have values. In this case innovation is strongly more important than price (for a value of 5) and quality is moderately to strongly more important than price (for a value of 4). These three values can then be entered into a pairwise comparison matrix as shown in Table 5.5.

The remaining cells of the matrix also need to be populated. First, we can place values of 1 in the diagonal because this is where each criterion is compared with itself. Second, the values below the diagonal are simply the reciprocals of those above the diagonal. For example, if the pairwise comparison between innovation and price is 5, or a ratio of 5:1, then it follows that the pairwise comparison between price and innovation is 1:5, or 1/5. This is then completed for the remaining reciprocal values. The final stage is to sum the values in each of the columns to leave a matrix as shown in Table 5.5.

Calculate criteria weights

The data in Table 5.5 can then be used to estimate the criteria weights. This is achieved by dividing each of the values in Table 5.5 by their column total and then computing the row averages. The calculations are shown in Table 5.6. In this example, the final criteria weights are 0.619, 0.284 and 0.096 for innovation, quality and price, respectively. This means that innovation is more than twice as important as quality, and about six times more important than price. Quality is slightly less than three times as important as price.

Table 5.6 Calculating criteria weights (adjusted matrix)

	Innovation	Quality	Price	Weights[a]
Innovation	0.652*	0.706	0.500	**0.619**
Quality	0.217	0.235	0.400	**0.284**
Price	0.130	0.059	0.100	**0.096**

* For example, this value was calculated by dividing the original value (1) (See Table 5.5) by the column total (1.533)

[a] The weights are the mean of the rows (for example, for innovation (0.652 + 0.706 + 0.500)/3 = 0.619)

Table 5.7 Pairwise comparison of suppliers for innovation, quality and price criteria

	Original			Adjusted			Weights
	S1	S2	S3	S1	S2	S3	
Innovation							
S1	1.000	9.000	2.000	0.621	0.882	0.250	0.584
S2	0.111	1.000	5.000	0.069	0.098	0.625	0.264
S3	0.500	0.200	1.000	0.310	0.020	0.125	0.152
Total	1.611	10.200	8.000				
Quality							
S1	1.000	0.200	3.000	0.158	0.153	0.231	0.180
S2	5.000	1.000	9.000	0.789	0.763	0.692	0.748
S3	0.333	0.111	1.000	0.053	0.085	0.077	0.072
Total	6.333	1.311	13.000				
Price							
S1	1.000	0.333	0.200	0.111	0.063	0.138	0.104
S2	3.000	1.000	0.250	0.333	0.188	0.172	0.231
S3	5.000	4.000	1.000	0.556	0.750	0.690	0.665
Total	9.000	5.333	1.450				

Evaluate individual suppliers

The next step is to compare each supplier against these criteria. The process is virtually identical to the previous two tables but with a separate table for each criterion. In this example, the Supply Strategist would start by comparing each pair of suppliers for the innovation criterion, followed by the quality criterion and finally the price criterion. To help illustrate the AHP technique, supplier 1 is the most innovative, supplier 2 has the highest quality and supplier 3 has the cheapest price. The results are shown in Table 5.7.

Calculate supplier weights

The final step of the AHP model is to calculate the final weights for each alternative supplier. The process is shown in Table 5.8. For each alternative supplier the criteria weights (from Table 5.6) are multiplied by the supplier weights for that criterion (from Table 5.7). The final weight is then the row sum of these values.

Table 5.8 Final weights and comparison of alternatives

	Innovation		Quality		Price		Weights
S1	(0.619)(0.584)*	+	(0.284)(0.180)	+	(0.096)(0.104)	=	0.423
S2	(0.619)(0.264)	+	(0.284)(0.748)	+	(0.096)(0.231)	=	0.398
S3	(0.619)(0.152)	+	(0.284)(0.071)	+	(0.096)(0.665)	=	0.178

* These values were obtained from the criteria weight for innovation in Table 5.6 (0.619) and the supplier weight for the innovation criteria in Table 5.7 (S1 = 0.584).

Box 5.4 Limitations of AHP

Like any MCDM model there are several limitations that the user should be aware of. First, AHP is driven by the judgements of the decision maker. Although the process is more transparent than making arbitrary decisions, the process is still susceptible to manipulation or simple errors. AHP is also reliant on relatively consistent decisions; for example, if criterion *i is* very strongly preferred to criterion *j* but only moderately preferred to criterion *k*, then it would logically follow that criterion *k* would be strongly preferred to criterion *j*. However, the pairwise comparison matrix allows for some inconsistency in these decisions. It is important that any inconsistency is kept within reasonable limits for the technique to remain effective. Lastly, the process is not particularly parsimonious. Because all values are relative, a new matrix must be calculated each time a new criterion or alternative is added.

Based on this analysis, supplier 1 has the highest weight with a score of 0.423, supplier 2 the second highest with a score of 0.398, and supplier 3 the lowest with a score of 0.178. Based on this simplified example the buyer firm should select supplier 1.

As can be seen from this example, AHP offers the Supply Strategist a systematic and transparent means of supplier selection. The technique helps to provide a step-by-step approach where large quantities of seemingly conflicting data can be handled in manageable chunks. With the recent Sarbanes–Oxley legislation AHP data can also give transparency to what otherwise can often seem a very subjective and sometimes biased process. However, there are a number of limitations to AHP, some of which are highlighted in Box 5.4.

Summary

Selecting the 'right' supplier has never been so important. This chapter provides a structured approach to the selection process, from initial qualification through to final selection. Our experience of using this process with various organisations has shown that it can be extremely useful in bringing people together to discuss otherwise implicit issues. It raises questions about the good or service sourced. It also has substantive benefits in creating transparency in a process that can otherwise appear murky and subjective. The next chapter examines the development of suppliers after the selection decision has been made.

Seminar questions

1. Discuss the strengths and weaknesses of the following sources of information that may be used to evaluate a supplier: information from suppliers, supplier visits, supplier performance measures.

2. Using a case study, undertake an AHP.

References

Agarwal, S. (2006) 'Managing Risk in The Supply Chain', *Supply and Demand Chain Executive*, August.

Cousins, P. D. and Lawson, B. (2007) 'The Effect of Socialization Mechanisms and Performance Measurement on Supplier Integration in New Product Development', *British Journal of Management*, 17, in press.

Cousins, P. D. and Menguc, B. (2005) 'The Implications of Socialization and Integration in Supply Chain Management', *Journal of Operations Management*, Vol. 24 (5), pp. 604–20.

Dale, B. (2003) *Managing Quality*, 4th Edn, Blackwell, Oxford.

De Boer, I., Labro, E. and Morlacchi, P. (2001) 'A Review of Methods Supporting Supplier Selection', *European Journal of Purchasing & Supply Management*, Vol. 7, pp. 75–89.

Dierickx, I. and Cool, K. (1989) 'Asset Stock Accumulation and Sustainability of Competitive Advantage', *Management Science*, Vol. 35, pp. 1504–14.

Fisher, M. (1997) 'What is the right supply chain for your product?', *Harvard Business Review*, Vol. 75 (2), pp. 105–16.

Gerwin, D. (1993) 'Manufacturing Flexibility: A Strategic Perspective', *Management Science*, Vol. 39 (4), pp. 395–410.

González-Benito, J. and Dale, B. (2001) 'Supplier Quality and Reliability Assurance Practices in the Spanish Automotive Components Industry: A Study of Implemenation Patterns', *European Journal of Purchasing and Supply Management*, Vol. 7, pp. 187–96.

Reese, A. K. (2004) 'Taking Performance Management Outside the Four Walls', *Supply & Demand Chain Executive*, April/May.

Saaty, T. L. (1980) *The Analytic Hierarchy Process*, McGraw-Hill, New York.

Schmid, R. (2000) 'Ericsson Falls Victim to Single Source Supplier', www.risk-engineering.com, 13 September.

Simon, H. A. (1957) *Models of Man, Social and Rational*, John Wiley and Sons, Inc, New York.

Useful sites

Dun & Bradsheet www.dnb.com

ISO 9000 www.iso.org

ISO 14000 www.iso.org

Endnotes

1. http://usa.visa.com
2. For a complete review of various models see de Boer et al. (2001).
3. See page 47 for a review of the Kraljic matrix.
4. AHP was developed by Saaty (1980) in the book *The Analytic Hierarchy Process*.

Chapter 6

Supplier development

Aim of chapter

The aim of this chapter is to discuss the development of a world-class supply base.

Learning outcomes

At the end of this chapter, readers will:

■ appreciate the strategic importance of supplier development;

■ have an understanding of best practices in supplier development;

■ understand the supplier development process.

Introduction

We have discussed previously how outsourcing and supply base reduction have led to close relationships with fewer suppliers. This increased dependence makes these strategic suppliers ever more important to the buyer for cost reduction, quality, on-time delivery and new product development. For example, 80 per cent of Honda's manufacturing costs and 70 per cent of Chrysler's costs can be assigned from purchased components (Hartley & Choi, 1996). Suppliers may also have been awarded long-term contracts, often for the life of the product, which makes supplier development attractive to both parties. In addition, many buyers have 'cost give-back' clauses with their suppliers, often amounting to 2 to 5 per cent annually. Supplier development is one means of helping suppliers meet these cost reduction goals.

Defining supplier development

The unit of competition has increasingly become about the supply network, rather than the individual firm or dyad. To compete, buying firms are increasingly focusing on the performance, capabilities and responsiveness of their supply base.

Rather than electing to in-source the component or switch to another supplier, many buyers are now actively intervening in the activities of their suppliers in order to generate the required performance improvements. This process of supplier development is most easily described as:

> any effort of a buying firm with a supplier to increase its performance and/or capabilities and meet the buying firm's short and/or long-term supply needs. (Krause, 1999)

These efforts may range from limited to extensive. Limited efforts include informal supplier evaluation and performance improvement requests, while extensive efforts often include training the supplier's personnel and investment in the supplier's operations. For example, the buyer may send their own engineers to the supplier's shop floor to help solve a specific problem, or to meet a particular launch date. They may also run training courses for suppliers' employees in techniques such as lean production, quality circles, value analysis and value engineering, and TQM. Within the auto industry, the vast majority of manufacturers have some sort of formal supplier development programme in place. Ford has 'kaizen[1] engineers' who run one-week workshops at supplier facilities, while Toyota has a Supplier Support Centre which helps their suppliers adopt lean manufacturing principles. Each of these automakers employs between 50 and 80 engineers whose sole task is to help improve supplier performance. John Deere, as a further example, has over 100 employees responsible for supplier development. Figure 6.1 illustrates the belief of these firms that supplier development can help build a world-class supply base with suppliers who are higher performing and more responsive to the buyer's needs. By providing a fresh outside perspective, buyers are able to question suppliers' underlying assumptions and provide the incentive for organisational change, thereby pushing suppliers up the slope to improved performance.

One of the advantages of a supplier development programme is that buyer pressure can act as a catalyst for process change within suppliers. Buyer involvement

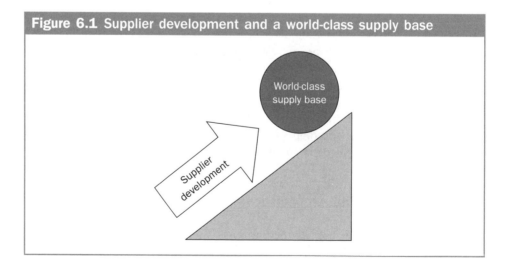

Figure 6.1 Supplier development and a world-class supply base

can provide a fresh perspective, challenging the underlying assumptions of the supplier, but also act as an external pressure point which legitimises the need for change, helping to overcome organisational inertia. The impact of supplier development can be immense. One study reported that as a result of a one-week workshop, General Motors were, on average, able to gain a 50 per cent improvement in supplier productivity, up to 75 per cent reduction in lead-time, and 70 per cent inventory reduction (Hartley and Choi, 1996). By changing the layout of a welding process, Honda of America's Best Practices team were able to reduce supplier costs by $200,000 per year. Another example is of a world-class customer and supplier who have had a close relationship for over nine years. During this time, the partners implemented integrated customer/supplier teams who worked within both companies to improve business and technical processes. Over the past four years the supplier has produced over 500 million items for the customer without a single item rejected, and attributes this perfect quality to the effectiveness of the integrated teams. Similar improvements have been recorded by numerous firms. The experiences of one such firm, John Deere, are described in Box 6.1.

Box 6.1 Supplier development at John Deere

John Deere, a Fortune 500 company that manufactures agricultural, consumer and commercial equipment such as tractors and lawnmowers, began a process of supply base rationalisation in the 1980s. As suppliers were reduced in number, the capabilities of those that remained became ever more important to John Deere, increasing pressure on suppliers. In the early 1990s, as suppliers were adjusting to the changes in Deere's manufacturing strategy, Deere found there was a sudden growth in demand for its portfolio of golf-course mowers, cranking the pressure up further on remaining suppliers. This led Deere to realise that if its suppliers were to improve, ultimately John Deere would benefit.

Fisher-Barton, who produced high-grade mower blades known as bed knives, was one such supplier. Deere offered to analyse and improve Fisher-Barton's operations to increase flexibility and efficiency of order fulfilment, but at first was greeted with scepticism. The president of Fisher-Barton stated that 'When someone mentions "partnership" I get nervous; I know its going to cost us money'. Despite these initial reservations, Deere convinced Fisher-Barton that they would not concentrate solely on their own needs, but would evaluate and improve the whole manufacturing operation.

The Deere supplier development programme worked successfully for Fisher-Barton, increasing quality, shortening order fulfilment times and improving margins and understanding of manufacturing operations. Deere does not rest on its laurels though; they claim to have been practising continuous improvement since the mid-1800s! Rating methods are reviewed annually and the emphasis changed as suppliers approach world-class standard, helping both firms achieve long-term success. Deere now pursues this strategy with its 'Achieving Excellence' programme, focusing on suppliers with a long-term business impact, particularly those with a unique capability or patent. This attitude is summed up by Deere's Supplier Development manager, who views supplier development as 'a standalone supply management strategy, not just one of many supply management tools'.

Sources: www.**deere**.com; Golden (1999); Aquent Consulting (n.d.)

Objectives of supplier development

Supplier development efforts typically have two main goals, either improving the supplier's operational performance or improving the supplier's *capability* to improve. In the first situation, development programmes tend to be relatively short-term and focused on working side-by-side with the supplier to directly *improve supplier performance* along dimensions such as cost, quality and delivery performance. This is a narrow perspective focused on bringing supplier performance up to the buyer firm's requirements. For direct improvement activities, the development team will often select one of the supplier's production lines for improvement. Typical changes include workflow simplification, layout changes and set-up time reduction. By applying these standard techniques across multiple suppliers and numerous factories, the buyer team becomes highly competent in its application. This approach may also be used as a form of pre-production emergency assistance where the development team helps the supplier meet deadlines or quality levels for a specific component. The disadvantages of this approach include the limited input of the supplier and the subsequent narrow understanding of the underlying problem-solving techniques. It also ignores the many socio-technical elements of the production system which also stand in the way of improvement.

The second type of supplier development effort is referred to as *supplier capability development*. Many supplier development programmes have moved beyond these short-term, standardised approaches and focus instead on building the supplier's capability for improvement from *within* the organisation. In essence, it is the buyer's attempts to transfer its own in-house capabilities across firm boundaries and into the supplier. The difficulty with replicating and then sustaining these practices within suppliers means that the second approach to supplier development is much more problematic to achieve, though the performance improvements are usually greater over time. Co-opting the supplier into the process helps build commitment to change, reduces resistance and facilitates the transfer of knowledge from buyer to supplier. In effect the buyer should be the trainer and facilitator, rather than driver of change. One of the key challenges is managing the transition out of the supplier's organisation. Change needs to be institutionalised, with continued feedback, rewards and monitoring on the part of the buyer. Without this follow-up support the supplier may slip back into old patterns or develop dysfunctional counter-reactions. This approach also has disadvantages. Large commitments of time and resources are required by the buyer, so potential candidates for capability development should be selected carefully. Results also may not come quickly. This approach has a slower pace of change than direct improvement efforts, so there is a danger of frustration on the part of the supplier.

Illustrating these issues, Sako (2004) examined the factors facilitating and constraining the development, and replication, of supplier capabilities. In a series of historical case studies of Toyota, Nissan and Honda she showed that supplier capability development occurred most effectively where companies share the practice, rather than the representation, of tacit knowledge. The rule of 'learning by doing', rather than observation, appears to apply. Despite the existence of manuals (which codify how the process should work), the most effective transfer occurs

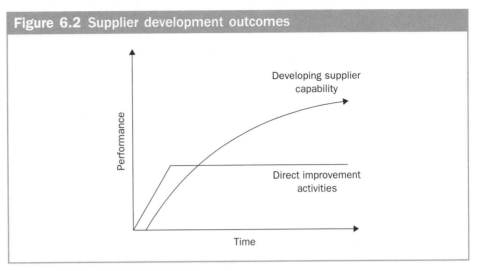

Figure 6.2 Supplier development outcomes

Source: Hartley and Jones (1997)

with hands-on instruction and classroom teaching. This makes the replication process highly labour-intensive (e.g. sending engineers to supplier plants), and expensive as economies of scale from this learning are difficult to achieve. In addition, Sako (2004) found that given the high levels of interdependence between buyer and supplier(s), the breadth of supplier development activities had also increased, leading to greater involvement of the customer (buyer) in the supplier's internal investment decisions. A systems approach to thinking sheds light on this problem. A systems approach recognises that improving the shop-floor operations impacts on only one element of the overall production system. To optimise the production system as a whole, the supplier development initiative needs to extend into other processes, such as purchasing and product development.

The relative impacts of *direct involvement* and *capability development approaches* are illustrated in Figure 6.2. Supplier development programmes focused on improving supplier performance along specific operational metrics have been effective in the short term. These results-oriented programmes employ standardardised, technically focused approaches (e.g. Toyota 5Ss, value analysis/engineering, workflow analysis) and have made step-changes to supplier performance. However, suppliers have been unable to sustain these improvement rates once the customer removes their on-site engineers and direct support for the initiative. By helping the supplier build the capability for change within its own organisation, the buyer can continue to realise performance gains, although the rate of improvement drops off as the supplier begins to tackle more difficult processes.

Summarising the points above, we can produce a typology of supplier development activity (see Figure 6.3). Effective supplier development programmes have multiple channels of contact with their supplier/s, ranging from individual to group assistance and from classroom teaching to joint problem solving on the shop floor.

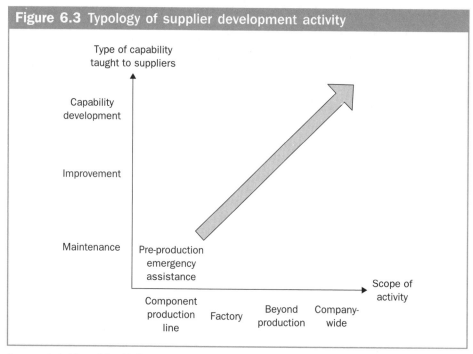

Figure 6.3 Typology of supplier development activity

Source: adapted from Sako, M. 'Supplier Development at Honda, Nissan and Toyota: Comparative Case Studies of Organizational Capability Enhancement', *Industrial and Corporate Change*, (2004) Vol. 13 (2), pp. 281–308, by permission of Oxford University Press

From a learning perspective, these efforts provide multiple opportunities to transfer both tacit and explicit knowledge to suppliers. Often these efforts begin at an individual component line in order to show the impact of supplier development and act as an exemplar to the rest of the organisation. These efforts gradually increase in scope over time, spreading into the rest of the factory, into product development systems and eventually into management systems. The nature of the supplier development initiative also changes as the scope broadens. Initially, supplier development may focus on achieving relatively short-term, narrow fixes to stabilise supplier performance (e.g. to launch a product on time). Improvement activities can then take place, seeking to improve dimensions of operational performance such as quality, reliability, delivery and cost. Over the longer term the partners will aim to build supplier capability, whereby improvement efforts on the part of the supplier become self-sustaining.

In some cases, the scope of the supply base development efforts may be immense. In setting up international operations, the local supply base may not be of sufficient quality or numbers to support the intended operation. In this situation, the buyer firm may have to take responsibility for evolving an entire supply base. Just such a challenge faced Ford at the start of the nineteenth century in their efforts to build a global supply base in the automotive industry. More recently, a similar challenge was faced by Saint Gobain when they sought to establish a float glass plant in Chennai, India. Their experience is detailed in Box 6.2.

Box 6.2 Saint Gobain

When the French company Saint Gobain decided to set up a float glass plant in Chennai, India, it ran into major technical problems with potential local suppliers. Firms were disorganised and scattered. Their technological capabilities were limited and they were unable to reach minimum standards unaided. Saint Gobain set up specialised teams to develop suppliers three years before even starting productive operations. The teams, comprising experts in several disciplines from India and abroad, provided assistance on raw material evaluation, engineering and technical services, information technology support, packaging materials development and logistics management. Each team worked with suppliers to develop cost and business models, train a largely illiterate labour force and educate firms in management concepts. The teams also acted as intermediaries to help firms obtain loans from financial institutions. Four years after the first teams were sent to India, 80 per cent of the raw material requirements were met locally, and several suppliers began selling to other transnational corporations in India.

Source: www.unctad.org

Supplier development strategies

Buyers can adopt a variety of strategies in an attempt to improve their suppliers' performance and develop capabilities. These strategies include: competitive pressure, evaluation and certification systems, incentives and direct involvement (Krause, Scannell and Calantone, 2000). The first three strategies represent externalised supplier development strategies since the firm uses external markets to drive supplier performance improvements. The final strategy, direct involvement, is an internalised strategy as it represents a direct investment by the buyer in their suppliers' activities. Each strategy is outlined below.

1 **Competitive pressure.** A buyer firm may apply competitive pressure on its suppliers by adopting multiple sourcing strategies. Using more than one supplier enables the firm to tap market forces by gaining bids from multiple suppliers. The firm can then distribute the volume of business across the supply base, ensuring that the best-performing supplier is rewarded with the higher volumes. The remaining suppliers are motivated to improve whichever dimension of performance (e.g. quality, delivery or cost) is deemed important by the buyer firm. It also maintains pressure on the primary supplier to ensure their performance does not slip.

2 **Evaluation and certification systems.** A buyer firm may use various assessment methods to evaluate the suppliers' quality, delivery, cost, technical and managerial capabilities. This assessment is then fed back, ensuring that the suppliers are aware of their performance and the customer (buyer) firm's expectation of their performance, and that they are provided with directions for improvement. Formal evaluation systems and supplier certification programmes communicate these expectations, as well as motivate suppliers to improve performance.

3 **Incentives.** The buyer firm may provide a range of incentives for improvements by their suppliers, including increased volume of current business, priority consideration for future business, use of award schemes and sharing of cost savings.

4 **Direct involvement.** The buyer firm may be proactive in developing suppliers through direct involvement. Direct involvement may include:

- *Capital and equipment investments in suppliers.* For example, buyer firms may invest in dies and fixtures.

- *Partial acquisition of the supplier firm.* This approach has been used widely by Japanese manufacturers, such as Toyota and Nissan who retain a 20–50 per cent equity position in their largest suppliers (Dyer, 1996). These 'vertical *keiretsu*' create intensive supplier–buyer linkages and high levels of intra-group trade, as well as dedicated investments in design and production equipment by suppliers. Often these relationships are replicated in overseas expansion, with buyer firm investments in a foreign location (such as the US), followed by the establishment of first- and second-tier supplier operations.

- *Investment of human and organisational resources.* For example, training of suppliers' engineers, on-site visits and mutual process adaptations designed to enhance the relationship.

Firms may adopt any one, or a combination, of the above strategies. For example, Dyer and Ouchi (1993) describe how Japanese *keiretsu* simultaneously use competition and cooperation within the supply base. For example, the buyer, let's say Toyota, may buy 50 per cent of its volume needs from one primary parts supplier, 30 per cent from a second, and 20 per cent from a third, with at least one of the suppliers being outside the *keiretsu* group. Toyota then encourages the second and third suppliers to match the primary supplier's performance through mechanisms such as sharing technical and process information or providing financial assistance. Toyota also strives to create supplier networks where supplier–supplier learning takes place, rather than the typical approach of buyer-driven supplier development. Elements of both cooperation and competition are thus present. If the supplier's performance improves, it may receive positive incentives of increased business; while if it fails to meet targets, it will have decreasing order volumes and may eventually be replaced. Toyota even assess their suppliers on the degree of assistance and knowledge transfer which takes place between suppliers within their overall supply base.

Research by Krause et al. (2000) suggests that the most effective strategy is one of 'direct involvement'. Strategies of supplier incentives and supplier evaluation and assessment provide a facilitating role in driving the success of the direct involvement effort. Recounting a discussion with a senior purchasing manager, Krause et al. (2000) observed that:

> despite his firm's intensive effort in supplier assessment and its practice of rewarding the best suppliers with increased business, suppliers rarely demonstrated significant performance improvement. He noted that his people would evaluate a supplier's facilities and processes, and leave the supplier with a list of improvements to implement in order to meet the buying firm's increasing performance requirements. However, suppliers rarely implemented the recommendations, either because of lack of know-how, lack of resources,

or indifference. The manager reported a different outcome when his firm initiated direct involvement activities, by sending engineering and purchasing personnel to suppliers to help implement the recommendations from the supplier assessment procedures. The suppliers reportedly embraced the direct involvement approach, and showed marked performance improvements. In turn, these improvements enhanced the competitiveness of the buying firm's end products. (p. 50)

Best practices in supplier development

A large variety of activities are used by buying firms to develop suppliers' performance and/or capabilities. These activities include:

- buying from alternative suppliers to generate competition for current suppliers;
- evaluation of supplier performance;
- raising performance expectations;
- recognition and awards for outstanding suppliers;
- promises of increased present and future business if supplier performance improves;
- training and education of a supplier's personnel;
- site visits by customer (buyer) to suppliers' premises;
- integrated teams to reduce supplier waste and help solve supplier problems;
- integrated technology roadmaps;
- access provided to CAD/CAM software;
- financial assistance (e.g. suppliers use customers' volume discounts, interest-free loans to suppliers, or advance payment).

The buyer should also examine the impact of its own systems on the supplier's organisation. Problems at the interface of the buyer's and supplier's systems can be an underlying cause of problems. For example, the buyer's forecasting, planning and scheduling systems may cause problems for the supplier in managing capacity at its factories. By modifying its own systems the buyer is able not only to deal with the problem, but also to demonstrate commitment to the improvement process. In turn, this interaction helps to build trust, communication and commitment, and may actually have a positive effect on the overall buyer–supplier relationship.

The supplier development process

Handfield et al. (2000) developed a seven-step process map for deploying supplier development initiatives. Their study found that most organisations were able to deploy successfully the first three or four of these steps, yet were less successful with the final steps aimed at sustaining the supplier development effort. The seven-step model is described in Figure 6.4.

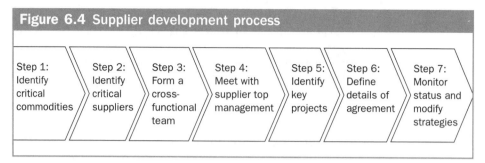

Figure 6.4 Supplier development process

Step 1: Identify critical commodities

Step 2: Identify critical suppliers

Step 3: Form a cross-functional team

Step 4: Meet with supplier top management

Step 5: Identify key projects

Step 6: Define details of agreement

Step 7: Monitor status and modify strategies

Source: adapted from Handfield et al. (2000). Copyright 2000 by Massachusetts Institute of Technology. All rights reserved. Distributed by Tribune Media Services

Step 1: Identify critical commodities

The Buyer may use a variety of frameworks to identify critical commodities where investment in suppliers is likely to be worthwhile. One useful model is Kraljic's (1983) matrix which identified a portfolio of commodities categorised according to 'routine', 'leverage', 'bottleneck' and 'critical'. The 'critical' category may represent commodities that are, variously, strategically important, have few substitutes, have few alternative suppliers, are high supply risk and purchased in large volumes. Suppliers of these commodities may be worthwhile candidates for investment by the buyer.

Step 2: Identify critical suppliers

In previous chapters we discussed how not all supplier relationships need be collaborative. Instead, a mix of arm's-length and collaborative relationships is generally required. The same principle operates for supplier development. Not all relationships require the buyer to engage in development activities. The buyer may already have a supply base operating at world-class level, or their purchasing power with the supplier may be so low that supplier development is not justifiable on strategic or financial levels.

Supplier development can involve a substantial investment of time, resources and money. Consequently, buyers must treat selection of suppliers as a strategic issue, and not a reactive, tactical decision to be made. There are a number of factors for selecting which suppliers to develop:

- *Amount of expenditure.* The higher the dollar amount of purchases the company makes from a supplier is an obvious, yet key factor in deciding on the focus of supplier development efforts.
- *Suppliers of strategically important component/s.* A supplier may have a low dollar amount of expenditure, yet the components they supply to the buyer may be strategically important.
- *Likely length of relationship.* Buyer firms should focus on those suppliers likely to remain over the long term. Shifts in technology, or product lines, can mean that current suppliers will not be suitable into the future.
- *Improving weakest suppliers.* Buyer firms can improve the competitiveness of their supply base by bringing their weakest suppliers up to par. This is done by

conducting a Pareto analysis of supplier performance, which reflects the observation that 20 per cent of suppliers may be responsible for 80 per cent of poor
performance. Suppliers failing to meet requirements for cost, quality, on-time
delivery or cycle times may be candidates for supplier development. Examples
of typical Pareto charts generated in practice include ranking suppliers based
on non-conformance levels in parts per million, the total number of problem
cases (or customer complaints), and other major quality/delivery impacts on the
buyer's production line. Successful implementation of this approach can lead to
greater competition among the supply base, which in turn results in lower prices
and better value for the customer.

■ *The type of manufacturing/administrative processes used by suppliers.* Not all
processes have the scope for cost improvement that is common to many supplier development efforts. For this reason, most development efforts tend to focus
on labour-intensive processes, rather than capital-intensive ones.

Step 3: Form a cross-functional team

Before the selected supplier is approached, the buyer should develop an internal
cross-functional team of employees from all relevant areas. This ensures that the
supplier is presented with a 'unified front' and sends the supplier consistent messages of what is expected of them in the initiative. The buyer also needs to be conscious of their supply chain strategy and the role of procurement and the supplier
within that strategy.

Step 4: Meet with supplier top management

Gaining the commitment of top management is a key success factor for virtually
any new organisational initiative. It is no different for supplier development, with
commitment of the supplier's top management particularly critical. Top management can push aside political barriers, assign resources and provide the drive to
make change happen. Gaining supplier commitment in the development process is
often even tougher, since it entails acceptance that processes can be performed better. In the words of one supplier manager, 'you have to eat your pride' (Hartley
and Choi, 1996). While some suppliers may be open about the need for change,
others may generate resistance to opening their plants to scrutiny, fearing spillover
of information about their cost structures and operations to the customer. One
effective way of getting the supplier's top management on side is to show how
supplier development would lead to greater profits or better quality, often through
supplier forums or meetings, where experiences are shared across the supply base.
Once the supplier's managers realise the opportunity, implementation is usually
much more straightforward.

The cross-functional team meeting with the supplier's top management also helps
to set the scene for relationship development. Communicating the buyer and
supplier's needs helps align the relationship, producing a total cost focus as well
as helping set the mechanisms for governing the relationship. For example, this
meeting should set out communication procedures, reporting and measurement

structures, and the commitments made by both parties. The depth of supplier commitment can also be gauged by examining the level of critical human resources, information sharing and management involvement in the change effort.

Step 5: Identify key projects

The next step is to identify key projects for the cross-functional team to implement. Many promising avenues for improvement will exist and it is necessary to evaluate each for feasibility, risk and return, and resource and time requirements. A common problem with many improvement efforts is that they target work on the 'hottest' items or the current crisis, rather than step back and assess the highest-priority improvements with the greatest impact on operational performance. The old saying 'a problem well defined is a problem half solved' is appropriate. Understanding the problem and selecting the right project are essential for successful supplier development.

Step 6: Define details of agreement

The implementation always comes down to the finer points. Supplier development is one route to the creation of value. This value needs to be shared between the two partners, and the metrics for doing so should be agreed prior to the commencement of the project. It is imperative that both buyer and seller are able to use the same criteria for determining the success or failure of the initiative. Metrics may include the percent of cost savings to be shared, percent of quality improvement to be achieved, percent of delivery or cycle time improvement, technology availability and system implementation targets. Some organisations may specify a 50–50 split of cost savings, while others require the supplier to forego price increases (aside from increases in raw materials) for the year following the project.

Step 7: Monitor status and modify strategies

To embed improvements from supplier development the partners must establish ongoing metrics for continuous improvement. The most sustained improvements occur where the supplier has been trained in capability development (and not purely performance improvement) and the customer (i.e. buyer) maintains an oversight and monitoring role on the supplier's operations. As the effort continues, the parties might also modify the original goals of the project, revisiting core assumptions and ensuring that the strategy remains aligned.

Barriers to supplier development

Numerous barriers to successful supplier development exist. They can usually be broken down into one of three categories: supplier-specific, buyer–specific and buyer–supplier interface. Table 6.1 briefly outlines each of these problems.

Table 6.1 Key barriers to successful supplier development

Area	Main issues
Buyer-specific	■ Lack of buyer top management commitment ■ Too small purchases by the buyer firm spread across too many suppliers ■ Supplier not important enough to buyer ■ Overly ambitious expectations that go unrealised
Supplier-specific	■ Lack of supplier commitment ■ Lack of buying firm power creates supplier reluctance to participate ■ Insufficient supplier human resources ■ Insufficient supplier technical capabilities
Buyer–supplier interface	■ Lack of mutual trust ■ Ineffective communication of potential benefits ■ Insufficient inducements to the supplier ■ Supplier is reluctant to share cost/process information ■ Poor cultural alignment

Summary

Ultimately, the strength of a firm's value chain determines its ability to extract a competitive advantage in the marketplace. Creating a supply base with fewer suppliers with whom you work closely is key to achieving this goal. However, continuous improvement in the supply base is critical to maintaining the advantage. By providing leadership, the right incentives and commitment, buyers have the opportunity to generate a supply base that exhibits not only continued operational improvement, but a self-sustaining capability to improve.

Seminar questions

1. Discuss, with examples, the strategies that may be adopted when developing a supplier.

2. Give examples of good and bad practice in supplier development.

3. Discuss how a particular supplier may be developed in a case study of your choice.

References

Aquent Consulting (n.d.) 'Partnering For Success: Eight Critical Success Factors in the Building of Deere & Company's Achieving Excellence Supplier Rating System', Case Study, http://it.aquent.com/Solutions/CaseStudies/index.html

Dyer, J. H. (1996) 'Specialized Supplier Networks as a Source of Competitive Advantage: Evidence from the Auto Industry', *Strategic Management Journal*, Vol. 17 (4), pp. 271–91.

Dyer, J. H. and Ouchi, W. G. (1993) 'Japanese style Business Partnerships: Giving Companies a Competitive Edge', *Sloan Management Review*, Vol. 35, pp. 51–63.

Golden, P. (1999) 'Quick Response Manufacturing Drives Supplier Development at John Deere', *IIE Solutions*, July.

Handfield, R. B., Krause, D. R., Scannell, T. V. and Monczka, R. M. (2000) 'Avoid the Pitfalls in Supplier Development', *Sloan Management Review*, Winter, pp. 37–49.

Hartley, J. L. and Choi, T. Y. (1996) 'Supplier Development: Customers as a Catalyst of Process Change', *Business Horizons*, Vol. 39 (4), p. 37.

Hartley, J. L. and Jones, G. E. (1997) 'Process Oriented Supplier Development Building the Capability for Change', *International Journal of Purchasing and Materials Management*, Vol. 33 (3), pp. 24–29.

Kraljic, P. (1983) 'Purchasing must become Supply Management', *Harvard Business Review*, September, pp. 110–17.

Krause, D. R. (1999) 'The Antecedents of Buying Firms' Efforts to Improve Suppliers', *Journal of Operations Management*, Vol. 17, pp. 205–24.

Krause, D. R., Scannell, T. V. and Calantone, R. J. (2000) 'A Structural Analysis of the Effectiveness of Buying Firms' Strategies to Improve Supplier Performance', *Decision Sciences*, Vol. 31 (1), pp. 33–55.

Sako, M. (2004) 'Supplier Development at Honda, Nissan and Toyota: Comparative Case Studies of Organizational Capability Enhancement', *Industrial and Corporate Change*, Vol. 13 (2), pp. 281–308.

Endnotes

1. The term '*Kaizen*' refers to continuous improvement. Firms often run '*Kaizen* workshops'. This is where a cross-functional team focuses on a specific problem assuming that there are no organisational constraints; the aim is to see how they would solve it. This process tends to develop simplified solutions that the firm then aims to put into practice.

PART 2

DEVELOPING SUPPLY STRATEGY

Chapter 7

Supply strategy: the development of the strategic supply wheel

Aim of chapter

The aim of this chapter is to introduce the 'strategic supply wheel' and to discuss briefly the concept and focus of supply strategy.

Learning outcomes

At the end of this chapter, readers will:

- understand the principles of the supply wheel;
- understand the difference between policy and strategy;
- appreciate the high degree of interaction between elements of the supply wheel.

Introduction

In Chapter 2 we discussed the idea of a framework for developing strategic supply in concept and practice. We term this the supply wheel, as the arrangement of factors that must be taken into account resembles such a structure and also there is a need to balance and align the organisation's activities in each of the areas, just as one balances a wheel that is to turn evenly.

In this chapter we introduce the supply wheel as developed by Cousins (2002). The wheel provides a way of analysing the behaviour and preferences exhibited by organisations as they approach the need for strategic purchasing and supply and also the means for planning such an approach in practice. This explanation will be in summary only – to show the nature and roles of the principal factors and the relationships between them. Each factor will be covered in more detail and at length in the remainder of Part 2.

The origins of the strategic supply wheel

It is important to note from the outset that the supply wheel is not simply a convenient way of setting down the important factors on the page: its constituent parts and their relationships were all developed from very thorough and rigorous research. This was completed in the usual way: an extensive exercise in *secondary research* (comprehensive assessment of what was already known about this subject, as recorded in formal management literature and related reports, over the past quarter of a century) and *primary research* (survey and interview work with organisations from a wide variety of sectors, to explore issues revealed by the desk work).

The primary research was conducted in 1999 and repeated in 2001 and 2005, using surveys to analyse over 500 organisations in North America, Europe and Australia. The survey research was followed up by interviews with 25 well-respected firms across a range of industrial and service sectors. The explicit purpose of the research was to understand how and why companies formulated a strategic supply policy.

The research showed immediately that it was useful and sound to consider the constituent parts of supply strategy under three broad headings: *process-based*, *procedures-based* and *policy-based*. It was clear that the main developments of supply strategy came from these drivers and it is worth reviewing their basic nature before considering the emergence of the 'wheel' structure itself.

Process-based approaches are those linked to specific organisational processes that need to be in place in order to facilitate strategy implementation. These include the development of appropriate skills and competencies and information systems.

Procedures-based approaches are those concerning the organisational procedures that are needed to facilitate implementation of a strategy through the organisational systems. These include use of performance measures and total cost–benefit analysis.

Policy-based approaches are necessary for the formulation of the strategy itself. These sit in the centre of the model (the 'hub' of the 'wheel') since without an understanding of the policies that the organisation declares in setting out its store, strategy formulation and deployment are likely to be made in isolation, thus lacking cohesion and robustness.

These three types of factor are naturally linked. Approaches to strategy that are closely linked to policy may be thought of as the 'most important' or influential, but those driven by the procedures (perhaps apparently the most mundane parts of management) are closest to what actually happens in practice. The three dimensions are thus all represented within the wheel, some in terms of the lines that link the elements and others in terms of the elements themselves. The simple beginnings of the wheel that stem from this basic observation are shown in Figure 7.1.

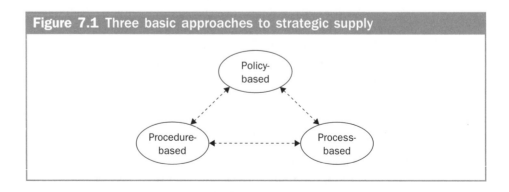

Figure 7.1 Three basic approaches to strategic supply

Once it is accepted that all the factors in strategic supply may usefully be classified in this way (note that it may not be the only way of classifying them) and that they must all be held together within a supply strategy that is itself linked to the corporate strategy of the organisation, arranging them as a wheel, with strategy as the hub, becomes a natural way of considering them. If such a hub were to be added to Figure 7.1, the wheel would have three circumferential elements – each generic. To make the model more useful, for purposes of analysis and planning, it is necessary to be more specific about these elements – and this is what our research explored. The outcome of this activity is the identification of five circumferential elements – approaches to strategic supply that are based in policy, processes or procedures, and which must be held together in a strategy. The supply wheel is shown in Figure 7.2.

The wheel shows the interrelationship between each of the strategic elements of the organisation. It also shows that because the elements are linked, if you want to change one element, you will need to change (or allow for change in) other elements within the model. For example, if you want to move towards more collaborative relationships, you will need to make sure that the organisation has the aligned measures, skills, cost/benefit model and appropriate organisation structure to deliver the change. A focus on one element of the model needs to be considered in relation to the entire model. The need to view all elements before making a decision is illustrated in Box 7.1.

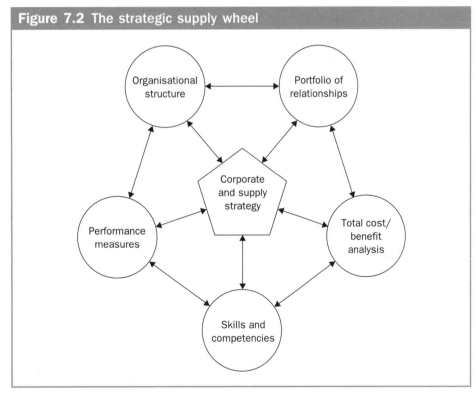

Figure 7.2 The strategic supply wheel

Source: Cousins (2002)

Box 7.1 Strategic alignment

A good case example of this was with a large computer company, early on in our research. The company saw itself as a leader in the marketplace and as such wanted to move towards more collaborative relationships with its suppliers. This move would mean reducing the supply base and focusing on higher-dependency relationships. Whilst this strategy was in vogue, the move could have been disastrous. Subsequent analysis showed that the firm did not have the appropriate measures (two-way measures) and the skills and competencies to operate in this manner. Therefore a strategic decision had to be made: should the company invest to acquire the new skills and implement new measurement systems, or not? If it did not, then it could not realise the potential medium- to long-term benefits that this strategy might have offered. The firm developed a business case, based on perceived benefits from the strategy versus the perceived costs, in order to make its decision – which ultimately was to proceed down the collaboration route.

The point from this case is that no strategy can be looked at in isolation – the firm had to consider the processes (relationships), procedures (measures) and policies (strategies) before making its business decision.

Rationale of the supply wheel

Appropriateness

The rationale behind the strategic supply wheel is one of making **appropriate** choices. It is vitally important to make sure that the most appropriate strategy is balanced against the other elements within the model. The wheel must stay in balance and in order for that to happen it must either contract or expand at the same rate.

Strategic planning tool

The wheel can be used as a strategic planning tool to analyse the organisation's strategic capabilities in a systematic manner. The strategist can use the model as a template for understanding where the organisation is (strategic analysis) and where the organisation wants to be (strategic choice) Any gap can then be identified, various elements of the model can be aligned and the strategy can be put into place (strategic implementation). The strategist should refer to specific models for each of the elements of the model (these will be explained in detail in subsequent chapters within this section).

Linkage with sourcing strategies and Kraljic's positioning model

The sourcing strategies discussed in Chapter 4 are also incorporated as part of this model. The central section of the model shows that the level of skills, measures, etc. must be appropriate to the sourcing strategy. This assumption will mean that a portfolio or range of each of the elements of the model is necessary. Furthermore, the variety or level of strategic attainment will be limited by the lowest common denominator within the model. For example, if the skills and competencies within the model are only able to achieve a tactical level of purchasing then the firm will be constrained to this level despite greater aspirations. The same is also true for each element of the model. Therefore, any assessment of sourcing strategies and positioning should be considered in the light of each element of the model. Of course, in the event that the firm has the capabilities to cover all sourcing approaches, it then becomes a matter of deciding how it wants to focus its resources.

Overview of each element

This section will give a brief overview of each element of the model. A more detailed discussion will then be given in each of the following chapters.

Alignment of corporate and supply strategy (Chapter 8)

This element of the model is concerned with understanding the alignment of an organisation's corporate and supply policies and the subsequent formulation of corporate and supply strategy. The 'policies' element of the model is particularly important here. It is essential that the policy of the firm be communicated through the supply process. For example, a policy of product design (rather than parts assembly) will have a profound effect on the way supply is organised within the organisation. Instead of buying from a wide range of suppliers and assembling in-house, the firm will move towards a method of modular production where large elements of the build programme will be built as sub-assemblies. Companies such as Westland Helicopters in the UK have become what they call 'systems integrators', that is, they put the aircraft together in the final stages and make sure that all of the complex systems 'talk to each other'. These elements have first been manufactured and assembled within 'first-tier' suppliers (see Chapter 4). This supply structure has to fit with the supply strategy and policies of the firm. Without the alignment of the corporate and supply strategies the firm will not be able to deliver on its chosen approach.

Skills and competencies (Chapter 9)

Variety of skills and competencies needed depending on strategy and relationships: The issue of skills and competencies is often overlooked by firms when developing their supply strategies. During research for this book one large UK automotive manufacturer's purchasing director said *'if I knew then what I know now I would not have embarked on half of the strategic approaches. We had to learn by making mistakes; this put us back to square one several times . . .'.* He was talking about implementing strategies such as supply tiering and delegation. His point (echoed by many of the practitioners that we interviewed) was that no matter how logical and innovative an organisation's strategy, the important question is 'what are the capabilities of the people?' It is the people that have to make the strategy happen. If they are not able to implement the new approaches then the strategy will simply not work.

The other point to make clear is that there will always be a variety of skills and competencies needed within a firm. Some of these will be more tactical or basic, while others will be more strategic or sophisticated. This will generally depend on the way the supply activity is organised. For example, London Underground has approximately 1500 people with signing authority in their organisation. That is, 1500 people can officially buy things on behalf of the company. This might sound like a lot of people – indeed it is. The company operates by giving anyone from managers to support workers the opportunity to take a 'competence exam'. If they pass, they are given access to purchase their own goods and materials. This is not quite as easy as it sounds. Goods and services are usually bought against an electronic catalogue, or a purchase card (effectively a corporate credit card) that is issued to an employee who then has to manage against a given budget. This means that the supply organisation can concentrate their efforts on the high-value items (such as outsourcing deals) and leave the day-to-day purchases to individuals.

Organisational structure (Chapter 10)

Three basic types: centralised, decentralised and hybrid structures: The way in which supply is structured within the firm can have a profound effect on how well and indeed what types of strategy will work. There is a vast array of names given to a variety of organisational structures such as 'clans', 'networks' or 'value configurations', and federal systems. These are discussed in Chapter 10.

Strategic performance measures (Chapter 11)

The importance of measures as the driving force of an organisation – 'the lubricant of the machine': Strategic performance measures are essential for the delivery of strategy; they ensure that both the internal and external elements of the organisation are aligned. Performance measures act as both a signal and motivating system to alert the organisation to act in a particular way. It is important that the firm employs the correct measures to achieve the maximum output from their chosen strategy. Measures can be considered as internal versus external, and efficiency versus effectiveness.

Cost–benefit analysis (Chapter 12)

This section of the model argues that companies need to understand the costs of doing business. The famous economist Milton Friedman put it very succinctly when

> ## Box 7.2 The cost of business
>
> A global energy company decided that it wanted to focus on strategic procurement. Its first move was to attempt to understand what it spent on products and services. After nearly a year of analysis (using a large consultancy company) the energy manufacturer was able to pinpoint its spend to regions, i.e. Europe, North Africa, etc. It was unable to say what it spent the money on and also in which countries the money was spent! In other words, it did not know the costs of doing business.

he said, 'the business of business is business'. In the private sector, firms are in business to make as much money as possible (within legal and ethical constraints). In the public sector, organisations try to maximise value or save as much money as possible. Either way, the motivation is driven by incomes or budget management. It is therefore important that firms and organisations understand the costs of doing business. While this might sound obvious to the reader, a small illustration from our research will certainly highlight this point. See Box 7.2.

This problem is further evident when firms decide to move towards collaborative strategies with supply. Often they do not consider the costs or indeed the 'real' benefits of the approach. When asked 'why have you moved towards collaborative strategies with your suppliers?', strategists typically respond that it was because other firms were adopting this approach, so it must be a good idea. It is argued that for a firm to follow any strategy it should make sure that it has a sound business case to support it and a clear understanding of the cost structure. The benefits and costs must align with the central strategy within the model and produce a business case for following any of the various relationship approaches.

Relationship portfolio (Chapter 13)

Range of relationships – brief summary of the literature – relationship themes: This segment of the model considers the types of relationship that the organisation operates. There is a wide literature on relationship management that tends to argue that relationships fall into a spectrum ranging from adversarial (traditional) types of relationships, very much transaction based, towards highly collaborative or partnership arrangements, which are much more strategically focused. Many authors offer a range of strategic relationship models, giving descriptions of the various relationships that a firm can have at a point in time. Some of these models are economically focused while others are much more behaviourally focused, e.g. considering the concept of trust and the role that people play within teams etc. It is important to be aware of all of these approaches and decide on the one that best fits a particular firm scenario.

The relationship as a process, focused on an output: The relationship literature will be explored in detail in Chapter 13. It is important to define what the term 'relationship' means in an inter-organisational sense. For the purposes of our book we refer to the 'relationship' as an organisational process. Any process must deliver an output of some description in order to add value. For example, communication is a process – in order for communication to have meaning it must deliver some output, for example to explain something to someone. The same is true of relationships. They must have a definable output. The output could be relatively simple, e.g. a reduction in price, in which case the process will be relatively simple and quite possibly very transaction focused. If the output is complex, e.g. to increase overall levels of innovation, then the process (relationship) will undoubtedly also have to be complex, e.g. work in a cross-functional team, develop a close relationship with the supplier, risk and reward sharing agreements, etc., in other words, highly collaborative relationships. This definition allows firms to decide, based on the output, what sorts of relationship they should create. More importantly, the procedures and policies that support this process can also be shaped. The various relationship outputs will need to be supported by the other elements within the supply wheel. If complex relationship processes are required to achieve complex outputs then it is likely that these will require highly skilled personnel. It is also likely that the measurement systems will have to reflect this output; they will need to be focused on effectiveness rather than efficiency.

Summary

This chapter has introduced the concept of the strategic supply wheel to the reader. The essence of the wheel is that no one element should be looked at in isolation. Each part of the model affects the other elements. Furthermore, the model reveals that firms and organisations should choose appropriate strategies that balance out each element.

The wheel can be used both as a diagnostic tool for understanding the many elements of supply within a firm or organisation and as an implementation tool to understand which areas of the wheel need to be developed and aligned with each other.

References

Cousins, P. (2002) 'A Conceptual Model for Managing Long-term Inter-organisational Relationships', *European Journal of Purchasing and Supply Management*, Vol. 8, pp. 71–82.

Further reading

Harland, C., Lamming, R. and Cousins, P. (1999) 'Developing the Concept of Supply Strategy', *International Journal of Operations & Production Management*, Vol. 19 (7), pp. 650–73.

Chapter 8

Aligning supply with corporate strategy

Aim of chapter

The aim of this chapter is to provide readers with an understanding of the process of strategic alignment between supply and corporate strategy.

Learning outcomes

At the end of this chapter, readers will be able to:

- define and identify levels of strategy;
- understand the importance of strategic alignment;
- understand and be able to apply strategic alignment within a supply chain context.

Introduction

This chapter focuses on the *alignment between corporate strategy and supply strategy*. It represents the hub and most important of the six elements in the strategic supply wheel. As discussed in Chapter 7, the other five elements (see Chapters 9–13) revolve around the outside and are driven by strategic choices made in the centre. Performance measurement, skills and competencies, organisation structure, relationship approaches and cost–benefit analysis should all be linked to the strategic direction of the firm. A reminder of the model is provided in Figure 8.1.

This chapter begins by defining strategy, levels of strategy and strategic alignment. This sets the scene for the development of the alignment between corporate and supply strategies. In particular, we focus on the process of alignment to help Supply Strategists make more informed decisions when both developing strategies and applying supply chain practices. The requirement for strategic alignment in the public sector is illustrated in Box 8.1.

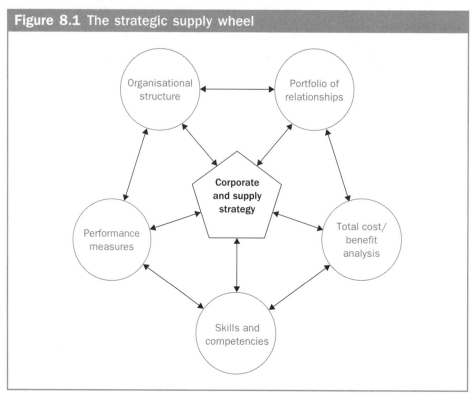

Figure 8.1 The strategic supply wheel

Source: Cousins (2002)

Box 8.1 Strategic alignment in the public sector

The need for alignment of purchasing and corporate strategy has gone beyond the private sector. In 2002 the chairman of the Society of Procurement Officers in Local Government pinpointed alignment of purchasing and 'corporate' strategy as central to performance improvement in local government. This task, he believes, will be as difficult as it will be important, as he identified it as 'The biggest challenge facing local government purchasers in the next year'. The root of the problem, he felt, was that procurement strategies lacked buy-in from the top, and consequently procurement officers were not involved in corporate strategy. Unsurprisingly, this had resulted in procurement and corporate strategies being misaligned. These concerns were supported by the fact that only 47 per cent of local authorities had procurement strategies agreed by chief executives and elected councillors. As taxpayers' expectations of greater value for money grow, the public sector will increasingly find itself under the same pressures as private enterprise to align strategy and reap the benefits.

Source: Arminas (2002)

What is strategy?

Before we can begin to understand the concept of strategic alignment, we will first need to define what we mean by the term 'strategy'. This is not an easy task, as many academics (and practitioners) have differing views on what strategy actually means. There are at least ten schools of strategy formation (Mintzberg, Lampel and Ahlstrand, 1998) ranging from the prescriptive and economic (e.g. the Positioning School) to the descriptive and behavioural (e.g. the Cognitive School).

For our purposes we will use Quinn's (1980) definition of 'strategy' which is replicated in Box 8.2. He argues that strategy is a pattern or plan from which an organisation can develop its major goals and objectives. Sometimes these strategies are written down in documents (explicit) but they may also be merely implied and understood by the organisation (implicit).

Three important points emerge from this definition:

1 *Strategy affects the scale and scope of an organisation's activities over the long term.* Strategy should clearly point to activities that the company should and shouldn't be involved with. This will help determine both the extent of vertical integration and the scope of markets addressed. Strategy should also guide any decisions to expand or contract (either horizontally or vertically) over the long term.

When easyJet started operations in 1995 it had a clear 'no frills' strategy to provide low-cost air travel within Europe. The company had clear characteristics, such as only one type of aircraft, no in-flight meals, high utilisation rates, direct sales and so on, that supported this strategy. Subsequent diversifications have been directed by this strategy and leveraged the low-cost image across a range of activities, from car hire to cruises. The boundaries of the organisation are therefore driven by the overall strategy.

2 *Strategy is about being responsive to changes in the external environment.* There are two major perspectives to developing strategy within organisations. The first is what we can call the 'outside-in approach to strategy'. This approach suggests that strategy should be aligned and responsive to current and future states of external markets.

For example, an organisation's strategy may need to change in response to technology innovation. This was recently highlighted by the shift from analogue to digital technology within the photographic industry. Although both film and digital photography are concerned with capturing images, they are substantively

---

Box 8.2 A definition of strategy

Quinn concludes that a **strategy** is the *pattern* or *plan* that integrates an organisation's major goals, policies, and action sequences into a cohesive whole. A well-formulated strategy helps to marshal and allocate an organisation's resources into a unique and viable posture based on its relative internal competencies and shortcomings, anticipated changes in the environment, and contingent moves by intelligent opponents.

Source: Strategies for Change: Logical Incrementalism, © The McGraw-Hill Companies, Inc., (Quinn, J. B. 1980)

different in methodology. While film photography dominated, Eastman Kodak was essentially a chemical company, producing silver halide and other chemicals for the development of film. However, as it became clear that digital technology was the future of the industry, Kodak was forced to reinvent itself as an electronics and hardware company. The change in strategy was driven by external pressures.

3 *Strategy is about aligning activities with strategic resources and capabilities.* The second perspective is what we can call the 'inside-out approach to strategy'. This is primarily aligned with the resource-based view (see Chapter 3 for detail), which suggests that competitive advantage is sustained by a firm's distinctive resources and capabilities. Strategy is therefore a question of matching activities with those distinctive capabilities.

This approach helps make sense of diverse, seemingly unconnected portfolios of business units within firms. For example, Honda manufactures an apparently diverse range of products, varying from cars and motorcycles to lawnmowers and power generators. Underlying these divergent activities are two distinctive capabilities: engines and power trains. Diversification occurs when it capitalises on existing resources and capabilities and will thus guide (and constrain) strategy development over the long term (see Prahalad and Hamel, 1990).

Having defined strategy, it is also important to discuss the various levels at which strategy is formulated within the organisation.

Levels of strategy *within* organisations

Strategy is usually developed at three levels within the organisation: corporate, business and functional. Corporate-level strategy asks *what business are we in?* Essentially, corporate-level strategy is a question of organisational boundaries. Strategy at this level will determine the extent of integration along the supply chain (the organisation's scale) and the range of activities in which it competes (the organisation's scope). Over the past decade we have seen many organisations reduce in scale and scope as they look to focus on core competences (Prahalad and Hamel, 1990) and outsource peripheral activities. This trend increases the importance of managing the supply chain (see Chapter 2).

Business-level strategy asks *how do we compete in our chosen markets?* Each market is likely to differ (in terms of levels of competition, rate of change, entry barriers, and bargaining power (Porter, 1980)) and therefore require a different strategy.[1] Business-level strategies deal directly with decisions over individual products within a given market. Strategies will involve assessment of internal factors, such as product life cycles, innovations to existing products, R&D spend, capital equipment and facilities, advertising, and external factors, such as competitor analysis, technology change and customer needs. Business-level strategy should therefore support corporate-level strategy by ensuring that product and market development is consistent with the overall strategic direction of the organisation.

Finally, functional-level strategy asks *how can our function support business- and corporate-level strategies?* Functional strategies will be developed by all of the major functions, including finance, marketing, operations, human resources, information technology and supply chain management. Strategies at this level involve the development (either internally or through acquisition – see Chapter 3) and co-ordination of resources and capabilities to help execute business-level strategy. Functions should ideally be involved in the process of strategy formulation at the business and corporate levels so as to integrate their proprietary knowledge of the function's skill and capabilities, customers and competition into these higher-order strategies. Functions can then translate the business- and corporate-level strategies into short- and medium-term plans for their discrete area of responsibility.

This section has defined strategy and considered three levels of strategy within organisations. The next section examines the process of strategic alignment.

What is strategic alignment?

By strategic alignment we mean that functional strategies should connect with business- and corporate-level strategies. Strategic alignment asks *does our functional-level strategy support business- or corporate-level strategies?* Alignment is important so that resource allocation and activities at the functional level are consistent with high-level objectives. For example, a company with a low-cost corporate strategy should be supported at the functional level by activities that help get the product to market for the lowest price possible. In this instance, it would be counter-productive for marketing or new product development to offer expensive optional extras. Strategies should be aligned.

However, that is not to say that functional-level activities should be constrained to passively accepting strategies handed down from the corporate level. On the contrary, strategy development can be both 'top-down' (from corporate to functional) and 'bottom-up' (from functional to corporate). Research by the authors has previously shown the importance of involving the operations and supply functions in corporate-level strategy development (see Brown and Cousins, 2004 and Brown, Squire and Blackmon, 2007). We found clear evidence that 'world-class' plants are far more likely to involve operations and supply personnel in the strategy planning process.

The alignment process is shown in Figure 8.2.

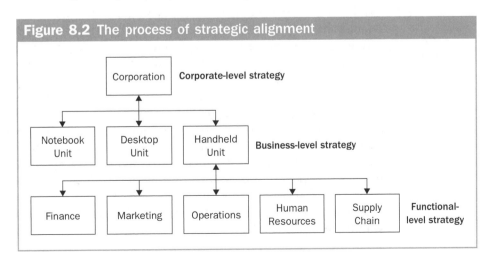

Figure 8.2 The process of strategic alignment

Figure 8.2 shows the process of aligning strategy between the three levels. Importantly, the arrows between the three levels are bilateral. This reflects our belief in the importance of functional-level involvement in the strategy development process.

This section has familiarised readers with the basic concepts of strategy that are important for the remainder of this chapter. In particular, the concepts of levels of strategy and strategic alignment are critical to the following discussion.

Aligning purchasing and corporate strategies

Strategic alignment between supply chain and corporate strategies is achieved where supply chain strategy supports and facilitates corporate strategy. This means that the goals of the supply function are aligned with the competitive priorities of the organisation. For example, if the organisation's priority is high quality then the supply chain function should be concerned with obtaining high-quality inputs from suppliers.

An organisation's competitive priorities will generally emphasise one or a mix of the following:

- cost
- quality
- flexibility
- delivery
- innovation.

Although the emphasis may shift across commodity groups, an organisation will usually develop a reputation based on one or two of these priorities. For example, easyJet has established a reputation for low cost, Dell a reputation for flexibility, and 3M a reputation for innovation. Such reputations do not come about by chance but are derived from specific corporate strategies that are supported at the business and functional levels.

Unlike other supply chain practices that may directly impact the external supply base,[2] aligning purchasing and corporate strategies is an internal activity (Narasimhan and Das, 2001). Strategic alignment does not require large capital investment but is more to do with information sharing, the status of the purchasing function, the knowledge and skills of purchasing personnel, and managing organisation change.

In particular, it is important that any changes to corporate strategy are discussed with the supply chain function. Although this may seem obvious, Tamas (2000) cites the case of a consumer products manufacturer where corporate strategy was revised to innovation but supply strategy was still focused on providing responsiveness and market share. In other words, because strategy should be dynamic, a previously aligned strategy will become misaligned if change is not communicated across the organisation. This case firm is certainly not alone. Related research has shown that only 13 per cent of firms believe their supply practices are fully aligned with business unit strategy.

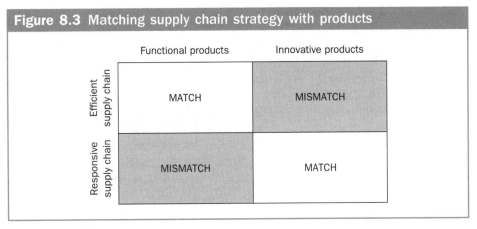

Figure 8.3 Matching supply chain strategy with products

Source: Fisher (1997)

Although many firms are not aligned, the performance implications of alignment versus misalignment are clear. Recent research by one of the authors (Brown and Cousins, 2004; Cousins, 2005) clearly demonstrates that misaligned firms will underperform aligned firms. This point is illustrated succinctly with a case study company who is a large retailer in the UK. The supply function spent over a year negotiating long-term agreements with suppliers, having already been through an aggressive resourcing programme. After the negotiations were complete and the contracts were running, the suppliers each received a letter from the CEO demanding a 10 per cent price reduction across the board. This letter was sent to the suppliers without Supply's knowledge. The result was mayhem, with suppliers refusing to supply and threatening legal action. The supply function became very demoralised and disillusioned with the senior management and a great deal of money was wasted on setting up deals that were not going to be realised. The point here is obvious. In order to survive, the firm needed to follow a cost-focused approach; it had to reduce costs. Supply, on the other hand, implemented long-term strategic collaborations. There was a mismatch between what the firm needed to do and how supply saw itself. This occurred because supply was unaware (until it was too late) of the strategic priorities of the firm.

The need for alignment can also be seen at the product level. Innovative products (such as an MP3 player) require a thoroughly different supply strategy from functional products (such as a can of baked beans). Whereas functional products require a strategy that emphasises efficiency and low cost, an innovative product requires quick response and inventory buffering (Fisher, 1997). A mismatch between product and supply chain strategy would cause significant under-performance, as shown in Figure 8.3.

The process of aligning supply and corporate strategies

Strategic management studies have long noted the distinction between the process of strategy and the content of strategy. The content of strategy examines the specifics of what was decided, whereas the process of strategy considers how such decisions

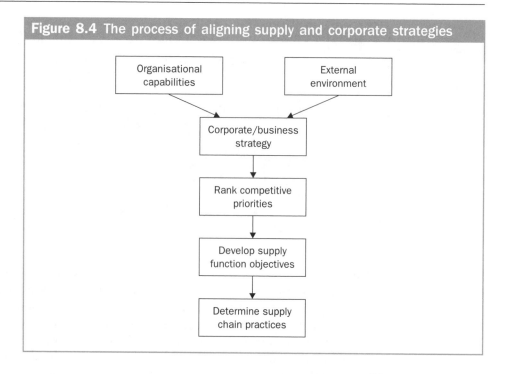

Figure 8.4 The process of aligning supply and corporate strategies

are made within organisations. This section is primarily interested in the process of how to align supply strategy and corporate strategy and incidentally touches on the content along the way.

The model shown in Figure 8.4 helps to depict the process.

Developing corporate strategy

We previously considered the link between the external environment, internal capabilities and the development of strategy. In summary, it was argued that there is need to consider both the current and future states of external markets and matching activities with distinctive resources and capabilities.

Critical to this process is the involvement of the supply function in strategy development. Supply involvement refers to the extent to which supply strategists actively participate in corporate- and business-level strategic decision making. Supply involvement has been argued to lead to improved performance (e.g., Narasimhan and Das, 2001); however, as long ago as the early 1970s studies were showing the divorce between the supply function and corporate strategy development (Farmer, 1972, 1973). Indeed, until the 1980s supply management was seen as part of the clerical function of purchasing, performing a purely tactical, reactive, buying function[3] (Reck and Long, 1988). Thus, supply's contribution to any strategic planning within the firm was largely ignored or, at best, was reactive in nature. By the time that supply personnel became involved, strategic plans had already been formulated by an elite planning group within the firm's hierarchy (Williamson, 1985) whose understanding of the strategic importance of supply was very limited.

To counter this, supply personnel need to be present at, and to have influence on, boardroom decisions related to business strategy. Strategy is ultimately the responsibility of senior-level managers within the firm even though a range of stakeholders (both stakeholders within the firm and those with external linkages to the enterprise) is vitally important to the strategy process. Excluding supply from such top-level discussions means that supply's capabilities and limitations are ignored in strategic decisions.

Our recent research confirms the need for greater involvement of supply personnel in strategy development. We sampled 750 UK manufacturing firms from a database held by the Chartered Institute of Purchasing and Supply (CIPS). Of the respondents, only 55 per cent agreed they had some involvement in strategy development and a mere 11 per cent agreed they had full involvement. These results clearly demonstrate the isolation still felt by many purchasing functions within the UK and show that further work is required to move the profession to a higher status.

Setting competitive priorities

Competitive priorities are generally developed by the operations/manufacturing function in conjunction with corporate planners. Because strategy is about focus (Porter, 1996) and competitive priorities are necessarily in trade-off, organisations will have to emphasise one or two competitive priorities. The operations function will therefore rank these priorities for the organisation[4] and thus determine their relative importance for the supply function.

Supply strategists can then set about operationalising these priorities for their function. The priorities as they relate to the supply function are described in Table 8.1.

Table 8.1 Competitive priorities for supply

Priority	Description	Typical measurement criteria
Cost	Supply, production and distribution of products at low cost	Total cost, pricing terms, exchange rates
Quality	Supply, production and distribution of products with high quality and performance standards	Product durability, performance reliability and conformance quality
Delivery	Supply and distribution of products on time and/or at short lead-time	Delivery speed, delivery reliability
Flexibility	Supply, production and distribution of different mixes and volumes of product with little or no impact on cost	Volume flexibility, mix flexibility
Innovation	Supply, production and distribution of new products	Supplier technological capability, speed of NPD

Translating competitive priorities into supply function objectives

Objectives translate strategy into specific measurable targets. Generally, objectives should be realistic but challenging and give functions a quantifiable goal to strive towards over the medium to long term. More specifically, objectives should conform to SMART, which stands for:

- Specific: Objectives should explicitly state what they want to achieve.
- Measurable: Objectives should be quantifiable to gauge achievement.
- Achievable: Objectives should be context specific and realistic.
- Relevant: Objectives should be relevant to the specific function.
- Time bound: Objectives should be set with an explicit time-frame for completion.

For example, SMART objectives for a supply function could be:

- Reduce inbound supplier costs by 10 per cent within two years.
- Reduce inbound product defects by 0.5 per cent within six months.
- Reduce supplier lead times from Hungary by three days by September.

The relevance of these objectives is determined by the weighting of competitive priorities. In this instance the first objective would be most relevant to an organisation emphasising cost or price, the second objective would be most relevant to an organisation emphasising quality and the third objective would be most relevant to an organisation emphasising delivery speed. The specific measures will be considered further in Chapter 11.

Translating supply function objectives into supply chain practices

The final step in the model is to move from objectives to specific practices. Supply chain practices are the major tools and techniques applied within the supply function. A number are considered throughout this book, including supplier base rationalisation (Chapter 4), supplier selection (Chapter 5), supplier development (Chapter 6), supplier performance measurement (Chapter 11) and relationship management (Chapter 13).

It is important that these practices are not applied in a vacuum but with full consideration of the competitive priorities and objectives of an organisation. Although practices such as 'partnering' and 'rationalisation' have received much attention by academics and practitioners alike, their successful application is entirely contingent upon the specific organisational context. While these practices can have a significant impact on firm performance, their implementation should be driven by firm-level priorities, not by tales of success from other firms or the press. For example, research by Cousins (1999) has shown that less than half of firms involved in supply base rationalisation have captured the benefits they first expected. However, further research by the author also uncovered that this figure was significantly moderated by the presence or absence of strategic planning within supply functions. In other words, rationalisation can have considerable benefits but only when it is aligned to the competitive priorities and objectives of the function. It is therefore critical that strategy, not best practice, drives the implementation of supply chain practices.

Summary

This chapter has considered the alignment between corporate strategy and supply strategy. We started by defining strategy and strategic alignment. We then discussed the alignment of supply and corporate strategies, with a particular focus on the process of alignment. Strategic alignment represents the central hub of the supply wheel and sets the scene for the following five chapters. These begin with an assessment of skills and competence development of supply strategists.

Seminar questions

1. Describe the development of strategy within a business (showing the difference between corporate, business and functional levels).

2. Discuss the importance of strategic alignment.

3. Apply strategic alignment within a supply chain context.

References

Arminas, D. (2002) 'Align Buying and Corporate Strategies, Chairman Urges', *Supply Chain Management*, 14 November, Vol. 7 (23), p. 13.

Brown, S. and Cousins, P. (2004) 'Supply and Operations: Parallel Paths and Integrated Strategies', *British Journal of Management*, Vol. 15, pp. 303–20.

Brown, S., Squire, B. and Blackmon, K. (2007) 'The Contribution of Manufacturing Strategy Involvement and Alignment to World-class Manufacturing Performance', *International Journal of Operations and Production Management*, Vol. 27 (3), pp. 282–302.

Cousins, P. D. (1999) 'Supply Base Rationalisation: Myth or Reality?', *European Journal of Purchasing and Supply Management*, Vol. 5, pp. 143–55.

Cousins, P. D. (2002) 'A Conceptual Model for Managing Long-term Inter-organisational Relationships', *European Journal of Purchasing and Supply Management*, Vol. 8 (2), pp. 71–82.

Cousins, P. D. (2005) 'The Alignment of Appropriate Firm and Supply Strategies for Competitive Advantage', *International Journal of Operations & Production Management*, Vol. 25 (5), pp. 403–28.

Farmer, D. (1972) 'The Impact of Supply Markets on Corporate Planning', *Long Range Planning*, Vol. 5 (1), pp. 10–15.

Farmer, D. (1973) 'Purchasing Myopia', *Journal of General Management*, Vol. 1 (Winter), pp. 56–66.

Fisher, M. (1997) 'What is the Right Supply Chain for your Product?', *Harvard Business Review*, Vol. 75 (2), pp. 105–16.

Mintzberg, H., Lampel, J. and Ahlstrand, B. (1998) *Strategy Safari: A Guided Tour through the Wilds of Strategic Management*, The Free Press, New York.

Narasimhan, R. and Das, A. (2001) 'The Impact of Purchasing Integration and Practices on Manufacturing Performance', *Journal of Operations Management*, Vol. 19 (5), pp. 593–609.

Porter, M. E. (1980) *Competitive advantage*, The Free Press, New York.

Porter, M. E. (1996) 'What is Strategy?', *Harvard Business Review*, Vol. 74 (6), pp. 61–78.

Prahalad, C. and Hamel, G. (1990) 'The Core Competencies of the Corporation', *Harvard Business Review*, Vol. 68 (3), pp. 79–91.

Quinn, J. B. (1980) *Strategies for Change: Logical Incrementalism*, Irwin, Homewood, IL.

Reck, R. F. and Long, B. G. (1988) 'Purchasing: A Competitive Weapon', *Journal of Purchasing and Materials Management*, Vol. 24 (3), pp. 2–8.

Tamas, M. (2000) 'Mismatched Strategies: The Weak Link in the Supply Chain? *Supply Chain Management: An International Journal*, Vol. 5 (4), pp. 171–75.

Williamson, O. E. (1985) *The Economic Institutions of Capitalism*, The Free Press, New York.

Endnotes

1. This assumes that the organisation serves multiple markets. If the organisation serves only one market, corporate-level strategy and business-level strategy will merge into one overarching strategy.
2. Such as make–buy (Chapter 3), supply base rationalisation (Chapter 4), supplier selection (Chapter 5) or supplier development (Chapter 6).
3. See Chapter 2 for more detail.
4. This may also occur at plant level for large manufacturing organisations.

Chapter 9

Competency and skills development for strategic supply

Aim of chapter

The aim of this chapter is to provide readers with an understanding of the process of aligning purchasing competencies within the organisation.

Learning outcomes

At the end of this chapter, readers will understand the:

- difference between skills, competencies and competences;
- competencies for strategic supply;
- methodology for the application of competencies to a practical situation.

Introduction

This chapter focuses on skills and competencies for strategic supply and is the first of five circumferential elements of the strategic supply wheel (Figure 9.1).

As we have seen, the concept of strategic supply has received increasing attention over the past two decades. Numerous authors have identified the evolution of supply management from a tactical to a strategic function (see Chapter 2), and that truly strategic supply requires strategies to be aligned with, and supportive of, overall corporate objectives (e.g. Narasimhan and Das, 1999; Brown and Cousins, 2004). These changes within the supply function also have implications for the skills and competences of the purchasing professionals within it.

An organisation is only as good as the skills and competencies that its personnel possess. Supply can only be strategic if the people working in that area possess the requisite skills and competencies to operate in that way. No matter how complex the measures, if the skills and competencies are not at the required level, the organisation will not be able to fulfil its strategic objectives (see Figure 9.2).

Figure 9.2 shows how this alignment process might work. The vertical arrow shows the desired level of strategic attainment; this is where a firm would like to be. The bottom axis shows the 'actual level of strategic attainment'; this is where

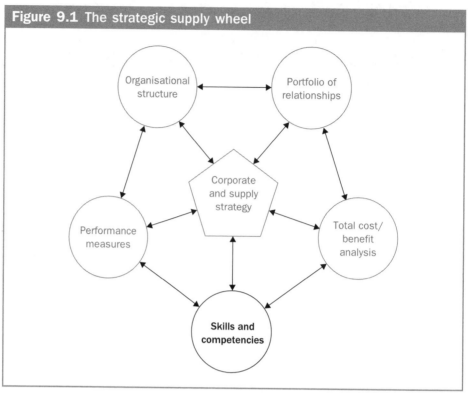

Figure 9.1 The strategic supply wheel

Source: Cousins (2002)

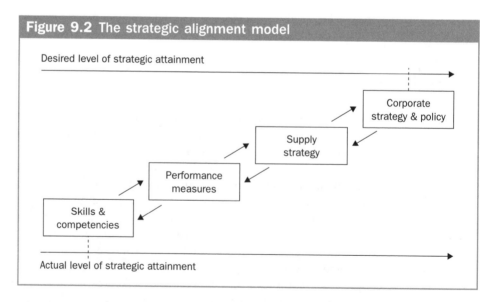

Figure 9.2 The strategic alignment model

the firm actually is (the direction of the arrows represent-time). The model reminds us that no matter how advanced the strategic thinking of the firm, if it does not possess the requisite level of skills and competencies, even the most sophisticated strategy will simply not be achieved. The skills and competencies of the individuals in the organisation will allow only a certain level of attainment.

The role of Purchasing has clearly evolved. It is apparent that supply is becoming a process undertaken by multi-functional teams, across the organisation, instead of a functional department reacting to the requests of other organisational departments. In addition to this, Purchasing is now required to undertake a much broader range of activities, often crossing traditional functional boundaries. In view of these developments, any approach towards competency development must look beyond the traditional functional boundary of Purchasing and consider the organisational requirements for the 'process' of supply management. Competency development that discriminates between organisational titles may fail to meet organisational goals and objectives, as it assumes that purchasing is an activity only undertaken by the Purchasing 'function' or department.

The rapidly growing body of literature on the subject of strategic supply management reflects a belief that organisations can influence their supply market by applying different strategies in different supply situations. Kraljic's supply positioning tool (see Figure 4.2, p. 47) clearly indicates that different purchasing environments necessitate different purchasing strategies. Following this line of thinking, it can be reasoned that different competencies will be required to support effective behaviour for different purchasing strategies.

In practice, it appears that 'Purchasing', in the traditional (administrative) sense of the word, has rarely been seen as a strategic department or role. As Purchasing becomes more strategic it must fill a role in such areas as logistics, make-versus-buy decisions, outsourcing and in-sourcing, supply chain management, inter-firm communication, strategy formulation, relationship management, performance assessment, inter-firm networking and innovation scanning. Competency development should thus be seen (and evaluated) in the light of a more comprehensive 'supply management' context.

This chapter explores the new skills and competences that are required of purchasing professionals operating within strategic supply. We start by exploring the nature of competence, competency and skills. Next we examine competences and skills within the context of purchasing. Finally we develop a model for competency development.

The nature of skills, competency and competence

Definitions of skills have traditionally been associated with the level of training a job requires. Historically, jobs have been termed 'skilled' or 'unskilled', a classification reinforced by mass production. Consequently, standard measures of skills have been derived mainly from the characteristic of technical skills. The literature contains extensive exploration of the concept of skill but no agreed definition exists. Strebler, Thomson and Heron (1997) summarise some of the inadequacies of traditional definitions, which include:

■ The nature of jobs has changed and will continue to change, thus the key elements of a job that determine whether it is 'skilled' or 'unskilled' may change.

■ Older methods of assessing skills (e.g. traditional apprenticeship) are no longer seen as relevant by employers, at least in some industries and occupations.

■ Employers are increasingly interested in defining the skills required for a particular job more objectively for pay and training purposes.

In the light of these inadequacies, researchers and practitioners alike have given increasing consideration to the concepts of competences and competencies. Many large organisations in the UK have invested heavily in structured programmes of education and training and development for their commercial personnel, typically within the objective of developing competence in order to improve performance.

It is important to note and differentiate between the terms 'competence' and 'competency', as these two terms are often used interchangeably, leading to confusion in development procedures. Competencies and competences have been the cause of numerous discussions, with some writers making no distinction between the two words and others stating they have very distinct and separate meanings. An often-used definition of a competency is: 'any underlying characteristic of a person which results in effective and/or superior performance in a job' (Klemp, 1980). An 'underlying characteristic' may be 'a motive, trait, skill, aspect of one's self-image or social role, or a body of knowledge which he or she uses' (Boyatzis, 1982).

There is also an argument that confusion over the meanings comes from a difference of definition between the North American language and the English. The competency approach first became popular in the USA through McClelland's work in the late 1960s and early 1970s. He founded the McBer consultancy which carried out a number of studies into identifying competencies, the first prominent one being that of Boyatzis (op. cit).

Boyatzis' model illustrated that effective job performance can only occur when three critical components – an individual's competencies, the job's demands and the organisational environment – fit together in a congruent manner. If only two of the components are present, this *may* result in effective performance in the short term, but it is less likely that this performance will be sustainable over longer periods. Other studies such as those by Spencer and Spencer (1993) built on Boyatzis' original research by concluding that the different *aspects* of competency – skills, knowledge, social role, self-image, traits and motives – are the clue to superior individual performance. Although the concept of 'competency' has grown in popularity worldwide, it differs greatly from the output-type 'competence' movement promoted within the UK.

Since the start of the 1980s, government agencies known as industrial lead bodies were involved in research into various occupational areas in the UK, identifying key roles, units of competence, elements of performance, performance criteria and range statements for various levels of employment. As a result of the research, the National Council for Vocational Qualifications was set up in 1986, providing the opportunity for individuals to be accredited with awards that were based on standards approved by the aforementioned industrial lead bodies.

National Vocational Qualifications (NVQs) concentrate on standards that define the knowledge, skills and experience required in the workplace. To gain accreditation, individuals are expected to produce a portfolio providing evidence of outputs they have achieved in areas relevant to their job. A common goal of competence development programmes is to promote greater flexibility, adaptability and mobility amongst employees.

In contrast to Boyatzis' competencies, NVQs specify the outcomes required of a person working within a particular job role. This distinction can be specified by thinking that a competence refers to aspects of the *person* that enable him or her to be competent whereas the NVQ-type competence is concerned with aspects of the job at which the person is competent: 'Competencies deal with the behaviours people need to display in order to do the job effectively [. . .] and not with the job itself' (Woodruffe, in Boam and Sparrow, 1992).

There is one final difference in the emphasis of the approach. The UK approach emphasises *assessment* of individuals. In contrast, the US approach is geared more to the *development* of individuals, being originally based on a study of outstanding performers. The different approaches, therefore, have assigned different meanings to the term 'competence'. Whereas to be 'competent' using NVQ standards will imply that an individual has reached the minimum requirements for his or her job role (performance is 'adequate'), the US meaning is more associated with reaching a level of 'excellence'. The two approaches both have advantages, in that there is clearly a need both to develop and to assess the purchasing capability.

The integration of competencies and competences

It is essential, when setting up development frameworks, for organisations to be aware of confusing competencies and competences. Each job requires a number of outputs, deliverables or roles (competences) which in turn require the demonstration of a number of competencies. If the output competences are confused with competencies, this will lead to problems with measuring individuals accurately against the framework at the assessment stage.

Roberts (1997) also accepts the different definitions but claims that the debate should not discourage organisations from taking advantage of the benefits of a flexible competency framework. Roberts has developed a practical framework that encompasses both Boyatzis' concept of competencies and the output-type competences. Roberts' approach involves four clusters: natural, acquired, adapting and performing, as shown in Figure 9.3.

■ *Natural competencies.* The 'natural' grouping is akin to the original concept of competency as developed by Boyatzis, referring to 'underlying traits' and personality dimensions. As these are more difficult to develop, it is recommended that individuals with the desired 'natural' competencies are selected rather than

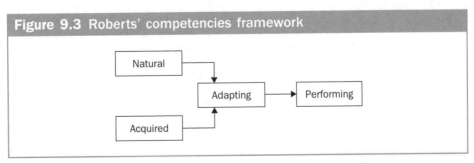

Figure 9.3 Roberts' competencies framework

Source: Roberts (1997)

developed into the required role. These competencies can often be assessed with relative accuracy through personality questionnaires.

- *Acquired competencies.* The 'acquired' competencies are the knowledge and skills that an individual has managed to accumulate through previous experience. This would include education, qualifications and professional knowledge.
- *Adapting competencies.* The 'adapting' competencies deal with the individual's aptitude in coming to terms with changing work environments. Someone displaying superior 'adapting' competencies would be able to move to a different department or organisation and have the ability to tailor their 'natural' and 'acquired' competencies to different contexts with a similar level of success as in their previous job role.
- *Performing competencies.* Finally, the 'performing' group lends itself to the UK brand of competence. It consists of outputs or observable behaviours that are produced as a result of the combination of the previous three clusters.

With many organisations choosing to adopt a hybrid system of competencies combining national standards with their own behavioural standards, Roberts' framework appears to provide clarification and a practical way of incorporating both the UK and US approaches to competence. Roberts argues along the same line, stating that viewing competencies as 'natural', 'acquired' and 'performing' can resolve the problems organisations presently encounter. Instead of attempting to view all competencies in the same manner, the four clusters can be used at different stages of the Human Resources cycle of selection, performance management and development.

Criticisms of competency-based approaches are given in Box 9.1.

Box 9.1 Criticisms of competency-based approaches

Meger (1996) provides the most complete criticism of the competency-based approach and suggests reasons to reject the 'subjective', behaviourally based systems for selection and evaluation of personnel. These are summarised in the table below.

No.	Criticism of behavioural competency
1	They can't be explained in simple rational terms. Only consultants understand them.
2	They are typically based upon the opinions of an elite group. What happened to empowerment?
3	They are designed to create a workforce of clones. What happened to diversity?
4	They are used in a highly situational manner. What happened to consistency and fairness?
5	Constructs are inherently difficult, if not impossible to validate.
6	They are not an open invitation to discriminate against anyone who does not fit in.
7	Legal challenges to these systems are inevitable. They simply raise too many questions.
8	They don't lend themselves to development. If they can't be trained – who knows what they really are?
9	They legitimise the concept of the glass ceiling by implying that those not at the top must not belong there.
10	Interviewers and evaluators cannot make judgements based upon a subjective evaluation of nebulous behavioural traits.

Source: Table from Meger (1996)

Box 9.1 (*continued*)

If competencies are to be used in the selection of candidates or for the measurement of employee performance, it is essential to ensure that they are predictive of performance. While authors such as Spencer and Spencer (1993) outline methods for defining and measuring competencies, and claim that research validates their approach, it is clear that, in practice, implementation is often complex. Meger (1996) emphasises the importance of having a competence system that can be explained, understood and applied fairly.

Munro and Andrews (1994) identify three main criticisms common to most competency frameworks. Firstly, they argue that proponents of the management competency idea do not acknowledge the organisational aspects of consistent, stable, effective performance, tending instead to focus on the role and the individual. Second, while there is recognition that organisations must develop for the future, their paths towards this strategic objective are constrained by the fact that current rather than future competencies dominate competency frameworks. Finally, it is important to understand which capabilities and competencies are of strategic and long-term value, as opposed to those that are essential for efficient operation in the short and medium term.

With the skills and competency literature in mind, in the next section we shall consider the implications for strategic procurement.

Competency and competence requirements for strategic supply

Supply competencies will vary depending on the type of supply and the level of its strategic intent within the business. In Figure 9.4 we use Kraljic's matrix to show how competencies may be populated against various areas of the matrix.

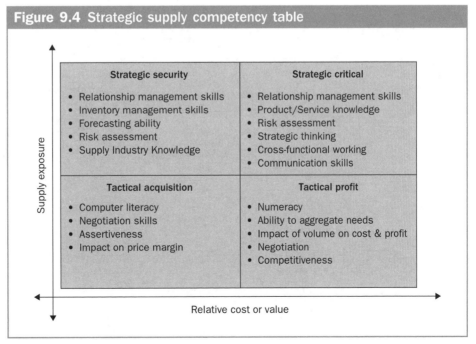

Figure 9.4 Strategic supply competency table

Source: based on Kraljic (1983)

The competencies shown in the above figure were selected from a listing of 97 descriptions of purchasing competencies drawn from the literature and from our research. The most important finding was that the competencies identified by companies varied greatly; clearly it is not appropriate to adopt a standardised approach towards competence development. It is perhaps curious that companies often spend a great deal of time attempting to differentiate their product offering, but remain content to standardise their competence development. It would appear important to align competence development programmes to strategic goals and objectives, rather than standardise through adopting generic purchasing programmes.

The conclusion that can be made here is that it is very difficult to identify a list of generic competencies that are supportive of effective purchasing behaviour for all companies. Each organisation operates within its own distinct environment, and therefore competencies may be viewed as situation specific. The key competencies that purchasing professionals require can be seen in Box 9.2.

Box 9.2 Could you be a world-class Supply Strategist?

Our research demonstrates that it is not valid to argue for one set of competencies for all purchasing professionals. Desirable competencies will vary across organisations and position on the organisation chart. However, despite this, we can still ascertain a number of attributes that will facilitate a shift towards strategic supply. These five areas and some of the key competencies are shown in the figure below. Tick off the competencies you possess!

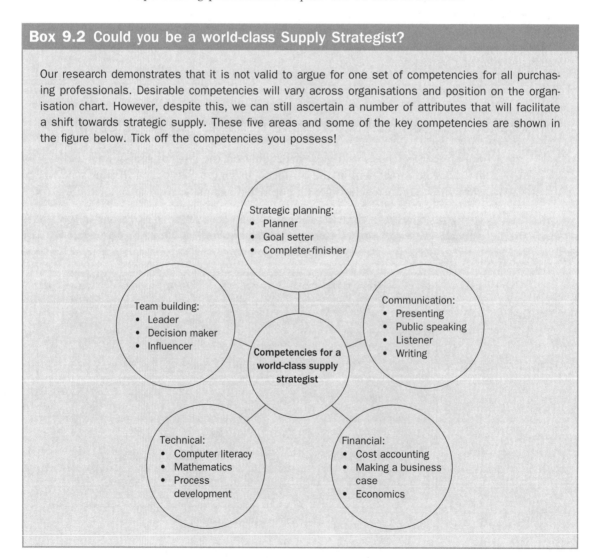

Purchasing Competency Development Model

The Purchasing Competency Development Model (PCDM) (see Figure 9.5) is characterised by a process that aligns Purchasing's capabilities to the role it is required to play within the organisation. It is designed to make Purchasing supportive of overall business goals and objectives. Use of such a model will require the input of individuals who are not labelled as Purchasing or 'Buyers'. The model is built on the thinking that purchasing is a process (rather than a function) at which an organisation must become competent in order to succeed in the marketplace.

The model is set out as a linear process, comprising six steps. It contains aspects of a cyclical nature, however, as the needs and requirements of the role of purchasing may be expected to evolve. Failure to include such a developmental process could result in the eventual misalignment of Purchasing's competence as organisational and purchasing strategies evolve.

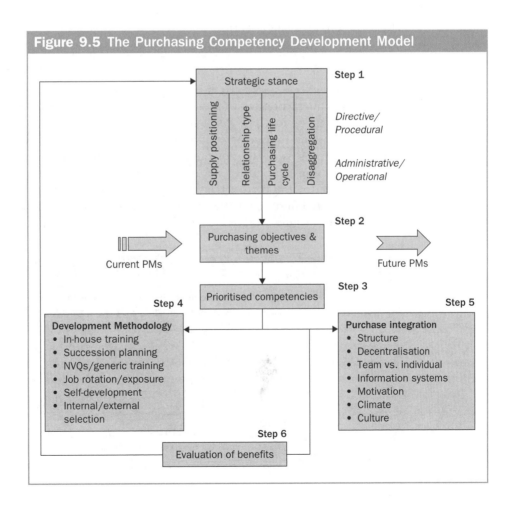

Figure 9.5 The Purchasing Competency Development Model

Step 1: Strategic stance

The first step is to clarify the strategic stance of the organisation and how the role of Purchasing is required to add value to the business operation. This first step comprises four further sub-steps identifying the functioning and positioning of purchasing as an organisational process. The starting point for this development model is the clarification of the firm's strategic stance. This will depend on the ways in which the organisation chooses to develop and define its strategy. For example, it should be clearly understood whether the business strategy is one of cost leadership or product/service differentiation. Without a clear understanding of this, Purchasing cannot ensure its efforts are aligned towards the achievement of overall business goals.

Supply positioning

The role and activities of Purchasing may be disaggregated using the supply-positioning tool (Kraljic, 1983). Appropriate purchasing strategies and procedures must be identified for the areas of tactical acquisition, tactical profit, strategic security and strategic critical purchases. We have used Kraljic's matrix again, to illustrate this (see Figure 9.4).

Relationship type

In order to realise the objectives of distinct strategies for different types of purchasing, the interaction with the supply base must be supported by the appropriate relationship option. The 1990s saw a trend of companies reducing their supply bases and striving to develop collaborative or partnership-type relationships with their suppliers. It is clearly not the most appropriate option to enhance all supplier relationships to partner status. In a similar manner to supply positioning, it is essential for the correct relationship options for the range of purchases to be identified and nurtured. Different relationships will require different purchasing competencies. Figure 9.6 represents four generic relationship types using the

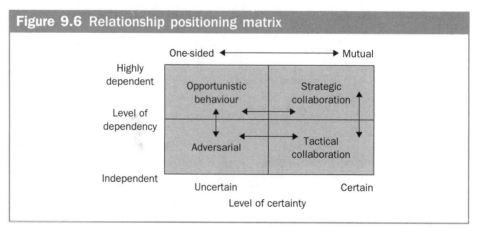

Figure 9.6 Relationship positioning matrix

Source: Cousins (2002)

certainty–dependency model as a useful frame (see Chapter 13 for more detail). Each relationship is characterised by different benefits but also different levels of effort required within the role of Purchasing.

Purchase life-cycle-assessment

Throughout the life cycle of any purchasing strategy, different activities will support the attainment of strategic goals. The variety of activities being undertaken at any one time will require different skills, capabilities and experience. Themes behind any strategy will have life cycles; it is important in the development of purchasing staff to understand the dynamics of activities that are seen to be supporting the current purchasing strategy. Some of the activities will continue to support the strategy; others will become redundant in the future, while new activities will emerge to support the evolution in the strategic stance of the organisation. For effective purchasing behaviour it is essential to identify the different purchasing activities and understand the nature of how they currently support strategy, and how they will continue to do so in the future.

Purchase disaggregation

In a similar vein, it is also essential to undertake a purchase disaggregation exercise. This involves mapping the many activities that comprise the purchasing process, identifying where the activities are undertaken. This will aid in identifying the most appropriate team structure and extent of centralisation for purchasing. Figure 9.7 demonstrates some of the typical issues addressed in a disaggregation exercise. The activities of purchasing can be 'outsourced' to other functional areas

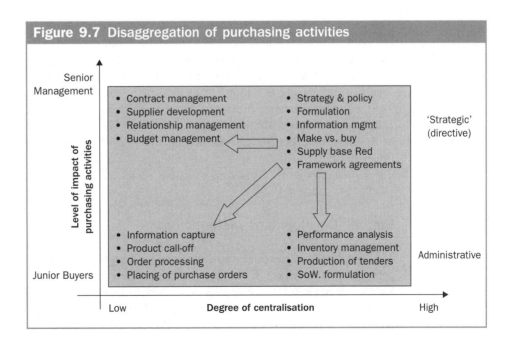

Figure 9.7 Disaggregation of purchasing activities

of the organisation if they are not deemed to be critical. The most important activities should be retained within 'purchasing' (whether centrally or not is another question).

The exercise of disaggregation confronts problems relating to organisational competence development, in that it makes the Purchasing manager understand *what* needs to be developed and *where*. Before any competence development takes place it is essential for the development manager to understand the audience for the training or development programme, and where in the organisation they will be located.

Step 2: Purchasing objectives and themes

Having built a clear understanding of the organisational requirements, the second step is to clarify the objectives of purchasing. When clear objectives have been derived the development programme can be themed, and broken down into more manageable categories. The process in Step 1 appears to be exhaustive, but its aim is only to confront all potential areas of conflict and to gain a clear understanding of the requirements of the purchasing process, allowing the correct competencies to be developed. Step 2 therefore is to clarify the broad objectives of purchasing, and break them down into smaller and more manageable themes for which supporting 'competences' can be clearly defined. The themes may well be described by a number of desirable output 'competences'. The development process will necessitate breaking down the output 'competences' into more specific 'competencies'.

Step 3: Prioritised competencies

The third step is to evaluate and list the supporting competencies for effective behaviour in each themed vein. A number of purchasing professionals should discuss and eventually prioritise the competencies that will support and enhance the purchasing activity. It is important to do this, as it will allow the time and resources spent on purchasing development to be utilised most efficiently and effectively.

At this stage, having produced a 'shopping list' of competencies, it is appropriate to undertake a 'gap analysis' exercise. The objective of this is to look at the existing competency base within the role of purchasing and gain a clear understanding of the current organisational shortfalls. This will allow competency development to be prioritised in the areas most requiring it.

Step 4: Development methodology

The fourth step in the development model is to understand the nature of the competencies that have been listed. This will give a view of the most appropriate method for the organisation to acquire the competence in the workplace. The flexible competency framework of Roberts (see Figure 9.3) will allow the nature and characteristics of each competence to be identified and developed or sourced.

When the competencies have been categorised according to Roberts' competency framework, appropriate development methodologies and plans can be developed, e.g. in-house training courses, selection, reward, education, NVQs, job rotation, and business sector exposure. Individuals should be recognised as experts for developing specific acquired competencies, enhancing the efficiency of future development programmes.

Step 5: Purchase integration

The competency development model has so far generated a lot of information pertaining to development requirements of the role of purchasing. It is essential that after such in-depth analysis of the role of purchasing, the competencies being developed integrate well with, and are supported by, other critical areas of purchasing. Areas to be considered are:

- purchasing structure;
- extent of decentralisation;
- team versus individual assessment and appraisal;
- information systems;
- corporate culture and purchasing climate;
- channels of communication;
- remuneration.

It is not enough to embark on an in-depth competency development programme: careful attention must also be paid to the motivation of the purchasing staff. Organisational success is dependent not only on the potential of the workforce, but on the 'top down' constraints placed upon employees, and the 'bottom up' choices that the purchasing staff have to make to perform their jobs effectively. In other words, employees may be able to meet their objectives, but might not choose to do so. Careful consideration of remuneration, corporate culture, and feedback will help to motivate the purchasing professional to achieve higher levels of performance.

Step 6: Evaluation of benefits

The final step, having created a competency development process, integrated within the normal operation of the business, is to evaluate the relative benefits that the programme is bringing to the role of purchasing. This is a vital step, allowing sceptics and enthusiasts to appreciate the true merits of such an exercise. It is also significant to evaluate the effectiveness of the integrated system and implement modifications where necessary.

Summary

This chapter has examined competency development for strategic supply. It was recognised early on that the role of purchasing personnel has evolved with the changing nature of supply management. Furthermore, it was argued that the level of strategic attainment was restricted by the skills and competencies within the supply function. The old adage 'you are only as good as your people' certainly applies here.

The chapter explicitly defined the difference between skills, competences and competencies. It was argued that a focus on skills was largely outdated within Western organisations and that competency development was more desirable. Unfortunately, there is a tendency for competence development to be historically focused. In an area such as Purchasing, which is undergoing rapid changes, it is essential that the competencies defined meet future rather than past needs. We conclude that there is a problem for lead bodies in producing competence descriptions that on the one hand need to be specific to avoid ambiguity, but on the other need to be general enough to apply across organisations. Generic competence descriptions are unlikely to relate directly to a particular organisation's needs. For this reason, many organisations have opted to build on the NVQ competences and develop their own hybrid competencies approaches (enveloping both competence and competency). In this manner, it is possible for the development effort to provide a possible source of competitive advantage.

The chapter has proposed an approach allowing a more strategic and proactive input into the development of purchasing competencies and competences. The approach addresses the issues of:

- alignment with organisational policy and strategic objectives;
- speculation of the future role of purchasing;
- consideration of organisational structure and where the purchase activity takes place;
- flexibility in the workforce.

Seminar questions

1. Discuss the difference between skills, competencies and competences.
2. Describe the competencies required for strategic supply.
3. Apply the competencies approach to a practical situation.

References

Boam, R. and Sparrow, P. (1992) *Designing and Achieving Competency*, McGraw-Hill, London.

Boyatzis, R. (1982) *The Competent Manager: A Model for Effective Performance*, Wiley, New York.

Brown, S. and Cousins, P. (2004) 'Supply and Operations: Parallel Paths and Integrated Strategies', *British Journal of Management*, Vol. 15, pp. 303–20.

Cousins, P. (2002) 'A Conceptual Model for Managing Long-term Inter-organisational Relationships', *European Journal of Purchasing and Supply Management*, Vol. 8 (2), pp. 71–82.

Kraljic, P. (1983) 'Purchasing Must Become Supply Management', *Harvard Business Review* (September–October), pp. 109–17.

Klemp, G. O. (1980) *The Assessment of Occupational Competence*, National Institute of Education, Washington, DC.

Meger, B. (1996) 'A Critical Review of Competency-based Systems', *Human Resources Professional*, Vol. 9, pp. 22–5.

Munro, A. and Andrews, B. (1994) 'Competences: Dialogue without a Plot?', *Executive Development*, Vol. 7 (6), pp. 12–15.

Narasimhan, R. and Das, A. (1999) 'An Empirical Investigation of the Contribution of Strategic Sourcing to Manufacturing Flexibilities and Performance, *Decision Sciences*, Vol. 30 (3), pp. 683–718.

Roberts, G. (1997) *Recruitment and Selection: A Competency Approach*, IPD, London.

Spencer, L. M. and Spencer, S. (1993) *Competence at Work*, John Wiley & Sons, New York.

Strebler, M. T., Thomson, M. and Heron, P. (1997) *Skills, Competencies and Gender: Issues for pay and training*, Institute for Employment Studies, Brighton, Report 333.

Further reading

Boyatzis, R. E., Cowen, S. S. et al. (1992) 'Implementing Curricular Innovation in Higher Education: Year One of the New Weatherhead MBA Program', *Selections*, Vol. 9 (1), pp. 1–9.

Cousins, P. (2002) 'A Conceptual Model for Managing Long-term Inter-organisational Relationships', *European Journal of Purchasing and Supply Management*, Vol. 8, pp. 71–82.

Prahalad, C. and Hamel, G. (1990) 'The Core Competencies of the Corporation', *Harvard Business Review*, Vol. 68 (3), pp. 79–91.

Chapter 10

Organisational structures for supply management

The aim of this chapter is to identify and assess a range of organisational structures for strategic supply.

Learning outcomes

At the end of the chapter, readers will:

■ understand the difference between centralised, decentralised, hybrid, atomised and federal structures;

■ understand the advantages and disadvantages of these different structures.

Introduction

This chapter focuses on organisational structures for supply management and is the second of five circumferential elements of the strategic supply wheel (Figure 10.1). As purchasing and supply management becomes a strategic part of the organisation and is expected to be a significant contributor to its competitive success, so its location, shape and form within the organisational structure becomes critical. The nature of the business will inevitably affect the choice of these factors, although trends such as outsourcing, information and communications technology (ICT) and globalisation may have an overarching impact.

In this chapter we explore the options available to Supply Strategists for structuring their resources and efforts in order to match the requirements of the markets.

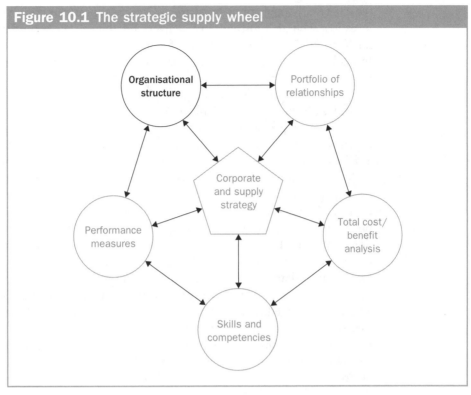

Figure 10.1 The strategic supply wheel

Source: Cousins (2002)

Conceptual framework

Selecting the right structure for the Supply department involves a combination of three schools of knowledge: strategic supply, competition, and organisational design. The last of these is a vast field with a rich literature and we do not attempt to summarise it here.[1] We shall borrow concepts that are directly useful for the present discussion but in addition to using their own initiative, experience and imagination, the good strategist will always consult the broadest possible literature before making decisions and designs, searching for ideas that others have not exploited in the search for competitive advantage. Competition is assumed to be the driver for strategy and changes in its nature will be considered. Where no competition may have existed traditionally (e.g. in public services) there is now usually sufficient pressure to perform, exerted by regulators that are intended to give the same effect.

Many of the modern strategic challenges facing organisations on the supply side do not fit within traditional purchasing and supply perspectives. As we saw in Chapter 9, the array of skills and competences required to meet these challenges is complex. New types of individual roles have emerged within the function, dividing it into two parts: day-to-day operations and leading-edge deal making.[2] For example, at Herman Miller (HM) the organisation of the purchasing function is split into two groups. Materials Managers and Buyer Planners are responsible for the day-to-day supply of material and their focus is primarily concerned with efficiency measures such as lead-times and delivery reliability. The second group is responsible for supplier development and effectively divorced from day-to-day operations. Instead, they have responsibility for developing suppliers, ensuring they have the capabilities to support HM and projecting what future needs are going to be.

The people who have been trained for traditional purchasing may find it hard to deal with these radical challenges and new perspectives. Whether they survive – and whether purchasing as a function remains in the organisational structure – depends to a great extent on how it is structured to meet the organisation's needs.[3] The long-running debate in the organisational design of Purchasing has been whether it should be *centralised* or *decentralised*. Much has been written on this, mostly by management consultants.[4] This may be because the moves between central and distributed functional organisation are not limited to Purchasing: they form a bread-and-butter activity for management consultants who are keen to develop organisational change. We shall review this debate and also consider some more recent aspects that must be taken into account in embarking on the design of Purchasing's shape, form and position within the organisational structure.

The types and extent of competition faced by business organisations in almost all sectors changed fundamentally in the closing decades of the twentieth century. Central to this change was the advance in ICT. As long ago as 1990, Venkatraman pointed out that those information systems represented a possibility for completely redesigning the organisation and the ways in which it earned its income.[5] His point was not that this was an interesting option but that organisations that did not do this would not survive. The chief executive of American Airlines at the time was famously quoted as saying that if he had to sell his aeroplanes or his information system, he would sell the planes. Venkatraman showed how information systems required organisations first to evolve and then go through a 'revolution'. In the 1990s, the rise of electronic commerce (variously including e-purchasing, e-procurement, e-business, e-supply, etc. – see Chapter 17) has been seen as a revolutionary stage in information systems and there is general acceptance of Venkatraman's maxim: business organisations have to join this wave or simply get left behind. The implications for Supply Strategists are extreme – we shall examine these in this chapter.

The broader implication of Venkatraman – that organisations would have to look anew at how they earned their keep – subtly combines with the technological impacts of the microprocessor (starting in the mid-1970s) and the development of global labour markets to present organisations with the need to reallocate activities, only undertaking internally those for which their own competences provide the best resource. This has meant that many organisations have stopped doing things they used to do and now have those activities carried out by others: subcontractors. This is not new, of course; for purchasing and supply the *'make or buy?'* decision has long been seen as a staple of the function. However, the stakes in outsourcing are so high that a new language has been invented for it – the concept of 'core competencies'.[6] It is wrong to think that these are things that an organisation must do for itself, however. As Roberto Testore, chief executive of Fiat Auto, said in 1997, his company's core competencies were styling and engines.[7] Despite this, Fiat has always outsourced both of these to some extent (for example, having its styling done by famous Italian automotive studios such as Pininfarina, Giugiaro and Bertone). The point is that Fiat needed to *know about* these competences – to be an intelligent, well-briefed customer.

Applying the concepts: the development of organisational design

Most modern business organisations still display the structures and mechanisms that nineteenth-century mass production concepts demanded – many are still close to a Weberian model of traditional *bureaucracy*.[8] A hierarchy is constructed beneath the board of directors, with vertical functional 'chimneys' or *'silos'* – ladders up which career paths are seen to lead – taking responsibility for the activities and specialisms into which the organisation divides itself (Finance, Marketing and Sales, Operations, Human Resources, and so on). Purchasing is rarely one of these silos – more often it fits within one of the first three. The silos were strengthened over the twentieth century by the 'professionalisation' of specialisms, complete with self-governing associations (mimicking the craft-based guilds formed two centuries before). Entry to these professional groups was controlled with centrally written examinations and qualifications (sometimes self-referential), and status differentials, largely based on time serving and practical experience, thus reinforcing the new status quo.

During the 1970s, much discussion began on the need for a more practical approach to the horizontal flows of communication (i.e. a member of staff might be permitted to speak to their opposite number in another department [silo] without 'going through' their manager). This was driven by the need to remove operational anomalies that the previous system had accommodated. Such accommodation was no longer possible because markets at this time began to demand responsiveness and price performance that had not been seen previously. The concept of bringing a product to market in a specific time (more quickly than a competitor) meant that organisations could not wait for procedures to run their course – short-cuts were needed; this gave rise to horizontal communication and the beginning of the end for functional silos.

The operational-level impact of this was the concept of *'cross-functional teams'* – in which people from different functional silos were put together to work as a unit, for a specific purpose. Breaking down the silo walls in this way was not easy and cross-functional teams still appear to present major problems for some organisations today. For Supply Strategists, many of the people with whom they work on a daily basis are from other organisations (suppliers and contractors) and their cross-functional teams should logically break not only the silo walls but also the organisation's own boundaries. A good example of this is given by the integrated project teams (IPT) developed within the UK Ministry of Defence (for example, at the major centre at Abbey Wood, just north of Bristol) where secondees from several defence contractors and MOD personnel are co-located on a long-term basis (actually working together as an integrated team, sometimes even sharing one large office) in order to focus their activities on a specific objective (e.g. developing a new class of submarine or refitting an older class). The IPT initiative developed for the MoD by management consultants was not without its teething problems but is widely seen as a success; it was soon copied by organisations within the defence industry for working on their own new products by collaborating with their suppliers.

The purpose of organisational design is to arrange the intelligent resources of the organisation (people and ICT) in such a way that it can engage with the market effectively. It follows that as the needs of the market change (e.g. computers have to become communicators in addition to calculators, or long-term peace breaks out in a previously troubled region, reducing the need for fighter aircraft as happened in the early 1990s), so the design of the organisation must be reviewed. As globalisation of customer markets forces organisations to face the need to be able to compete anywhere in the world – selling products and procuring goods and services – so their operations must reflect a strong core and flexible operating divisions. Purchasing is directly and profoundly affected by such design changes and cannot expect to live cosily within a traditional silo.

Such forces have been under way for some time and most organisations have already felt the wind of change. These concepts and developments must be addressed constantly in practice by Supply Strategists: we shall look at how they might face the challenge.

Challenges, issues and practical aspects: principal choices for organising purchasing

In this section, we consider the basic choices that are available to the Supply Strategist when deploying people and resources to provide the organisation with effective service. The actual choice made will depend on the market pressures – there can never be one best way. It is also not possible to draw simple connections between external pressures and organisational design; for example, market globalisation might mean entirely different things to an insurance company and a producer of motor cars. A buyer sourcing indirect materials, or 'MRO' (the American term for maintenance, repairs and overhaul[9] expenses), may have different concerns about e-procurement from those of a colleague buying components for production. However, in discussing the differing structure types we shall consider situations in which each might appear prima facie appropriate. In each case we shall also consider the practical advantages and disadvantages that may be associated with the approach.

Centralisation

The original silo format of organisations was based upon co-locating all the functions on one site (see Figure 10.2) – often quite literally 'beneath' the board of directors (who would occupy the top floor of the office block). This simple idea naturally brought the Purchasing department together as one entity. When divisions were formed in the organisation, so satellite plants would be managed from the centre, where the expertise, records and political power lay. Once the divisions

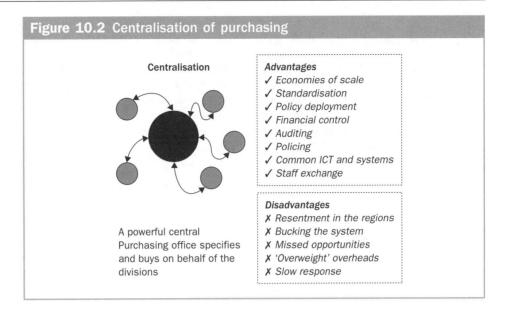

Figure 10.2 Centralisation of purchasing

Centralisation

A powerful central Purchasing office specifies and buys on behalf of the divisions

Advantages
✓ Economies of scale
✓ Standardisation
✓ Policy deployment
✓ Financial control
✓ Auditing
✓ Policing
✓ Common ICT and systems
✓ Staff exchange

Disadvantages
✗ Resentment in the regions
✗ Bucking the system
✗ Missed opportunities
✗ 'Overweight' overheads
✗ Slow response

began to gain different political power and expertise (local knowledge, language, etc.), tensions built up between them and the centre. From these early developments in the twentieth century, centralised Purchasing inherited advantages and disadvantages. Naturally, when the divisions originated outside the organisation (i.e. acquisitions) the political difficulties in centralising Purchasing might be very complicated.

Advantages

Economies of scale

Perhaps the most obvious advantage of centralisation is the ability of the organisation to amalgamate its requirements – across the divisions – and buy in large quantities, negotiating for lower prices: traditional economies of scale. If commodities are to be bought, this makes even more sense – the size of requirements is a powerful bargaining tool in such purchasing and even more important if the trader is to balance a portfolio of futures and stocks in various places in the world – perhaps dealing on several exchanges at once. In some industries this is not even seen as the role of the Purchasing department – for example, in the UK, the giant confectioner, Mars, refers to the people who buy cocoa, sugar and butter for them as 'Economists.' (We shall examine this in Chapter 18.)

The amalgamation of requirements (see Box 10.1 for an example) is only a paper exercise, of course. The delivery requirements may be much more diverse (for example: Head Office in London might make a corporate deal on photocopier paper or electronic components but require shipments to be delivered to several operating divisions on sites across Europe). This can detract from the economies of scale as the supplier will need to charge for the delivery complexity – thus removing the single, optimised price (note that the supplier will charge for this, whether the customer realises it or not).

Box 10.1 North West Universities Purchasing Consortium Limited

The North West Purchasing Consortium Limited (NWUPC) is a not-for-profit company that aims to 'secure value for money' in the purchasing of goods and services. It is open to any Higher Education Institute in NW England, North Wales and Ireland.[10] By pooling requirements, the NWUPC has greater bargaining power to drive costs lower than any single institution could achieve. Beyond this the consortium also seeks to promote standards and good practice in an industry that traditionally lagged behind the private sector.

Source: based on www.nwupc.ac.uk

Standardisation

With the amalgamation of requirements comes the ability to standardise. This should provide operating cost reductions as well as the possibility of a lower overall price. For example, in 1999, SmithKline Beecham (SB), now GSK, developed a global purchasing database that enabled its Purchasing staff and divisional managers to know the price that should be paid for many items across a wide range of requirements, wherever in the world they were purchased. At the same time, head office did a deal with Compaq for laptop computers. Through this deal, SB personnel in, say, Sydney, Australia could buy a computer at the lowest price possible, under the deal (price saving). When they brought their laptops to a meeting in London and needed to replace a part that had been broken on the flight, the standardisation would mean that their machine was the same as that used by their UK colleagues, and the part could be procured and fitted easily. The Internet hardware manufacturer Cisco has a similar policy, linked to its strategy of growth through acquisition in the 1990s: when it took over another company, all existing computers were removed and replaced with a standard model so that all PCs throughout the organisation are the same.

Policy deployment

Standardising should support the vital concept of policy deployment. This means constructing organisational mechanisms that ensure the policies developed by the board of directors are actually followed in practice. It is important to note that policy is a much more profound and long-term feature than strategy, which may change at a moment's notice. A policy is a public statement to all stakeholders (the community, shareholders, employees, customers and suppliers) of what the organisation stands for and the values by which it will operate. Failure to deploy policy appears to be a key weakness in many organisations. For example, it is often the case that the chief executive tells the shareholders that the firm now operates a policy of collaborating with suppliers (perhaps calling it 'partnership') while at the supply interface the Buyer is still instructed to negotiate for every penny possible (and their performance is assessed on this) regardless of the impact on the supplier, or any value there may be in the relationship. The weakness comes from a lack of credibility in the marketplace (first the supply market, then the stock market).

Centralised Purchasing should mean that the decisions taken centrally can be manifested in divisions by controlling what is bought. The logic is that procedures to control Purchasing in the organisation as a whole can be more easily managed if they are run by one office (rather than several, perhaps located in countries thousands of miles apart, by people who speak different languages and have different customs, in different time zones).

Financial control

Financial Centralised Purchasing should lead to better control of financial issues, for reasons similar to those associated with policy deployment. This should include the costs of purchase, the financial implications for investment (capital) and cash flow (revenue) and the integration with other parts of the organisation that are responsible for such matters. Once again it is the geographical proximity and the homogeneity of the business culture that are employed to engender the benefits.

Auditing

The inspection of procedures is a complex and difficult process, made simpler by the co-location of all the areas that must be examined; it is rarely popular with those whose actions are under scrutiny! Centralising the Purchasing activity should ease the complexity (and thus reduce its process costs) and make for more effective, responsive auditing, though disdain for a central authority may be difficult to dispel.

Policing

The bane of the Purchaser's life is so-called 'maverick' buying – where an individual decides to procure something outside the agreed specifications or takes action that compromises the commercial freedom of the Buyer to gain value for money for the organisation. Even when individuals are spending on their own budgets, the lapse in control represented by non-standard choices is perceived as a weakness in the system. We shall visit this again later – it is not that simple, of course – but for now, it appears that a basic advantage of centralisation should be the ability of the Purchasing system to stop maverick buying, or any other departure from the agreed procedure (whether or not the act itself represents criminal, moral or ethical corruption, or just someone exercising their imagination and autonomy).

Common information and communications technology and systems

Ever since the advent of the microprocessor in the mid-1970s, business organisations have struggled to get to grips with the information systems presented to them by an avid and avaricious supply industry (hardware and software manufacturers and consultants). The complexity of the systems coupled with the complexity of the processes and structures they are attempting to manage has meant that stories of failure and duplication are legion. The need to incorporate communications in the package (and thus move from IT to ICT) in the late 1980s complicated matters even further. From materials requirements planning in the 1970s to enterprise resources planning in the 1990s (and e-procurement at the turn of the century), IT/ICT systems appear to have provided solutions in theory and problems in practice with e.g. the £30bn NHS system. They are seen, nevertheless, as a sine qua non and Purchasing is required to fall in line with its share of them. This may be seen as rather general in its assertion but it is depressingly obvious in practice.

This is not the place to explore all this complexity (and the despair in implementation): suffice it to say that a centralised system should logically be simpler to develop, implement and run than one that has to take in the complexity of de-centralised decision making. This should be reinforced by the possibilities represented by the Internet. The fact that it is not so in practice suggests that communications between the centre and the operating units can never be assumed to be a simple matter in a divisionalised organisation.

Staff exchange

The staff in a centralised purchasing organisation develop skills and expertise, coupled with an overview of the corporate position, that may be rare and valuable attributes within the divisionalised organisation. This 'view from the hill' may be shared with divisions by seconding staff from the centre. This may be coupled with the common practice in purchasing and supply of moving buyers from commodity to commodity periodically in order to give them a broad view of the items that the organisation needs to acquire. (This also has the effect of preventing individual buyers from building up too personal a connection with any one supplier, or the reverse – demotivation from being stuck with a difficult supply relationship.)

It is an assumed benefit of centralisation, therefore, that someone has a view of the total organisation. Whether or not this is so will depend on the degree to which there is transparency and communication within the organisation, as we shall see.

Disadvantages

The disadvantages of centralisation stem largely from attitudinal problems and the difficulty of controlling processes remotely. The feelings of people in divisions towards headquarters may include resentment of perceived hierarchy or privilege and it is likely that any anomaly or mishap will be blamed upon those in the central office who 'don't know what is going on at the coalface'. Thus, a system that runs well may still be criticised simply because it is imposed, while one that leads to errors will be grasped with enthusiasm as an opportunity to show dissent.

Beyond criticism, of course, lies sabotage. Staff in divisions (in purchasing offices or operating units who are, in effect, the 'customers' for Purchasing's services) often feel they have a right to autonomy, since it is they who answer for the performance of their operation. This commonly leads to 'bucking the system' (the maverick buying referred to above). Local staff express their preference by ignoring the standard systems and preferred sources, and conceal this in order to avoid penalties. Once this starts (and it is observed to be a very common practice) the integrity of the centralised system can never be assured.

People in the divisions who criticise the central system may have good reason to do so. Local knowledge at the divisional level may be very valuable and a system that seeks to suppress this may lead to missed opportunities. For example, when the Japanese television manufacturers came to South Wales in the 1970s, they set about developing local supply bases. This was not just for political or even logistical reasons – they needed to localise design of televisions with the people who would watch them. When their very successful Accord saloon was redesigned in 1996, Honda ended up with three different models for the three principal regions, allowing for varying tastes. 'Global' need not mean standardised (Akio Morita, founder of Sony, invented the word '*glocalisation*' to describe this combination of global economies of scale combined with local preferences). This may apply to ways of working (including systems and procedures) as well as to products and services.

A negative feature of centralised control that grew during the first three-quarters of the twentieth century was what might be called 'corporate obesity' – excessive overhead costs and even opulence in some cases. In the 1970s, large companies would often have elaborate headquarters buildings in fashionable areas, justifying them as symbols of success that would appeal to potential share-holders. Centralised Purchasing can also suffer in this way, presenting another reason for those in divisions to criticise it. Oversized central offices also typically work with a slow response to divisional matters – despite the extra people, the system may appear not to provide good service to its remote customers. Indeed, many of the 'corporate palaces' were removed in the last two decades of the twentieth century as funds were redirected to improve operations: takeover deals often revealed decadence and profligacy at the heart of the old empires. Some firms boasted of light, or lean, central offices with few staff and modest style.

Decentralisation

Many of the advantages of *decentralisation* (see Figure 10.3) come from removing the disadvantages of centralisation, discussed above. As the constraints of the centrally run system are removed, those in the divisions gradually take more control of their day-to-day affairs and can develop previously unexploited opportunities. The basis for this is the human instinct for autonomy.

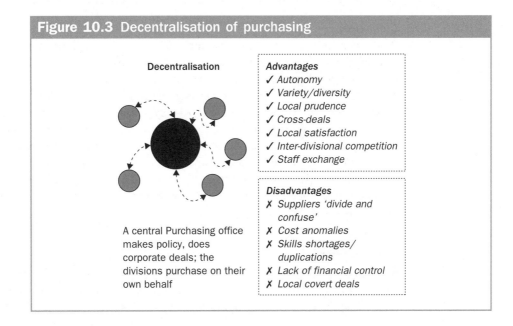

Figure 10.3 Decentralisation of purchasing

Decentralisation

A central Purchasing office makes policy, does corporate deals; the divisions purchase on their own behalf

Advantages
✓ Autonomy
✓ Variety/diversity
✓ Local prudence
✓ Cross-deals
✓ Local satisfaction
✓ Inter-divisional competition
✓ Staff exchange

Disadvantages
✗ Suppliers 'divide and confuse'
✗ Cost anomalies
✗ Skills shortages/duplications
✗ Lack of financial control
✗ Local covert deals

Advantages

Autonomy

For managers in divisions to control their own purchasing, critical resources must be made available by corporate planners. Such resources may include information systems that are designed in one location (centrally). For the divisions to enjoy autonomy, therefore, requires consultation with staff about designing and implementing standardised ICT provisions. This seemingly obvious requirement apparently eluded Purchasing and IT strategists for many years (and still does in some fields).

Autonomy, once agreed, should enable divisional purchasing staff to exploit the diversity and variety of local supplies, and to exercise prudence (that may reflect, for example, local or national culture that would be offended by insensitive edicts from a remote central office). As the responsibility for divisional purchasing to obtain best value for money for their funds becomes real, so the carping about anomalous systems must logically disappear ('If it doesn't work for you then change it yourself – to your own requirements').

The divisions themselves become the focus for activity and planning in decentralised systems; however, a central office usually remains. Often it is seen as a 'staff' role (as opposed to a 'line function') or internal consultancy. In very large global organisations, the central (or 'corporate') office often has no executive control over purchasing in the divisions and may be chiefly concerned with consolidating policies (removing anomalies between divisions), education and training, and process development (i.e. genuine consultancy). This may need to be funded as an overhead, or on the basis of the central team charging its customers (divisional purchasing directors) for its services. The latter is often fraught with difficulty in practice because hard-pressed operating divisions are likely to remove, say, 'education' from their budgets in favour of more immediately beneficial investments, even though they would probably all agree that education is vital, in the long term.

Cross-deals

Partly as a result of the 'bridging' mechanism of a central office but also as a part of everyday operating, it is likely that senior staff in the divisions will communicate amongst themselves as a natural network. This can lead to opportunities in one region being exploited by Purchasing in another – a 'cross-deal'. This can include making other divisions aware of especially good suppliers, exchanging members of staff on secondment, and so on. Often, however, such sharing of benefits is curtailed by a Buyer in one region fearing that by sharing a good supplier, they might lose the position of preferred customer, with a consequent drop-off in service. This is a good example of the failure of mechanistic organisational logic in the face of organic human nature.[11] Intra-corporate secrecy and competition tend to flourish in decentralised Purchasing systems.

Disadvantages

Being able to respond to local requirements without the need for central approval should lead to purchasing offices in divisions improving the satisfaction felt by their 'customers' in their operating units. Despite this, the disadvantages of decentralisation can lead to situations as corrupted as the one we saw above under Centralisation.

Lack of communication between divisions

The lack of communication or collaboration between divisions, unchecked by a central, common system, can provide a perfect opportunity for suppliers to exploit their customers by charging different prices across the corporate organisation. This was the situation in the National Health Service as recently as the early 1990s, where one health authority would typically be paying significantly higher prices for an item (e.g. hypodermic syringes) than its neighbour, just a few miles away. The problem was addressed by the formation of a central purchasing authority for the NHS but the predictable wrangles over local autonomy continued (for example, surgeons often like to use their favourite particular brands of latex gloves and will not be prepared to have this preference compromised by a clerk in a central purchasing office, simply to save a little money, when lives might be put at risk. There may be no logical connection between the preference and saving the patient's life, but who is going to argue with the surgeon?).

Duplication of resources

Decentralisation inevitably involves duplication of resources – each divisional office has its own range of skills and competences. In addition to the obvious corporate cost of this (which might, however, not exceed the cost of the excessive overheads in the centralised system), a situation of scarcity may arise (e.g. just how many experts in e-commerce can a corporation hope to employ?).

Difficult to control spending

A combination of these factors may give rise to difficulty in controlling the financial reporting in a decentralised organisation – if only for purposes of corporate reporting. The tendency for divisions to conduct local, covert deals may lead, in fact, to a loss of intelligence at the corporate level that could be considered destabilising for the organisation – not a situation that is tolerable for long. An extreme example of this is provided by the case of the North American Walt Disney Corporation, which reached a point in the 1980s where the chief financial officer did not know how much was being spent on the very diverse and exotic range of products and services that the company had to procure. Decentralisation had gone haywire. His only chance of regaining control was to stop all payments being made and see who complained. Then, one small central office was set up where all cheques would be raised for payment. Gradually, a picture emerged of the spend that was being made across the corporation. Such draconian measures are not uncommon!

Atomisation

So far we have considered corporations in which there is a central 'headquarters' office (which presumably doesn't do anything productive; i.e. it is an overhead cost) and operating divisions, where all the action takes place. It is not just in such a large, divisionalised organisation that the debate on central control takes place; in

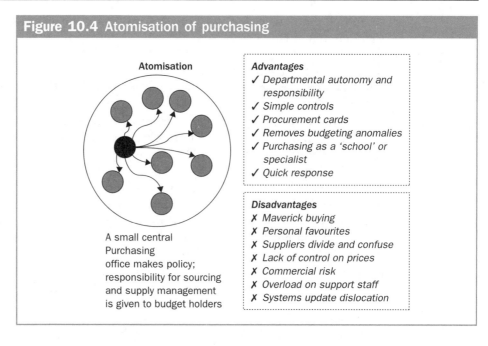

Figure 10.4 Atomisation of purchasing

Atomisation

A small central
Purchasing
office makes policy;
responsibility for sourcing
and supply management
is given to budget holders

Advantages
✓ Departmental autonomy and
  responsibility
✓ Simple controls
✓ Procurement cards
✓ Removes budgeting anomalies
✓ Purchasing as a 'school' or
  specialist
✓ Quick response

Disadvantages
✗ Maverick buying
✗ Personal favourites
✗ Suppliers divide and confuse
✗ Lack of control on prices
✗ Commercial risk
✗ Overload on support staff
✗ Systems update dislocation

any situation where Purchasing provides a service to budget-holding 'internal customers' there will be a tension between the constraints of a formal system in the former and the wishes and preferences of the latter.

One way of overcoming this is to *atomise* (see Figure 10.4) responsibility for expenditure – to 'explode' it from the centre to the budget holders. This has radical implications for both Purchasing and the organisation as a whole. The budget holders may assume that they can make their own purchases but find that it is not as simple as it seems to get good value. Rather than fall back on traditional centralised purchasing, they may require different types of support, including advice on policy, tactical activity, legal and contractual matters, and so on.

As with decentralisation, atomisation brings autonomy to the budget holder. It may be possible to temper this with fairly simple controls; for example, the advent of corporate credit cards for budget holders – the so-called procurement cards of the 1990s – represented an attempt to do just this. The early offerings from providers of e-procurement systems take this concept to a more advanced level: budget holders can buy materials and services through a computer interface that can actually show them the product. Such a system seemingly transforms the role of the Buyer from one of processing requisitions to a more strategic activity of setting up corporate contracts and deals that may be exploited by those wanting to acquire items for themselves (for production or MRO). Once again, in practice, the organic nature of organisations often overpowers the mechanistic design: the difficulty arises when the human nature of the budget holder takes effect.

Budgets are a complex (and, some would say, flawed) concept. It is not in the interests of someone to whom an annual operating budget is given to reduce the amount allocated to them. So, if someone in Purchasing offers to reduce the cost of the items that the budget holder needs to acquire, it might easily be seen as a threat to the level of budget that could be claimed next year. Giving budget holders responsibility for purchasing may not result in corporate savings, therefore, and is open to all the problems of maverick buying, local preferences and supplier exploitation that we saw earlier. Atomisation of purchasing may thus require a review of budgeting procedures.

The budget holders may see atomisation as increasing their workload and bid to employ their own specialist (i.e. a Purchaser in every department or project). This has all the resourcing problems (scarcity and duplication) that we saw above. The activity involved in purchasing by the budget holders must thus be reduced to a minimum. To do this, the Purchasing department has an important role as a 'school' or internal consultancy – to help the budget holders buy for themselves with all the commercial skill and wisdom of a traditional purchasing person. This must be held together with a robust policy, which makes it clear to everyone how the organisation conducts its relationships with other parties and how dealings must proceed.

Atomisation is still a relatively rare approach to structuring purchasing within an organisation, even in those that are project-based. As technology (e-supply) eases the physical burden associated with conducting one's own buying, so the concept appears to have major attractions, in reducing organisational dislocations that traditionally occur between the person who wants something (whether it is a piece of equipment or components to be used in production) and the remote purchaser who acquires it for them.

Federal structure

The expression 'federal' has suffered from bad press in recent times, perhaps due to its use in a derogatory manner in political and economic reform in Europe. It is actually a more general concept and has major implications and opportunities for business organisations (Figure 10.5). Charles Handy, in his book *The Age of*

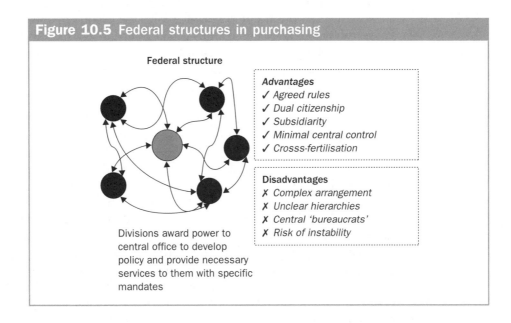

Figure 10.5 Federal structures in purchasing

Federal structure

Advantages
✓ Agreed rules
✓ Dual citizenship
✓ Subsidiarity
✓ Minimal central control
✓ Crosss-fertilisation

Disadvantages
✗ Complex arrangement
✗ Unclear hierarchies
✗ Central 'bureaucrats'
✗ Risk of instability

Divisions award power to central office to develop policy and provide necessary services to them with specific mandates

Unreason, explains the basic rules of federalism.[12] Briefly put, Handy explains them as:

- Common rules and procedures: basic ground rules are agreed and used throughout the organisation. Within these, local ways of working may vary, but not in conflict with the corporate policies and strategies.

- Dual citizenship: people in the organisation are genuinely content to wear two hats – showing concern for the good of the corporation as a whole, and for their own local division.

- Subsidiary: literally 'giving away power' by the centre to the divisions. This concept means that activities are carried out, and decisions taken, at the lowest level possible. The centre then becomes a coordinating device, but answerable to the divisions.

For Purchasing, the implications are profound. In a federal system, the role of the central office is to serve the divisions, not control them. Since its personnel are seconded from the divisions, there should be less chance of the centre becoming remote – the headquarters 'syndrome' may be avoided. For their part, the divisions are in constant and intimate contact with one another – sharing sourcing information and maintaining a dual perspective – and they are as concerned for the success of the whole organisation as they are for their own local prosperity. This is not easy in a business organisation because it is quite possible for one division to be set against another in the need to decide, for example, which plant to invest in and which to close (especially if the two are in different countries). Thus, Ford's decision in 2000 to cease car production at its highly visible main plant in Dagenham was eased because the motor giant's purchasing is closely controlled globally from Dearborn in Michigan, and locally from Cologne, in Germany. The same company had realised long before the benefits of central control on purchasing in its industry, enabling it to economise on 'platforms' (the standardised base for a car, on which several different bodies might be produced, appearing to be independent designs). For example, this enabled Ford to produce new Jaguar saloons (the 'S' type, effectively a remodelled Lincoln Town Car, and the X400, based on the Ford Mondeo – the latter built well away from Jaguar's traditional base in Coventry, in a Ford plant).

Hybrid systems

In fact, Ford's purchasing, like that in many global giants, has to be a hybrid of the forms discussed above – combining the strengths of central planning with the necessities and opportunities of local sourcing. When the company began making its famous Model T, all the parts were produced in Michigan and then shipped to assembly plants around the USA. This technique was used throughout the twentieth century to enable developing countries to produce complex products from a kit of parts that could not possibly be sourced locally. The practice is called CKD (standing for completely knocked down) and is still in use today. As developing countries grow, however, their politicians want jobs for their people not just in assembly (in 'screwdriver plants') but in the more valuable activities (i.e. greater value is added in creating components from raw material than in simply screwing them together). The challenge for purchasing is to be able to source locally (sometimes under the pressure of 'import substitution' or, in the more complicated world of defence procurement, as part of an 'offset' or 'counter-trade' deal).

The most common form of hybrid is seen in organisations that decide to buy some commodities centrally and others locally. The rationale is typically based upon the principle of economies of scale – major deals that can be struck for items such as energy (often an organisation's largest spend after labour), company cars, legal services, information systems, travel services, etc. True commodities (the word is used loosely for many items that are not actually commodities in the economic sense: see Chapter 18), such as cocoa and sugar for confectioners or steel for car producers, are almost always bought centrally unless the global nature of the organisation provides sufficient bargaining strength for traders in several countries to buy independently. Even then, such traders within the organisation will need to keep constantly in touch, to share market intelligence and trading dynamics such as the chance of arbitrage (buying in one market where the price is low and selling in another where it is high – such practice helps to reduce anomalies on world markets).

In parallel with this central activity, the hybrid organisation will require (or allow) its divisions to purchase other requirements locally. Take the example of a catering company firm with a chain of restaurants (owned or franchised); items where large-scale deals can bring low prices, reliable delivery and quality, resulting in standardised offerings to customers, will be bought centrally. Items such as fresh vegetables or bread, meanwhile, will be bought in local markets at the discretion of the local manager (or chef) to take advantage of daily deals and specialities.

Pseudo-commodities (such as technological items whose supply and demand fluctuates with innovation and fashion) pose a problem for manufacturers. The latest technology must be available globally but there is no formal market (i.e. a network with all the information, analysis, communication and stable dealing of a true commodity market) to support sourcing. An example of this would be dynamic random access memory chips (DRAMs) in the computer industry. Producers of such vitally important components regularly employ the oldest form of economic power (make an item scarce and thus drive up the price) to support their industry. Consequently, computer manufacturers have to vie with one another to get hold of the precious components (which are said to be worth more than their weight in gold). To inform themselves, such producers set up mechanisms within their global structures to ensure that they know what is going on. One global giant, IBM, calls these 'commodity councils'. The members of such councils become the experts for IBM on the commodity in focus (e.g. 'memory' or 'packaging'), communicating constantly through electronic mail and video conferencing, etc. and actually meeting only occasionally. The councils are features of the purchasing structure within the global organisation, although they may include specialist non-Purchasing people (such as engineers or logisticians).

Another traditional approach to the problem of intelligence on sourcing and technology is to appoint one division as 'lead buyer' for the commodity; the organisation's 'brain' for sourcing, say, high-performance metals, might lie in its Singapore purchasing office: all others communicate with colleagues in Singapore for direction on this commodity. The problem with this approach is that as the commodity becomes global (e.g. a new source for high-performance metals is set up in Brazil) the single specialist division may find it difficult to maintain sufficient intelligence. The solution to this would seem to be IBM's commodity council approach.

From classical to radical

Inevitably, structuring purchasing within organisations is a matter of 'horses for courses'. There are, however, some trends that might shed some light on where the topic is heading. The twin forces of globalisation and technology development (which are, of course, heavily intertwined) encourage both traditional approaches such as economies of scale and radical concepts such as networked intelligence and atomisation. A large organisation with stable infrastructure (e.g. a local government system in one country) may face constant change but is unlikely to shut down divisions quite as readily as, say, a producer of televisions or a retailer. A federal system may work well in such a situation, since the divisions themselves compete in only some respects (e.g. for inward investment) but collaborate in most others (e.g. to drive down prices and improve quality levels for basic services).

The advent of electronic exchanges may be expected to encourage centralisation, or perhaps federal structures, since the Internet makes geography almost irrelevant – at least at the sourcing stage. It is too early to assess the impact of such 'rational' approaches to purchasing on the strategic approaches of collaboration and partnering, in which, it would seem, personal connections and face-to-face meetings are all-important.

The possibilities of e-supply may be extrapolated to a scenario in which much day-to-day purchasing is done by computers with minimal human input (as, for example, wages and other 'book office' functions are managed currently), while the really value-adding deals in the supply market are done by powerful and dynamic individuals who see the world as their marketplace and work in very short time scales, possibly from a remote location. This scenario would encourage a centralised basis for the majority of purchases, coupled with a high degree of flexibility in the entire system for divisions to take advantage of special opportunities which must be managed as projects of change. The lesson for the structure of purchasing is clear in all these possibilities: it must change to adapt to the requirements of the organisation. Such requirements cannot be assumed static, even over the briefest planning period.

Summary

This chapter has reviewed various organisational designs for purchasing. It was shown that there are advantages and disadvantages to each of the considered approaches. Organisational design should be contextual and appropriateness therefore lies within the resources of the firm, the market forces and the corporate and purchasing strategies. We identified a number of these moderating conditions and in particular considered the twin effects of globalisation and technology development.

Seminar questions

1. Describe the difference between centralised, decentralised, hybrid, atomised and federal structures.

2. In groups, examine the advantages and disadvantages of centralised, decentralised, hybrid, atomised and federal structures.

References

Burns, T. and Stalker, G. M. (1961) *The Management of Innovation*, Tavistock Publications, London.

Cox, A. and Lamming, R. (1997) 'Managing Supply in the Firm of the Future', *European Journal of Purchasing and Supply Management*, Vol. 3 (2), pp. 53–62.

Daft, R. L. (1997) *Management*, The Dryden Press, Fort Worth, TX.

Galbraith, J. (1973) *Organization Design*, Addison Wesley, Reading, MA.

March, J. and Simon, H. (1958) *Organization*, John Wiley & Sons, New York.

Handy, C. (1998) *The Age of Unreason*, Business Books Limited, Hutchinson, London.

Ouchi, W. G. (1980) 'Markets, Bureaucracies, and Clans', *Administrative Science Quarterly*, Vol. 25 (1), pp. 129–41.

Prahalad, C. and Hamel, G. (1990) 'The Core Competencies of the Corporation', *Harvard Business Review*, Vol. 68, pp. 79–91.

Scott Morton, M. (ed.) (1991) *The Corporation of the 1990s: Information Technology and Organisational Transformation*, MIT Press, Cambridge, MA.

Endnotes

1. Galbraith (1973) and March and Simon (1958).
2. Cox and Lamming (1997).
3. See Chapter 17 for a discussion on how technology may remove some of the traditional need for Purchasing's role in the acquisition process.
4. Ouchi (1980).
5. For a good development of Venkatramen's work and many other linked concepts, see Scott Morton (1991).
6. Prahalad and Hamel (1990).
7. Ing. Testore was addressing the IPSERA Conference in Ischia.
8. Daft (1997).
9. MRO is also sometimes referred to as 'maintenance, repair and operating.'
10. There are 6 regional HE purchasing consortia in the UK.
11. *Mechanistic* and *organic* are terms originated by the early seminal work of Burns and Stalker (1961).
12. Handy (1998).

Chapter 11

Performance measurement

Aim of chapter

The aim of this chapter is to provide readers with an understanding of the elements of performance measurement of the supply base.

Learning outcomes

At the end of this chapter, readers will:

- understand the basic elements of performance measurement systems;
- appreciate the interaction between performance measures and strategy;
- understand the differences between different types of supplier performance measures.

Introduction

This chapter focuses on performance measurement systems, and is the third of five circumferential elements of the strategic supply wheel (Figure 11.1).

Performance measurement is critical for the successful management of a firm's supply chain, and is a key means of monitoring and evaluating the actions of individuals and work groups within the function. Traditionally, Purchasing has lagged behind other functions in developing sophisticated performance measurement systems, although this situation is slowly changing. In addition, most measures of performance have focused on the internal operations of the purchasing function, with few outward-looking measures assessing supplier performance.

The fundamental objective of a purchasing and supply chain performance measurement system is to aid in strategy implementation through a formal, systematic approach to monitoring and evaluating purchasing activities. Managers can use several types of information to achieve this goal: the most effective blend financial information with non-financial information. As managers have limited spans of attention, performance measurement can act to preserve their attention by helping ensure supply-related operations are 'in control' and flagging up any variances from planned

Figure 11.1 The strategic supply wheel

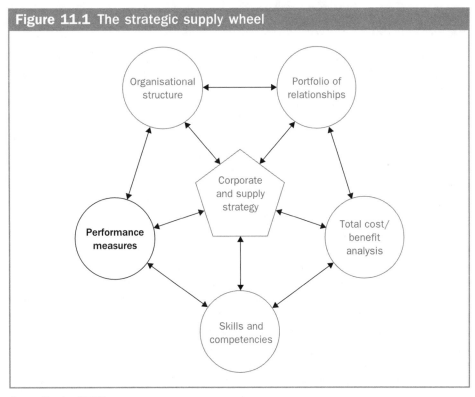

Source: Cousins (2002)

performance. Many firms have harnessed information technology to provide them with information necessary to manage performance. One such firm is Comet, a UK-based retailer, whose approach is discussed in Box 11.1.

In the past, when acquiring raw materials was relatively simple, when manufacturing processes were straightforward, when engineering changes were few, when masses of stock were considered an asset and when the term 'quality' was reserved for engineers, the procurement function could survive as an island tasked to cut costs. This approach is no longer feasible. Although the vital role of purchasing in the achievement of the firm's strategic goals has been recognised, there has generally not been a corresponding change in the types of measure used. The ways in which many efficiency and financially based measures are employed reflect the outdated idea that purchasing is an add-on cost to the business. As purchasing has become more strategic, these traditional short-term efficiency measures have become less useful in assessing how well Purchasing achieves its aims. Indeed, they may be undermining the credibility of purchasing managers and their buyers, whose activities the performance measures should be designed to support.

Performance measures as signalling devices

Moreover, management can use performance measures as a means of signalling and influencing the actions of the people who are responsible for performing the tasks. Employees may not necessarily stop to evaluate the suitability of the criteria

---

Box 11.1 Comet introduces supply chain performance measurement

Comet, a large UK-based electrical goods retailer, decided in 2005 to improve the level of visibility and control it had over its supply chain. Using a custom-designed measurement tool, designed in conjunction with an external consulting company, they designed a new scorecard measuring system. The scorecard, to be fit for purpose, had to allow Comet to rank suppliers and identify specific issues in the supply chain, such as late deliveries and quality-related issues.

The scorecard was compatible with Comet's warehouse and business intelligence system to help ensure widespread adoption and consistent measurement. For a pan-European firm such as Comet, compatibility throughout all its regions was of utmost importance. The actual system itself measured supply issues such as order fill success (i.e. is what is ordered actually delivered?), availability cover (i.e. does the supplier have enough stock to cover forecasts?) and 15 items related to delivery performance, including method of delivery, quality of goods on arrival and the number of rejects per batch. Comet centralised the information the scorecard collected, offering a single point of reference for supply staff to identify problems.

The system also allowed ranking of suppliers according to various criteria such as product line and delivery location. Specific supply issues could be addressed based on performance in each area. The system in and of itself, however, could not solve supply problems. The system had to be managed correctly and information kept up to date. Comet update their system weekly and offer reports the day after the system is updated, ensuring that their scorecard system remains a valuable management tool, rather than an expensive source of obsolete data. Comet believe the system has been a resounding success. Since the installation of the scorecard system, Comet has seen customer service improve along with supplier relations, and, more importantly, profitability.

Source: www.conchango.com

---

on which they are judged, but instead will take their lead from these criteria to maximise their own performance. For example, if the quality of inputs gets only lip service from top management, and only the cost of inputs is measured, then quality essentially becomes a secondary issue. Similarly, performance measures may send conflicting signals to your buyers, with measures often disconnected from both corporate and supply strategy. Thus, performance measures must be carefully designed to suit the needs of the organisation in order to avoid resources being allocated in a sub-optimal way. A well-balanced and well-structured system should support and encourage performance in the areas which are critical to the firm's success, while poorly designed systems serve only to encourage the wrong goals and reward the wrong achievements.

Cascading performance measures

Effective performance measurement systems should also cascade the high-level corporate strategy down into the lowest levels of the organisation, signalling expectations and desired behaviours to employees. The aim is to create an alignment between the corporate strategy, supply strategy, goals and objectives, performance measures, and ultimately, the actions of the individuals responsible for carrying

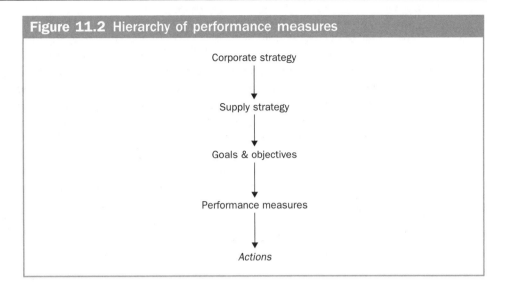

Figure 11.2 Hierarchy of performance measures

Corporate strategy

Supply strategy

Goals & objectives

Performance measures

Actions

out the work. For Purchasing to contribute to the success of the organisation, it is vital that it derives its strategy from the corporate strategy. Purchasing therefore requires a clear alignment with the broader corporate thrust: operating according to any other criteria will mean that resources are being misallocated. Figure 11.2 reflects this approach.

The benefits of measurement

The benefits of a well-directed and well-balanced performance measurement system for purchasing are extensive. Performance measurement can help focus Purchasing on adding value in a number of ways.

- **Decision making.** The right type of measures enables improved decision making, by directing activity which is aligned to the needs of the organisation and identifies variance from planned results. In addition, the cause-and-effect relationship between processes and their outcomes will be more readily apparent, facilitating greater ease of planning and control and coordination of activities across the organisation.

- **Communication.** Establishing targets which are relevant to both Purchasing personnel and their internal customers can facilitate an improved level of communication throughout the organisation. It is important that other functions are aware of the contribution which Purchasing can make, so they may draw on it to their own advantage.

- **Visibility.** A well-structured set of objectives and targets will improve the visibility of activities both within the purchasing process and with other departments, identifying areas of waste in terms of defects, delays, surpluses and mistakes. It may also contribute to the status and profile of Purchasing within the organisation.

- **Motivation.** Measurement motivates people to act in certain ways. If targets are related to the overall success of a particular objective, then employees will feel more motivated. One theory of worker motivation states that people feel the need to contribute; and when they see an objective being fulfilled at least partially as a result of their actions, they will find increased satisfaction in working to achieve those goals. Conversely, if measures have no apparent purpose or link to the overall working of the company, there will be little attraction in achieving them. Within large companies, it is often difficult for employees to grasp the larger purpose of their efforts or to see how they can add value in a way that can make a difference. Saunders (1994: 144) claimed 'what is measured not only provides data that can inform judgements about the standards of performance achieved but also provides signals as regards to what is important. Measurements have a motivational influence, therefore, and they help to shape perceptions of what is important and to concentrate energies on actions relevant to them.'

Problems with measurement

Measurement, particularly where the determinants of performance cross organisational boundaries, is an extremely difficult process. Numerous problems may emerge, which limit the effectiveness of the purchasing performance measurement system. These problems are now discussed.

- **Conflicting messages.** Problems arise when conflicting messages are received by managers and buyers regarding what is expected of them, or when measures are derived which are not directly related to the organisation's purpose. Conflicting messages may be transmitted regarding the 'real' performance measures that an organisation uses. Often, a piecemeal approach to performance measurement means that particular initiatives will be overrun by other corporate priorities which affect activities going on elsewhere.

- **Collection of inappropriate information.** Problems also often arise because the measurement system in use was not originally designed as a measurement tool, but rather to meet operational requirements. Order processing and inventory tracking in purchasing might be examples of this. A common error has been to assume that the by-products of such systems provide suitable information for management reporting and decision making. Measurement systems have traditionally been designed for senior managers to gather information 'upwards' so that they can impose decisions 'downwards'. Business functions end up with their own measures, based on results but not indicating either how they arrived at their current situation or what to do differently.

- **Lack of goal congruence.** Fundamentally there is no point in measuring an activity unless the results inform the recipient of how well various goals are being met. It is often not so much the measures that are being used that make a difference but actually how they are being used and what they contribute to decision making. This requires that they be related to the strategic objectives of the organisation, via the goals of the particular department or process. The performance measurement system must be derived directly from corporate strategy, synthesising an analysis of the external environment with internal capabilities which reflect the purpose, technology available, and the nature of the activity.

Key performance measurement concepts

Efficiency versus effectiveness

Traditionally, purchasing performance concentrated on achieving price savings in the supply market, and other efficiency-based measures. These, however, do not reflect the full extent of purchasing activities, and the preoccupation with such measures may actually detract from the more useful indications of how Purchasing performs across this range of activities. Van Weele (1984) argues that there are two dimensions to performance in any activity, efficiency *and* effectiveness. *Efficiency* is the relationship between the planned and actual sacrifices which are made to achieve agreed goals – it is, in effect, an operating ratio of effort against results. This may depend on organisational factors such as the workload, certain procedures, the information system used, and headcount, often focusing on transactions. *Effectiveness*, meanwhile, is the extent to which a goal can be met, using a chosen course of action. Supplier development, value analysis, forward buying programmes and lead-time reduction all impact on assessments of Purchasing's effectiveness. These two categories of performance measurement are described in Figure 11.3.

Clearly there is an important relationship between the two definitions – efficiency may be an important part of whether a function is effective in meeting its goals – but they remain distinct from each other. Price performance, therefore, which is a common expectation of Purchasing, is a legitimate element of purchasing efficiency – and therefore Purchasing performance – but not the only one. One firm that we studied received 35,000 requisitions, raised 28,000 purchase orders, and arranged and managed 26 contracts with a total value of £18m. These are simply statistics: they do not give information as regards measures of efficiency or effectiveness. A more useful measure of efficiency might be that the average time from receipt of order requisitions to the placement of orders was 1.5 days. In this

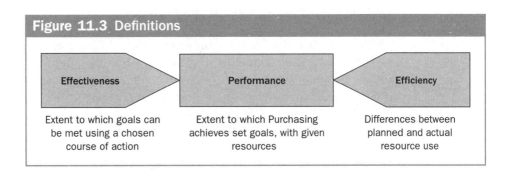

Figure 11.3 Definitions

Effectiveness	Performance	Efficiency
Extent to which goals can be met using a chosen course of action	Extent to which Purchasing achieves set goals, with given resources	Differences between planned and actual resource use

case, order turnaround time is a useful efficiency measure which indicates how well internal customer needs are being met. In addition, 75 per cent of deliveries on all orders placed were either early or on time. This gives a more meaningful indication of effectiveness against a particular criterion (delivery performance), and can be tracked over time.

Why can cost-based measures be dysfunctional?

Price performance indicators may be misleading in many ways. Assessing buyers against the price they have paid is not as easy as it may first appear. The real price may be blurred by quantity discounts, payment terms, credit, and currency fluctuations. Also, the price paid in one period compared to the previous may be meaningless, as the difference between the two may depend on the relative success of the buyer in securing price concessions on different occasions. The factors which contribute to this are unlikely to be constant. For example, in the case of inflation indices, simply to be better than an index is no guarantee of profitability – competitive tenders only provide a 'snapshot' of a particular point in time, and inflation may not be passed on to customers continuously.

Another problem might be in identifying who is actually 'responsible' if a fall in the market price occurs. Closer cross-functional cooperation may result in improved design specifications but it is difficult to attribute the success in securing a lower price to any one function. To be meaningful, price savings should be considered in the light of those planned, predetermined actions undertaken by Purchasing, or by Purchasing and other departments, which result in measurable cost/price reductions, value improvements (e.g. through value analysis projects, quality control circles) or avoidance of higher costs. In this sense, across-the-board price reductions by a supplier should not necessarily count as a measure of purchasing success. Similarly, savings which may result in an increased overall cost to the customer organisation should be avoided, such as volume discounts which lead to increased stockholding costs, or quality failures: the danger of many price savings, in an efficiency-orientated environment, may simply result in a cost being incurred elsewhere in the business. Again, the attention is drawn to the effectiveness of such decisions in achieving a lowest total cost of acquisitions, throughout the product life cycle.

Financial and non-financial measures

Purchasing can add value to an organisation in a number of ways, as summarised in Table 11.1. While a number of these areas may be important to the final price obtained from a supplier, to focus entirely on price performance may be counterproductive, when other issues, such as product quality or delivery reliability, may be more immediately important to the well-being and smooth functioning of the organisation, and the achievement of lower costs overall. If these activities are not measured, then the traditional argument that you cannot control what you cannot measure may be seen as important opportunities are overlooked.

Table 11.1 Value-adding activities which Purchasing may undertake

Strategic	Tactical
Supplier relationship management	Contract negotiation
External resource management	Contract management
Customer satisfaction	Improved utilisation of money/getting better value
Product/range development	Provision of commercial acumen
Process reengineering	Improved productivity
Supply chain management	Reduction of internal operating costs
Customer & supplier education	

Source: adapted from Butler (1995)

A further problem with an over-reliance on efficiency-based measures is that, in addition to focusing resources on only a limited part of purchasing activity, the nature of much financial data means that they may not be useful in decision making, when considered in isolation. Simple workload statistics, such as the number of Purchasing employees, number of purchase orders raised, the number of requisitions received, and department costs (all still in common use), do not necessarily reflect the key areas of significance to the organisation as a whole. It is therefore doubtful that departments which are still primarily expected to deliver the best price savings or efficiency statistics, and which are measured on these criteria, will be effective in contributing to the organisation's overall goals. Financial accounting systems were never originally designed as a tool for business control. In consequence, performance measurement systems in many of today's companies focus on historic rather than future performance, financial rather than operational indicators, internal rather than external data, and numeric rather than qualitative results. These results-based measures are naturally important, in that they allow organisations to 'keep score', but they do not enable managers to monitor the activities and capabilities that enable them to perform a given process.

Various attempts have been made to integrate non-financial measures of performance into organisational measurement criteria. These measures can help shift attention away from short-term financial goals towards medium- and long-term goals emphasising causality: 'suitable non-financial measures are the cause, and successful financial performance the effect'. While it is difficult to quantify performance in such areas as supplier development, interdepartmental relationships and negotiation skills, they are often the very activities which need to be monitored and stimulated, in order for purchasing to deliver the appropriate goods and services to internal users effectively. It would be pointless to continue to measure buyers on the price concessions that they may achieve with suppliers, through applying pressure, when the priority for a particular product or service might be to secure regular and reliable delivery, or a particular level of quality. Lip service may be paid to the stated priority but actions will always be directed first towards achieving that target on which they are measured, especially if the target is linked to remuneration.

Identify the stakeholders

Any assessment of performance 'should be brought about with the active involvement of all those who are affected by the activity'. Indeed, Dumond (1991: 37) argues that 'good or bad purchasing is largely determined by the perception of internal customers to whom purchasing provides its services . . . purchasers will clearly be at their best when they fully appreciate that their performance will be evaluated in the light of its impact on the performance of their internal customers.' In a process, the customer is the next person or function for whom Purchasing provides goods, materials, products or services. However, identifying who the internal customers are, and gathering the information they actually need to gauge performance, can be frustrating steps in the performance measurement exercise.

Gaining buy-in

A further important principle of performance measurement is that the measures designed at each organisational level should include specific input of the teams which will be responsible for delivering the progress against those goals. Managers will be required to set the strategic context but should allow the teams to think about the most effective ways in which they can achieve them to suit that strategic context. In this way, the measurement system will achieve a greater degree of credibility with employees than if the measures are imposed on them from the top down. Firms often impose measures on employees to enable senior management to pull information up, so that they can manage downwards. This ignores the fact that people who do the job routinely and who are 'closest to the action' will know more about the nature of their work and should be able to judge which measures will be relevant and effective. Objectives 'owned' by those responsible for achieving them are far more powerful motivators of performance.

Categories of performance measures

There are literally hundreds of different ways of measuring the various elements of supply chain performance. Some measures assess the supply base, others assess the performance of the Purchasing department, while still others may be used to monitor the interfaces between Purchasing and other internal functions. The most effective performance measurement systems will assess performance across the entire length of the firm's supply chain, from suppliers through internal processes to customers. Figure 11.4 illustrates the major categories of supply chain performance measurement. Each category is discussed in the remainder of this section.

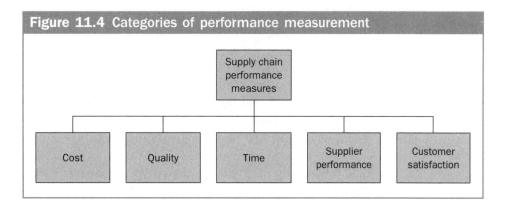

Figure 11.4 Categories of performance measurement

Cost

Cost-related performance measures help evaluate the efficiency and effectiveness of the purchasing spend. At a simple level, this relates to variance analysis examining the deviation from actual and planned spending. The benchmark may relate to budget, market values, or be benchmarked across multiple plants or divisions of the organisation. Commodity products (e.g. raw materials) are most usefully judged against actual price to market price index.

Specific performance measures at this stage may include:

- *Total distribution cost.* Efficient and cost-effective distribution systems are critical. Thus, firms need to measure the various distribution cost elements to identify trade-offs between different modes of transport and warehousing.

- *Total inventory cost.* Inventory is one of the biggest hidden costs for many businesses. Up to 50 per cent of a company's current assets may be tied up in inventory, with excess inventory a key reason for long lead-times. Inventory should be evaluated with the use of suitable performance measures. These may measure levels of inventory on hand, obsolescence, and inventory in transit. The accuracy of forecasting techniques should also be included as it is a key determinant of inventory levels.

Quality

Quality is key. It may be assessed across three levels, being manufacturing-related, supplier-related and customer-related.

- *Production quality.* Numerous approaches exist to assess the level of defects for a particular item, product or sub-assembly. Most often it is expressed as yield rates, or 'good' product as percentage of total production. Also, parts per million, made popular under Six Sigma initiatives, may be used to judge conformance to specification.

- *Defects per supplier.* Measuring defects received from suppliers can be a useful means of monitoring performance and target setting, as well as encouraging competition among the supply base. Defects are most commonly assessed by inspecting or sampling the suppliers' deliveries and calculating the acceptable items or assemblies as a percentage of total delivered. This approach allows trend analysis of individual suppliers, helping identify variance in their performance. Setting a minimum quality benchmark also helps enforce certification and incentive schemes. Finally, by making performance levels public across the supply base it provides social norms for improving performance, where suppliers want to be seen at the top, and certainly would not want to remain at the bottom of the list.

■ *Customer returns.* The buyer can trace the causes of failure of their final products to specific items, components or assemblies provided by a supplier. The usual benchmark is zero failures. Failures also represent an opportunity for supplier improvement and new product development, as well as being a key driver of customer satisfaction.

Time

A company will have little success if it manufactures a great product, but delivers late to the customer. The ideal goal is to deliver 100 per cent of orders on time. However, in order to deliver goods on time to customers, they must also be produced in time. Thus, we assess time based on responsiveness to customer and the reliability of the delivery process.

■ *On-time deliveries.* This measures whether a perfect delivery has taken place, and acts as a measure of customer service levels.

■ *Customer response time.* The time lag between an order being placed and its delivery. Firms might measure elements such as manufacturing lead-time, shipping errors, and customer complaints.

■ *Backorder/stockout.* The level of item, order or product availability, assessed as number of backorders, number of stockouts and average backorder level across all product/service ranges.

Supplier performance

Typically, more subjective, non-financial measures are used to assess supplier performance. These include the level and degree of information sharing, the number of buyer–vendor cost-saving initiatives, and extent of mutual assistance in problem-solving efforts. In addition to measuring the degree of collaboration, firms should also examine the characteristics of the supply base. For example, the percentage of suppliers who are certified, or the number of suppliers per commodity purchased.

Customer satisfaction

Companies may measure not only their operational performance within the function, and across their supply base, but also the final impact on customers. Purchasing have internal customers in manufacturing and operations, whose satisfaction with the procurement service may be measured. External customers may also be assessed through measures such as customer query time (for example, about stock availability or delivery), and other post-transaction measures of customer service.

Developing a performance measurement system

Developing a performance measurement system requires top management support, organisational buy-in, and resources to set up procedures for appropriate data collection. Top management need to communicate their support for the new system, and emphasise the link with incentives and remuneration, where appropriate. Figure 11.5 overviews the various stages in developing a purchasing performance measurement system.

1. Determine goals to measure

Driven by the cascading of corporate strategy, business strategy and functional supply strategy, the first step is to identify the critical areas for measurement. Different categories (discussed in the section above) are going to be more or less important across firms. Specific performance measures are not necessary at this stage, just creating alignment between firm strategy and performance measurement. A key pitfall for many firms at this stage is selecting goals which do not reflect the corporate- and business-level strategy of the firm, or which have not been revisited as the firm's strategy and operations change.

2. Establish performance measures

Ideally, the specific performance measures used to monitor and evaluate performance should possess certain characteristics. The SMART test (Specific, Measurable, Actionable, Relevant, and Timely) is frequently used to provide a quick

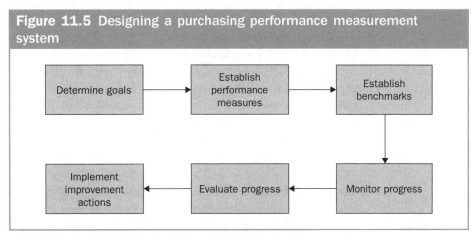

Figure 11.5 Designing a purchasing performance measurement system

Source: adapted from Monczka et al. (2005)

Table 11.2 Characteristics of effective performance measurement systems

Measurement systems should:

1 Be linked to corporate objectives ('goal congruence')
2 Combine different measures to meet the requirements of different organisational levels ('cascading goals' – i.e. the goals of one level are the means of another)
3 Capture elements of both efficiency and effectiveness
4 Allow the identification of trade-offs between different dimensions of performance
5 Include a balanced mixture of qualitative and quantitative measures
6 Include a mix of leading and lagging indicators of performance
7 Be incapable of manipulation
8 Allow data to be collected systematically and analysed over time
9 Differentiate between incremental/control measures and radical objectives
10 Encourage cross-functional working

reference to determine the quality of a particular performance metric. Table 11.2 highlights key characteristics of effective performance measures.

Firms face many challenges in establishing the 'right' kind of performance measures. Performance measures can lack 'power' to influence behaviour where they are not linked to employee evaluation or incentive plans. Organisations may select too many measures, leading to a lack of focus, or alternatively, select too few measures which may lead to missing information. The measures may also have a short-term focus, or generate conflicting signals as to desired behaviours.

3. Establish standards for comparison

Three main approaches are possible for establishing standards. It is no good measuring performance without having a standard or expectation against which to compare the result. Furthermore, personnel should be allowed to participate in setting the standards, as it generally leads to higher commitment to meeting those standards.

■ **Analysis of historical data.** Firms can gather past data about an activity as a basis for setting the performance standard. Where a firm has lots of experience with the activity, this can provide a good basis for predicting future performance. A continuous improvement aim may also be embedded in the target to aid in cost saving. This approach is often used in purchasing for efficiency-related measures, such as price. However, it is important to guard against relying on these measures excessively. Even seemingly minor changes in the way in the product is manufactured or sourced can make the standard irrelevant. For example, a Northern Irish weaving company recently sourced to China and experienced significant reductions in their input costs – clearly the target would have to be reset!

■ **Planned performance.** Firms may also look at other internal divisions or groups to identify company-wide best practice. For example, TNT, a courier company, would publish a league table of the highest-performing depots, with the performance of the top depot being the 'stretch' goal for the others. This can create a more realistic 'stretch' target, but can lead to dysfunctional rivalry among internal business units as they compete, rather than cooperate. In any case, best practice internally may not match the capabilities of the external competitors.

■ **Competitive benchmarking.** Goals may also be set based on detailed analysis of competitors, or firms in other industries, but who manage similar activities. For example, airlines and hotels may collaborate on benchmarking as they both conduct food and beverage purchasing, but compete in distinct industries. By identifying the practices and performance of external companies competitive benchmarking can be motivator for best practice and world-class manufacturing.

4. Monitor progress

At this stage, firms must make decisions about the type of feedback they require from their performance measures. They must identify who the users are, what information they require, how frequently and how this data will be collected. Measuring progress too often leads to excessive cost and effort for little value. Conversely, measuring progress too little may lead to potential problems not being recognised until it is too late.

5. Evaluate progress

The purchasing performance measurement system must ensure that it has feedback mechanisms: i.e. close the loop. The performance measures should capture performance, and identify exceptions to what is planned. For example, the system may identify an unfavourable material price variance for the month. This would be a signal that follow-up investigation is required. One problem faced at this stage is over-aggregation of the data, which can lead to masking of potentially important events or trends.

6. Implement improvement actions

The final step of the performance measurement process is to undertake corrective action. The firm must move to correct the problems or issues identified. However, a number of cautions are appropriate at this point. Firms must ensure that they are not driving the wrong performance; they must be sure that the measures used will result in the desired actions. Some measures may encourage internal competition and discourage teamwork if performance is measured vertically, rather than horizontally across the entire work process.

7. The Purchasing Balanced Scorecard

The Balanced Scorecard, developed by Kaplan and Norton (1992, 1996), was originally conceived as a means of measuring corporate performance in a manner which reflects not only financial indicators of performance, but also those other critical value drivers that enable an organisation to compete successfully. The Balanced Scorecard attempts to foster a balance between disparate strategic measures, as no single type of measure can provide a clear focus for attention. It is a useful planning tool which does not place undue emphasis on simple control measures but rather pulls activities into line with corporate strategy. The Balanced Scorecard thus becomes a tool for focusing the organisation, improving communication, setting organisational objectives and providing feedback on strategy.

The Balanced Scorecard shows not only the critical measures of firm success, but also the relationship between those measures in a cause-and-effect manner. It is not simply a 'laundry list' of measures, but rather individual measures within the four perspectives must be linked together explicitly. The scorecard is based on four perspectives: financial; customer; internal business processes; and innovation and learning.

- **Financial perspective** reflects the underlying financial performance of the firm. It typically includes more traditional measures of corporate performance, focusing on profitability, cash flow, and shareholders. Accounting information is also backward-looking – showing the results of actions already taken – thus the remaining three measures are seen as measuring the drivers of performance.

- **Customer focus** is essential to understanding how customers view the business, because without customers, no organisation can create value. This area forces managers to translate their broad goals on customer service into measures that really matter to the customer. It is composed of such issues as time, quality, performance and service, and essentially tries to get managers to see the company from the customers' point of view.

- **Internal business processes** refer to the way operations are carried out within the company, which enable customer satisfaction to be achieved. The focus should be on the internal processes that have the greatest impact on customer satisfaction, and therefore which affect cycle time, productivity, quality and design, for example. A capable information system is vital for this to be achieved.

- **Innovation and learning** is the ability to change and improve on a continuous basis. While customer and internal business processes reflect the parameters that the company considers vital for success, continuous improvement is also necessary in a turbulent business environment. It recognises the intellectual assets which are inherent in any organisation and the importance of human resources.

The scorecard approach provides a potentially useful way of approaching purchasing performance measurement. Purchasing and Supply departments must satisfy not only certain financial targets, such as cost reduction and price performance, but also other important areas. Notably, a fifth perspective may be added measuring supplier performance, and assessing how well purchasing performs vis-à-vis its suppliers. Figure 11.6 illustrates a sample Balanced Scorecard, complete with potential performance measures. *Financial perspective* may assess the price performance, such as material price variances, the total purchasing costs, and other firm-specific measures, such as foreign currency matrices. The *Internal Business Process perspective* may measure the on-time delivery, order cycle time, or percentage of spend covered by e-procurement techniques, such as reverse auctions. Under *Innovation and Learning*, the levels of professional development, in terms of qualifications or the levels of training of staff, may be important. For *Supplier Performance* the firm may measure the percentage of the supply base that is

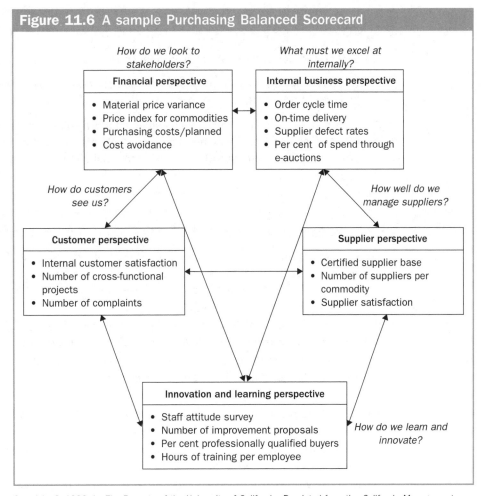

Figure 11.6 A sample Purchasing Balanced Scorecard

certified, the level of supplier satisfaction or the depth of supply base for particular commodities.

Summary

This chapter has overviewed the characteristics of effective performance measurement in supply chains. Although Purchasing has traditionally had difficulty in measuring inter-organisational performance, it is slowly developing more sophisticated systems which assess purchasing performance both internally, with regard to internal customers, and externally, with regard to their suppliers. The chapter also offered a framework for the development of a purchasing performance measurement system, and provided a sample Balanced Scorecard, which might be used for monitoring and evaluating purchasing performance.

Seminar questions

1. Outline the basic elements of performance measurement systems.

2. Discuss how performance measurement and strategy interact, giving examples of good and bad practice.

3. Develop a set of performance measurements for evaluating purchasing performance in a firm competing: (a) as an innovative, high-tech manufacturer; (b) a low-cost provider; and (c) a manufacturer of medical equipment.

References

Butler, R. (1995) 'What You Measure is What You Get – an Investigation into Measurement of the Value Added by the Purchasing Function', in Lamming, R. (ed.), *4th International Purchasing Supply & Education Research Association Conference (IPSERA)*, University of Glamorgan, Glamorgan.

Cousins, P. D. (2002) 'A Conceptual Model for Long-term Inter-organisational Relationships', *European Journal of Purchasing and Supply Management*, Vol. 8 (2), pp. 71–82.

Dumond, E. J. (1991) 'Performance Measurement and Decision Making in a Purchasing Environment', *International Journal of Purchasing and Materials Management*, Vol. 27 (2), pp. 21–31.

Kaplan, R. S. and Norton, D. P. (1992) 'The Balanced Scorecard – Measures that Drive Performance', *Harvard Business Review*, January–February, pp. 71–9.

Kaplan, R. S. and Norton, D. P. (1996) 'Linking the Balanced Scorecard to Strategy', *California Management Review*, Vol. 39 (1), pp. 53–79.

Monczka, R. M., Trent, R. J. and Handfield, R. B. (2005) *Purchasing and Supply Chain Management*, 3rd edn, South Western, Cincinatti.

Saunders, M. (1994) *Strategic Purchasing and Supply Chain Management*, Pitman, London.

van Weele, A. (1984) 'Purchasing Performance Measurement and Evaluation', *Journal of Purchasing and Materials Management*, Fall, pp. 16–22.

Further reading

Lee, H. L. and Billington, C. (1992) 'Managing Supply Chain Inventory: Pitfalls and Opportunities', *Sloan Management Review*, Vol. 33 (3), pp. 65–73.

Chapter 12

Cost–benefit analysis

Aim of chapter

The aim of this chapter is to discuss the cost and benefits of strategic supply management.

Learning outcomes

At the end of this chapter, readers will:

- understand the role that cost has to play in making the purchasing decision;
- have a clear overview of how to apply the Total Cost of Ownership (TCO) concept in making a business case.

Introduction

This chapter focuses on the issues of balancing costs, benefits and relationship strategies within the supply chain, and is the fourth of five circumferential elements of the strategic supply wheel (Figure 12.1).

Supply management decisions, like any other business function, should be based on sound management principles such as transparency, analysis and alignment. In order to achieve this, firms often produce a document known as the 'business case'. The development of the business case is seen as central to the management decision-making process. In any major project or strategic initiative a business case should be produced and presented.

The traditional role of Purchasing (as discussed in previous chapters) often led to purchasing decisions being taken without the production of a business case, or certainly in areas such as IT outsourcing, the business case was prepared by technicians and not by Purchasing professionals. This led to some well-documented cases where companies were commercially exposed on service level agreements (SLAs). With supply management being seen as a strategic player, there is much more emphasis on providing accurate information for management decision-making purposes.

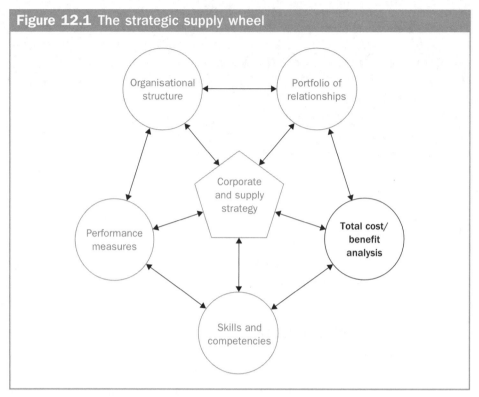

Figure 12.1 The strategic supply wheel

Source: Cousins (2002)

For example, if a firm wishes to outsource elements of its business it will need to clearly understand the supply implications, similarly for strategies such as supply base rationalisation or reduction, supply tiers, and major collaboration deals. All of these decisions should require the production of a business case. This chapter will discuss some of the issues involved in the production of business cases for supply. It will suggest and present some frameworks and models for consideration.

The measurement of costs

How firms measure the cost implications of their strategies has been the subject of constant debate for many years. However, within supply chain management, measuring the performance or suitability of supply strategy has traditionally been viewed as relatively simple. Typically, management will look at how much money Purchasing has managed to save, usually against a year-on-year target, e.g. the price paid last time versus the price paid today. This system was also known as *zero-based pricing*. This method of price comparison appeared to work well until firms started to consider the 'cost of quality', or rather 'cost of poor quality', arguments. A customer experiences the quality of the product only after it has been manufactured, branded, distributed and sold. If the product fails, perhaps due to a defective supplier-made component, the customer automatically attributes the failure to

Box 12.1 Dissatisfied customers

A retired couple recently purchased a top-of-the-line, class A motor home for cross-country travel. During their first 5000-mile inaugural trip, the travellers experienced over 25 quality-related problems with the unit, some quite serious. Before they left their home state, the power steering failed, making the motor home difficult and dangerous to drive. Soon after, the camera that provided visibility to traffic and obstacles behind the vehicle stopped working. Eventually the water pump broke, leaving the travellers with no use of their showers, toilets or sink. Later, the internal electrical systems failed, leaving them in the dark and rendering their refrigerator useless. One of the most difficult problems occurred when the steps that allowed passengers to enter and exit the motor home failed to retract. This required the travellers to drive with the steps extended away from the vehicle. Eventually, the transmission began to fail during the last several hundred miles. After limping home (with frequent stops for less than responsive service) the weary travellers concluded, quite dejectedly, that a recreational vehicle was probably not for them. They eventually sold the motor home several months later at a significant loss!

Source: Trent and Monczka (1999)

the manufacturer and not to the supplier. There is an often-quoted statistic that one dissatisfied customer will tell ten others. This problem can be illustrated by an extract from a paper by Trent and Monczka (1999: 927), shown in Box 12.1.

As Trent and Monczka point out, the name that the customers saw was the brand name and not those of the suppliers. The cost of quality issue here was substantial. Therefore, when measuring costs it is important that we measure the right things. In an effort to allow companies to take a wider view of cost measurement, the Balanced Scorecard was developed (Kaplan and Norton, 1992). However, in order for this to work, supply management needs to be seen as being strategic as opposed to tactical. It needs to be viewed as contributing towards the development and support of the final product or service as opposed to simply processing the purchase orders. Therefore, there is a linkage between the type of cost measure used and the strategic capability of the supply function. If Purchasing is going to act strategically then it needs to be measured in that way. As well as being measured, it needs to think more along the lines of total cost management as opposed to the management of price.

Price versus cost

It is worth discussing a few definitions, primarily the difference between cost and price. Figure 12.2 gives a simplified representation of the issues, showing three broad categories of cost:

1 *Fixed costs*. These costs are fixed, at least in the medium to long term (e.g. plant and equipment, and buildings).

2 *Variable costs*. These costs vary with each unit of production (e.g. material and labour costs).

3 *Profit*. The level of mark-up required to invest back into the business and/or to distribute to shareholders.

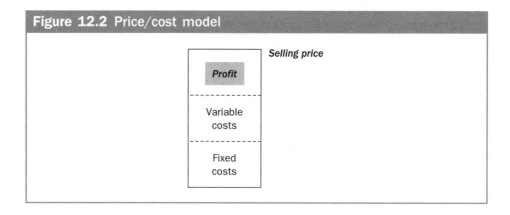

Figure 12.2 Price/cost model

A focus on price?

Looking at this diagram and taking a price-focused approach, what are the implications? A *price-focused* approach means that you (as a customer) want to pay less than you did last time you bought the product or service. As a supplier you face a limited number of choices. Fixed costs do not enter into consideration as they are fixed, or at least non-variable in relation to production. This leaves variable costs and profit. Variable costs are inevitably influenced by the relationship between the customer and supplier (not all but a reasonable proportion), so only a small adjustment could be made without the help of the customer. Joint efforts for cost reduction and improvement by the buyer and supplier can help here. This leaves profit. The level of profit made is largely at the discretion of the supplier, who may increase or decrease this at will. Therefore when customers adopt a price-focused approach they generally expect the supplier to reduce its price, leaving it the only alternative (in the short term) of reducing its profit margin. Whilst this may seem like a perfectly reasonable thing to do (particularly as a customer/buyer), consider what is likely to happen in the medium term. Price reduction strategies drive down profit: profit that was used for reinvestment and to pay shareholders a dividend. If the profit is significantly reduced over the medium term then this will have dire consequences for the business.

The supplier's firm, therefore, has several broad strategic decisions that it can make:

- *Stay in the marketplace* and attempt to survive.
- *Leave the marketplace* and find another that is more lucrative.
- *Go out of business.*

What tends to happen when customers adopt this strategy is a 'business cycle' effect. That is, starting with many suppliers and a few buyers, buyers have the market power so drive towards price reduction. Suppliers reduce profit and attempt to cut cost (usually resulting in poor-quality products). Suppliers begin to move out of the industry to find more lucrative markets, whilst some are able (with the help of reserves and cross-subsidisation) to stand their ground and others go out of business. After a period of time the market dynamics have changed. There are now, relatively speaking, few suppliers and many buyers (customers). The risk has now turned. Suppliers see that they are now in the dominant position and push up price and therefore profit in an attempt to recoup the losses made over the previous time period. The customer (buyer) must therefore pay more for the product, and decide whether to absorb the cost or pass it on to the final customer, potentially losing valuable market share. Once again the actions of a transactional supply process have had large consequences for the strategic positioning of the firm in its market.

However, this situation is not static, but rather dynamic. As prices rise, other new sources of supply see a lucrative market. Indeed they may well be exiting from a marketplace that is experiencing low profits. They begin to enter the market, thus increasing the number of suppliers relative to the number of buyers, equilibrium is reached, prices stabilise and the process begins again. The business cycle effect continues. This mechanism operates when companies have a traditional view and measure of supply.

Total cost of ownership

Total cost of ownership considers all the costs involved in the company's supply chain, typically focusing on a particular supplier, a particular good or service, or a particular process. Total cost of ownership (TCO) takes a 'big picture' perspective, considering costs beyond simply price. Other cost factors are critical, including costs related to quality, delivery services, ordering, reception, inspection and transportation. For example, a company making a decision to source a critical component may develop the following TCO analysis. A higher cost per kilogram of raw material sourced from a local supplier, with shorter lead-times and less required inventory, may be balanced against an overseas supplier with greater risks of supply disruption. Balanced against these additional risks, the lower TCO supplier may be local, rather than overseas.

Many consumers, businesses and governments fail to understand and calculate TCO and instead rely on total cost of acquisition (TCA) to make buying decisions. The TCO can and often does vary dramatically against TCA, although TCO is far more relevant in determining the viability of any sourcing initiative. For example, it is suggested that if the financial success of an international transaction is based solely on reducing unit costs, commodity managers will inevitably seek material from suppliers that meet that objective, thinking they are reducing costs by 30 to 50 per cent when they are actually inadvertently draining profits from the bottom line. The projected savings do not accurately model the total cost of ownership. Box 12.2 highlights just such a situation.

Uncovering the hidden costs of ownership

The TCO concept requires an analysis of all activities performed by the firm that incurs costs. By identifying explicitly the activities incurred across the entire purchasing value chain, and the cost of those activities, buyers can calculate the

---

Box 12.2 The true cost of ownership?

'I'm in for a big promotion!' exclaimed Ken, seasoned commodity manager for a UK aerospace manufacturer. 'I found a new low-cost supplier in China that cut my unit costs by over £7 million annually. Based on this 35 per cent unit-cost savings, the purchase price variance in my next review will be off the charts!'

'Way to go, Ken,' said Brian, Ken's long-time co-worker.

Ken continued: 'The steel we use to make ball bearings amounts to half of our annual material expenditures. So life is good! For the first time in my career, the CEO personally thanked me for my work.'

Unfortunately, Ken's assumptions were wrong. He actually increased his company's total costs by over £4 million annually. Increased transportation costs, greater inventory-carrying costs, taxes and insurance collectively exceeded his projected 35 per cent savings in material costs.

---

true costs of supply. Key purchasing activities as they relate to TCO are shown in Figure 12.3, together with examples. The six categories identified relate to management, delivery, service, communications, price and quality.

Buyers have long recognised that some suppliers are easier to work with than others, implicitly recognising that suppliers with better service help to reduce the firm's internal costs, time and efforts. However, existing managerial accounting systems have not enabled firms to track these cost savings. The TCO concept, together with activity-based costing (ABC) systems, today enable Purchasing managers to estimate these costs and/or savings.

A simple matrix, developed by Degraeve and Roodhooft (2001), can be used to help firms uncover all these relevant costs of procurement. The matrix enables managers to assess costs along the length of the procurement value chain, and at all levels of its supplier relationships. Table 12.1 on p. 168 illustrates this total cost of ownership matrix.

Along the horizontal axis are the sequential steps in the procurement value chain, from initial acquisition, through reception, possession and use, and finally, to disposal or recycling of the product. These five stages are:

- *Initial acquisition.* These costs relate to activities which take place prior to receiving the product from the supplier. For example, the product price, costs related to negotiation and contracting, and supplier vetting costs.

- *Reception.* Reception costs occur when receiving goods, processing invoices and payments, and performing inspections on a sample of goods received.

- *Possession.* Possession costs occur between receiving goods and actual utilisation of goods in production or service. Typically, these would include internal transportation from storage to factory floor, along with inventory holding costs.

- *Utilisation.* Costs of use may include installation, personnel training and impacts of product failure.

- *Elimination.* Elimination or reuse costs are often omitted from the initial procurement decision, but can represent considerable cost to the buying firm. For example, electronic equipment such as mobile phones, computers and consumer electronics can often be recycled at the end of their useful lives. However, many

Figure 12.3 Purchasing's activities contributing to total cost of ownership

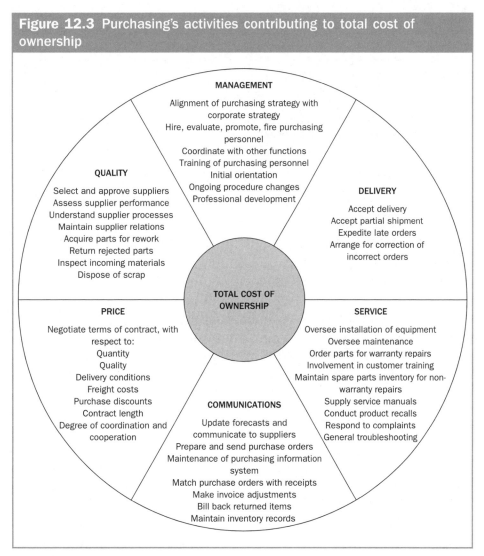

Source: Ellram and Perrott-Siferd (1993)

firms do not consider these costs of recycling or safe disposal of their products in the initial purchase decision. Tighter environmental controls and government legislation are increasingly forcing firms to consider these issues upfront.

The vertical axis represents three main levels at which costs may be aggregated: supplier, order and unit. At each cost level, we distinguish between potential savings that are realised as cash, versus savings that result from freeing up capacity or other resources (non-cash). Using such an approach also facilitates an analysis of trade-offs between various cost categories and alternative purchasing strategies. The three hierarchical levels are discussed:

■ *Supplier-level*. Supplier-level costs occur each time a given supplier is used. For example, the cost of supplier audits and the salary of the buyer responsible for managing the relationship.

Table 12.1 The total cost of ownership matrix

TCO-matrix	Acquisition	Reception	Possession	Utilisation	Elimination
Supplier-level					
Cash	Total purchase discount				
Non-cash	Supplier vetting costs RFP costs Contract administration Supplier follow-up costs Supplier change costs	Legal costs for breach of contract		Engineering costs Personnel training costs Systems adaptation costs	
Order-level					
Cash	Payment delay savings or costs	External transportation costs			
Non-cash	Ordering costs	Receiving costs Invoice and payment processing costs Quality testing costs Quantity testing costs Legal costs for problems with quality	Internal transportation costs	Quality control costs Production delay	Waste collection costs
Unit-level					
Cash	Price Product discount			Intrinsic efficiency Replacement costs	Recycling costs or revenue Disposal fees or revenue
Non-cash	Service costs for installation and assembly Testing costs		Inventory holding costs Order picking costs	Production failure costs Maintenance costs Installation costs	Cost of removing obsolete materials Disposal management costs

Source: Degraeve and Roodhooft (2001)

- *Order-level.* Order-level costs occur each time an order is placed with a supplier. These costs might include receiving, invoicing and external transportation.
- *Unit-level.* Unit-level costs are incurred on a per unit basis, and are often incurred in the utilisation and elimination phases of the procurement life cycle. They might include costs of a production shutdown caused by a supplier's faulty product, inventory carrying costs, disposal/recycling, pallet movement and damaged items.

In constructing the TCO matrix, all relevant activities that generate costs must be identified. Many firms will use some variant of activity-based costing to identify their various cost drivers as the product moves through the value chain and assign them to activities. After identifying the activities, the next step is to calculate the cost of each activity by measuring its resource usage. At the supplier level, the cost of negotiating and managing each supplier could be calculated by dividing the Purchasing manager's annual salary by the average total time spent with the supplier. Construction of such an analysis enables the buyer to identify the major cost elements in the purchasing process and to investigate possibilities for cost reduction, along with the impacts (cash and non-cash) on total purchasing cost.

Summary

This chapter has described the fundamental difference between price paid and the total cost of ownership. We stressed that the unit price is not the only factor that needs to be considered – all costs along the entire procurement value chain should be evaluated. Developing a TCO model can help managers make clearer purchasing decisions, such as outsourcing components, third party logistics (3PL), and evaluating different suppliers or supply contracts.

Seminar questions

1. Discuss the role of cost versus price in a purchasing decision.

2. What are the major benefits of adopting a total cost of ownership (TCO) perspective?

3. Thinking about the procurement value chain, how do you think a firm could calculate the cost of recycling and disposal in a TCO model? Give examples of these activities, and how you might identify the relevant costs of these activities.

References

Cousins, P. D. (2002) 'A Conceptual Model for Managing Long-term Inter-organisational Relationships', *European Journal of Purchasing and Supply Management*, Vol. 8 (2), pp. 71–82.

Degraeve, Z. and Roodhooft, F. (2001) 'A Smarter Way to Buy', *Harvard Business Review*, June, pp. 22–3.

Ellram, L. M. and Perrott-Siferd, S. (1993) 'Purchasing: The Cornerstone of the Total Cost of Ownership Concept', *Journal of Business Logistics*, Vol. 14 (1), pp. 163–84.

Kaplan, R. S. and Norton, D. P. (1992) 'The Balanced Scorecard – Measures that Drive Performance', *Harvard Business Review*, January–February, pp. 71–9.

Trent, R. and Monczka, R. (1999) 'Achieving World-class Supplier Quality', *Total Quality Management*, Vol. 10 (6), pp. 927–38.

Further reading

Sako, M. (1992) *Prices, Quality and Trust: Buyer Supplier Relationships in Britain and Japan*, Cambridge University Press, Cambridge.

Chapter 13

Managing inter-firm relationships

Aim of chapter

The aim of this chapter is to give the reader an overview of the complex field of relationship management. The chapter will also provide frameworks for thinking about measuring, managing and implementing relationship strategies and put relationship management in context with other elements of the supply wheel.

Learning outcomes

At the end of this chapter, readers will:

- have a clear understanding of the main models, concepts and theories of relationship management;
- be able to see relationship management in context and understand that it can be viewed from a variety of perspectives, e.g. economic, strategic, behavioural and marketing;
- appreciate the complexities and difficulties in implementing a relationship management approach;
- have an understanding of how to approach and implement relationship management techniques.

Introduction

This chapter focuses on the portfolio of relationships which is the fifth of the five circumferential elements of the strategic supply wheel (Figure 13.1).

Milton Friedman, a famous economist and Nobel Prize winner,[1] famously said when commenting on how businesses work, *'the business of business is business . . .'*. This simple yet insightful quotation positions how we should think of business relationships. Friedman reminds us that firms are in the business of making or saving money. In the private sector we are in the business of making as much money as possible (constrained by various moral, ethical and legal requirements) to satisfy our shareholders and increase firm profits. In the public sector it could

Figure 13.1 The strategic supply wheel

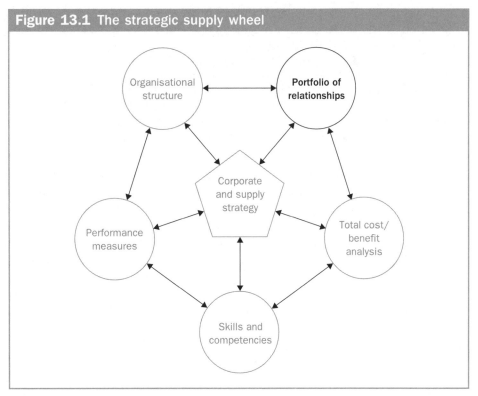

Source: Cousins (2002)

be argued that we are in the business of saving money, i.e. to make the most of the funds that we have available for certain projects. Either way, the business of procurement is the same: to achieve the best deal for *your* organisation.

This chapter will examine inter-firm relationship management from a strategic perspective. It will set out what we define as a business relationship; it will then discuss the development of a relationship management model, present the certainty–dependency model and discuss the implementation of business relationships.

The topic of inter- (between) and intra- (within) firm relationship management is one of the most discussed and potentially least understood topic areas within supply chain management. This is because relationship management can be viewed from a variety of perspectives: from the level of the firm, e.g. company A's relationship with company B; from the level of a particular project or group within and between firms, e.g. a major alliance between a manufacturer and key partner; and of course, at the level of the individual, e.g. relationships managed by individuals and key account holders. All of these relationships are important – and perhaps they are not mutually exclusive. In other words, when we consider the concept of inter-firm relationships we should think of all three levels, and what's more, not just between firms but also within firms.

If defining the level of analysis is complex, then defining business relationships is perhaps even more difficult. Whilst this sounds very simple, the more you think about it the more difficult it becomes. To illustrate, let me give you an example (Box 13.1) from my own extensive experience working in this field.

Box 13.1 How hard is it to define a relationship?

As a new consultant I was asked by a major aerospace firm to ascertain the 'relationship' between them and one of their major suppliers. I immediately thought that this should be a simple process and would only take a matter of weeks to determine. How wrong I was! After several weeks I had to report back to the managing director that I was none the wiser. The problem was that I had asked some people who reported that the relationship was great; others said it was fine, whilst others would prefer not to deal with the company at all! The problem of relationship definition falls into several key dimensions:

■ At what level (or levels) should the relationship be defined? For example, defining the relationship at the level of the firm is impossible as there are so many different experiences and views. Following on from the above case study, after six months I found a total of 1504 of what could be termed relationships. Naturally these could be classified into a variety of different types. However, it would be impossible to say that Firm A's relationship with its major supplier was good, bad or indifferent.

■ A further complication to this definition problem is what we might call an asymmetry of understanding. To put this simply, if the relationship was symmetrical Firm A would understand what Firm B thought of them and vice versa (perfect information). However, in reality what Firm A thinks of Firm B and B thinks of A might be completely different. Therefore when examining business relationships we must appreciate the views of both buyers and suppliers.

■ Having argued that it is difficult to assess the relationship at the level of the firm, perhaps we should move to the level of the group or product/commodity team. This definition starts to make a bit more sense. We can define the relationship at the level of the product or service being bought, as opposed to at the level of the firm. This would mean that we could conceivably have a variety of different relationships with the same firm, depending on the type of commodity or service being bought, its level of importance to our business, our level of importance to their business and so on. This type of thinking is inevitably more complex, but is starting to mimic reality more closely. However, it is missing a vital ingredient: interpersonal relationships.

■ Examining relationships at the level of the person is important. Organisations consist of people and it is interpersonal relationships that drive (or not) organisational processes. But individuals are not unconstrained. They are governed by rules, professional and personal ethics and motivated by the organisation's performance measurement systems. They are therefore constrained and in a sense controlled on how they will act. So whilst we accept that these relationships are important, in today's businesses an individual's effect is greatly reduced, rather it is how the team(s) works. Therefore whilst we acknowledge that interpersonal relationships have an effect on the business relationship, they are guided and focused by the organisation's strategy to achieve its business success.

Having outlined our arguments we still need to define what is meant by a business relationship. Let's begin by saying what it is not – it is not a 'thing', an 'entity' of some description. It has no physical presence or being, much the same as organisation culture, or communication. This leads us to an important part of our definition. We define relationships as *processes*, much the same as culture and communication (see Figure 13.2).

Processes have several important properties – firstly, they require inputs in the shape of resources and secondly, they will require an output. For example, communication (which is a process) will require resources, e.g. a lecturer is a resource

Figure 13.2 Relationship resources

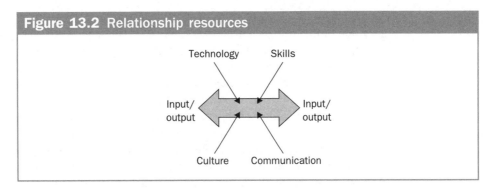

who uses the communication process to achieve the output of knowledge transfer to the receivers of the communication. Much the same as communication, relationships also require resources such as people, technology, time and effort (cf. Figure 13.2). They also should have an outcome focus, for example price or cost reduction[2] (these are two distinct strategies and should not be confused), technology sharing and development, risk sharing and so on. Processes need to be viewed as both efficient (how quickly they are conducted) and effective (how well they meet the strategic focus of the firm). To make a process efficient it is important to consider the allocation of resources to the expected output. It is also important to make sure that the firm has the requisite resources to manage the process. For example, the buyer firm may not have the relevant skills and competencies to carry out the project. The objective of efficiency in this case is to allocate the minimum amount of resources to achieve the maximum amount of output.

Effectiveness as previously defined means delivery to the strategic objectives of the 'firm',[3] which in essence means making sure that the relationships are business focused on a series of outcomes that are expected by both parties within the relationship. So, for example, if we had a simple output such as price reduction we would need a relatively simple level of inputs in order to achieve it, e.g. a buyer focusing on price negotiation. Whereas if we had a complex output such as technology development, risk and reward sharing, etc., we would require a complex relationship process to achieve this task, e.g. cross-functional teams, inter-firm teams, etc. Naturally the cost of the resources will escalate depending on the complexity of the relationship output. It is therefore important to realise that there is a cost–benefit analysis equation (see Chapter 12) that will need to be balanced when deciding on various relationship strategy approaches. We therefore define inter-firm business relationships as:

> *[Inter firm relationships are a set of . . .] complex business processes that require resource allocation from the buyer and supplier to achieve a set of complex outputs. These outputs and inputs may be asymmetrical depending on the desired outcomes for the buyer and supplier. In addition, these relationships will be influenced by their respective external environments and constrained by the parties' strategies, goals and power mechanisms.*

It is worth pointing out at this point that there are substantial rewards for those firms who can successfully manage their business relationships. Successful relationship management has been demonstrated to lead to lower costs, higher quality, greater product innovation, reduced risks and even enhanced market value. Take, for example, the often-quoted example of Japanese automobile manufacturers. In the late 1980s the Western economies witnessed a 'new' phenomenon: Japanese manufacturers quite literally invaded safe home markets of domestic manufacturers like GM, Ford and Chrysler, supplying higher-specification vehicles with fewer defects, higher reliability and at cheaper prices than their domestic counterparts. Naturally, it did not take too long before consumers began switching away from their staple brands to the 'new' Japanese vehicles supplied by the likes of Honda, Toyota and Nissan. Despite various attempts at trade, tariff and non-tariff barriers[4] it soon became apparent to the incumbents that they were either going to have to change or quite simply go out of business!

The question that firms asked in the late 1980s (which incidentally they still seem to be asking today) is: *what makes Japanese firms successful?* The early 1990s saw a massive amount of effort by academics, consultants and practitioners attempting to answer this simple yet complex question. One of the critical success factors was found to be the differences in the way Japanese and Western manufacturers managed their supplier relationships. It was clear from the research that Japanese firms viewed their subcontractors (or suppliers) as essential to their business; indeed Japanese firms viewed relationship management as the primary role of the procurement professional.[5] This view was not the same as that of Western manufacturers, who viewed relationship management as *in addition* to their main procurement management role.

A strategic approach: the development of supply chain and relationship management

SCM is now well established within the literature and is becoming more recognised by firms as a strategic business process. Whilst there is a variety of definitions used to describe what supply chain management actually is, perhaps the most succinct definition is provided by Lambert et al. who refer to SCM as *'the integration of business processes from end user through original suppliers that provides products, services, and information that add value for customers'* (p. 504). Lambert et al. develop the argument that whilst there is a range of definitions with varying detail, the common factors are supply chain actors or institutions, such as suppliers and customers.

Further elaboration in the literature has led to the development of the definition of 'strategic supply' management. Ellram and Carr (1994) point out that the literature takes three distinct themes: first, specific strategies employed by the Purchasing function; second, Purchasing's role within those strategies; and lastly, Purchasing as a strategic function within the firm. This research found that whilst there was a reasonable amount of literature on the subject, most of it was of a conceptual nature and lacked empirical rigour. In a recent paper Tan (2001) explores the development of the supply chain literature and argues that there is a convergence of two areas: logistics and purchasing. The conclusion is that there is a variety of 'buzzwords' but little empirical substance. It is clear that the development of supply chain management requires more rigorous, empirical work.

Other authors (Farmer, 1972; Reck & Long, 1988) have put forward four- and five-stage models to show how organisations can attain 'strategic status', whilst others (Carr and Smeltzer, 1997) have taken a more pragmatic view, analysing the constituent ingredients required to make supply strategic. Carr and Smeltzer (1997) argue that its status, knowledge and skills, risk and available resources directly influence the level of strategic supply within the organisation. The overall consensus is that supply should be seen as 'strategic', as integral to the decision-making mechanisms of the firm, although more rigorous empirical work is required.

The research on supply management tends to base itself either in the transaction cost (Richardson, 1994; Williamson, 1975) or resource-based view (RBV) or in the marketing literature. Some authors have put forward the view that the firm should be seen as a 'nexus of contracts' and that the firm should manage its resources to maximise advantage for the business; relationships are seen as a key resource of the business. Others see the management of supply as part of the wider production system.

The implications of managing supply strategically are debated in the literature. It is widely agreed that the involvement of Purchasing in a strategic context can enhance a company's financial performance and improve the firm's overall competitive position. Others argue that the integration of strategic purchasing practices can directly affect manufacturing performance and therefore added value to the customer. This integration manifests itself in the selection of sourcing strategies for technological innovation as well as in the design of the appropriate business network within which to manage the supply strategy.

Regulating the relationship is an integral component of managing sourcing strategies. Authors argue this point from a variety of perspectives, some from the viewpoint of the relationship in a general behavioural sense, e.g. Kanter (1989) refers to successful partnerships being needed to manage the relationship and not just a focus on the business deal; she calls it becoming best PALs (pooling, allying and linking). Other scholars argue that the move towards relationship management will change the very role and strategies of how firms behave, moving them away from their traditional structures and towards 'hub and spoke' focused organisations. Other writers see relationship management from a much more economic viewpoint, utilising game theory to demonstrate how various strategies and relationships can be aligned. This discourse clearly shows that there is a variety of ways of viewing relationship management; however, the key question appears to remain the same: *How should a firm organise to manage its complex relationships?*

Relationship definitions and misconceptions: towards a management model

Whilst this question sounds very simple, the answer to it is in fact very complex. This complexity is in part caused by the fact that relationship strategies are only one dimension of a much more sophisticated management system. Referring back to the

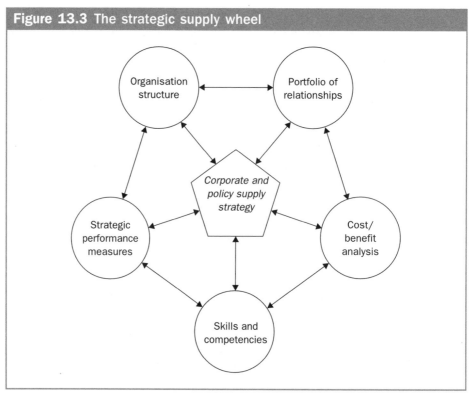

Figure 13.3 The strategic supply wheel

Source: Cousins (2002)

supply wheel (see reminder in Figure 13.3), the supply strategist can see that the management of business relationships must be considered in conjunction with other elements of the supply process. As we will show, the management of relationships will vary according to both the strategy of the organisation and the product sourced.

Firms that are cost focused will require the supply activity to deliver a range of business and marketing benefits that will put the firm into a stronger cost management position (i.e. savings). The firm is not interested in Supply forming closer working relationships, or implementing complex sourcing strategies, rather it is interested in short/medium-term direct business benefits. The key focus for the firm has to be on competing based on cost reduction (see Figure 13.4). Supply in these organisations will undoubtedly be seen as an important function, with the key focus on purchasing as a tactical weapon as opposed to a strategic process. For Supply to be seen as important within this type of firm it must deliver savings.

Differentiation-focused firms, on the other hand, have a more enlightened and long-term view of the business. They will tend to view Supply as strategic to their business organisation. Their competitive advantage is gained from manipulating their competencies and capabilities and Supply will be seen as a core capability. Differentiated firms will compete by using a differentiated approach; this could focus on improving time-to-market, increased innovations within the firm and co-makership. Differentiated firms will see supply as a strategic activity to achieve these aims. Supply may achieve these business aims through supply tiers (delegated and/or parallel sourcing), outsourcing and co-design agreements.

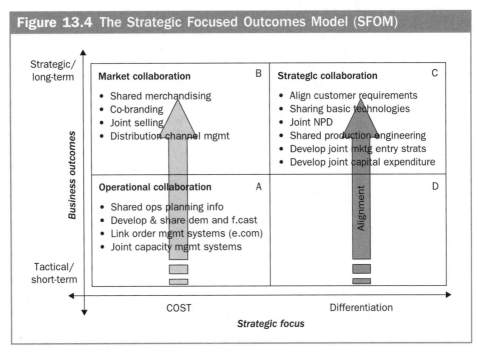

Figure 13.4 The Strategic Focused Outcomes Model (SFOM)

Source: Cousins (2005)

These approaches will require more complex collaborative approaches utilising strategic collaborations. Firms following this approach can expect to achieve higher visibility of the partner's business through cost transparency and information sharing. The development of risk and reward sharing agreements, which divide the level of risk and return between the strategic partners, will generally focus on major collaborations such technology development programmes and customer and/or market development activities. Relationship development outcomes will also deliver improved integration of business processes, with a view to improving efficiency and overall levels of effectiveness of these processes. Finally, relationship development outcomes will also allow the partner firms to develop joint shared capital investment projects such as development of new factories, warehousing, etc. In short, the differentiated approach requires a much broader and more strategic view of Supply's role within the firm.

The model shown in Figure 13.4, the Strategic Focused Outcomes Model (SFOM), indicates which strategies should be followed dependent upon the strategic approach taken by the firm. The emphasis here is appropriateness and allocation of resources. If the firm sees its competitive advantage in a cost-focused approach then Supply has the opportunity to follow two strategic approaches (illustrated in quadrants A and B), operational collaboration or market collaboration.

This SFOM model was developed from a two-year research project examining a range of medium to large firms. The research indicates that a short-term strategy would only allow for what is termed 'operational collaboration' to be achieved. This strategy consists of actions such as sharing operations planning information, developing and sharing demand forecasts, linking order management systems, usually via an intranet, and joint capacity planning management systems to align operational flows. Should Supply want to develop longer-term relationships with the suppliers under the cost-focused approach, they have the ability to develop what is termed 'market collaborations' (see quadrant B). Market collaborations are concerned with tactics such as shared merchandising, co-branding, joint selling and management of distribution channels. These types of collaboration tend to be move long term; however, their main focus is firmly embedded in the activity of cost reduction. The SFOM illustrates the available strategic alternatives to match the strategic focus on the firm. If Supply is aligned in cost-focused organisations it should peruse both operational and market collaborations.

Firms that have a 'differentiation' focus will tend not to have any short-term strategic foci. Their main concern will be to develop long-term sustainable business outcomes, based around strategic collaborations (see quadrant C). Strategic collaborations are concerned with aligning the customer requirements with the supplier, the sharing of technological processes and products to enhance offerings to existing and new customers that may lead to new product development activities. Furthermore, this type of collaboration will also focus on sharing production-engineering resources, developing joint capital investment and expenditure plans; these are typically in the shape of risk and reward sharing agreements between the buyer and supplier. Firms that have a differentiation focus will require Supply to align its approach to achieve the various goals and objectives outlined above. Failure to do so will result in a misalignment of the strategic focus of the organisation and supply management and will undoubtedly lead to tensions and non-achievement of the firm's organisational focus.

Development of a relationship management approach

The concept of a 'relationship' is much discussed and generally misunderstood. A good deal of this confusion comes from not understanding the unit of analysis and indeed not really considering what a 'relationship' is in a practical sense. Most purchasing professionals tend to think of a relationship as an entity (a thing), they will often refer to 'the relationship that exists between us and Supplier X'. Often in discussions with purchasing professionals they tell of away days to discuss 'the relationship' between buyers and suppliers. Whilst there are some socialisation benefits to be gained from this, there is no clear evidence that these events enhance the relationship between the two firms. This is because it is unclear to both parties what the relationship actually is. To put it another way, think of the relationship that exists between Buyer A and Supplier B as a business process (or course of action). This process will lead to some type of output. For example, communication is a process or course of action, which leads to the communicator delivering (via a medium) a range of information. It is deemed to be successful if, when tested, the recipient has clearly understood the message. If managers think about relationships as a process or course of action, then their role is to deliver some sort of business outcome. This could be in the form of price reduction, cost information exchange, technology or innovation exchanges and so on. In other words, relationships need to focus on business deliverables; they need to deliver something if they are deemed to be successful. This is an important point and worth recapping: *relationships can be thought of as a process or course of action, which should be designed to deliver business outcomes.* Now building on this point, in order to deliver business outcomes, relationship processes need to focus at the level of the product or service (and not the firm). For example, some products and services that are bought from suppliers will require a relatively simple relationship process to achieve a relatively simple business outcome, i.e. negotiation to achieve price reduction. Other business outcomes may be much more complex; for example, innovation exchange or long-term joint cost reduction targets will require much more complex relationship processes in order to deliver them. Therefore, the type of business outcome will dictate the level of relationship process or detail of course of action required to achieve it. Again, this is another important point. Taking this to its logical conclusion, it will mean that there will probably be a portfolio of relationships with any particular supplier depending on what business outcomes are required from the various products and services procured from that supplier. Furthermore, both buyers and suppliers need to be aware that when they develop a relationship strategy they focus the relationship process on the delivery of business performance outcomes.

The management of dependencies and certainties

Managing inter-firm relationships is a difficult task, which, as previously discussed, is made much more difficult when practitioners have to consider the range of issues involved in using the relationship to achieve significant business success. Figure 13.5 builds on the previous discussion and presents a model for thinking

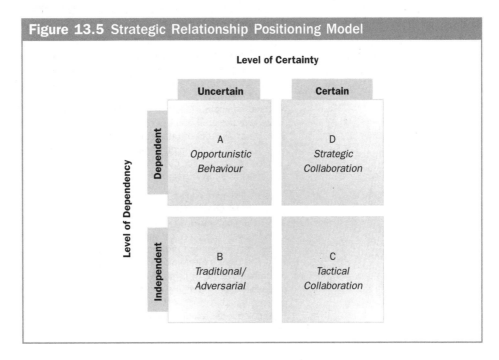

Figure 13.5 Strategic Relationship Positioning Model

about the management of inter-firm relationships. The model considers two key variables for the management of relationships: dependency and certainty. Dependencies are defined as mechanisms that create a reliance on either the buyer/ supplier or both. There are four key dependencies (see Cousins, 2002): economic, historic, technological (product and process) and political (defined in Table 13.1). These dependencies are not mutually exclusive, i.e. all, some or only one of these may be in effect at a particular point in time.

These dependencies can be identified by both the buyer and supplier firms as drivers for the development and manipulation of the relationship. In order to use these to gain business success the firm must take a strategic stance. The aim of either side would be at worst to create 'inter-dependence' (or mutual dependency); this occurs when the buyer and supplier are relatively equally dependent on each other. This would be an equilibrium situation; neither party will try to gain advantage over the other as they each have as much to lose as the other. This situation is often referred to as 'win/win'; however, as is obvious from this illustration, it

Table 13.1 The four key dependencies

Dependency	Description
Historic	The parties have had previous interactions with each other; this has built up a level of knowledge and shared experiences. These could be positive as well as negative and will act to inform the parties on what they can expect in the future from the relationship.
Economic	Economic dependencies refer to what is traditionally termed 'switching costs'. These are the costs incurred of moving the supply relationship from one supplier to another. These costs are generally easy to quantify, e.g. tooling costs, investment in labour, training, patents, investment in plant, machinery and so on. By investing in these types of costs the buyer and supplier become dependent on each other for the delivery of the product or service. Naturally, the higher the level of investment the more difficult it becomes to switch from one supply source to another.
Technological (product and/or process)	Technological dependencies refer to dependencies centred on technological competencies and capabilities. These could either be product based, i.e. a physical technology of some description, or software or process based. Process technologies would refer to knowledge-based competencies such as a consultancy firm. These dependencies are very powerful and also demonstrate that dependencies can be created on other aspects of business and are not confined to purely economic size. For example, large multinationals can be highly dependent on small software houses for development and maintenance. This can represent a significant supply chain risk if it is not managed carefully.
Political	Political dependencies are interesting and often highly influential, but often ignored by practitioners; these can be in the form of a large 'P' or small 'p'. They can have a large influence over which suppliers are selected and deselected and how the relationship is managed. Government policy in some industries (particularly military and aerospace applications) can have a significant impact on which suppliers are chosen for particular contracts (large 'P'). Internal politics can also drive supplier selection and management. Suppliers can become quite adept at playing the 'political' game (small 'p'). This is another very good reason to manage the internal organisational relationships.

is effectively 'lose/lose' as neither party can gain substantial advantage over the other; they in effect sub-optimise.

Another strategy, which might be referred to as the 'best' or optimal approach for creating or maximising value, occurs when either the buyer or the supplier creates a one-sided dependency on the other, i.e. the supplier is dependent on the buyer or the buyer is dependent on the supplier. This situation will allow the dominant party to exploit their relationship position. This naturally has a time limitation, as if one party over-dominates then the other will tend to search for either a new source of supply or a new customer. However, there is a variety of strategies that can be executed around this approach. For example, the dominant party might use its dominant position only in situations when maximum advantage can be gained; this would leave the other party tolerating the relationship without being prepared to divest it.

The level of dependencies within the relationship is, however, only one aspect of the management of these complex processes. The other aspect that needs to be considered is the level of 'risk' that is involved with the management of this interaction. The term 'risk' is used here instead of the usual term, 'trust'. In the interests of brevity this report will not go into a long discussion of this issue, but a brief explanation is required. The concept of 'trust' is extremely difficult to understand and define, especially when it is used to refer to something that exists between two companies as opposed to two individuals. Durkheim,[6] who was a famous sociologist, referred to trust as 'blind faith'; other philosophers such as Hume and Kant refer to it as 'promise keeping'. When we think of these definitions between two humans it makes sense, but between firms (which consists of thousands of individuals pursuing a variety of goals and objectives) it becomes much more difficult to comprehend. To summarise, 'trust' in an academic sense is often used to refer to individuals and not to collectives (such as firms). Firms and more importantly relationships as a unit of analysis tend to involve a variety of people pursuing a mix of aims and objectives. Perhaps what firms mean when they refer to 'trust' between firms is the minimisation of risk; in the language of economics this is referred to as 'opportunistic behaviour', i.e. one party taking advantage of the other. Economists often refer to the concept of risk as 'certainty'.[7] This definition has been used to construct the second variable that should be considered when managing inter-firm relationships; these are certainties or risks.

Building on the work of Mari Sako (1992), who explored differing contractual mechanisms such as arm's-length (adversarial) and obligation exchanges (collaborative), four levels of certainty have been defined: contractual, competence, goodwill and political. These are described in Table 13.2.

The balancing out of dependencies and risks will yield a variety of possible relationship management strategies. These are illustrated in Figure 13.5, the Strategic Relationship Positioning Model (SRPM). The available strategies are: adversarial, opportunism, tactical collaboration and strategic collaboration.

The SRPM uses the previously discussed concepts of dependency and certainty as a mechanism for developing relationship management strategies at the product/service level. It offers a range of available relationship strategies. The key point to remember here is that either the buyer or the supplier should choose the most appropriate strategy for them to follow, i.e. the strategy that will achieve the most

Table 13.2 The four levels of certainty

Certainties	Description
Contractual	How certain are the parties that one or other will perform to the specifications and standards of the contract?
Competence	How certain are the parties that one or other has the capabilities to perform to the contract, e.g. the required levels of skills, competencies and capabilities?
Goodwill	How certain are the parties that the one or other will be willing (or not) to go beyond their contractual duties and go beyond the straight contractual terms and conditions should they need it?
Political	What is the political risk or gain of dealing with the party either from an internal or external perspective?

Source: based on Sako (1992)

value. This will naturally depend on the time horizon (i.e. whether it is seen as a short-, medium- or long-term game) and also on the amount of value (or expected value) that is to be gained from the relationship.

The four key generic strategies that have been identified will now be briefly discussed. Adversarial strategies refer to arm's-length contractual relationships. These are where there are low levels of dependency (independent) and low levels of risk (generally due to multiple sources and the product or service having low technology). Opportunism occurs where either the buyer or the supplier is dependent (one-sided) on the other party. This will allow the dominant partner to take advantage of this situation (if that party desires to use the situation in this way). Opportunism will only generally take place if the dominant partner believes that they are in a position to sustain this additional value over time and if the interaction is relatively short-term and discrete, i.e. project-type environments. The management process here is around dependencies. Opportunism occurs where dependency is one-sided and levels of certainty are low, i.e. contractual terms may be short (this will allow the other party to see this as short term and therefore take advantage of the situation), competencies are undefined, goodwill is unproven and the level of political 'fallout' is also low.

The two remaining strategies deal with varying degrees of collaboration activity; these are split into tactical and strategic collaboration. Tactical collaboration occurs when the levels of mutual dependency have increased, for example because a modularity strategy or supply base reduction strategy has been followed. In addition, certainties have also increased, perhaps through offering long-term contracts, development of some risk and reward sharing arrangements, etc. Whilst these relationships do not represent what has become known as 'partnership' arrangements, they do represent a significant level of collaborative activity.

The final strategy available is 'strategic collaboration'. This occurs where there are high levels of mutual dependency (or inter-dependency) and high levels of certainty. These collaborations focus both parties on working the relationship for mutual gain; these would consist of risk and reward sharing arrangements, co-makership, and joint product and technology development teams and so on. They require a large amount of investment, with large returns for both parties involved.

Having outlined the key relationship strategies, it is now important to see where they fit into the overall sourcing process. Figure 13.6 offers an 'alignment' model

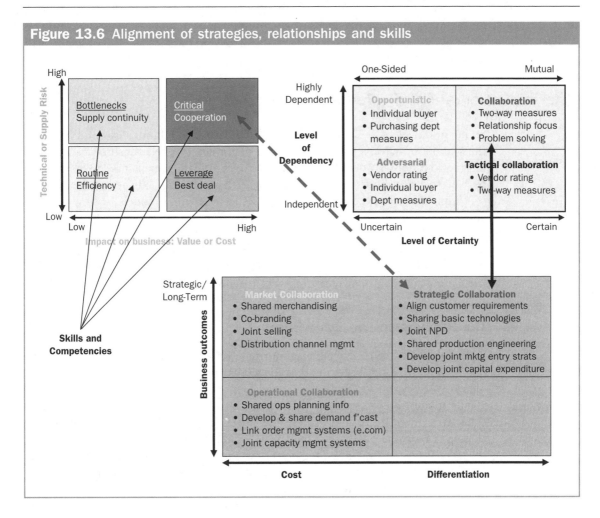

Figure 13.6 Alignment of strategies, relationships and skills

to help consider this approach. As previously discussed, relationship strategies should be focused at the level of the product or service being purchased.

The alignment model shows the interaction between the relationship focus, the type of product and service being purchased and the strategic nature of the supply function. The model also shows the link between skill and competence development, the argument being that firms need to align all of these issues if they want to maximise value from their inter-firm relationships and, more importantly, that these relationships are built up from interactions at the product/service level. In other words, a buyer may have any number of different relationships with a supplier depending on the importance of the product, the amount of risk that is being taken and the balance of power/dependency within the relationship.

The point that should be emphasised here for the firm is that the choice of the relationship approach or strategy should be based on focusing the *appropriate* relationship type to the outcomes required from the business transaction. These are indicated from the various linkages within this model. Furthermore, in order to operate these relationships the model indicates that the firm will need to have the requisite skills and competency mix and performance measurement systems.

Practitioners should refer back to the supply wheel at this stage to remind themselves of the broad and interrelated issues that need to be considered (see Figure 13.1).

The implementation of relationship management

So far in this chapter we have discussed the nature of relationships and begun to think about how (on a strategic level) we might design a relationship strategy. The next few sections go deeper into the relationship management process itself, with the key focus on how we might implement change within business organisations.

Within this context we will consider some conceptual models of how the cost and benefits of relationships vary over time. These models, which have all been developed by one of the authors, will be explored individually, but they are all interrelated. These models, specifically, the Partnership Life Cycle Effect, Partnership Expectations Effect and the Partnership Desert, form the total strategic framework for the management and measurement of the relationship.[8]

The Partnership Life Cycle Effect

Partnerships can be described as conforming to a life cycle. The product life cycle has been used as the basis for this conceptual model. Our model of relationship life cycles is shown in Figure 13.7.

The model shows conceptually how relationships operate. Note that relationships are viewed as having a finite life. Regardless of whether it is project purchasing or recurrent purchasing, the only element that differs is the time scale. Further, the team's construction will often need to change as the relationship moves through its life cycle. Our research showed that different skills were required from the selection and partnership teams during the first three stages of the life cycle. For example, during the embryonic stages, the team needed to think laterally to solve potentially huge barriers to the project's implementation. During the growth stages, different skills were required and these aligned much more with traditional management activities such as measurement, control and general problem resolution. The third

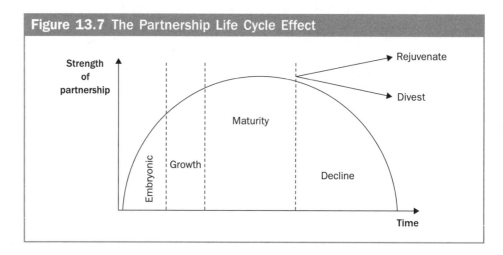

Figure 13.7 The Partnership Life Cycle Effect

phase requires an amalgamation of the two previous approaches. It requires management monitoring and general problem solving. In addition, managers need to consider how to develop the relationship, i.e. rejuvenate, divest or maintain.

The fact that these sourcing relationships will end at some point in time tends to engender fear into the organisations that want to operate them. The spectre of 'opportunistic behaviour' is certainly not welcome. An exercise known as the Red/Blue game or Prisoner's Dilemma reflects this view. The exercise was conducted with all of the case study companies, though one of the best reactions came from a group of final-year students. Having played the game and claimed a victory, viewed as 'slaughtering' the opposing team, the students commented that they had behaved in this manner because they knew that the game was coming to an end. This was a fair point, and one that has been raised continually throughout this research, especially from the oil companies, who are predominantly operating in a project-type environment. However, when the students returned the following week for the next lecture, they were told that they would be playing the game again, and against the same team that they played the previous week. Their faces dropped and they became confused and apprehensive. This point illustrates that even in a project environment buyers and suppliers may have to work with each other several times and past performance tends to predict future attitudes.

The Partnership Expectations Effect

The life-cycle model is limited in its description of what occurs within and between organisations. A more detailed framework that may more accurately describe the building of partnership relationships is the 'partnership achievement and growth model', which illustrates the expectations effect of relationship development. The model suggests how relationships appear to develop over the short (t1), medium (t2) and long term (t3) against given returns (return on partnership – ROP). The model also suggests how, as the relationship develops over time, different levels of return can be expected. Sako's (1992) contractual, competence and goodwill trust will be utilised to illustrate this point. The Partnership Expectations Model is illustrated in Figure 13.8.

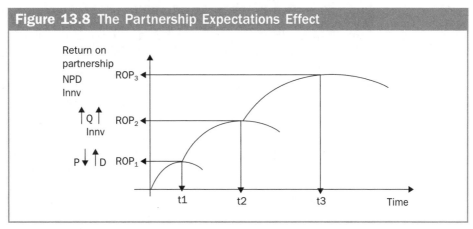

Figure 13.8 The Partnership Expectations Effect

Source: Sako (1992)

In the short term (t_1), as the relationship is building, the buyer and supplier will set measurable benefits such as improvements in pricing and delivery performance. To illustrate, we describe a research interview with an electronics component supplier who, when starting a partnership arrangement with a supplier of high-volume stock, required (in exchange for a five-year contract) a reduction in prices and an improvement in delivery performance. The supplier found these targets acceptable because with long-term orders they could plan their scheduling arrangement much more easily. In turn they were able to reduce their stock levels and gain improvements in economies of scale through 'piggy-backing' on short-term orders. Interestingly, as the relationship developed the expectations were constantly raised to improve the overall performance levels, indicative of a '*kaizen*' approach. The supplier was able to achieve this because the buyer altered its working systems to improve communications to the supplier of ongoing scheduling activities that were previously not released to the supplier. The research also revealed that high levels of contractual and competence trust were being realised by both parties.

In the medium term (t_2), the buyer and supplier have the opportunity to take a further decision: they could engender or rejuvenate the relationship to look at a wider sphere of deliverables, such as improvements in quality and possible joint innovation projects, or they could leave the relationship on its present level. Quite often the choice to develop the relationship was predetermined by past performance, by the levels of competence and to an extent the goodwill trust that had built up between the parties. The initiative to develop the relationship seemed to come from the buying organisation in most of the cases. When the relationship was developed further, typical criteria for measurement were 'improvements in quality' and 'possible innovation activity'. Interestingly, as the relationship developed the measurement appeared to become more subjective. For example, companies were asked how they define quality. A spectrum of definitions was used, ranging from defect rates through to the quality of the documentation and the quality of response from the sales department representative. A large manufacturer further emphasised this point: 'We need to build products to a very high standard. Therefore our quality requirements are very stringent. This benefits both our customers and our suppliers as other buyers know that our supplier can produce to the highest quality standards.'

A similar principle applies at the t_3 level. As the relationship reaches its mature stage, the levels of goodwill and competence trust have again been built up, communication systems are well aligned and now the partners have to make a decision to further develop the relationship or to leave it as it stands. This decision is again based on a cost–benefit analysis approach. The choice to develop the relationship appears to be dependent on the amount of competence and goodwill trust between the parties – contractual trust having already been established during the past two phases of the relationship life cycle. Once the decision has been made to develop the relationship and move into the area of new product development, the rejuvenated relationship begins once more. An example of this can be seen from the Westland case study (Cousins, 1997) where the joint venture was so successful that a 'spin off' company was created to manage the new development.[9]

At the t_3 level, the organisation also has to make decisions about the types of sourcing strategies it may use to generate collaborative benefits. These are outlined in Figure 13.9.

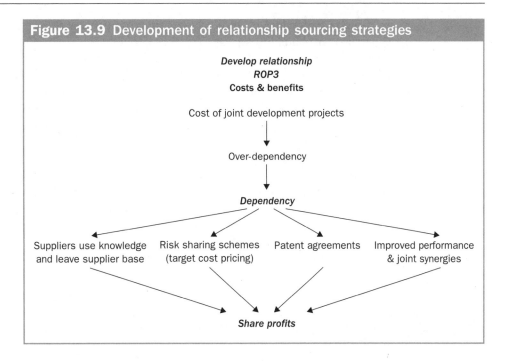

Figure 13.9 Development of relationship sourcing strategies

The Partnership Desert Effect

The final conceptual model is known as the 'Partnership Desert Effect' (see Figure 13.10). This model shows how in the short (t1), medium (t2) and long term (t3), the parties receive the benefits from entering into relationships.

The model depicts an oscillation effect, with 'deserts' (D1, D2 and D3) occurring at various time intervals. The partnership 'desert' can be thought of as a barren and inhospitable place, where no returns/benefits are received from the partnership approach. In the short term, when the relationship is first established, an initial return is realised which may be in the form of a price reduction, improvements

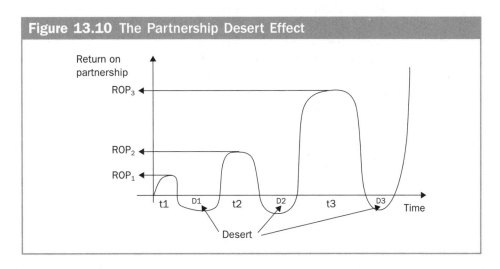

Figure 13.10 The Partnership Desert Effect

in delivery performance, offer to hold stock and so on. This occurs when contractual trust is building up between the parties.

A period where no benefits are received then follows: the desert (D1). This occurs during the growth stage of the relationship; communication systems and cross-functional teams are being put into place and all parties are getting used to a new collaborative way of working. Once these have been established and the philosophy is clearly understood, benefits from the improved business relationships begin to flow once more. Improvements in pricing, delivery and quality performance may be generated.

As time progresses and the partners work more closely together, the potential collaborative returns from the relationship increase and the 'deserts' become smaller. This approach depicts how the benefits accrue and decrease throughout the life of the relationship. Unfortunately, many firms lose the drive for partnerships after hitting the first 'desert', without realising that it is a normal part of the evolution of their relationship. They are merely laying the foundation of future benefits.

Implications for managing relationships

There are several management implications that should be drawn from this discussion so far:

1 The management of inter-firm relationships is complex; it is not sufficient simply to set up an agreement: action plans need to be followed to instigate change. The supply wheel demonstrates the complexity of areas that need to be considered simultaneously.

2 It is important to consider what a 'relationship' is, i.e. defining the term; in this chapter, relationships are referred to as processes that drive or facilitate changes in behaviour. Naturally these can be positive or negative depending on how they are used.

3 It is important to consider relationships at the level of the product or service and not at the level of the firm, e.g. it is impossible to say that the relationship with firm X is good bad or indifferent, as there will be as many views on this as there are people involved. The point is that firms need to consider strategically what they buy and then apply the appropriate relationship which will deliver the maximum value for their business. Milton Friedman's famous quote, 'the business of business is business,' applies here.

4 Inter- and intra-firm relations. Relationship management should not begin with changing the way a firm manages its suppliers. It should start with how the buyer firm interacts with itself (intra-firm relationships). It is vitally important that relationships are aligned internally first, before any attempts are made at changing, enhancing or refocusing existing inter-firm relationships.

5 Building a business case. There *must* be a business benefit from refocusing relationship approaches. Firms (both buyers and suppliers) need to think through clearly what these benefits are, and also if the costs of getting them outweigh the actual benefits. Whilst this may sound obvious, it has certainly become

apparent during this research with major firms how few consider these important decision drivers. Firms tend to reduce supply bases with little cost knowledge, move towards higher-dependency relationships without performance measurement or skill changes and so on. The point here is that if a firm is going to adopt a different way of working then it must consider all of these aspects and build a business case for doing so.

6 Relationship strategies are dynamic; they need to be thought through and managed over time. At different stages they may require different people/skills to manage them. It is important that firms choose appropriate relationships to deliver the maximum value for their transaction. This can be achieved through manipulating and managing the dependency/certainty mix.

Summary

This chapter began by discussing and defining the term 'relationships'. We presented a view which suggested that relationships in and of themselves were not entities but rather should be thought of as processes. These processes have inputs and also need to have focused outputs. We discussed a variety of models and concepts to show how we might think about developing a relationship strategy. Finally we concluded by discussing a range of implementation issues which challenge firms when redesigning their relationship management processes.

Seminar questions

1. Discuss, giving examples, the main models, concepts and theories of relationship management.

2. Discuss how relationship management can be viewed from the economic, strategic, behavioural and marketing perspectives.

3. Using a case study company of your choice, show the complexities and difficulties in implementing a relationship management approach.

4. Using a case study, discuss how you would implement relationship management techniques.

References

Carr, A. S. and Smeltzer, L. (1997) 'An Empirically Based Operational Definition of Strategic Purchasing', *European Journal of Purchasing and Supply Management*, Vol. 3 (4), pp. 199–207.

Cousins, P. (1994) 'A Framework for the Measurement and Management of Strategic Inter-firm Relationships,' Unpublished PhD Thesis, University of Bath.

Cousins, P. D. (1997) 'Flying High: the Westland Experience', in Taylor, D. (ed.), *Cases in Strategic Operations Management*, Wiley, pp. 89–96.

Cousins, P. D. (2002) 'A Conceptual Model for Managing long-term inter-organisational relationships,' *European Journal of Purchasing & Supply Management*, Vol. 8 (2), pp. 71–82.

Cousins, P. D. (2005) 'The Alignment of Appropriate Firm and Supply Strategies for Competitive Advantage', *International Journal of Operations and Production Management*, Vol. 25 (5), pp. 403–28.

Cousins, P. and Crone, M. J. (2003) 'Strategic Models for the development of obligation based inter-firm relationships: A Study of the Automotive Industry', *International Journal of Operations and Production Management*, Vol. 23 (12), pp. 1447–74.

Ellram, L. and Carr, A. (1994) 'Strategic Purchasing: A History and Review of the Literature', *International Journal of Purchasing and Materials Management*, Vol. 30 (2), pp. 10–22.

Farmer, D. (1972) 'The Impact of Supply Markets on Corporate Planning', *Long Range Planning*, Vol. 5 (1), pp. 10–15.

Hines, P. (1994) *Creating World Class Suppliers: Unlocking Mutual Competitive Advantage*, Pitman, London.

Kanter, R. M. (1989) *When Giants Learn to Dance*, Simon & Schuster, Boston, MA.

Lambert, D. M., Stock, J. R. and Ellram, L. M. (1998) *Fundamentals of Logistics Management*, Irwin/McGraw-Hill, Boston, MA.

Lamming, R. (1993) *Beyond Partnership: Strategies for Innovation and Lean Supply*, Prentice Hall, New York.

Nishiguchi, T. (1993) *Strategic Industrial Sourcing: The Japanese Advantage*, Oxford University Press, New York.

Reck, R. F. and Long, B. G. (1988) 'Purchasing: A Competitive Weapon', *Journal of Purchasing and Materials Management*, Vol. 24 (4), pp. 3–6.

Richardson, J. (1994) 'Parallel Sourcing and Supplier Performance in the Japanese Automobile Industry', *Strategic Management Review*, Vol. 14, pp. 339–50.

Sako, M. (1992) *Prices, Quality and Trust: Buyer Supplier Relationships in Britain and Japan*, Cambridge University Press, Cambridge.

Seligman, A. (1997) *The Problem of Trust*, Princeton University Press, Princeton, NJ.

Tan, K.-C. (2001) 'A Framework of Supply Chain Management Literature', *European Journal of Purchasing and Supply Management*, Vol. 7, pp. 39–48.

Williamson, O. E. (1975) *Markets and Hierarchies: Analysis and Antitrust Implications*, The Free Press, New York.

Womack, J. P., Jones, D. T. and Roos, D. (1990) *The Medicine that Changed the World*, The Free Press, New York.

Further reading

Burt, D. and Doyle, M. (1994) *The American Keiretsu: A Strategic Weapon for Global Competitiveness*, Irwin, IL.

Carlisle, J. and Parker, R. (1989) *Beyond Negotiation: Customer Supplier Relationships*, John Wiley and Sons, London.

Carlson, P. (1990) 'The Long and the Short of Strategic Planning,' *Journal of Business Strategy*, May–June, pp. 15–19.

Cousins, P., Lawson, B. and Squire, B. (2006) 'An Empirical Taxonomy of Purchasing Functions,' *International Journal of Operations and Production Management*, Vol. 26 (7), pp. 775–94.

Cox, A. (2004) 'The Art of the Possible: Relationship Management in Power Regimes and Supply Chains, *Supply Chain Management: an International Journal*, Vol. 9 (5), pp. 346–56.

Farmer, D. (1985) *Purchasing Management Handbook*, Gower Publishing, London.

MacBeth, D. and Ferguson, N. (1994) *Partnership Sourcing: An Integrated Supply Chain Approach*, Pitman Publishing, London.

Porter, M. (1980) *Competitive Strategy*, The Free Press, New York.

Porter, M. (1985) *Competitive Advantage*, The Free Press, New York.

Endnotes

1. For a history of Professor Friedman please see the following link: http://nobelprize.org/nobel_prizes/economics/laureates/1976/friedman-autobio.html
2. Please note cost and price reduction are two distinct strategies. Price reduction focuses on negotiating the overall price whereas cost reduction examines how the price is made up and attempts to focus on reducing the various cost elements within the price. This is more beneficial as a method for long-term relationship management.
3. Firm in this case refers to both of the firms engaged in developing the relationship.
4. For an interesting historical discussion see Womack, Jones and Roos (1990) – including the development of transplants. Also, for a discussion on Japanese subcontracting arrangements see Nishiguchi (1993), Lamming (1993) and Hines (1994).
5. See Cousins and Crone (2003).
6. **Émile Durkheim** (15 April, 1858–15 November, 1917) was a French sociologist whose contributions were instrumental in the formation of sociology and anthropology. See also Seligman (1997).
7. We can translate risks into probabilities of actions. Certainties can also be viewed in the same way, e.g. how certain (chance) is it that something will happen or not happen (one minus the probability).
8. These models were developed by Cousins and can be found in Cousins (1994).
9. An up-to-date version of this case is available on the website for this book.

PART 3

STRATEGIC ISSUES IN SUPPLY CHAIN MANAGEMENT

Chapter 14

Environmental and ethical issues in supply management[1]

Aim of chapter

The aim of this chapter is to provide readers with a clear understanding of the growing importance of environmental and ethical concerns to purchasing and supply management

Learning outcomes

At the end of this chapter, readers will:

- understand why purchasing and supply management should be concerned with environmental and ethical supply issues;
- have a clear understanding of the contribution purchasing and supply management can make to environmental soundness;
- be able to identify a range of implementations issues that are important to 'green supply'.

Introduction

The purpose of this chapter is to explore the connections between the sourcing decisions made within purchasing and supply and some of the effects those decisions have on the world, in terms of biophysical (for example, air, water and soil pollution), economic (for example, loss of habitat and even warfare) and ethical (for example, the use of slavery and child labour). Traditionally, little attention would have been given to such remote and exotic issues within the Purchasing office. Now, however, the issues are increasingly real challenges for the Supply Strategist.

We shall demonstrate why purchasing and supply professionals should be concerned about the environmental[2] aspect of supply chain management, defining such concepts as sustainable development, corporate social responsibility and environmental soundness. We shall discuss the Supply Strategist's potential contribution to increasing environmental soundness. Lastly, the chapter identifies and discusses several important implementation issues.

Why should Purchasing be concerned?

In October 2000, as part of its weekly investigative programme *Panorama*, the BBC aired an exposé on supply chains in the sports clothing industry. The programme televised scenes of children in Cambodian factories making products for well-known global brands (in this instance for Nike® and The Gap®).[3] The episode was widely discussed by the British media and engendered considerable public outcry. The two companies' purchasing strategies were immediately front-page news; both immediately sought to quell the adverse publicity with promises to remove such practices from their supply chains. A year later, the American journalist Eric Schlosser published *Fast Food Nation* in which he exposed abusive labour practices in the factories processing the hamburgers and potatoes served in US restaurants. The book cites damage to American agriculture as a result of the massive commercial power of a small number of large firms (seemingly in league with federal and state governments). In addition, Schlosser describes several very unsavoury and possibly dangerous ingredients in the food that Americans consume. While several large industrial food companies immediately criticised Schlosser, they were unable to cite any specific errors in the damning book he had written (Schlosser, 2002: 276). The book was widely reviewed in the international media, generating much exposure and considerable public discussion. The debate in the connection between obesity and fast food was fuelled by the evidence Schlosser provided, driving some chains to reduce the excessive portions and introduce salads as alternatives to hamburgers.

In the UK, the code on child labour in the supply chain developed by the high-street retailer Marks and Spencer has become something of a general standard.[4] In the food industry, issues such as the BSE crisis[5] have led to stringent legislation and control of supply. The public, it seems, have begun to realise that their purchasing decisions have an impact on the earth and its inhabitants.

Before the early 1990s, the notion that Purchasing and Supply managers might have a significant interest in environmental or ethical issues was barely evident – it was limited to the activists of non-governmental organisations (NGOs) such as Greenpeace or Friends of the Earth. Managers in Purchasing and Supply were able to maintain this 'hands-off' approach because organisations had for some time created specialist environmental science departments, to whom, it was assumed, all such issues could be referred. By the end of the twentieth century, this approach often proved untenable.

Firms increasingly assessed their own environmental 'footprints' and those of their suppliers. A standard emerged – first as BS7570 and then ISO 14000 – as a reference or proxy for good environmental practices. These standards became widely accepted by industry as a business 'totem', much like the ISO 9000 quality standard two decades earlier, and were used as promotional points for those firms that gained accreditation. For example, a visitor to Toyota's massive Takaoka plant near Nagoya in Japan in 1998 would be greeted first not by a showroom of new cars but by the proud display of the factory's accreditation to ISO 14000. (See http://www.iso-14001.org.uk/ and Carter and Narasimham 1998.) This was a major part of the giant firm's strategy between 1996 and 2000, signalling its intention to position itself as the leader in developing cars that used fewer natural resources.

From using the accreditation of its factories as a marketing device, Toyota went on to develop and successfully market a 'hybrid-powered' car (the petrol/electric Prius), sold on the benefits of its reduced biophysical impact and fuel economy.

The popular press further highlighted environmental and ethical concerns. For example, rainforest destruction in South America was linked to garden furniture bought by British consumers. Television exposés such as *Panorama* documented the role of African slave labour in the production of coffee beans destined for European cafés.[6] The European Union subsequently established Directives on recycling consumer products – including motor cars and packaging/packaging waste.

Such emerging concern for the environmental impacts and ethics associated with purchasing decisions mirrors the concern for quality, health and safety that emerged in the 1970s. These concerns are clearly vital to sustainable business but were viewed as nuisances and unwelcome extra costs. Yet in the 1970s it became increasingly clear that quality management could be self-financing (through reductions in costs of non-quality). The question facing Operational managers and Supply managers in the early part of the twenty-first century is whether environmental and ethical concerns in the supply chain could also be self-financing.

While goods, materials and services acquired by an organisation may be assessed in terms of their biophysical or social impacts – even if this is limited to the imperfect understanding of the issues in the minds of consumers – the difficulty for Purchasing and Supply managers is establishing the scope of their responsibility for activities in the operations of their direct and indirect suppliers. There appear to be two good reasons for acting in a responsible way in this matter. The first is a genuine concern for the sustainability of the Earth's ecology. The second is improved risk management – avoiding the penalties associated with breaking civil or criminal law. We will now turn to a discussion of both.

In many Western countries (especially in the member states of the European Union), businesses face mounting pressures from consumers, regulators and even stock markets to assume more responsibility for their environmental performance. These pressures appear to fit a cyclical trend that is closely correlated with economic prosperity (Downs, 1973). As the effects of pollution become more visible and affect more people over time, it is likely that the peak of concern at the last cycle will form the base level of concern for the next cycle.

This trend is visible even in the more *laissez-faire*, market-driven Anglo-Saxon economies. In North America in the early 1990s, 75 per cent of consumers held that their purchasing decisions were affected by a company's environmental reputation; 80 per cent would pay more for environmentally 'friendlier' goods (Drumwright, 1994). A British government survey of public attitudes, conducted in 1994 by Environmental Data Services Ltd (ENDS), revealed that concern for the environment was third on a list of the most important issues that the public believed government should be addressing, ranked just below unemployment and health but above crime, education and the economy in general. The survey also showed a dramatic shift of public opinion in favour of a 'polluter pays' principle, even if enforcing such a principle resulted in paying higher prices for goods and services (62 per cent). Eighty-seven per cent of respondents wanted more information from companies on the environmental impact of their products, and 88 per cent wanted better labeling to enable consumers to make more informed buying decisions (ENDS 232, 1994). Other studies, however, have concluded that while consumers claim these preferences in surveys, their buying activities do not reflect these preferences in practice. Ten years on, there is still no evidence that anyone will pay a 'green premium'. It appears likely, nevertheless, that faced with a choice between two otherwise identical products, consumers would buy the more environmentally sound of the two.

Although consumers may not explicitly ask for ethically produced items, Knight (1996: 65) argues they expect them. When consumers suspect or discover that goods are not environmentally sound, they become disappointed. As Knight points out, disappointment is vastly inferior to the aim of 'customer satisfaction', and even further from that of 'customer delight or excitement'.[7] These are the necessary conditions to encourage repeat buying and personal recommendation of a product/ service. These may have been the concerns in the boardrooms and Purchasing offices of Nike and the Gap after the *Panorama* broadcast.

Environmental and ethical problems are thus intrinsically linked to supply chains. While these problems are manifested at one point in the chain – for example, disposal of electrical goods with harmful chemicals – their root cause is often located two or three links earlier in the chain.[8] Thus, a Supply manager's perspective must include provision for potential problems – and opportunities – elsewhere in his or her organisation's respective supply network. Policies and strategies must be formulated accordingly, to address several complicated issues. For example, what is meant by terms such as 'environmentally friendly', 'environmentally sound', 'sustainable development' and 'corporate social responsibility'? Even a brief encounter with the subject area reveals an amazing lack of clarity and considerable ambiguity.

Sustainability, green, and environmental soundness

The environmental pressures that affect a business may come from sources inside and outside the firm. External sources include industry requirements (i.e. customers and suppliers), financial institutions, regulatory authorities and public bodies (i.e. local, national, regional and even global authorities and other organisations). These pressures form the external environmental context in which a business operates and that its overall strategy should be designed to address. Internal pressures, however, are increasingly important. Internal sources include the desires of marketing departments to 'green' their respective organisation's image; the legal mandates of health and safety inspectors; the fiduciary and stewardship concerns of board members; and the desire of employees who feel the effects of pollution personally not to be associated with recognised polluters. Employee motivation is a key factor in business productivity. Although companies may be expected to withstand these pressures to some degree, there are limits to this resilience (see Cramer, 1996).

Developing environmentally sound supply chain policies and strategies to address the related market needs therefore requires a clear understanding of each of the stakeholders' perspectives and priorities. This should be fitted into a framework that may be used to guide the firm's activities. For the Purchasing and Supply manager, this framework would serve as the basis for formulating the firm's environmental supply strategy. One should be able to predict the outcome of any chosen path with regard to its environmental consequences and its likely impacts upon the objectives of the business.

As public appreciation of the importance of the issues grows, the blanket term 'environmentally *friendly*' (i.e. applied to products that in some unspecified way claim to have less environmental impact) finds few supporters today. Concern is now expressed in more sophisticated terms, often referring to the concept of sustainability or corporate social responsibility (CSR). There has been a transition from a generalised wish not to harm the environment to a focused concern for specific, carefully dimensioned impacts. One example of this is the UK taxation regime for the benefits employees are deemed to receive from company cars. In addition to the engine size, the tax calculation formula includes the published emissions data for the vehicle. Another development in this direction is the increasing use of 'mass balance' (see Jones, 2004).

Corporate social responsibility is an overarching term that encompasses many aspects of environmental and ethical performance. Most large companies now publish reports on their CSR policies and performance – data that are considered by the investment community. For purposes of focus, CSR can be seen as the endeavours of the organisation to achieve sustainable development.[9]

However, a firm may have difficulty determining whether its product or service may be labelled 'sustainable'. The Brundtland Report 'Our Common Future' (WCED, 1987)[10] is recognised as the basis for understanding this subject. It defines sustainable development as seeking to meet 'the needs of the present without compromising the ability of future generations to meet their own needs'. The report gives particular prominence to food security, institutional and legal change, access to democratic processes, and health, education and population control. Emphasis is placed on equity and the 'essential needs of the world's poor' with the major objectives of development set as 'the satisfaction of human needs and aspirations'. The report asserts that sustainable development is not incompatible with economic growth provided the content of growth does not involve the exploitation of others. As has been pointed out before, 'sustainability is meaningful *only* at the global level; to attempt to affect it at the corporate level leads inevitably to rhetoric and sophistry (for example, in corporate reporting)' (Lamming, Faruk and Cousins, 1999).

In describing sustainability as it applies to business organisations, it is common to speak of 'the triple bottom line'. The triple bottom line refers to an organisation's responsibilities in the areas of economic behaviour, environmental impact and social policy. It may be argued that firms should not aim for developing social policies, since policy matters are the responsibility of elected representatives in each country or region. While the purchaser may expect political intervention to prevent social impacts, it is necessary to know the origins of raw materials and the impacts of their production and possibly take strategic action, as illustrated in Box 14.1.

For everyday sourcing decisions, firms need to develop policies and strategies for environmental and economic performance according to governments' and agencies' definitions of what constitutes socially accepted behaviour. As Figure 14.1 shows, the combination of these first two 'bottom lines' provides a definition of 'environmental soundness' that should be seen as 'a continuous process with respect to improving environmental performance' (Miller and Szekely, 1995). Miller and Szekely go on to observe that 'it would be erroneous to suggest that green is a fixed state that users of the environment can eventually reach . . . Companies do not become green; they become greener.' Over time, therefore, as part of development within defined social policy, environmental soundness – 'greening' rather than 'greenness' – could be said to deliver sustainability.

Box 14.1 Social policies

National and regional governments and international agencies provide many guidelines, ranging from advice to legal requirement, to ensure that organisations know the social policies within which they should work. On child labour, for example, Convention 182 from the International Labour Office (ILO) of the UN provides guidance (http://www.ilo.org/public/english/standards/ipec/index.htm) that is accepted by national governments. An organisation may choose to develop its own policy within this or mimic one set up by a reputable company. For example, many retailers use the Marks and Spencer code as the basis for their own approach; this reflects well on them and on M&S.

More general environmental performance may be developed in the context of a standard from the International Standards Organization (ISO) – starting with ISO 14000, which is a scheme for accrediting the firm's activities and policies. ISO 14000 grew from the world's first Environmental Management System (EMS) Standard, British Standard BS7750 (1992), itself derived in the early 1990s from the quality assurance standard BS5750 (later the ISO 9000 series). See http://www.iso-14001.org.uk/ and http://www.bsi-global.com

While these two are voluntary standards – companies may choose to eschew them but then face the wrath of the market – regulations such as the European Commission's Directives on Packaging and Packaging Waste (94/62/EEC) requires member states to set up return, collection and recovery systems and provide consumer information. Other Directives in Europe include Civil Liability for Waste, Landfill and Air/Climate Change.

The European Commission also has voluntary standards, such as EMAS: Eco-Management and Audit Scheme, which obliges accredited companies to report on their performance at least once every three years.

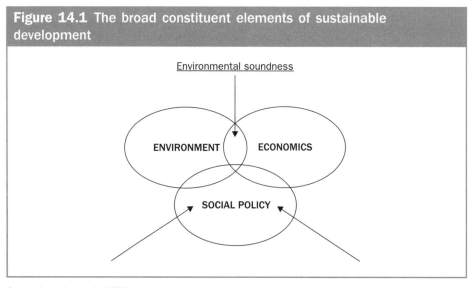

Figure 14.1 The broad constituent elements of sustainable development

Source: Lamming et al. (1999)

Purchasing and supply management's environmental contribution

For Purchasing and Supply managers, environmental soundness may be seen as the degree to which their activities comply with the framework of requirements their parent organisation has identified as its policy and strategy on the subject. This is a subtle point but one that should enable managers to establish an appropriate scope of responsibility. Using the corporate framework, Purchasing and Supply strategists can formulate their own economic and environmental plans and stances to ensure they conform to the firm's intentions and preferences. The issues addressed may be very significant, as illustrated in Box 14.2.

Box 14.2 Mobile phones and African wars

There is growing pressure on purchasers to understand the far-reaching social impacts of their sourcing decisions for raw materials on the countries that produce them. These impacts can be literally catastrophic, combining the economic, environmental and social aspects of the triple bottom line. For example, in March 2001, The World Conservation Union, IUCN, called for a ban on a mineral called 'coltan' (short for columbite-tantalite – a form of tantalum). Users of mobile phones are probably unaware that this mineral exists in their handsets, their children's computer game consoles, and their computer chips. It is essential in the manufacture of electrical components known as pinhead capacitors, which regulate voltage and store electrical energy. The reason for the IUCN request was that coltan mining in the Democratic Republic of Congo (DRC – formally Zaire) provides wealth for warring factions and countries, takes away the livelihoods of people who live on the land, and destroys wildlife. DRC has 80 per cent of known deposits of the mineral, while 80 per cent of processing takes place in Australia. Over 10,000 miners had moved into two World Heritage sites: Kahuzi-Biega National Park and Okapi Wildlife Reserve, and were largely relying on meat from wild animals (bushmeat) for food. David Sheppard, IUCN's Head of Programme on Protected Areas, said: 'Mining, together with the presence of so many people looking for food, is severely impacting on the ecology of these sites, and is in flagrant violation of World Heritage principles. Streams and forests are being degraded, the livelihoods of the indigenous people, the Mbuti, in the Okapi Wildlife Reserve are threatened, and wildlife is being destroyed at an alarming rate.' Sheppard emphasised that species such as elephants and the endangered eastern lowland gorillas were being hunted by the miners. 'It is feared that a large proportion of the elephant population in Kahuzi-Biega National Park has been killed as well as a significant number of gorillas, leaving the population at a dangerously low level', says Sheppard.

IUCN believes that companies who use coltan in their products have an obligation to help find a satisfactory solution to the crisis and launched appeals, calling on buyers of coltan to ensure that the product they purchase did not come from these World Heritage sites in the DRC. While supporting the current efforts to remove miners from the Okapi Wildlife Reserve, it called on the DRC authorities, and the neighbouring States of Rwanda and Uganda, to help enforce an immediate removal of miners from within the boundaries of both the affected World Heritage sites. Third, IUCN called on the buyers of coltan and the governmental authorities in DRC, Rwanda and Uganda to do everything in their power to find acceptable alternative livelihoods for all miners removed from the two World Heritage sites.

Sources: Trade and Environment Database: http://www.american.edu/TED; ICE Inventory of Conflict and Environment: http://www.american.edu/TED/ice/ice.htm; for a full version of this case, all references, and up-to-date news on this situation and many other ethical difficulties in supply chains, see http://www.american.edu/TED/ice/congo-coltan.htm and http://www.worldpolicy.org/

A checklist of the Purchasing manager's basic environmental concerns would include:

- an understanding of the types of pollution associated with goods and services being purchased;
- a policy on environmental soundness in purchasing and supply;
- a strategy to minimise the impacts of sourcing decisions;
- a plan for working with the risks associated with environmental performance.

Understanding pollution

Pollution can be broadly defined as matter that is in the wrong place. Matter can neither be created nor destroyed – it is simply converted from one medium into another. For example, burning paper does not destroy it; it simply turns it into billions of smaller particles, i.e. smoke. Similarly, using gas 'scrubbers' to reduce sulphur dioxide emissions from a smoke stack does not eliminate the problem; it just converts pollution in one medium into an environmental problem in another, i.e. from gas to liquid. When the liquid is precipitated, it becomes a problem of solid waste. This is illustrated in Figure 14.2. This, of course, is supply chain thinking – everything has a source and a destination. In economic terms, it is clear that pollution often represents a form of economic waste. Peter Jones, of Biffa, calculates that in the UK 'in terms of private consumption, we pour 600 million tonnes of resources into the economy each year and get 60 million tonnes out at the other end' (Jones, 1996). So, for every tonne consumed or used, there are nine tonnes of waste, packing, and so on. Jones finds the same is true of business; 90 per cent of everything a Buyer purchases (by weight) is eventually likely to end up as waste. Put this way, the immensity of the problem is clear.

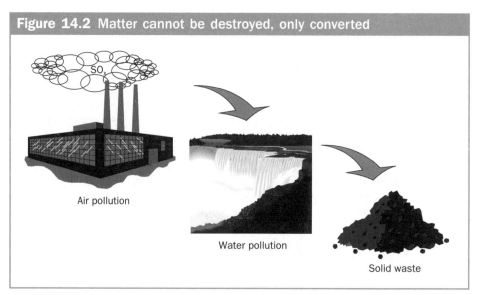

Figure 14.2 Matter cannot be destroyed, only converted

Air pollution

Water pollution

Solid waste

Source: Lamming and Hampson (1996)

Establishing a policy on environmental soundness

It is not too harsh to conclude that pollution is indicative of some business inefficiency, showing that resources have been used incompletely, inefficiently or ineffectively. It also requires additional cost, for example in terms of dealing with hazardous materials, double handling of returned or recycled products, and disposal or clean-up activities, all of which add cost, but little value.[11] Like defects, pollution often reveals flaws in the product design or production processes (Porter and van der Linde, 1995). Traditional costing systems have ignored these 'external costs' as they may not impact on the business, and thus may not need to be attributed to the product (e.g. the cost to the environment of dumping the packaging in landfill sites). As regulation changes (e.g. landfill taxes and the rights of consumers to return packaging to the manufacturers), the external costs cease to be negligible and must be added to the direct costs of the product. In effect, the supply chain implications of the product must be managed at the primary costing level (a factor that will have repercussions right along the supply chain if not properly managed).

Walley and Whitehead (1994) represent an alternative view on this issue. They underline the high costs associated with implementing environmental technologies and the lack of any real economic payback. As an alternative they suggest that the firm's goal should be to develop a strategy that internalises the external costs brought about by environmental pressures. To do so, managers must adopt a value approach, carrying out 'trade-offs' between the costs of responding to environmental issues against the benefits. Such an approach would run counter to the commonly observed practice of simply passing on the responsibilities for environmental impact to the suppliers. Experience with quality, timeliness, effectiveness and innovation in supply relationships suggests that there is little to gain by such abdication of responsibility. A supply strategy must be developed to face the implications of environmental responsibility head-on. It is also important to remember that when a supplier develops a new technology that provides real environmental benefits, it will see it as an advantage – one that it may choose to offer first to its best customers. For example, when Du Pont developed a replacement for CFCs, it was one of the first to press for their eradication (from, for example, refrigerators). A first-mover advantage such as this will provide knock-on advantages for customers whom suppliers (innovators) perceive as embracing challenges.

The implication of this is that environmental issues should be dealt with in the same manner as, say, the design, logistics or quality improvement processes, by integrating the issues into overall management, and assigning management responsibilities and goals, on a continuous improvement basis, which will minimise the possibility of mistakes occurring.[12] This does not mean that no environmental impact will occur, but rather that no management mistakes will be made, which might lead to an environmental 'incident'. This approach has been dubbed 'Total Quality Environmental Management' (TQEM) (Welford and Gouldson, 1993; Shrivastava, 1995). The parallels with quality principles are clear: it is most expensive to return a faulty product for repair after it has left the factory; it is less expensive to inspect the quality at the end of the production line, but it is most cost-effective to design any faults out of the system initially. Quality is essentially about limiting the cost of failure: 'when a product fails, you must replace it or fix it. In either case, you must track it, and apologise for it. The losses are much greater than the costs of manufacturing; none will recover your reputation, leading to the loss of market share' (Taguchi and Clausing, 1990). Similarly, with environmental quality, it will be most costly to pay for clean-up and fines after a spillage or a leak, for example (assuming regulatory frameworks operate effectively). It will be less expensive to use pollution abatement technology to minimise any pollution that is produced. The most effective solution would be to eliminate the risk of problems occurring by designing those problems out of the system in the first place. In terms of market image, any business process that is inherently wasteful, risky or controversial could be argued to be poor quality, by definition.

Taking a process view, and considering the supply network (Figure 14.3), it can be argued that as a company uses inputs from suppliers to produce outputs for its customers it will pollute the three environmental media of land, water and air. This apparently obvious analysis is in fact the practical basis for an assessment of the environmental impact caused by a company or its supply chain, and is reflected in the legislation with which firms must comply. The management system needs to address each of these stages, by translating customer requirements back up to suppliers, and by combining with the various functions and other parties within the extended organisation (i.e. including suppliers and customers where appropriate) to manage the inputs and control the outputs. A purchasing and supply environmental strategy might start with putting details of the company's situation onto such a map.

This view of environmental management fits well with the concept of 'lean'. If a lean enterprise seeks to produce goods and services using significantly lower levels of input (materials, time, labour, space) and avoiding all forms of waste, it is likely to adopt the principles of environmentally sound supply easily: the elimination of all costs incurred that do not add competitive value to a product.

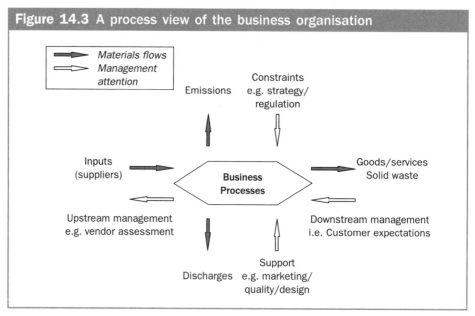

Figure 14.3 A process view of the business organisation

Source: Lamming and Hampson (1996)

Secondary principles include the reduction of waste, utilisation of space, the elimination of inventories, and the integration of quality control within the production process (Warhurst, 1994). The same principles can be applied to supply relationships and networks in lean supply (Lamming, 1993). If organisations are to produce greater product value from fewer resources, and with less waste (the 'more from less' approach: Hindle, White and Minion, 1993) then environmental management is an integral part of this – the use of fewer natural resources should be a key aim of environmental strategies.

Rather than concentrating on pollution control and clean-up, therefore, Purchasing and Supply managers could encourage their suppliers to examine the potential for pollution avoidance, which is ultimately related to improved resource productivity, and understanding the opportunity costs of pollution. In this sense, recycling, although commonly understood as a 'green' activity, is an 'end-of-pipe' solution, in that it deals with pollution and waste only after it has been produced. When one considers that all 'waste' was once bought into the company as an asset (or part of one), it becomes logical to think about minimising the amount of waste produced. Once one starts thinking this way, it is useful to consider a hierarchy of five main levels of approach (see Figure 14.4), each of which provides opportunities to improve process efficiency and product value:

- reducing the total amount of resource (materials, energy, etc.) used in the production and use of a unit of service or goods;
- the extension of the life of that unit;
- the reduction of the unwanted side effects of the unit throughout its life, including pollution and waste;
- reuse, recycling or incineration with energy recovery at the end of a product's normal useful life, instead of disposal to landfill. At this point it is useful to make the distinction between closed-loop and open-loop supply chains. The 'ideal' closed-loop supply chain would be one in which all material was recycled, remanufactured or reused without the introduction of any 'virgin' materials. Although completely closed loops are very hard to achieve in practice, many companies are using reverse logistics to recover end-of-life products, saving both costs and the environment.

Figure 14.4 The waste hierarchy

Source: Lamming and Hampson (1996)

It is important to retain a market focus in dealing with environmental management. Traditionally, 'green' products have sold on the basis of what they do not contain, as opposed to what they do. Frequently, this resulted in a loss of functionality (and therefore value to the consumer) of the product, i.e. 'less from less'. The 'more from less' approach can only be realised if the improved product sells in place of its less environmentally sound competitors. If it does not, the improvements will have been made in vain (Hindle et al., 1993).

Strategy for minimising impacts

A key aim of supply management is to minimise the costs and non-value-adding activities associated with each stage of the chain, while increasing the value-added, with a primary focus on achieving profit for the organisation from satisfying the end user. In environmental terms, there appears to be a clear link between supply chain management and product stewardship (Figure 14.5). This concept illustrates that the extent of a company's influence lies well beyond the traditional boundaries of a firm: it includes the environmental impacts of goods upstream and downstream in the supply chain, from raw materials extraction to end-of-life disposal. To understand the full impact of products throughout their whole life cycles, therefore, proactive companies need to examine not only their own processes, but also those along the full chain of materials sourcing, production, distribution and use (Smart, 1992).

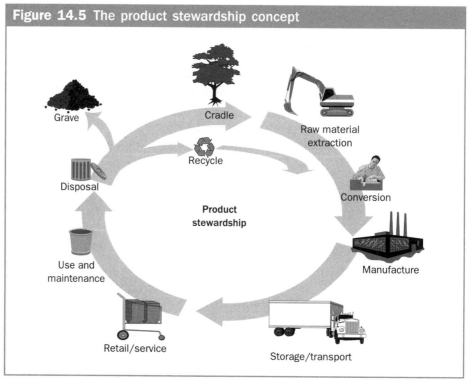

Figure 14.5 The product stewardship concept

Source: Lamming and Hampson (1996)

Suppliers need to be drawn into the process of environmental improvement if an organisation is to make substantial improvements in the environmental performance of its products and processes. Suppliers' own sourcing decisions and activities determine the nature of the inputs into a system, and are also integral to the competitive survival of the organisation in the business environment.

In some respects, the 'polluter pays' principle – a fundamental driver behind much environmental legislation – is a misnomer. If the polluter is not caught, then 'society' pays, in the form of external costs. If the polluter is a supplier, and is caught and fined, then additional costs may be passed along down the chain to the customer, who is, in effect, paying for that supplier's poor environmental management, i.e. buying at prices that reflect the cost of production and waste (Burt and Los, 1995). This will also be the case even if the supplier is complying with legislation, but is still producing unnecessary waste.

The challenge, then, is to urge suppliers to improve their environmental performance at each stage of the supply chain, through implementing the appropriate features of the waste hierarchy at each stage. Some of the key areas (Burt and Los, 1995) to address in this process include:

- customer specification;
- quality requirements;
- interface waste due to distance, and differing customer–supplier processes;
- company internal processing of materials: scrap, stock, and transport requirements;
- progression to the next processing/manufacturing firm in the value chain;
- post-consumption waste, not consumed by the end user.

With each of these, the aim should be to instil a philosophy of continuous improvement, without simply pushing particular environmental problems back to the previous stage in the supply chain – thus avoiding transference of the immediate risk of penalties, rather than an improvement in the overall environmental performance of a product. What would be the point, for example, of eliminating transport packaging, which as a result causes more damage or breakages to goods in transit? As we saw earlier, 'green' is not a fixed state – organisations can only become 'greener', and so companies should focus on the quality of supply as a whole (which will include environmental issues) rather than just the constituents of the product. Standards, legislation, expectations and competition will only become tighter and more stringent over time, so continuous improvement is the key to succeeding in this area of business. Many firms already have quality improvement programmes in place with their major suppliers, of which environmental management forms a part (see Bowen et al., 2001, 2002; Faruk et al., 2002).

Risks for Purchasing and Supply managers

Environmental issues pose a number of risks to Purchasing and Supply managers. Understanding these risks, and working with them, is an essential task for the supply manager who has to achieve environmental soundness. We outline a number of the risks below:

1 *Non-compliance with legislation/protocol.* Any non-compliance is likely to lead to company fines, the threat of imprisonment for directors, and potentially the loss of public and market place 'goodwill'. If suppliers are having problems with compliance, then it is likely that they are passing these costs down the chain to customers.

2 *Bought-in liability.* Customers must be confident that the goods, which they buy into their own processes, will not cause them to pollute once they are in use. This is related to the duty of care principle, which states that any company that produces, holds or is concerned with controlled waste (commercial or industrial) is responsible for its safe passage downstream through the supply chain. Contract cleaners, for example, may expose a company to duty of care legislation if they are responsible for disposing of some wastes.

3 *Security of supply.* This is perhaps the major issue which the environment poses for purchasing managers. Legislation will increasingly restrict the availability of certain key items. Types of available packaging may be one example. Another is that of the UK dry-cleaning industry in the 1980s, which, unaware of the impending ban on CFC manufacturing, proceeded with investment decisions in equipment which was dependent upon using those CFCs. As production capacity has declined subsequently because of the ban, so the price of CFCs has risen by over 800 per cent per litre. These companies also face the possible early obsolescence of that relatively new capital equipment (Business in the Environment, 1995). Similarly, the requirements of the Clean Air Acts have led some states in the USA to require the reformulation of gasoline to include more methanol. As a result, the anticipated increase in consumption has caused a tighter supply, and short- or medium-term price increases. Those companies with more secure sourcing arrangements might be expected to cope better during this period – before new production boosts capacity – than those with less foresight (Colby, 1995).

4 *Resource productivity.* As mentioned previously, the management of resources – and deriving the maximum possible value from the minimum input – is becoming increasingly important. Indeed, with the growth in global sourcing and the intensity of competition, it is no longer enough simply to own or have access to resources – the key is how they are managed, to get the most out of them (Porter and van der Linde, 1995). The opportunity cost of not maximising this, while competitors do so, may affect the cost performance of products in their end markets.

5 *Loss of competitive positioning.* Major industrial and corporate customers are increasingly asking questions of their suppliers as regards their environmental performance and, in some cases, how they assess their own suppliers' environmental performance. Those suppliers which can respond to these questions proactively, and demonstrate improved resource efficiency and cost effectiveness, will be able to realise some benefits vis-à-vis their competitive positioning.

Developing an environmental purchasing policy is therefore not about buying 'green' goods, with sub-standard performance, to be socially responsible: it is about working to minimise a growing strategic business concern, simultaneously reducing costs and improving added value.

Implementation issues

There is a range of implementation issues that a Supply Strategist must consider when thinking about environmental and ethical issues. We discuss the major hurdles to successful green supply management in this section.

Measuring environmental effectiveness

For environmentally sound purchasing to be achieved it becomes necessary to develop techniques for measuring the purchasing function on its performance in meeting these objectives. As the nature of purchasing changes, so what constitutes good performance in purchasing must also be redefined. This issue must be considered in the light of the wider debate on performance measurement in purchasing (see Chapter 11).

An environmental purchasing policy must be supported by open, credible, stated measurements which reflect the goals of that policy: otherwise, it will become side-lined. There appear to be many companies that claim to have implemented an environmental purchasing policy, but which have actually achieved little in terms of improvements, because measurements have not been put in place against which buyers may be assessed. For example, it is pointless to state that the company will buy only from suppliers that can demonstrate that they have made significant steps towards addressing their own environmental performance, if the prevailing measurement system simply assesses purchasing on the amount of savings made compared to the previous period.[13] In addressing these issues, the longer-term competitive implications (such as total cost of ownership, quality improvements and continuity of supply), with which environmental improvements might be associated, need to be considered. As such, the development of an effective performance measurement system that reflects the environmental priorities (derived from top-level strategy) requires a shift in management attitude.

Companies can measure environmental performance on many levels. The most basic of these might be on the number of incidents or prosecutions faced by the company over time, as most companies which publish environmental reports disclose. However, such measures can be deceptive. More sophisticated systems include progress against corporate goals, improvements against environmental audit results, waste tracking, etc., and develop a balance between process and results-based measures.

Supplier assessment

Life cycle inventory (White, 1996: 65) is potentially one tool which could enable Buyers or Purchasing managers to build an 'impact profile' for suppliers, forming a baseline for assessing their future performance. Another method, used by the British DIY retailer B&Q, is based on the management practices of suppliers. The practices reviewed are translated into buyers' appraisals, and may ultimately affect their bonuses. Once a general profile of the key actors in the supply base has been constructed, however, appropriate actions need to be in place for dealing with the information received: there is little point in investing time in setting up such an activity if plans for what to do with the information do not exist.[14]

A useful exercise would be to analyse all of the sources of supply, integrating environmental concerns with regular commercial analysis. One approach to this might be to develop existing supply management tools to incorporate environmental considerations. For example, as we have seen earlier, Kraljic's supply positioning matrix adopts a portfolio approach to the market, traditionally based on a classification of products according to:

- the value added by product line, the percentage of purchased items in total costs, and their impact on profitability; and
- the complexity of the market, depending on scarcity of supply, the pace of technology, materials substitution, and monopoly or oligopoly conditions.

This might be extended to add a 'third dimension' for environmental costs in each sector (see Figure 14.6).

Issues to consider in using this matrix, with which most Purchasing managers have been familiar for many years, would typically include the supplier's capacity utilisation and flexibility, past variations in capacity utilisation, the uniqueness of the product, volumes purchased and their expected demand, levels of technology, quality history and organisational culture. The consideration of environmental issues (derived from an analysis of internal and external stakeholder concerns and requirements) may well cause some suppliers to be positioned in different areas of the grid, according to the strategic impact of the environmental issue. For

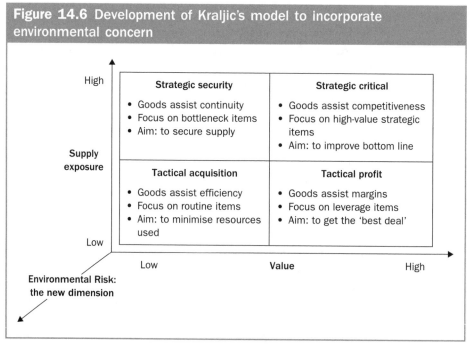

Figure 14.6 Development of Kraljic's model to incorporate environmental concern

Source: Lamming and Hampson (1996)

example, in the case of the dry-cleaning industry mentioned above, CFC suppliers may have moved from the Tactical Acquisition box to the Strategic Critical box, and would therefore require buyers to deal with such suppliers in an entirely different manner from that to which they were accustomed.

Strategy and senior management commitment

As with most management initiatives, the need for a senior management figure – a 'champion' – to promote the cause, both within the organisation and to customers and suppliers, is vital to the long-term success of pursuing environmental soundness in supply chains. It appears that this is not always the case: a survey in the mid-1990s showed that although most UK environmental managers claim to have board-level approval for their work, 74 per cent cite the lack of senior management commitment as the key obstacle in their work (ENDS 241, 1995). This issue also relates to the importance attached to those factors which are measured; the prominence of such a senior manager will help to communicate the message that the initiative is important to the company, and worthy of senior management time. Environmentally sound sourcing decisions may initially give rise to increased costs, posing difficulties for departments assessed financially at a local level. This would be difficult for Purchasing to support as an initiative, without the endorsement of senior management.

Alignment between the purchasing and supply environmental strategy and the overall environmental goals of the organisation is clearly vital. Effective implementation requires that the environmental objectives be integrated with day-to-day activities, as part of overall business performance, rather than as a separate add-on.

As with any project that introduces something new into working practices, requiring a change in attitudes, it is important for the Purchasing and Supply manager to produce successful results in the short term. In this way, general confidence and credibility for the project and the concept may be created. The way to do this is to identify potentially successful pilot projects – small scale, with high visibility, and well supported, to 'harvest the low-hanging fruit'. Waste management practices provide many opportunities to remove costs, simply though corrective action. As discussed above, poor-quality products that do not work are a waste of resources, and vice versa. In an early case of this, improvement processes applied by packaging engineers at Xerox, to reduce the impact of supplier and product packaging, enabled the company to avoid 10,000 tonnes of waste, and save $14 million per year (Smart, 1992). One useful initial measure, as part of a waste audit, might be to compare the quantity of waste produced by the organisation with the purchase value of those wasted products (Biffa, 1994). This would not only highlight the cost savings potential of such initiatives internally, but also bring together disparate parts of the organisation, focusing not only on the symptoms (i.e. excess waste) but also on the causes.

Once the appropriate management and measurement system has been constructed and short-term improvements have been realised, it is important to use those results to communicate the performance to all stakeholders, including suppliers, based on their respective needs for information (as opposed to what Purchasing thinks those stakeholders want to know).

Summary

This chapter demonstrated why purchasing and supply professionals should be concerned about the environmental aspect of supply chain management. The chapter introduced and defined the concepts of sustainable development, green supply chains and environmental soundness. It outlined and reviewed purchasing and supply management's contribution to increasing environmental soundness. Lastly, the chapter identified and discussed several important implementation issues.

Environmental soundness in supply management may now be classed as an essential business requirement. Although the full effects of the various pressures may take some time to filter through to purchasing in some industries, in others it is already a mainstream issue. Companies that consider environmental issues (and, perhaps, related public image issues) to be 'strategic' will not wait for the repercussions of inactivity to have an effect – they will seek proactively for the potential impacts on their business and attempt to minimise the risk before it is fully manifested. There is no quick fix and there are still many uncertainties in the area. It is likely, however, that as with cars, which are sold on the merits of such technologies as side-impact bars, airbags, ABS brakes and other safety features, so sound environmental management will become a defining feature for the goods and services of modern companies. The competitive pressure that this market development may be expected to place upon firms will surely find its way rapidly to Purchasing and Supply managers.

Seminar questions

1. Why should purchasing and supply management be concerned with environmental and ethical supply issues?

2. Describe some of the ways purchasing and supply management can make a contribution to environmental soundness.

3. Describe a number of implementation issues that are important to 'green supply'.

References

Biffa Waste Services Ltd (1994) *Waste: A Game of Snakes and Ladders?* UK Report.

Bowen, F. E., Cousins, P. C., Lamming, R. C. and Faruk, A. C. (2001) 'The Role of Supply Management Capabilities in Green Supply', *Production and Operations Management*, Vol. 10 (2), Summer, pp. 174–90.

Bowen, F. E., Cousins, P. D., Lamming, R. C. and Faruk, A. C. (2002) 'Horses for Courses: Explaining the Gap between the Theory and Practice of Green Supply', *Greener Management (International Issue)*, Vol. 35, Autumn, pp. 41–60.

Burt, D. and Los, R. (1995) 'A Value Chain Approach to Pollution Avoidance', *Proceedings of the Strategic Supply Management Forum*, University of San Diego, September.

Business in the Environment (1995) Supply Chain: the Environmental Challenge, London.

Carter, J. R. and Narasimham, R. (1998) *Environmental Supply Chain Management,* CAPS, Tempe, AZ.

Colby, E. (1995) 'The Real Green Issue: Debunking the Myths of Environmental Management', *The McKinsey Quarterly,* Vol. 2, pp. 132–43.

Cramer, J. (1996) 'Experiences with Implementing Integrated Chain Management in Dutch Industry', *Business Strategy & the Environment,* Vol. 5, pp. 38–47.

Downs, A. (1973) 'Up and Down with Ecology: The Issue-Attention Cycle', in Bain, J. (ed.), *Environmental Decay: Economic Causes and Remedies,* Little, Brown and Company, Boston, MA.

Drumwright, M. (1994) 'Socially Responsible Organisational Buying: Environmental Concern as a non-Economic Buying Criterion', *Journal of Marketing,* Vol. 58, pp. 1–19.

ENDS (1994) Public Concern for the Environment Rides the Recession, *ENDS Report* 232, May.

ENDS (1995) Environmental Managers Call for Greater Support from the Boardroom, *ENDS Report* 241, Feb.

Faruk, A. C., Lamming, R. C., Cousins, P. D. and Bowen, F. E. (2002) 'Analysing, Mapping and Managing Environmental Impacts along Supply Chains', *Journal of Industrial Ecology,* Vol. 5 (2), pp. 13–36.

Jones, P. (1996) 'Producer Responsibility and Resource Recovery from Waste: The Grave', in Lamming, R. C., Warhurst, A. C. and Hampson, J. P. (eds) *Purchasing and the Environment: Problem or Opportunity?,* Chartered Institute of Purchasing and Supply, Stamford, UK.

Jones, P. (2004) *Mass Balance Movement,* Biffa Ltd.

Hindle, E., White, P. R. and Minion, K. (1993) 'Achieving Real Environmental Improvements Value Impact Assessment', *Long Range Planning,* Vol. 26 (3), pp. 36–48.

Knight, A. (1996) 'Driving Continuous Environmental Improvement: the Role of the Retailer', in Lamming, R. C., Warhurst, A. C. and Hampson, J. (eds), *The Environment and Purchasing: Problem or Opportunity?,* Chartered Institute of Purchasing and Supply, Stamford, UK.

Lamming, R. C. (1993) *Beyond Partnership: Strategies for Innovation and Lean Supply,* Prentice Hall, New York.

Lamming, R. C. and Hampson, J. P. (1996) 'The Environment as a Supply Chain Management Issue', *British Journal of Management,* **Special Issue,** Vol. 7, March, pp. 45–62.

Lamming, R. C., Faruk, A. C. and Cousins, P. D. (1999) 'Environmental Soundness: A Pragmatic Alternative to Expectations of Sustainable Development in Business Strategy', *Business Strategy and the Environment,* Vol. 8 (3), pp. 177–88.

Miller, J. and Szekely, F. (1995) 'What is Green?', *European Management Journal,* Vol. 13 (3), September, pp. 322–33.

Porter, M. and van der Linde, C. (1995) 'Green and Competitive: Ending the Stalemate', *Harvard Business Review,* Sept–Oct, pp. 120–34.

Schlosser, E. (2002) *Fast Food Nation,* Penguin Books, London.

Shrivastava, P. (1995) 'Environmental Technologies and Competitive Advantages', *Strategic Management Journal,* Vol. 16, pp. 183–200.

Smart, B. (1992) *Beyond Compliance,* World Resources Institute, USA.

Taguchi, G. and Clausing, D. (1990) 'Robust Quality', *Harvard Business Review*, Jan–Feb, pp. 65–75.

Walley, N. and Whitehead, B. (1994) 'It's Not Easy Being Green', *Harvard Business Review*, Vol. 72 (3), pp. 46–52.

Warhurst, A. C. (1994) 'The Limitations of Environmental Regulation in Mining', in Eggert, R. G. (ed.), *Mining and the Environment: Resources for the Future*, Washington, DC, pp. 133–72.

Welford, R. and Gouldson, A. (1993) *Environmental Management and Business Strategy*, Pitman, London.

White, P. (1996) 'Life Cycle Assessment: What Can it Tell the Buyer?', in Lamming, R. C., Warhurst, A. C. and Hampson, J. (eds), *The Environment and Purchasing: Problem or Opportunity?*, Chartered Institute of Purchasing and Supply, Stamford, UK.

World Commission on Environment and Development (WCED) (1987) *Our Common Future*, Oxford University Press, Oxford.

Further reading

Center for Advanced Purchasing Studies (2000) *Purchasing's Contribution to the Socially Responsible Supply Chain*, CAPS, Tempe, Arizona.

Center for Advanced Purchasing Studies (2000) *ISO 14000: Assessing its Impact on Corporate Effectiveness and Efficiency*, CAPS, Tempe, Arizona.

Hedstrom, G. and McLean, R. (1993) *Six Imperatives for Excellence in Environmental Management*, PRISM: Arthur D. Little, New York.

Lamming, R. C., Cousins, P. D. and Notman, D. (1996) 'Beyond Vendor Assessment: Relationship Assessment Programme', *European Journal of Purchasing and Supply Management*, Vol. 2 (4), pp. 173–81.

OECD (2002) *Corporate Social Responsibility: Partners for Progress*, The Brookings Institute, Washington, DC.

Roy, R. and Wheelan, R. (1992) 'Successful Recycling Through Value Chain Collaboration', *Long Range Planning*, Vol. 25 (4), pp. 62–71.

White, P. R. (1995) 'Environmental Management in an International Consumer Goods Company', *Resources, Conservation and Recycling*, Vol. 14, pp. 171–84.

Useful sites

http://www.ethicaltrade.org/

http://www.ends.co.uk/

http://www.american.edu/TED/ice/

http://worldpolicy.org/

http://www.iso-14001.org.uk/

http://www.bsi.org.uk/Education/Enquiries/LeafletPdf/ISO14000DV.pdf

http://www.greensupply.org.uk/escf.htm

http://www.eea.eu.int

http://www.societyandbusiness.gov.uk/

Endnotes

1. The authors would like to thank Jon Hampson of Cap Gemini Ernst and Young for his important contribution to this chapter.
2. In this chapter 'environmental' refers to the 'natural environment' rather than the 'business environment'
3. 'Gap and Nike: no sweat?', BBC *Panorama*, 14 October 2000.
4. But see also http://www.eti.org.uk/ for a discussion on the definitions of child labour.
5. In 2000, British cattle herds were culled of animals infected with the disease Bovine Spongiform Encephalopathy (BSE, or 'mad cow disease'). Consumption of contaminated meat from BSE-infected animals was associated with the fatal and untreatable human condition new variant Creutzfeldt Jacob Disease (CJD). The spread of BSE within herds was traced to contaminated bone meal (from infected animals) added to livestock feed.
6. See, for example, http://www.fairtrade.org.uk/ or http://www.cafedirect.co.uk/our_business/fairtrade/ifat/ for a discussion and more information on the supply chain for coffee and the efforts made to reduce social impacts of the processes involved.
7. For more on this topic, see www.singleplanetliving.com
8. European Community Directives: the Waste Electrical and Electronic Equipment Directive (or WEEE) and the Restriction of the Use of Certain Hazardous Substances in Electrical and Electronic Equipment Directive (or ROHS) came into force on 13 February 2003 and Member States had to turn them into law by 13 August 2004. The main producer responsibilities came into effect in August 2005. The WEEE Directive is about collecting, treating, recycling, and recovering waste electrical and electronic equipment. It explicitly recognises that manufacturers have some responsibility for this.
9. For a comprehensive discussion on the subject of corporate responsibility, see Harvard Business Review: *HBR on Corporate Responsibility* (September 2003) Harvard Business School Press ISBN: 1491392748
10. For a full review of the Brundtland Report and many other topics, see The Encyclopaedia of the Atmospheric Environment on http://www.doc.mmu.ac.uk/aric/eae/Sustainability/Older/Brundtland_Report.html
11. See detailed discussion of value adding activities (VA) versus non-value adding activities (NVA) in Section 4.1.
12. This is the purpose of the environmental quality management systems: BS 7750, the Environmental Management & Audit Scheme (EMAS), and ISO 14000. All of these systems are based on the principle of continuous improvement.
13. Green measures should therefore be built into both supplier selection (see Chapter 5) and performance measurement (see Chapter 11).
14. The leading UK hardware and garden equipment retailer, B&Q, has extensive information about its Social Responsibility policies on its site at http://www.diy.com/bq/templates/contentlookup.jhtml?content=%2Faboutbandq

Chapter 15

Involving suppliers in new product development

Aim of chapter

The aim of this chapter is to describe the key issues surrounding involvement of suppliers in the new product development process.

Learning outcomes

At the end of this chapter, readers will:

- understand issues in selection of suppliers;
- be aware of criteria for the extent and timing of supplier involvement;
- understand key managerial practices which enhance successful involvement outcomes.

Introduction

Today's business climate is all about change. The forces of globalisation, the growth in computing and communications technologies, and increasingly demanding customers and markets have made innovation increasingly central to firm competitiveness. The changes and challenges forcing firms to innovate may be summarised in an old African parable: 'Every morning, a gazelle wakes up knowing it must run faster than the fastest lion. Every morning a lion awakens knowing it must outrun the slowest gazelle. It doesn't matter if you are a lion or a gazelle – when the sun comes up you'd better be running.'

New product development (NPD) is a key source of competitive advantage for firms. Historically, many firms would have undertaken NPD in-house. However, today's business environment has meant that individual firms are often unable to undertake NPD initiatives alone, and instead have turned to other entities in their supply chain. Key drivers have been escalating R&D costs, increasing product complexity, reduced product life cycles, difficulties in managing technological change and the greater amount of resources and knowledge required to innovate. Other firms may also have experienced downsizing and have little choice but to outsource

Box 15.1 Supplier involvement at Delphi

'Bridge builder' are the words that Tom Miklik of Delphi Electronics and Safety (DES) uses to describe his job at DES' global supply management organisation (GSM). Miklik's duties as manager of advanced product development in the global supply management organisation are to work with Delphi engineers and suppliers to make sure Delphi gets the latest technology for the automotive systems that it builds for its OEM customers. Delphi designs and builds a number of high-tech systems for automakers, including keyless entry, theft protection and safety warning among others. Miklik must make sure suppliers not only provide a needed technology, but can support Delphi's requirements for capacity, delivery, quality and cost.

'What we try to do is build a bridge between the corporation and suppliers to address the technology needs that our engineering community has identified,' says Miklik. 'There are times when we need to have a supplier bridge the technology gap that we have.' To bridge that gap, Miklik spends a high percentage of his time with engineers at Delphi as well as with suppliers' engineers. His involvement with design occurs very early in the new product introduction cycle. Often his role is to find capable suppliers for new technologies as technology gaps are discovered between what Delphi needs and what its current supply base can provide. 'When we find a technology gap that needs bridging, I sit down with engineering and discuss it,' says Miklik. 'We ask: "Who do we know that can give us the technology we need?" Then we define expectations and I go out to suppliers along with the engineering.'

Engineering often tend to look at the technical advantages of a supplier. Miklik sees his job as having a more comprehensive perspective. 'Engineering often has the view: "I want the technology. I want to go in that direction." They don't have the whole organisational view of what that means to the company,' says Miklik. 'I bring in that commercial business piece.' A supplier may have a great technology, but may not be able to deliver in the volumes that Delphi needs or support it globally, or deliver on time with short lead-times. The bottom line is that suppliers must have the technology and still be competitive in their marketplace. 'For the most part, we direct engineering to suppliers who we have a history with and can deliver the technology that we need,' says Miklik. 'Suppliers need to bring enough to the party for us to leverage and help us be more competitive.'

Source: Abridged version of Carbone (2006)

a number of operations. Consequently, as key partners in the supply chain, suppliers are often one of the first ports of call in seeking to improve outcomes of NPD programmes. Involvement of suppliers earlier and more extensively in the NPD process has thus become increasingly commonplace. Box 15.1 illustrates the approach of Delphi Systems to early supplier involvement.

Various terms have been used to describe the practice, including early supplier involvement (ESI), supplier integration in new product development (SINPD), and collaborative product development (CPD). Recent experiences of firms across numerous industries, including automotive, health care, information technology and construction, have all reported NPD projects being significantly enhanced by supplier involvement, particularly early in the life cycle. Many firms are even outsourcing their research and development. For example, in North America and Europe it is not unusual for firms to outsource around 30 per cent of their R&D budgets (Roberts, 2001). Indeed, managing technology outsourcing may be becoming a core competence of the organisation – with some evidence suggesting that in-house NPD efforts actually increased R&D costs across 12 different industries (D'Aveni & Ravenscraft, 1994).

Decisions made early in the development cycle have a significant impact on quality, cycle time and cost of the product. Considering that 80 per cent of the product cost is committed by the time the product is designed, involving the Procurement function early has vast scope for adding value to the process. To quote Petersen, Handfield and Ragatz (2005), 'Unless you can impact sourcing early in the NPD process, you have almost no impact on the resulting design of the supply chain'. Involving Procurement in the process does not mean squeezing supplier margins, which in any case is eventually a zero-sum game that does not enhance revenue for either buyer or supplier. Rather, Procurement can add real value by adding their knowledge of the supply market, selecting the right partner, and then managing the relationship.

Moreover, as the design proceeds, engineering changes become more difficult and expensive to make. This is illustrated in Figure 15.1. We see that at the start of the process there is a wide range of alternative possibilities for the product, with accompanying choice of sourcing options. As the design progresses and decisions on materials, technology and product specifications are made, any changes cost money and increase the time to reach the market. Thus, effective product management means involving all parties early, resolving conflict early, and through this achieving the consensus required to move the product quickly to market. For this reason, cross-functional teams, consisting of representatives from Marketing, R&D, Purchasing, Manufacturing, Sales, and increasingly suppliers, have become popular means of structuring the development project.

The processes associated with 'best practice' in supplier involvement in new product development have often been characterised by managers and researchers as a 'black box'. This chapter attempts to shed light on various aspects in managing ESI. We first look at the advantages and disadvantages of the practice, before

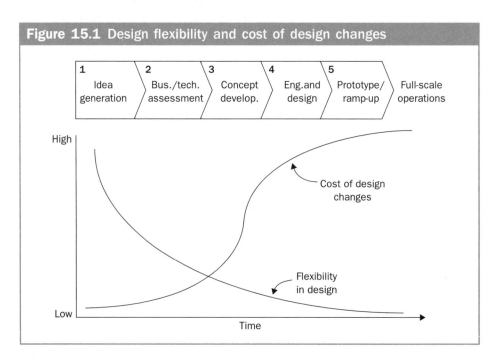

Figure 15.1 Design flexibility and cost of design changes

moving on to issues of timing of involvement, extent of involvement and effective practices for managing the relationship.

Advantages of ESI

Working with suppliers creates many benefits for the buyer. We examine two key categories of benefit: product related and organisation related. At the product level, early and extensive involvement of suppliers in the development process has been associated with improvements in the end product, as well as the development project. These benefits include:

- improved product quality;
- increased manufacturability of product;
- reduced cycle time (i.e. faster speed to market);
- reduced development costs;
- decreased product cost.

At the organisational level, ESI provides numerous strategic benefits. These include:

1 *Learning effects.* The buyer can leverage the investments made by the supplier in their area of core competence. Since the supplier is expert in their area, the buyer is able to gain economies of scale and scope in learning, without having to make the physical and time investments. For example, the supplier of a multinational furniture company has been integrated into product design: '. . . suppliers are involved right the way through and have a transparent vision of seeing what our internal design engineers are seeing'. The supplier has a member of staff who sits on the buyer's design team, attends design reviews and inputs into design changes as they happen. The result is that ESI has reduced lead-time for one component from 21 to 5 days.

2 *Access to new capabilities.* Particularly in fast-moving technology environments, working with suppliers provides access to new capabilities which the buyer could not ordinarily access. For example, a plastic injection moulding company were able to provide a large Australian automaker with new capabilities in plastics technology. The supplier demonstrated the benefits of stereolithography (which creates plastic prototypes based on a CAD system) in prototyping new designs. Lead-time on that component dropped from over 2 weeks to a handful of hours.

3 *Technology roadmapping.* Working closely with a supplier can provide access to the supplier's technology roadmap. The technology roadmap outlines the future directions for the supplier's product range. This advance knowledge can enable the buyer to plan and incorporate the supplier's technology more quickly into their own product architecture. Indeed, a close relationship can sometimes enable the buyer to influence the direction of the supplier's technology development efforts to benefit the buyer. Box 15.2 illustrates the process of developing a joint technology roadmap at Cisco Systems.

4 *Risk reduction.* ESI can help spread the risk of undertaking new product development. For example, many automakers have in place risk–reward sharing

Box 15.2 Developing joint technology roadmaps

It's not uncommon for electronics OEMs to involve purchasers in new product introduction when design engineers begin work on a new product. Cisco Systems, however, is taking purchasing involvement in design to a new level. Commodity managers are not only involved in new product introduction, they often influence what technology will be used before design on a new Cisco router, switch or other product begins. They work with engineers to determine which technology is the best fit for future networking products. For instance, commodity managers worked with engineering to determine when Cisco's switch from synchronous DRAM to double data-rate DRAMs should occur and which suppliers should be used. Commodity managers also helped determine Cisco's switch from ASICs made on .13 micron technology to 90 nm process technology, and are now monitoring when it makes sense to move to 65 nm technology.

Commodity managers also help determine which suppliers will be included in new product development efforts and carefully monitor technology roadmaps to make sure suppliers are investing in the technologies that Cisco will need in the future. Such up-front early involvement by commodity management in design is having far-reaching impact on Cisco's products and overall business, says John Kern, senior director for global supply commodity management. 'Engaging with engineering, understanding technology roadmaps and getting lined up with the right suppliers allows us to make the right decisions to meet the requirements for our products,' he says. 'At the same time, we can make decisions that really mitigate potential issues downstream. If you do a good job up front you have fewer quality issues, pricing-related problems and delivery problems. You can focus on prevention vs. chasing issues,' says Kern.

'One of the things we have learned over the years is that decisions made in sourcing at the design phase today have a big impact in the success of the supply chain. That's why we believe in partnering up front to make the right sourcing decisions,' says Kern. Commodities managers also spend a lot of effort on technology roadmaps. 'We have a consolidated roadmap for each one of our products. Of those products, from an architecture standpoint we try to reuse technology where we can. Other times we need to customise technology for that individual product set,' he says. 'From the suppliers' perspective, they also get a better understanding of our technology roadmaps and what we are looking for,' he says. 'They can align their investments with our technology investment so we get the technology when we need it when we launch the product.'

Source: abridged version of Carbone (2006)

arrangements with their strategic suppliers, which transfer much of the development risk for the component or sub-assembly to the supplier. Similarly, Dell seeks to reduce the risk of product failure by integrating suppliers at the design stage to maximise compatibility between components.

Disadvantages of ESI

Despite the numerous benefits outlined above, there are disadvantages to partnering with suppliers in new product development. A number of these key issues are outlined below:

1 *Early involvement is not always beneficial or appropriate.* In previous chapters we discussed how not every supplier need be a collaborative partner. In a similar vein, not every collaborative partner needs to be involved in product development. For example, it would make little sense for an automaker to involve the exhaust supplier early in the design process before the engine architecture had been stabilised.

2 *Loss of bargaining power.* Once the supplier has been 'locked in', they may lose incentive to deliver the 'best' project possible, as well as gaining a bargaining position in negotiations on price and other terms. Close partnerships are one means of guarding against the exercise of supplier opportunism, although buyers should remain mindful of the dependencies created in such relationships.

3 *Leakage of key information.* In many situations, the supplier may also trade with several of the buyer's competitors. Working closely with the supplier and exchanging sensitive technology or trade secrets runs the risk of leakage of information to competitors about future plans, product specifications or technical know-how. Care must be taken to manage these risks, including confidentiality agreements, appropriate monitoring and reporting structures, and physical security of documentation and prototypes. Numerous buyer firms have worked closely with suppliers to develop new products only to turn up to trade fairs to find the supplier selling an exact replica under their brand name!

4 *Financial burden on manufacturing.* Partnering is both a time-consuming and resource-intensive process. Moving to supplier involvement, without appropriate support for the functions affected, can be detrimental to their performance. In particular, ESI initiatives can place extra burden on the manufacturing department who may already be struggling to implement the latest manufacturing initiative or deal with outsourced production.

5 *Locked into wrong technological trajectory.* In fast-paced environments, choosing the right technology standard is critical. ESI means that the supplier's technology is incorporated into your product at an early stage of the design process. However, how do you know that the supplier's technology wave you are riding is going to be the one that reaches the shore? Many a product has failed because the technology has moved on by the time the product reaches the market. Where this is an issue, many firms use some form of 'postponement' to delay making technology selection decisions to as late as possible in the development cycle.

Selecting the right suppliers

Selecting the right supplier is critical to the success of the product and the future health of the firm. The supplier will typically be involved in both the design and volume production of the component or sub-assembly. Thus, decisions of supplier selection take on an added dimension – the supplier must be not only an effective design partner, but must also be able to ramp-up production smoothly to meet demand after product launch. The supplier selection criteria should reflect this requirement.

Although the specific weighting to be placed on each criterion may vary from company to company, at a minimum the supplier selection criteria should include assessments of:[1]

- design and engineering capability;
- willingness to be involved in design;
- cultural compatibility with the buyer;
- ability to meet development schedule;
- willingness to co-locate design/engineering personnel;
- willingness to share cost and production information.

Perhaps the key success factor in supplier selection is the technical and cultural alignment of the buyer and supplier. Each party must be clear on their respective roles and responsibilities, and commitment to the project. Without this common understanding it is difficult to reach agreement on key issues in development. At the micro level, it is important for the product development and commodity teams to work together effectively. Moreover, in long-term partnerships it would be important to consider not just current supplier capabilities, but also their potential future capabilities. Technology evolves and as such a peripheral supplier may become more important as time moves on.

The timing of supplier involvement

Once the supplier has been selected, the buyer faces the decision of when to involve the supplier. Figure 15.2 shows a simple linear representation of the new product development process, along with the different points at which suppliers may be involved. The actual process of product development is chaotic, iterative and messy, but the diagram does serve as a useful approximation.

The general rule for supplier involvement is that if supplier design expertise is strong and their potential impact on the final design high, then the earlier they should be included in the process. Suppliers of complex or critical items, systems or sub-assemblies and 'black box' suppliers would fall into this category. The management of these types of suppliers would be much more interactive, with frequent

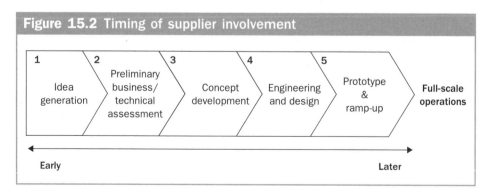

Figure 15.2 Timing of supplier involvement

face-to-face meetings and highly intensive information exchange. Such an approach is taken by a large Japanese computer maker with its supplier of microprocessors. Conversely, the simpler, less critical or standard the component, the more likely it is to involve suppliers late in the process. In this situation, the same Japanese computer maker would treat its suppliers of keyboards and mice in such a manner. Information systems are used to transfer demand forecasts and ordering information, rather than personal contact.

The extent of supplier involvement

A buyer also faces the decision of the appropriate extent or depth of supplier involvement in product development. Typically, the earlier the involvement, the more extensively the firm will rely on its supplier for development of a given component. Figure 15.3 illustrates the range of approaches available for supplier involvement, with supplier responsibility for design increasing from 'none' to 'black box'.

1 *No supplier involvement.* A traditional approach of tendering may be used in this situation, with the buyer providing set specifications to the supplier. This would be appropriate for routine, standard items, such as nuts and bolts.

2 *White box involvement.* The least complex of the approaches to supplier involvement. Suppliers are involved in a relatively *ad hoc* manner, with the buyer 'consulting' the supplier on their design. This may be appropriate where some customisation of parts is required for a given component.

3 *Grey box involvement.* Perhaps the most interesting, yet also the most difficult approach to manage, grey box involvement is the formal integration of the supplier into the buyer's NPD team. The buyer and supplier in this situation undertake joint design, prototype manufacture and testing. Consequently, high levels of trust must be present – along with practices such as co-location of staff, intensive knowledge transfer and richer interpersonal communication.

Figure 15.3 Extent of supplier involvement

None	'White box'	'Grey box'	'Black box'
No supplier involvement. Supplier 'makes to print'	Informal supplier integration. Buyer 'consults' with supplier on buyer's design	Formalised supplier integration. Joint development activity between buyer and supplier	Design is primarily supplier driven, based on buyer's performance specifications

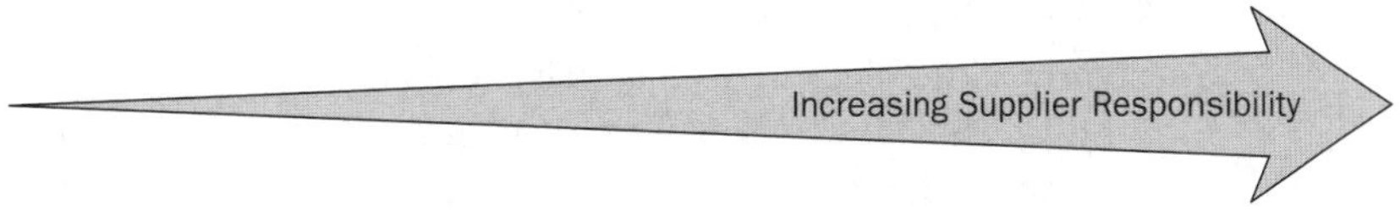

Increasing Supplier Responsibility

Box 15.3 ESI at Smart

In the case of the DaimlerChrysler SMART car plant in Hambach, for example, the product architecture is designed around an assembly consisting of five principal modules: the platform, the power train, the doors and roof, the electronics and the cockpit. The modular configuration of SMART extends to the organisation of the production plant where a small number of first-tier suppliers are integrated into the facility and take responsibility for their operations in final assembly. SMART supports the idea that the impact of modularisation increases collaboration in buyer–supplier relationships.

---

4 *Black box involvement.* Black box involvement is a highly effective approach to product development, when used effectively. The Japanese automakers have used this approach of shifting design responsibility to a trusted supplier to strong advantage over the years. In this situation, the buyer has little involvement in the activities of the supplier. The design directive is based on desired functionality and performance specifications – it is then up to the supplier how these objectives are met. Unsurprisingly, high trust is a necessary element as the design process takes place out of sight of the buyer in a 'black box'.

Recent research by one of the authors (Howard and Squire, 2007) confirms this continuum approach. A survey of UK manufacturing firms found that product modularisation increased information sharing and collaboration in buyer–supplier relationships. In particular, collaboration helped reduce any interface constraints that arose during product design. This is further supported by the example of the SMART car (see Box 15.3).

Managing the involvement

Not only is the timing and extent of involvement important, we must also consider the *quality of the relationship* and *the way it is managed*. The effectiveness of the relationship is determined by a complex interaction of organisational and managerial processes. Some of the successful practices identified by the research include:

1 *Supplier selection procedures.* Selecting the right supplier (see section Selecting the right suppliers, p. 221) is key to a successful project.

2 *Degree of supplier responsibility for design.* As a general rule, the more supplier responsibility for design, the more effectively the goals of the design project are met.

3 *Communication processes between buyer/supplier.* Product development is inherently a knowledge-based activity. Effective communication between the engineers and technical staff of the buyer and seller is critical to transferring knowledge between the parties; combining and recombining each firm's knowledge base is what creates added value for the product or service.

4 *IP agreements*. The ownership and sharing of the risk and rewards from the joint development effort must be spelled out prior to commencement of the project. Who owns the IP? Who collects royalties?

5 *Alignment of buyer/supplier technologies*. Constructing a technology roadmap helps determine the future working potential of the two parties. Each party must ensure that their respective technology plans are aligned currently and into the future.

6 *Project team structures*. Organisational structure determines the environment in which the work will be carried out. Cross-functional teams have proved effective across numerous settings, beyond just product development. A team which draws on all relevant functions, including Purchasing, is able to speed products to market by compressing decision-making time and handovers.

7 *Supplier membership on project teams*. Recent research suggests that the single biggest determinant of ESI success is supplier membership on project teams. Often members of the buyer firm's team will not trust the supplier representative, at least not initially. For example, an engineer for a buyer firm we interviewed commented that '. . . there is no way I am going to share commercially sensitive information with them [the supplier] on our team. How do we know they won't turn around and use that information with our competitors?' Even so, by making conscious effort to build trust within the team, such obstacles can be overcome and superior performance achieved. Supplier membership enables information about the product's requirements to be transmitted directly back to the supplier, with the representative acting as a official liaison and champion for the project inside the supplier.

Summary

This chapter has overviewed the niche, yet rapidly emerging, area of supplier involvement in new product development. The majority of firms engage suppliers to some extent within their product development processes – yet with little knowledge of the key issues for consideration and most effective practices. We highlighted the advantages and disadvantages of supplier involvement, together with the key decisions of when to involve, and degree of responsibility to be awarded to suppliers. We concluded with a number of key managerial practices that are associated with ESI success.

Seminar questions

1. Identify the main drivers of the trend toward collaborative new product development. What benefits might buyers expect to gain from this approach?

2. What do you consider to be the key factors that are commonly used to promote supplier innovation?

3. Make suggestions as to when different approaches to supplier design involvement (e.g. white box, grey box, black box) would be most appropriate.

References

Carbone, J. (2006) 'Delphi Builds Bridger to Designers & Suppliers', *Purchasing Magazine Online* (www.purchasing.com), 16 March.

D'Aveni, R. A. and Ravenscraft, D. J. (1994) 'Economics of Integration versus Bureaucracy Costs: Does Vertical Integration Improve Performance?', *Academy of Management Journal*, Vol. 37 (5), pp. 1167–206.

Howard, M. and Squire, B. (2007) 'Modularisation and the Impact on Supply Relationships', *International Journal of Operations and Production Management* forthcoming (2007).

Petersen, K. J., Handfield, R. B. and Ragatz, G. L. (2005) 'Supplier Integration into New Product Development: Coordinating Product, Process and Supply Chain Design', *Journal of Operations Management*, Vol. 23 (3–4), pp. 371–88.

Roberts, E. B. (2001) 'Benchmarking Global Strategic Management of Technology', *Research Technology Management*, Vol. 44 (2), pp. 25–36.

Endnotes

1. Each of these criteria can be incorporated into a selection model as exemplified in Chapter 5.

Chapter 16

Public and regulated supply management[1]

Aim of chapter

The purpose of this chapter is to describe the special nature of public procurement. The reader will gain an understanding of the development of European procurement regulations and be aware of how this regulation affects decision making and behaviour within the public sector.

Learning outcomes

At the end of this chapter, readers will:

- understand the special nature of public procurement;[2]
- know something of the historical development of the European procurement regulations, as an example of regulated supply management;
- understand the European Commission Procurement Directives and how they are applied;
- understand how regulation affects decision making and behaviour in public procurement;
- access links to information available publicly on this subject.

The context

In 2002, total public procurement in the EU, i.e. the purchases of goods, services and public works by governments and public utilities,[3] was estimated at about 16 per cent of the Union's GDP or €1500 bn. Its importance varies significantly between member states, ranging between 11 and 20 per cent of GDP. The opening up of public procurement within the internal market increased cross-border competition and improved prices paid by public authorities. There remains potential for significant further competition in procurement markets and for further savings for taxpayers (www.simap.europa.eu).

Introduction: the difference

Central and local government departments, from the Treasury to the local borough council, and other public sector organisations (such as health, defence, utilities, police and fire services and education), buy goods and services and work with money that is mainly generated from taxation. The fact that it is 'public' money makes a fundamental difference to all aspects of the ways in which it is spent and accounted for. Not surprisingly, public procurement has traditionally been seen as very different from its counterpart in private sector organisations. In recent years, the basis for this difference has been questioned and initiatives have been run by national governments to achieve 'value for money'[4] – attempting to instil a more business-like attitude into those spending public funds.

Nevertheless, the combination of public scrutiny over sourcing decisions (including a sometimes mischievous press and the partially informed 'barrack-room lawyer') and the need to provide services to an insatiable client base (can publicly provided health care *ever* be totally satisfactory?) leads to a situation in which public procurement has to operate in a different manner, and this is reflected both in its processes and in its organisation.

A further special aspect affects public procurement, born of the fact that the organisations do not have competitive markets in which to operate. For a private sector firm, competitive pressures are translated and transmitted to its purchasing and supply management activities as demands for cost reductions, timeliness and innovative solutions to next-customer requirements. For a public body (say, a government department) there is no equivalent pressure. In lieu of competition, therefore, public procurement employs regulation – stipulated performance requirements (including budgets) that put pressure onto the operating unit to be efficient. Regulation may take the form of pricing policies (as in the case of the privatised utilities who have, in effect, monopolistic or oligopolistic positions), budgetary constraints (typically used in central funding to local government) and stipulated procedures to be followed (in pursuit of efficient supply markets). It is not certain that regulation can have the same impact as competition in practice but it is the established approach for putting pressure on public sector organisations to perform.

Thus, while any or all of the principles and concepts covered elsewhere in this book can be applied within public procurement, it is worth dedicating a chapter to its special nature.

What is public?

Countries vary in their preferences for public ownership of national infrastructure and services. For example, from 1945 until the late 1970s in the UK, the telephone, health, gas, electricity, water, rail, bus and coal industries were publicly owned – administered either by civil servants or by managers characterised as having a public sector 'mentality'. Such public services are called 'utilities'. In addition to the utilities, there were other organisations, such as parts of the automotive manufacturing industry and the national airline, that were in public ownership, for a variety of historical reasons. Since that time, European governments, often led by a post-Thatcher UK, have gradually transferred utilities from public to private ownership, on the basis that managers motivated by shareholder pressure and the profit principle will run a more efficient operation. This was further fuelled by the rise in standards of living since the Second World War, leading to labour costs that were not affordable if inefficiency was to be tolerated. Keynes' principle of spending public money to provide jobs and thus lower unemployment was seen by many as no longer tenable by the 1980s.

Whether or not this 'privatisation' was a good idea is not to be discussed here. Suffice it to say that many countries have followed this path. Gradually, the parts of everyday life that are serviced by government-run organisations have become fewer – with consumer choice steadily increasing. Meanwhile, public debates rage about the amounts of personal fortune made by private individuals and foreign speculators, and media exposés reveal examples of poor service or wasteful practices.

Coupled with the move towards privatisation during the 1980s were centrally led drives to outsource activities in all types of public sector organisations. Local councils were required to test markets for easily specifiable services (such as street cleaning), transferring employees from council employment to the successful contractors that won the competitive tendering, or bidding, exercise.[5] The same activity ('compulsory competitive tendering') took place within central government, with building maintenance ('facilities management' or FM), security, transport and information systems being favourite candidates for outsourcing. At central government level in the UK information systems were outsourced by individual departments apparently without sufficient discussion. This led to a situation in which, by the mid-1990s, over two-thirds of central government information systems were under the control of one – North American – private sector contractor. Furthermore, regulation meant that the same contractor could not be prevented from bidding for – and winning – further contracts.

For European countries, this change in the ways services are procured by public sector organisations happened at a time when the focus for economic activity was moving from national to regional. The European Union had been developing for almost half a century by the time the efficiency drives took a hold and the result was that competitive tendering for services was met with bids from contractors outside the usual area of activity for the procurer. For example, an early outsourcing exercise for the street-cleaning services in the East Sussex town of Brighton resulted in a Spanish firm being awarded the business. The furore in the local press ranged from the puerile to the xenophobic. Local politicians, mindful of their need to gain votes, must have had a dreadful time. They had no choice, however, as the processes that governed the procurement were now in place at the European level and failure to comply could mean not only loss of office but possible personal disaster. We shall explore this further, later in this chapter.

So, public sector procurement is driven by the need for efficiency, 'value for money' or 'best value',[6] public scrutiny, national and regional regulation and legislation, and political expediency: clearly, a complex matter. There is a further level of influence – members of the World Trade Organization (WTO – previously GATT, the General Agreement on Tariffs and Trade) have a 'Government Purchasing Agreement' (the GPA, signed in Marrakesh in April 1994) that applies to a growing list of major spending public bodies (e.g. central and regional government offices, museums, national health services); in effect, this simply draws the constraints of regional (e.g. EU) regulation tighter for such bodies.

In order to illustrate these principles we shall use one example: the European Commission's Procurement Directives and the manner in which they are introduced into national law. It would not be possible to cover all countries in the world here but similar situations do exist. For example, the NAFTA (the North American Free Trade Agreement) applies similar conditions to public purchasers in Canada, the USA, Mexico and the countries of the Caribbean – although the process of adoption lags that in Europe.[7]

Why is the European Union relevant to UK public procurement?

The European Union exists to support political and economic peace and development in the region. There is a constant debate over which of these two aspects is the more important. Fundamental to both is the notion of a single (or 'common') market for goods and services.[8] The Treaty of Rome, upon which the European Union is built, contains several clauses dedicated to encouraging free competition (especially Articles 85 and 86) – equally applicable to private or public sector organisations. In the public sector, these have been translated into nationally enforced regulations, via European Commission Directives[9] which require those spending taxpayers' money to do so within certain formal procedures. There are two basic purposes behind the procurement Directives:

- to ensure that those spending significant amounts of public funds explore the whole of the single market and thus have the best chance of getting value for money;

- to ensure that firms in member states throughout the EU get the chance of bidding for business throughout the whole market.

The Directives are translated into Regulations at the national level and voted into law under national legal systems.

What is a 'significant' level of spend?

The procedures that must be followed may be seen as unreasonably burdensome for small purchases. Therefore, when someone in a public sector organisation needs to spend public money on provision of goods or services (including construction work), it is important to establish whether or not the amount is significant in the context of the EU principles and purposes. This is done by the setting of 'thresholds' – financial levels above which the expenditure is deemed to be significant. In the jargon of public procurement, the contract under consideration is said to be 'caught' if it is above the threshold.

The thresholds are set in euros and translated into national currencies when the directive is adopted into national law. However, for purposes of global dealing, a platform for agreeing fixed exchange rates is necessary, to allow planning and audit to have some stability. The unit employed by the global financial community for these purposes is called 'Special Drawing Rights' or SDR. Originally exchange rates against the SDR were fixed for a year but now they are set each day. For example, on 19 July 2006 the euro was worth .8515SDR, and £1 was 1.24722SDR.[10] Changes made to the EC Directives in 2005 mean that, in practice, most users of the system no longer need to be concerned with SDRs.

It should be noted that although the Directives apply to all qualifying contracts above the respective thresholds, the Treaty principles of 'No discrimination on the grounds of nationality, equal treatment of potential bidders, proportionality, mutual recognition and transparency' apply to all purchases by the public sector, including below-threshold purchases and contracts outside the full scope of the Directives, such as Category 'B' services and concession contracts.

The EC Directives and UK Contracts Regulations

Note: Details below are correct at the time of writing this book (summer 2006) but the Directives are modified from time to time and the financial data are bound to change. While the principles and purposes may be assumed to remain, therefore, it is essential to check the up-to-date information in studying or using this chapter in practice. This is relatively easy, however: the European Commission's services and UK government's Internet information are very comprehensive and useful web addresses are given in the endnote.[11] *The Official Journal of the European Union (OJEU)*[12] can be viewed simply by using any standard browser. See http://simap.europa.eu; the UK goverment's Office of Government Commerce (OGC) site is also very helpful (http://www.ogc.gov.uk).

Having committed themselves to non-discrimination against, and the freedom of movement for, individuals, firms and their goods and services, the member states of what was then the European Community (effectively the forerunner of the European Union) agreed on the first public procurement Directives (from the European Commission) in the early 1970s. In reviewing this development, the 1988 Atkins Report concluded that they had had little impact – with only between 2 and 5 per cent of public contracts being awarded to non-national firms or individuals. The Report showed that ECU 440bn was being spent on contracts by central and local government (representing 15 per cent of European GDP) while a further ECU 600–750bn (>20 per cent of GDP) was going into civil and defence spending.[13] The report advised that significant economic benefits must be available within such spending by increasing the degree of cross-border contracting. The later Cecchini report (1988) concurred, coining the phrase 'the cost of non-Europe' and going some way to quantifying it.[14]

Originally, the Directives were developed to guide public procurers in three separate types of contract:

- supplies: where items or materials are to be bought or leased;
- services: which may range from street cleaners to opera singers for public concerts;
- works: buildings, bridges, roads, etc.

To reflect the fact that utilities might be public or private (and indeed were being privatised at varying rates in the different EU countries), a special Directive was developed for what were initially called 'the excluded sectors'. The logic behind this special 'Utilities Directive' (which was to cover all three of the contract types) was that privatised public service organisations (e.g. British Telecom) had to compete with established private companies and should be less constrained in their procurement than government organisations. This easing was generally achieved by setting thresholds higher (i.e. so that less of their procurement would need to follow the burdensome procedures and fewer of the contracts they put out for tender would be 'caught').

In addition to these, two further Directives were developed – to deal with enforcement of the requirements. These were called 'Compliance' and 'Remedies'. The procurement Directives were also linked to other, more general Directives (for example, the Public Services Directive 2004/18/EC).

As the Directives were developed and released at various times over a period of 30 years they became 'messy' – increasingly complicated as they tried to accommodate complex political and economic pressures while the European Union itself grew.

In March 2004, the EU adopted two new public procurement Directives: one for the public sector (2004/18/EC) and one for utilities (2004/17/EC). This was followed in 2005 by a long-awaited major revision to the complex arrangements of the Directives (Commission Regulation 1564/2005, 7 September 2005), passing into law in the UK in January 2006 as public regulations (with a separate enactment for Scottish law). Thus, the regulations based upon Supplies, Services and Works Directives were replaced with the 2006 Public Contracts Regulations and the Utilities Directives by the 2006 Utilities Contract Regulations. The next stage is a review of the Remedies Directives. Draft proposals have been issued by the Commission and, at the time of writing, these are currently being reviewed by the member states. The legal niceties of remedies and compliance were integrated into the two documents.

The essential elements of these Regulations require those spending public money to:

- invoke competition for purchases over a certain value by requiring the purchaser to place an advert in the *OJEU*;
- allow specified periods of time for contractors throughout the EU to tender if they wish to bid for the contract;
- ensure that tenders are evaluated in an open, fair and transparent way;
- provide an opportunity, through an accelerated debriefing process, for all bidders to challenge an award decision before the award is made;
- require the purchasing organisation to publicise details of the contract awarded (also through the *OJEU*).

Some of the new features of the 2006 Regulations also encourage purchasers to utilise electronic commerce technologies, where they can be used to speed up processes.

For most public sector bodies, the regulations catch contracts exceeding €211,000 (or £144,371) for the provision of goods and services (bought, leased or hired) and above €5,278,000 (or £3,611,319) for works (such as new buildings, bridges, roads, etc.) For public sector bodies covered by the WTO GPA (including central government departments and the Health Service), however, the thresholds are lower – or tighter – at €137,000 (or £93,738). This extra constraint reflects the commitment the WTO countries have for making the GPA work. For utilities, the threshold is less strict, at €288,741, once again recognising the need to let newly privatised organisations a little off the hook. The rates at January 2006 are shown in Tables 16.1 and 16.2.

'Prior Indicative Notices' (generally known as PINs) are issued by public sector bodies when they wish to give advance notice to the market of future requirements. The issue of PINS is not mandatory, but if a qualifying PIN is issued purchasers have the facility to reduce contracting time scales. For this reason, PINS may be issued for all contracts above the relevant thresholds.

Table 16.1 Thresholds from 31 January 2006

	Supplies	Services	Works
Entities listed in Schedule 1[1]	£93,738 (€137,000)	£93,738[2] (€137,000)	£3,611,319[3] (€5,278,000)
Other public sector contracting authorities	£144,371 (€211,000)	£144,371 (€211,000)	£3,611,319[3] (€5,278,000)
Indicative Notices	£513,166 (€750,000)	£513,166 (€750,000)	£3,611,319[3] (€5,278,000)
Small lots	£54,738 (€80,000)	£54,738 (€80,000)	£684,221 (€1,000,000)

Source: http://www.ogc.gov.uk/index

[1] Schedule 1 of the Public Contracts Regulations 2006 lists central government bodies subject to the WTO GPA. These thresholds will also apply to any successor bodies

[2] With the exception of the following services, which have a threshold of £144,371 (€211,000)

- Part B (residual) services
- Research & development services (Category 8)
- The following telecommunications services in Category 5
    - CPC 7524 – Television and radio broadcast services
    - CPC 7525 – Interconnection services
    - CPC 7526 – Integrated telecommunications services
- Subsidised services contracts under regulation 34

[3] Including subsidised services contracts under regulation 34

Table 16.2 Thresholds: Utilities sectors from 31 January 2006

	Supplies	Services	Works
All sectors	£288,741 (€422,000)	£288,741 (€422,000)	£3,611,319 (€5,278,000)
Indicative Notices	£513,166 (€750,000)	£513,166 (€750,000)	£3,611,319 (€5,278,000)
Small lots	£54,738 (€80,000)	£54,738 (€80,000)	£684,221 (€1,000,000)

Source: http://www.ogc.gov.uk/index

The regulations ensure that purchasers keep to the spirit of the Directive in their contracting. Some of the penalties for failing to use the procedures correctly can be very severe, including suspending or setting aside a contract awarded incorrectly and payment of damages. They are triggered by complaints against the award of contract – perhaps by an unsuccessful bidder who feels the process was not correctly followed (see below). To date, however, no contract has been set aside once it has been awarded.

Observing the thresholds

An obvious way of avoiding the need to use the procedures would be to break up a contract into several parts, each of which would be below the threshold. The Directives had foreseen this and contain a principle that addresses it. It is called 'aggregation'.

The rules of aggregation state that the thresholds apply to 'one-off' purchases and to a series of contracts with similar characteristics. Similar characteristics means 'Similar products and services, for a single or recurring need, available from the same or similar suppliers, bought in the same period and perhaps capable of being bought on the same contract'. If a set of purchases within an organisation could be said to reflect these conditions, then the Directive requires the purchaser to aggregate them into one contract, regardless of whether this takes the overall value above the threshold.

When estimating the value of contracts for threshold purposes purchasers are required to aggregate the value of all purchases/lots of a like type and if the total value of contracts to be let within laid-down timescales exceeds the thresholds then all contracts must be let in accordance with the rules even though individual contracts may be below the thresholds. The Directives provide some flexibility and allow small lots below specified values to be let outside the scope of the Directives providing the total value of these lots does not exceed 20 per cent of the total value.

It is worth noting here that the burden of proof lies with the purchaser. Put simply, this means that if the eventual value of a contract is above the threshold, it is assumed that the purchaser should have foreseen this and followed the procedures. If a purchaser has estimated the value of a contract to be below the threshold but all bids received exceed the threshold, both the UK government and the Commission have advised that the purchaser does not have to start the process again under the rules providing they can demonstrate due diligence in estimating the value of the contract and the contract has been let in accordance with the Treaty principles. The nature of evidence to show such diligence would clearly be complex! In practice, purchasers err on the side of caution, and use the procedures for any contract that has the smallest possibility of being caught.

But, is it fair to ask the organisation to aggregate similar purchases into one contract? Perhaps the parts of the organisation that require similar items are actually very separate entities. The Directives allow an organisation not to aggregate where it can show that the separate parts of the organisation are 'discrete operating units' or DOU. A DOU is defined as 'a part of a business which buys goods for its own purposes, has devolved authority to purchase those goods, and takes decisions independently.' (This has interesting implications for the choices made over the organisation of purchasing.)

Once again, if a complaint is raised about a contract, the burden of proof lies with the purchaser – to show that the un-aggregated contracts (which perhaps all fell below the threshold) were made by genuine DOUs.[15]

The procedures

As we have seen, the first part of the Directives is concerned with whether or not the contract in question is significant – driven by the overall goals of single market integration and value for taxpayers' money at the local or national level.

When the Directives began to be taken very seriously, in the late 1980s, a great deal of concern was expressed by public procurement officers. This had two main parts:

- that the stipulation of strict procedures would in some way compromise the 'professional' autonomy, skills and style of the purchasers;
- that the processes in the procedures would be cumbersome, time consuming and costly.

In practice, almost two decades after these concerns were common, it is broadly felt that, while they represented sound practice, the Directives have proven particularly time wasting and costly for the purchase of standard products and services; it was for this reason that time scales have been addressed in the new Directives. Public sector purchasers have taken on the procedures without major upsets and, in general, they appear to work well.

Within the Utility sector, it is possible for an organisation to have its in-house procedures inspected for compliance with the procedures so that, provided they are always followed, the organisation will be viewed as having followed the correct path. This process, originally contained in the Utilities Compliance Directive and not included in the Public Sector legislation, is called 'attestation'. It enables organisations to develop acceptable (and thus 'owned') procedures that make sense in local terms (and perhaps terminology) while also ensuring that the requirements of the Directives are met.

Whether or not the Directives have worked will be reviewed later. First, we must examine the procedures themselves. There are five sets of procedures and, having decided that a contract is 'caught', a purchaser must choose one of them to follow:

- open procedure;
- restricted procedure;
- competitive dialogue;
- negotiated procedure:
  a) without a call for competition (including urgency procedure);
  b) negotiated procedure with a call for competition;
- dynamic purchasing system.

In each case, the procedure stipulates how much time must be left for the market to respond between the key stages of the process: initial invitation to tender (ITT) – published in the *OJEU* for all contractors in the EU to see; closing date for tenders to be submitted; award of contract; notification of award (again, via the *OJEU*).[16]

Open procedure

In the open procedure (Figure 16.1), the ITT ('Notice') is submitted to the *OJEU* in an acceptable form; in particular, the process must not discriminate in favour of local suppliers. The *OJEU* is published electronically, daily, in all the languages of the EU. Its operating title is 'Tenders Direct' (see www.tendersdirect.co.uk).

The purchaser must then allow 52 days to pass before making the award of the contract. The purchaser can reduce this period, under the terms of the regulations, in various ways. For example, if an electronic contract notice is used, this period may be reduced by 7 days and by a further 5 days if all contract information is available electronically from the day the ITT is sent to the OJEU. Note that the basis of the additional reductions is the issue of a PIN. If a PIN is issued the period may be reduced further to 'generally not less than 36 days and in any event, not less than 22 days'. In practice, time scale reductions for use of PINs have become common practice. It is important to maintain the principle that, whatever time scale is used, purchasers must allow sufficient time for suppliers to bid.

In normal contracting, the purchaser may wish to discuss the tender with the bidder – either for clarification or to negotiate terms before deciding on the award. In a perfect situation, the tenderers will respond simply to the ITT and the award will be made without further ado. In practice, the ITT will need interpretation and, provided all parties are content that fairness has been maintained (i.e. all clarification is provided to all bidders before bids are made), this is considered normal practice. Under the Directives, queries by suppliers regarding clarification of the ITT before bids are received are allowed, as is clarification of bids after receipt (i.e. queries from purchaser to supplier). However, another common practice, changes to the bid after the closing date for receipt of tenders, via post-tender negotiation,

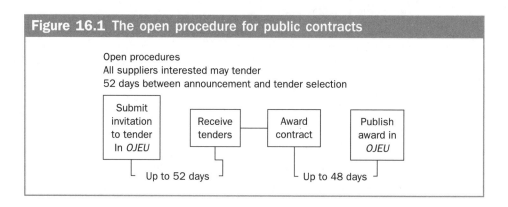

Figure 16.1 The open procedure for public contracts

Open procedures
All suppliers interested may tender
52 days between announcement and tender selection

Submit invitation to tender In *OJEU* → Receive tenders — Award contract — Publish award in *OJEU*

Up to 52 days   Up to 48 days

is not allowed under the open or restricted procedures. It is a complex subject (e.g. there are stipulations such as the time within which the purchaser must provide enquirers with information) and the websites identified in the endnotes may reveal examples of actual cases and formal rulings and advice.

Having made the decision to award a contract and selected the preferred bidder(s), the purchaser must comply with the requirements of the 'mandatory standstill period' and provide all bidders with details of their scores against the contract award criteria and the name and scores of the preferred bidder(s). They must then offer them an accelerated debrief within laid-down time scales. If, as a result of this debrief, a tenderer is not satisfied that the award has been made properly and in accordance with the rules, they may seek court action. In these circumstances the purchaser may not proceed to award the contract until any court actions are finalised.

With these provisos, having made the award, the purchaser may start the contract at any time after completion of the mandatory standstill period and place the award notice, including the actual value and the name of the successful contractor, in the *OJEU* within 48 days of that date.

In practice, a period of 52 days between sending out an ITT and placing the contract for complex purchases is not unusual even without such procedures. Thus, the Directives do not appear to delay the process for purchasers (one of the original worries). While the Directives do not lay down a format for an ITT, they do have standard notices for advertising the contracts and these have proved in practice helpful to some organisations whose established practices were improved as part of compliance. Lastly, since public money was concerned, the value and contractor identity would have been public knowledge in any case and it is always good practice to debrief unsuccessful bidders. All in all, then, the Directives could be said to have helped, rather than hindered, public purchasers. The 'downside' for the public sector,[17] however, lay in subtler aspects. They had now to advertise their requirements to all contractors across the EU, not just their local taxpayers' favourites (potentially a problem for vote-catching and local credibility) and the transparency of the contract was increased (they had to publish the details, not simply accede to requests for such information (perhaps sluggishly) from voters wanting to find out where their money was being spent, or contractors keen to know who had beaten them in a bidding process).

The one credible complaint about the open procedure is that, as all applicants that meet the purchaser's minimum standards must be invited to bid, large numbers of bids must be sought for some contracts, which can be expensive for both purchasers and suppliers. The advantage of the open procedure is that the contracting time scales are shorter than for the other procedures.

However, the open procedure is not suitable for contracts where the costs of bidding and assessment of bids are high unless there are only a few suppliers in the market. Thus, whereas using the open procedure (properly) should ensure that a purchaser is safe from subsequent attack, it may be preferable to opt for less open procedures, bearing the burden of justifying the restricted invitation. The Directives present a number of ways of doing this; the first is called the restricted procedure.

Restricted procedure

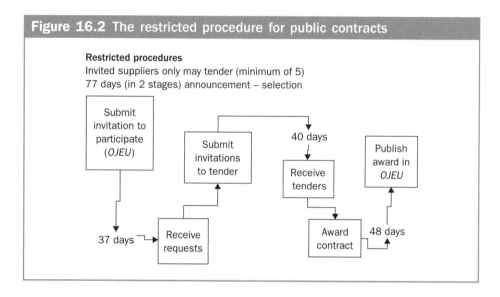

Figure 16.2 The restricted procedure for public contracts

Restricted procedures
Invited suppliers only may tender (minimum of 5)
77 days (in 2 stages) announcement – selection

The restricted procedure (Figure 16.2) allows the purchaser to short-list contractors that they deem competent and invite them to tender. Clearly, this compromises the basic tenet of the single market, so the procedure is designed to allow the purchaser to proceed carefully, to ensure fairness: in effect, the ITT is conducted in two stages. The first stage is an invitation to participate (ITP), published in the *OJEU*. This indicates the nature and scope of the contract that is envisaged and also the specific expectations and requirements of suppliers. These details are checked carefully before the ITP is raised as they must be seen as fair if subsequent complaints (and related delays) are to be avoided. There is a clear connection between this process and the idea of keeping a register of approved suppliers – a normal feature of supplier assessment schemes; logically, any approved supplier on such a list should be competent for a possible contract in their area of expertise. Unlike the Utility sector in which organisations may use lists of approved suppliers as a basis for selecting suppliers to bid, the public sector must issue a call for competition for every contract and can only consider suppliers that responded to a call for competition. Once again, the Commission has lengthy guidelines about this and cases and advice are given on the website.

Having invited participation, the purchaser must allow 37 days for suppliers to apply and provide the qualifying information requested. Ensuring that unsuccessful applicants are debriefed, the purchaser can now send the full ITT directly to the selected bidders and must wait a further 40 days before making the award. Once again, the purchaser is allowed to reduce this period, if a PIN has been issued or in a case of urgency, to 15 days (or 10 if the contract notice has been made via certain electronic means). As before, the details of the contract awarded must be published in the *OJEU* within 48 days.

Clearly, the restricted procedure will appear attractive to purchasers who want to ensure that they do not waste time dealing with incompetent contractors;

37 days is not long to wait to clear such potential problems away and this may be shortened (although the purchaser must justify their action if challenged). While the public sector may use either the open or restricted procedure without having to justify their decision, the reasons for refusing permission to tender must be 'water-tight' and there must be no possibility of interpreting them as, for example, a way of favouring local (or national) contractors. The previous Directive suggested only two reasons for using the restricted procedure: 'When there is a need to maintain a balance between contract value and procedural costs' or 'Because of the specific nature of the goods'. The 2006 Regulations have rather more comprehensive cover. Nevertheless, it still appears that the wording has been kept as loose as possible – and disputes will be left for national courts to resolve.

In practice, the restricted procedure is favoured for complex purchases because the purchaser may short-list the number of suppliers to a minimum of five, pro-viding five qualified applicants are available. The effect of this has been to subject purchasers' systems and processes to scrutiny, e.g. having your 'Preferred Supplier' list vetted, as part of attestation (as noted above, this is for Utilities only and not allowed in the public sector).

For more complex purchases, the purchaser may be unable to define their require-ments to a degree that suppliers may bid if the purchaser were to assess bids under the rules for open or restricted procedures. Purchasers may need to specify their requirements in output or performance terms or they may be genuinely unaware of the solutions the market can offer. In cases such as these, the Directives allow the use of the competitive dialogue and the negotiated procedure.

Competitive dialogue

This procedure may be used by the public sector when they cannot define their requirements in detailed terms or are not aware of what the market can offer in relation to their output requirements.

This is a two-stage process that is available to the public sector for complex purchases where the requirements are expressed in output terms. Under this pro-cedure there are three parts to the process. The first stage is similar to the first stage of the restricted procedure. A contract notice is issued in the *OJEU* and applicants are requested to provide the qualifying information requested by the purchaser. Based on this information the purchaser may short-list down to a minimum of three applicants to go forward to the bidding stage. For the award stage the process is divided into two parts. Part one is the dialogue stage and part two the bidding stage.

During part one the bidders put forward initial proposals or solutions based on the outputs specified by the purchaser. Dialogue may than take place with the indi-vidual bidders with the aim of agreeing solutions that meet the required outputs. The dialogue must take place on a confidential basis and must follow the rules relating to no discrimination and equal treatment.

During the dialogue stage the number of bidders may be reduced using the award criteria specified in the tender documents. Once several solutions are agreed, the process moves to the second part of the award procedure which is the final bid stage. Once the bids have been received they may be clarified and some fine-tuning may take place but no significant changes are allowed. The purchaser must then select a preferred bidder with whom they may agree other fine-tuning of the bid which may include changes to price but again the changes must not be significant.

The competitive dialogue procedure is not available to the Utility sector because they have the freedom to use the negotiated procedure with a call for competition without having to justify the use of this procedure.

Negotiated procedures

There are two negotiated procedures: one with a call for competition and one without a call for competition.

The rules in relation to the use of the negotiated procedure without a call for competition are very restrictive and apply to both the public and utility sectors. They include urgency for reasons not due to the purchaser or reasons which were unforeseeable by the purchaser, in other words urgency due to reasons outside the control of the purchaser. Other reasons include that contracts have been advertised under the open and restricted procedures and no responses have been received or that there is only one supplier available or the requirements are additions to existing contracts where to change suppliers would result in major technical problems.

The negotiated procedure with a call for competition (Figure 16.3) may be used by the public sector when they have advertised under the open and restricted procedures and received only non-compliant or unacceptable bids or when the purchaser is unable to define their requirements to the level that would allow them to award the contract under the rules applicable to the open and restricted procedures. The utility sector may use this procedure without having to justify its use.

Negotiated procedures require the purchaser to issue an ITT in the same way as for the other two cases, but it may be indicated that a contractor is already identified. The purchaser must allow 37 days for the contractors to respond and provide the qualifying information requested in the contract notice or the prequalification questionnaire (PQQ). The purchaser must select a minimum of three suppliers to go forward to the award stage. The Directives do not detail the

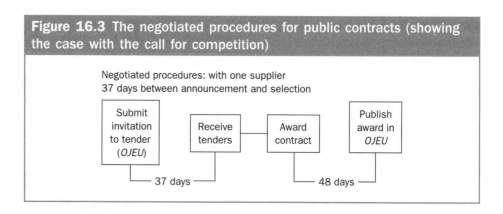

Figure 16.3 The negotiated procedures for public contracts (showing the case with the call for competition)

process or time scales for the award stage but in practice most purchasers require an initial bid on which to commence negotiations. The time scales allowed must be sufficient for the contractors to respond and the procedures must be non-discriminatory. The negotiations must not lead to significant changes from the originally advertised requirements to the level that would have affected suppliers that did not respond to the original notice or the manner in which applicants did respond.

The purchaser is not allowed to show preference for a specific contractor and must indicate that they are competitive in a general sense.

A special feature of the negotiated procedure is the permit it gives a public body to act in times of crisis (e.g. flood or major fire) when it would clearly be impossible to follow the requirement to wait before contracting with an organisation able to help.

Once again, the 2006 Regulations are rather more comprehensive on the conditions acceptable for using Negotiated Procedures. They still reflect the original advice of the previous Directives, which allowed purchasers to use negotiated procedures when open and restricted procedures do not result in good tenders (the purchaser would have to show very clear reasoning and audit trail to substantiate this); products are for research and development only (R&D is often treated as a special case in sourcing regulation); the source is unique (e.g. artistic or exclusive rights); additional deliveries by the existing supplier are warranted (for example, for spare parts to fit existing equipment, or extra items in the same range for which common spare parts are kept that would not fit other makes); or there is extreme urgency (but not of the purchaser's own making!).

Dynamic purchasing system (DPS)

This is a new, all-electronic procedure most suitable for the purchase of standard products. Under this procedure, purchasers may set up lists of suppliers who have responded to an open procedure notice which seeks suppliers to go onto the list. Qualifying procedures are laid down in the Directives and all suppliers that comply with the purchaser's qualification requirements must be included on the list. The lists must be open at all times for new suppliers to request to be included. When a purchaser wishes to place a contract under the system they must first place a second notice in the *OJEU* giving other suppliers the opportunity to qualify. When all responses to this notice have been assessed, all suppliers on the list must be given the opportunity to bid electronically.

Do the Directives work?

While the initial worries over excessive bureaucracy, delay and restriction of professional style may appear now to have been overstated, there is still some doubt about the effectiveness of the Directives, in the light of the bold assertions of Atkins and Cecchini. Some of the most common criticisms have been:

- The Directives do not help small and medium-sized enterprises (SMEs). A significant proportion of employment in most national economies, and within the EU as a whole, is within SMEs. However, the thresholds are set at levels that exceed typical contract sizes for many SMEs. It is likely that contracts below thresholds are being let to local firms, for the reasons indicated above; SMEs, it seems, are stuck with local business only.[18]

- Rather than firms in each of the EU countries bidding for business, there has been a tendency for large organisations to set up operations in those countries to bid for local contracts.

Examples of public sector procurement

The public sector is broad and the organisations within it have very different agendas and pressures. The Ministry of Defence, for example, has perhaps the greatest responsibility – defence of the realm, as it is termed in the UK – and potentially the highest costs. The National Health Service has perhaps the broadest and most complicated customer base and constraints on its procurement freedom (from specifying very expensive equipment to never running out of bedpans, from the apparent caprice of a surgeon over what type of rubber gloves are to be used to the confidence in a new drug). Local government procurement faces the turbulent pressures of small-town politics and top-down pressures, while central government suffers from a legacy of 'mandarin'-governed departments that do not speak, and layers of administration in which staff have perfected ways of justifying their existence. In the UK, this situation led to a commissioned report by Peter Gershon, then managing director of Marconi Aerospace, in which the state of central government civil procurement was portrayed as parlous. Gershon recommended the setting up of an Office of Government Commerce (OGC) and was subsequently asked to lead it himself. The advice and activities of OGC has led to major savings in public procurement in the UK and indeed reforms in administrative infrastructures; the reader is recommended to visit its extensive website for a very comprehensive explanation, update and illustration of public procurement issues (http://www.ogc.gov.uk/).

Summary

For the reasons shown at the outset, public sector procurement has a special nature and must be regulated to ensure value for money for the taxpayer. The European Directives are designed to provide this value and there is some evidence that they do so. The 'professionalisation' of public sector procurement, required by adherence to the regulations, must be seen as good thing, although there is a strong suggestion that national organisations, especially in member states lower down the table of prompt adoption of Directives, still find ways to keep public money in the country.

Seminar questions

1. Compare and contrast the procurement activities of one public sector or government organisation and one private sector enterprise and discuss the reasons for any different approaches.

2. Regulatory frameworks such as the EC Procurement Directives are intended to achieve better value for public money. What barriers might there be to realising this objective?

3. Access the information available publicly on this subject and describe if and how the EC Procurement Directives have developed since the writing of this book.

References

As mentioned in the text, there is much to read for this chapter on the official websites, including that of the OGC. Books and articles on the subject tend towards macroeconomics, as opposed to the very practical focus we have tried to maintain in this chapter. There is also the problem that texts go out of date very quickly; again this presses the researcher towards internet sources.

Very comprehensive research sites include:

- Public Procurement Research Group (http://www.nottingham.ac.uk/law/pprg/)
- International Research Project on Public Procurement (http://www.irspp.com/)
- Centre for Defence Economics (http://www.york.ac.uk/depts/econ/research/associated/index.htm)
- Journal of Public Procurement (Florida, USA) (http://www.fau.edu/pprc/journal.html)

Atkins, W. S. (1988) *Technical Barriers to Trade*, Study for the Single Market Review, subseries III.1, OO PEC, Kogan Page, Luxembourg and London.

Cecchini, P. (1988) *The European Challenge 1992: The Benefits of a Single Market*, Wildwood House, Aldershot.

Further reading

Arrowsmith, S. and Davies, A. (eds) (1998) *Public Procurement: Global Revolution*, Kluwer Law International, London.

Arrowsmith, S. (2005) *The Law of Public and Utilities Procurement*, Sweet & Maxwell, London.

Bovis, C. (2005) *Public Procurement in the European Union*, Palgrave Macmillan, London.

Martin, S., Hartley, K. and Cox, A. W. (1997) 'Public Purchasing in the European Union: Some Evidence from Contract Awards', *International Journal of Public Sector Management*, Vol. 10 (4), pp. 279–93.

Quayle, M. (1998) 'The Impact of Strategic Procurement in the UK Government Sector', *International Journal of Public Sector Management*, Vol. 11 (5), pp. 397–413.

Smart, A. (2005) 'Exploring Supply Chain Opportunities in the UK Utilities Sector and the Supporting Role of eMarketplaces', *Supply Chain Management: An International Journal*, Vol. 10 (4), pp. 264–71.

Somasundaram, R. and Damsgaard, J. (2005) 'Policy Recommendations for Electronic Public Procurement', *Electronic Journal of e-Government*, Vol. 3 (3), pp. 147–56 (http://www.ejeg.com/volume-3/vol3-iss3/SomasundaramRamanathanandDamsgaardJan.pdf)

Endnotes

1. The authors would like to thank Mr Fred Harvey for his very detailed and extensive help, guidance and input to this chapter. Mr Harvey is the UK's leading authority on the European Procurement Directives and Regulations. In addition to guiding his many clients, he is also a senior advisor to the European Commission in the development of the rules.
2. We have already discussed the fact that 'procurement' and 'purchasing' are used synonymously and interchangeably in practice and concluded that differentiation between them is nugatory. Both are used in public sectors but 'procurement' is perhaps the more common; accordingly 'procurement' will be used throughout this chapter.
3. 'Public' can include utilities that are in fact privately owned, as countries vary in their policies on the balance of such ownership and time scales for transitions such as 'privatisation'.
4. These were UK initiatives but others have been launched in the USA, Australia and other European countries. The UK's Office of Government Contracts has a comprehensive provision of advice and explanation on all matters to do with the subject: www.ogc.gov.uk/
5. For details on Transfer of Undertakings (Protection of Employment) – the law covering this transfer, see http://www.tssa.org.uk/ or http://www.dti.gov.uk/employment/trade-union-rights/tupe/page16289.html
6. 'Value for money' was the term developed by the UK Conservative government in the early days of the efficiency drive (c.1990); the incoming Labour government changed it to 'best value' in 1997. For practical, rather than political purposes, the two terms appear to be synonymous.
7. For discussions on the impacts of NAFTA, see www.nafta-sec-alena.org/; www.ustr.gov/Trade_Agreements/Regional/NAFTA
8. There is a concomitant implication for open markets for labour and capital, but these are not discussed here. For information on the Treaty of Rome, see http://www.hri.org/docs/Rome57/
9. Directives are one of the main instruments of the European Union. The European Commission develops Directives constantly – on every aspect of daily life. EU countries agree to install the EC Directives in national law. They do so, however, with greatly varying degrees of promptness!
10. See www.imf.org/external/np/exr/facts/sdr.HTM. For daily valuations, see http://www.imf.org/external/np/fin/rates/rms_five.cfm
11. See http://www.ogc.gov.uk/index. The 2006 regulations may be downloaded from this site.
12. Formerly the *Official Journal of the European Community (OJEC)*.
13. For these purposes, the ECU – the European Currency Unit – may be seen as the forerunner and equivalent of the euro.
14. It should be noted that the figures derived and used in such reports are notoriously unreliable in anything other than a general sense. Few would disagree with the findings of the

Atkins and Cecchini reports but few would defend the precision of the figures, as illustrated by the expressions shown here.

15. Complaints can come from a variety of sources. The two principal ones are disgruntled unsuccessful bidders and the Commission itself, which regularly takes national governments to task over major contract decisions. The websites identified earlier contain current news of such cases and often make interesting reading.

16. See http://www.ogc.gov.uk/resource_toolkit.asp

17. It should not be inferred that this was a problem for procurement officers: a preference for local suppliers, where it exists, may be attributed to elected members within local government.

18. However, the ability of any firm to advertise itself on a well-designed website can counteract this. The problem experienced by some SMEs as a result, however, has been the need to supply and maintain items to customers spread across the world.

Chapter 17

Electronic supply

Aim of chapter

The aim of this chapter is to provide readers with an evolutionary perspective of how technology impacted on strategic supply management.

Learning outcomes

At the end of this chapter, readers will:

■ be able to differentiate Electronic Data Interchange from internet technologies;

■ be able to identify different forms of electronic exchanges;

■ understand the implications of electronic technology for strategic relationships and the supply base.

Introduction

In this chapter we shall discuss the development of the technology underlying the Internet. The chapter first outlines the emergence of electronic data interchange (EDI). We show how Internet-based supply markets were the technological successor of these earlier electronic supply approaches. The chapter then discusses the emergence of supply hubs on the Internet in which many customers are connected to many suppliers. We continue the discussion of hubs by examining the different types of content on offer by the exchanges. Finally, we conclude the chapter with a high-level overview of electronic reverse auctions.

Development of the enabling technology

The Internet is older than most people think; its origins lie in the American military world of the 1970s.[1] For the next two decades it remained a worldwide network of computers connected by an infrastructure of communications technologies serving Western defence establishments, academe and, finally, business/commerce.

During the early 1990s, this communications network emerged as a source of fundamental change in the way that businesses operated and engaged their customers. The parallel rise of low-cost, powerful hardware and software meant that by the time the Internet was enabling widespread electronic communications, consumers had already grown comfortable with the technology.

To appreciate the magnitude of this change, one need only to consider the business-class cabin of any transatlantic flight in the late 1990s. A good proportion of the occupants would be busy working on their notebook computers. That same scene 30 years earlier would scarcely have included executives working away on portable typewriters! Yet by the first decade of the twenty-first century, the ability to link in real time an airborne personal computer (PC) through mobile communications to the Internet – and thus to any computer on the planet – seems perfectly natural. Furthermore, the ability to contact any individual carrying a personal communications device in his or her pocket – the stuff of science fiction a mere 15 years ago – is also now taken for granted.

By the late 1990s nearly every business process was becoming or had already become 'e-enabled'. New business thinking was rife. Start-up businesses considered physical presence to be unimportant: virtual identity alone would suffice. Many a start-up firm had only a website and an address when its shares were initially tendered to, and enthusiastically purchased by, the investing public. At the very end of the twentieth century it seemed that investors would rush to fund any firm with the dot.com soubriquet in its IPO filing, regardless of whether its respective business were profitable or not. We are now all too familiar with the result of the infamous 'dot.com' stock market run-up. The speculative bubble, fuelled by what the US Federal Reserve Bank chairman referred to as 'irrational exuberance' by investors, eventually burst. Surviving firms soon returned to the more rational concerns of businesses, including the need to secure physical premises, maintain appropriate inventories and ensure profitability in the medium term.

These concerns are, of course, areas of great interest to the supply management field. Most purchasing and supply management professionals therefore need to thoroughly understand the implications of e-commerce. New technology (a website and sophisticated appearance on the Internet) would need to be combined with more traditional concerns (the physical ability to deliver goods and services) to develop a business strategy encompassing both 'clicks and bricks'. Amazon.com, for example, one of the longest-surviving dotcoms, combined its impressive 'front end' (web presence) with a physical network of very large warehouses to store its merchandise.

But the implications can be even more profound. Some hark back to the basics of trade – control of supply and demand – and the nature of information upon which sourcing is conducted. This is reflected in a new terminology which frequently blurs the demarcations of traditional business functions: e-commerce, i-business (i for Internet), business to business (B2B), business to consumer (B2C), etc. 'e-commerce' connects the act of buying with that of selling, and includes both downstream and upstream perspectives. When purchasing online via an electronic exchange, purchasing and supply professionals cannot restrict their thinking to the immediate purchase transaction if they are charged with getting the best deal, i.e. reducing overall cost or TCO for the enterprise.

By developing a taproot into the Internet, a business is simultaneously able to obtain massive benefits and to make huge mistakes in a global trading environment. Let's examine the development of this electronic connection by purchasing and supply management professionals.

Electronic data interchange

The first technology to be used by supply management was rather modest, entailing the mere exchange of basic coded data. EDI represented most firms' initial foray into electronic interactions with their respective suppliers and customers. EDI was an outgrowth of the 'paperless office' movement that became almost a management holy grail in the 1980s.

The idea behind EDI was and remains quite simple. Computers send, receive, process, store and present operating information in the form of electronic signals. The process of entering data via a keyboard and retrieving data later as text on a screen or as printed output is merely the translation between electronic signals and physical media. Two computers can exchange data directly as electronic signals via a phone line (or slightly more sophisticated networks),[2] bypassing this intermediary translation. Although the idea may seem obvious and simplistic today, it was near revolutionary at the time.

As EDI developed, it became the standard way of doing business in many sectors until it was eclipsed by e-commerce in the late 1990s. The difference between the two is important to note. EDI represents a communications link between two companies' respective information systems. Although companies sometimes employed a third-party communications vendor, EDI commonly implied direct sender-to-receiver communications. In contrast, e-commerce usually entails communications between a company's information system and a general marketplace system. A major difference is found in the specific technological platforms used by EDI versus e-commerce. The role played by suppliers and customers in shaping, defining and selecting those technical platforms has not always been clear-cut.

Connecting computers is 'messy', a reflection of the evolution of information systems technology. For example, when EDI was still developing in the 1980s, the computer systems industry was in the initial stages of its technical evolutionary trajectory.[3] Providers of systems employed many different ways of generating and using electronic signals; few cared whether their respective methods were compatible with those of others. This is common in the early days of any technological innovation: every provider wants to establish the standard. It is not in every player's individual interests to accept a common protocol at the onset.

When EDI was introduced, therefore, it was typical for the customer to dictate to suppliers which system to use – its own. Suppliers faced with this ultimatum experienced two problems: the customer's system was usually different from the suppliers' and customer systems were most often incompatible with each other. The customer dominance in some industries (e.g. automotive – an early adopter of EDI) meant that the problems remained the suppliers'. Gradually, industry clusters emerged to solve this problem. For example, the North American transportation

Figure 17.1 Electronic data interchange

1980s: EDI
Electronic data interchange

Problems of standards and
need for many systems

industry was first to achieve widespread acceptance of EDI after a handful of truck-ing and shipping companies developed a standard which customers were then forced to use. A similar development occurred in health care, where hospitals ordered goods from the materials supplier, American Hospital Supply, using its proprietary, vendor-supplied EDI protocol (the ASAP system) which subsequently became the *de facto* industry standard.

As customers began to realise that EDI needed standardisation, business applications became aligned with those that had been in place for some time in technical developments. This is illustrated by the development of Open Systems Integration (OSI), often in the form of sector or industry-wide collaboration. For example, the automotive industry set up several special panels and developed their own standards, although the large players were loath to dismantle their indivi-dual – and in some cases, idiosyncratic – systems. In financial services, meanwhile, the push towards standardisation led more easily to agreed use of OSI-based sys-tems. The aim of OSI was to provide a standard platform upon which any EDI system could work. This would enable suppliers to 'translate' between their own EDI protocol and that of a customer, or between two customers' differing systems (see Figure 17.1). OSI coupled with consolidation of third-party communications vendors ensured that EDI gradually became a useful technology.

By the time this happened, in the late 1980s, the Internet had developed to the point where more attractive, powerful systems were available, enabling the buyer to access global supply markets. Investments in EDI could not be simply ditched, however, and the limitations of one-to-one, customer-specific communications had given way in some instances to more appropriate network systems, as we saw above. Although EDI is still widely used today, companies are simultaneously exposed to the broader possibilities of the Internet. Many MIS professionals no doubt long for the day when their firms' EDI legacy systems may be converted.

Early Internet markets

The major investments in EDI made by early adopters led to successful systems and there are many cases where it is still in use. An alternative to EDI, made pos-sible by the Internet, was the provision of supply services from one organisation

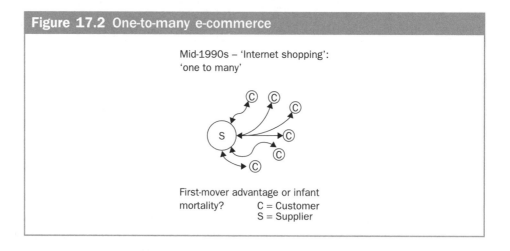

Figure 17.2 One-to-many e-commerce

Mid-1990s – 'Internet shopping':
'one to many'

First-mover advantage or infant
mortality?   C = Customer
                    S = Supplier

to many customers. This approach is clearly a marketing strategy and has its natural home in consumer business; the example of Amazon.com is perhaps the best known but the approach is now ubiquitous. An organisation establishes and promotes a system through which its customers may purchase its products using an online catalogue.

The technical spares and products supplier, RS Components, was an early example of this e-commerce architecture in the UK. In the early 1990s, RS launched an electronic version of its existing, paper-based catalogue. The company initially sent the electronic catalogue on CD-ROM to its vast customer base and provided the technology that would enable them to connect to RS automatically through a phone line. Once customers evolved technologically and used the Internet, it became possible for them to access the catalogue online, conducting searches, filling 'shopping carts' and so on in a manner that is now familiar to most consumers in the Western world (see Figure 17.2).

For suppliers, this 'one-to-many' arrangement is beneficial. It ties customers to the supplier as they become accustomed to the supplier's system and perhaps personalise their interactions with it. In addition, new offerings or changes in prices could now be added in real time. In contrast, CD-ROM or paper catalogues were 'frozen' in time – often for a year – requiring careful cost forecasting and risk management since margins were often hurt by supply-side fluctuations.

RS Components is a very old and well-established company and had little difficulty in linking its 'clicks' to its 'bricks'. Less well-established organisations found this strategy more difficult to implement in the 1990s. As with any innovation, early adopters sometimes gained first-mover advantages. In other cases 'fast-followers', i.e. those who waited until all the mistakes had been made, saw more success (and the early pioneers caught the arrows!).

The one-to-many marketing arrangement is the opposite of the customer-dominated EDI system described earlier. In a one-to-many architecture, the supplier determines the technology. Since the system is the Internet, however, there is little need for the customer to invest in special technology. A standard browser plus some form of protection ('firewall') may be all that is necessary.

Many to many: the emergence of hubs

Suppliers selling on the Internet soon began to buy in the same way, forcing other suppliers to sell to them via the Internet. This process encouraged suppliers further up the supply chain to get up to speed with Internet trading. As suppliers learned to sell on the Internet, so their customers were encouraged to use e-commerce, and so on. Customers sometimes still wished to use EDI to specify delivery requirements or technical work (e.g. sharing Computer-Aided Design – CAD – specifications). In time CAD drawings were being sent as e-mail attachments, however, and shortly thereafter suppliers were accessing a customer's 'intranet' (i.e. an organisation's internal communications network) to obtain specifications of the customer's requirements.

Once the technology was available to buy and sell simultaneously on the Internet, the idea of a marketplace, or exchange, emerged much as commodity exchanges emerged (see Chapter 18). The exchange was seen as the 'hub' of the market – a place where suppliers could exhibit their wares and customers publish their requirements. This is shown in Figure 17.3.

Like commodity exchanges, Internet marketplaces are commercial concerns and each has to compete for business. In the early days of Internet trading, some international industries established 'vertical' exchanges and exerted powerful pressure on one another and on their suppliers to join. The best known of these, COVISINT,[4] was launched by the largest vehicle assemblers in the automotive industry. There is no requirement for all the industry players to join, however, and several vehicle manufacturers chose to develop their own hubs – in some cases, an upstream version of the one-to-many we saw above. Suppliers, meanwhile, were pressured to join in as their customers averred that they would only purchase this way in future. The problems that beset EDI, however, are not present. Whilst a supplier may have to trade on several different systems if its customers use different exchanges, the technology is neither expensive nor difficult to use.

At the turn of the century, Internet trading on exchanges or hubs was becoming commonplace, with some industries following the automotive example (Exostar in the aerospace industry, formed by BAE Systems, Boeing, Lockheed and Raytheon;[5] Aeroexchange in the airlines industry[6]). Some were dealing in bespoke

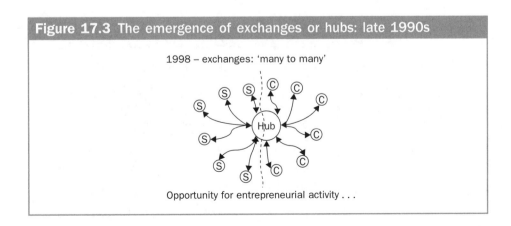

Figure 17.3 The emergence of exchanges or hubs: late 1990s

1998 – exchanges: 'many to many'

Hub

Opportunity for entrepreneurial activity . . .

requirements – items for which complicated specifications were required. Others dealt in standard equipment – office supplies, for example.[7] The American expression MRO began to appear outside the USA at this time, largely as the providers of the large exchanges for standard items emerged from there. MRO had been traditionally used in the USA to refer to shop-floor items.[8] Its migration to the office product scene prompted the rather odd soubriquet 'white-collar MRO'.

Purchases such as staplers and photocopier paper, personal computers, rental cars and temporary labour can be fairly simply specified (this does not mean they are necessarily easy to purchase!). An energetic industry quickly arose to provide systems for such purchases.[9] Software vendors Ariba, Commerce One and Oracle[10] marketed to professionals charged with developing e-commerce applications for their respective organisations. These systems were often functionally linked to ERP systems; the vendor Oracle provided both systems.

The hub that connects many customers to many catalogues enables the customer company to put its users (purchasing's internal customers) in touch with the broad supply market to do their own buying. The company's internal purchasing system contains both standard items, whose information is often extracted from suppliers' catalogues (e.g. office supplies) and customised items such as part-time temporary labour services. The catalogue is sometimes part of an atomisation strategy (see Chapter 10) in which budget holders spend their own funds, often using a corporate procurement card to do so. In this case, the Purchasing and Supply manager has set up the system (dealing with the provider of the software that connects the company to the hub) and can have some direction over where supplies are sourced. If users cannot find what they want in the systems' default catalogues, they may be permitted to 'punch out' – to be connected to a further catalogue in which a broader range is available. The practical problems of this are clear, especially when payment is concerned (the system will deal with all the payment issues as well as the ordering).

A recent trend has been to link hubs together in order to offer customers a broader range of products and services. This arrangement provides 'punch-out' facilities enabling comprehensive 'one-stop shopping' similar to the retail strategy of a department store (with specialist 'concessions') or a shopping mall. This arrangement is represented in Figure 17.4. There are some novel combinations of firms – many of them previously competitors – who link up in this way.

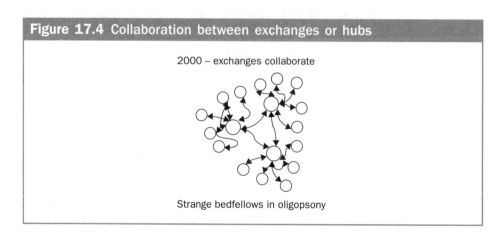

Figure 17.4 Collaboration between exchanges or hubs

2000 – exchanges collaborate

Strange bedfellows in oligopsony

The risk is that such alliances will distort competition if big players form an oligopsony – a market state in which there are only a few principal buyers. Most customers for the many-to-many hub systems are very large organisations. Since catalogue providers (e.g. office stationery) may already have established standalone one-to-many systems, it is not always clear whether these vendors will benefit from selling through an exchange (and paying a commission to do so) or whether their customers will force them to do so. Either way, the possibilities for supply management are enormous.

As exchanges deal with less simply specified requirements, customer enquiries must be treated in a more controlled manner. Suppliers must be vetted before being allowed to bid for the business and the process of accepting bids must be carefully managed. In such situations, the concept of the online or 'reverse' auction emerges (this is also referred to as a Dutch auction).

Content on offer from exchanges[11]

The service that an exchange can offer its customers (and thus the features of which a Purchasing and Supply manager should be aware) vary with the structure of the exchange. Where the customer sets up their own system to buy from separate suppliers, possibly including an online auction facility, they must go to several external sources to find what they need and bring the resultant information or supplies together themselves. This is termed 'direct content' (see Figure 17.5).

Where the buyer may access one site which has on it many potential suppliers, the content may be termed 'aggregated', in much the same way as a consumer may shop from a department store (Figure 17.6).

In accessing aggregated content in this way, however, the customers still have to integrate the various purchases themselves. They are also limited to the sources that are on the site. A more developed state is where the site acts not as a location for the various suppliers, but as a route to them for the customer. This is termed a 'portal'. This is shown in Figure 17.7.

Clearly, the portal implies that any source to which it connects the customer is in some way recommended (although legal commitments may well be circumscribed).

Figure 17.5 Direct content from several suppliers to a private exchange

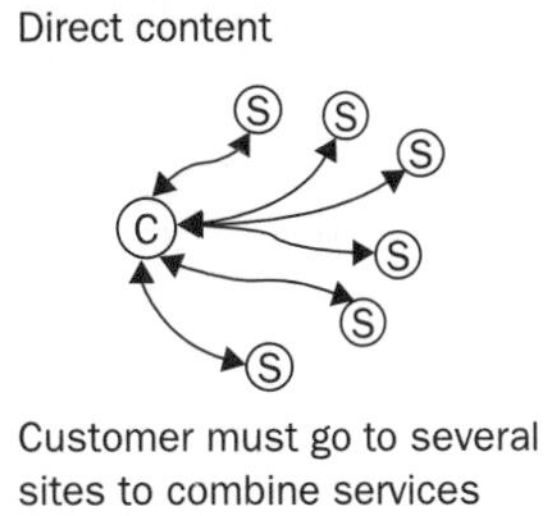

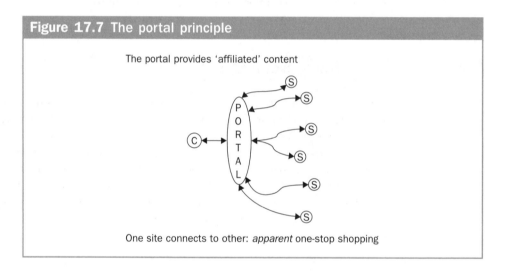

Figure 17.6 Aggregated content from a site containing several sources of goods and services

Aggregated content

One site contains all the customer needs – 'one-stop shopping'

Figure 17.7 The portal principle

The portal provides 'affiliated' content

One site connects to other: *apparent* one-stop shopping

In a developed form of the portal, the needs of the customer may be more technically taken into account – the portal offering the 'value-added service' of finding the right source for the customer, with explicit recommendations. This is shown in Figure 17.8.

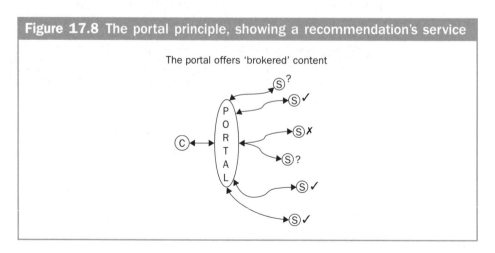

Figure 17.8 The portal principle, showing a recommendation's service

The portal offers 'brokered' content

As the sophistication of the exchange increases, the value-added services on offer become more extensive. Typical inclusions are finance, supplier accreditation, intelligence reports and perhaps the most central – the online auction.

Online auctions

The online (or 'reverse') auction process employs the Internet to provide secure, real-time dealing in a controlled environment between a customer and a set of invited suppliers, each of whom has been fully briefed. The event is similar to a traditional auction, except that the price of the business up for bidding is driven down by the process, rather than up. The suppliers log on to the system, using a password, and over a set period (perhaps an hour or two) they register bids through their Internet connection, for a clearly described 'parcel' of business (e.g. a year's supply of a component). Each supplier can see the current bid price and decide whether or not to compete by bidding lower. At the end, the customer has several choices (which will be made clear at the outset): either to take the lowest bid, or the lowest two or three and pursue them 'off-line', or to continue the auction a little longer (so-called 'dynamic closing').

Online auctions are usually run by individual specialist providers, sometimes incorporated in exchanges. It is possible for an individual organisation to have its own online auction activity but the special skills and investments required for it have meant that outsourcing the activity to a specialist has become the norm.[12]

Setting up an auction for suppliers to bid for business may be seen as the opposite of collaborative strategies in supply that have been so popular for over a decade. However, collaborative strategies are not intended to make the customer pay more than the market price for an item and the online auction appears to provide the best way of revealing that price – especially as they can easily be global. Provided the specification makes the terms of engagement clear (i.e. the manner in which the customer wishes to work with the successful supplier), then the competition can be said to go beyond simply bid prices, to include the extra benefits that should be available from collaboration. If an incumbent supplier is required to take part in the online auction, the customer will value the special relationship (i.e. track record of effective dealing) accordingly. Where a relationship is so well developed that the customer believes other ways are available to ensure the market is being tested, online auction may be seen as unnecessary.[13]

As with any market situation, there must be sufficient liquidity (plenty of suppliers wishing to bid for the business) in order for an online auction to function. In the early days there was a danger of suppliers forming cartels – effectively banding together to refuse to respond to requests to take part in online auctions. Gradually, however, firms came to realise that this was nothing new – simply the enquiry process being brought up to date with e-commerce technologies. Recent developments in online auctions include value packages (rather than simply buying on price) and cascade auctions – where a supplier may be bidding for business and simultaneously running an auction with its own suppliers for the component parts and materials it would need to support the business.

Many auctions result in a reduced price being paid to the incumbent rather than a resourcing activity; the actual market price has been revealed in many cases. Provided the proper behaviour is maintained (a requirement of any type of auction), there is no reason in theory why any purchase cannot be made using the online auction.

Summary

E-commerce includes a great deal more than just exchanges and online auctions. Application Software Provisions (ASP) provide a broad spectrum of tools and support services for buyers, including sophisticated tools for strategic sourcing, assessment tools for developing buyer–supplier relationships, systems for organising payment of invoices, contracts archives, and much more. The development of e-commerce may be expected to produce a wide range of threats and opportunities for those with existing skills. As with any innovation, the discretion, diligence and intelligence of the practising supply manager will determine what benefits are actually realised and what mistakes made.

The operating challenge of e-commerce for purchasing and supply is clear. Powerful tools must be used properly and, in this respect, e-commerce represents a major step in the sophistication and maturation of purchasing and supply. Exchanges have, for centuries, required the highest levels of professional behaviour from their members and exacted the fiercest of penalties for malpractice. As buyers, managers and strategists in purchasing and supply seek benefits and advantages through e-commerce, so they must look to their moral and professional codes, training and development, and monitoring of policy deployment, in order to increase the likelihood of success.

Seminar questions

- Discuss the difference between electronic data interchange and Internet technologies.

- Identify, with examples from your experience or case studies, each of the different forms of electronic exchange.

- Discuss, using case studies, the implications of electronic technology for strategic relationships and the supply base.

References

CAPS Research (2003) *Evaluating E-Procurement Solutions*, Tempe, AZ.

CAPS Research (2003) *The Role of Reverse Auctions in Strategic Sourcing*, Tempe, AZ.

CAPS Research and McKinsey & Company (2002) *E-Commerce Exchanges: Making Informed Decisions and Applying Best Practices*, Tempe, AZ.

Lamming, R. C. (1993) *Beyond Partnership: Strategies for Innovation and Lean Supply*, Prentice Hall, New York.

Nelson, R. and Winter, S. (1977) 'In Search of a Useful Theory of Innovation', *Research Policy*, Vol. 6 (1), pp. 36–76.

Nelson, R. and Winter, S. (1983) *An Evolutionary Theory of Economic Change*, Harvard University Press, Cambridge, MA.

Further reading

Croom, S. (2001) 'Restructuring Supply Chains through Information Channel Innovation', *International Journal of Operations and Production Management*, Vol. 21 (4), pp. 504–15.

Essig, M. and Arnold, U. (2001) 'Electronic Procurement in Supply Chain Management: An Information Economics-Based Analysis of Electronic Markets', *The Journal of Supply Chain Management*, Fall, pp. 43–8.

Griffiths, A. and Williams, R. (2003) 'Trusting and Auction', *Supply Chain Management: an International Journal*, Vol. 8 (3), pp. 190–4.

Laudon, K. C. and Traver, C. G. (2002) *E-commerce: Business, Technology and Society*, Addison-Wesley, Reading, MA.

McKinsey & Company and CAPS Research (2000) *Coming Into Focus: Using the Lens of Economic Value to Clarify the Impact of B2B e-marketplace.*

Min, H. and Galle, W. P. (1999) 'Electronic Commerce Usage in Business to Business Purchasing', *International Journal of Operations and Production Management*, Vol. 19 (9), pp. 909–21.

Parker, J. (ed.) (1999) 'Electronic Opportunities and Electronic Commerce – New Technologies for Purchasing', in *The Purchasing Handbook*, 6th edn, McGraw-Hill, New York.

Endnotes

1. See http://www.isoc.org/internet/history/ and http://www.isoc.org/internet/history/cerf.shtml. For suggested readings/videotapes on the history of the Internet, consult 'Fast Forward: Science, Technology and the Communications Revolution' at www.fastforwardproject.org
2. EDI was made possible by 'open systems integration' – see the ISO website at http://www.iso.ch/iso/en/ISOOnline.frontpage
3. The term 'natural trajectory' was developed by Nelson and Winter (1977, 1983). For a brief explanation see Lamming (1993, pp. 78–80).
4. For full details, see www.covisint.com
5. See http://www.exostar.com
6. See http://www.tdctrade.com/shippers/vol23_5/vol23_5_log_08.html
7. For a detailed overview of industry-sponsored marketplaces, consult the white paper 'E-Commerce Exchanges: Making Informed Decisions and Applying Best Practices' published in 2002 by CAPS Research and McKinsey & Company. The white paper is available at www.capsresearch.org

8. Note that MRO is also sometimes used to mean Maintenance, Repair and Overhaul.

9. For a detailed study of electronic procurement systems, see the Focus Study 'Evaluating E-Procurement Solutions' published by CAPS Research in 2003.

10. See: www.ariba.com, www.perfect.com, and www.oracle.com

11. The authors are grateful to Henry Kinniburgh, of HP Consulting, for his input to this section.

12. Examples of reverse auction providers include www.freemarkets.com and www.vendigital.com

13. For a more detailed overview of online auctions, see the Focus Study 'The Role of Reverse Auctions in Strategic Sourcing' published by CAPS Research in 2003. The study is available at www.capsresearch.org

Chapter 18

The relevance of commodities

Aim of chapter

This chapter aims to give the reader an overview understanding of the sophisticated area of commodity management. This is a highly specialised and important area of procurement. As such we have focused this chapter on giving the reader a working knowledge of what commodity management is and its implications for supply management.

Learning outcomes

At the end of this chapter, readers will:

- have a clear understanding of the definitions and operations of commodity markets;
- be able to distinguish various types of commodities, for example hard and soft;
- have an overview understanding of the workings of the commodity markets themselves;
- understand the implications of active and professional commodity management on the supply process and ultimately the effect that they have on the firm's output.

Introduction

One of the curious aspects of business is the laxity with which language is used. In any other branch of professional practice, specialist terms are carefully defined and used in a way that ensures they are understood immediately and precisely when they are used. In business, however, some words are used to mean several different things and new words are invented all the time. 'Commodity' is not a new word but it is used to mean many things. A dictionary definition gives only a general guide: 'A kind of thing produced for use or sale; an article of commerce; an object of trade. In plural: Goods, merchandise, wares, produce' (OED 2004).

In business, the term *commodity* is used to refer to an item which is specified so closely, in terms of its form and quality, that it may be bought and sold purely on price; the price reflects the availability or scarcity and the level of demand. Commodities are the stuff of national prosperity and disaster. They have frequently caused wars and still suffer from the effects of them.[1] They are affected by weather; if the coffee harvest fails in a South American country, the price of coffee is bound to rise in Europe. They are traded globally and require elaborate financial mechanisms to support them. In many organisations the people who buy commodities do not see themselves as part of Purchasing and Supply. The cocoa buyer for a maker of chocolate bars, for example, is more likely to have the title 'Economist' than Purchasing manager, or even Buyer. The cocoa is not simply being bought, but traded.

The principle of commodity

The *principle* of commodity actually runs through every purchase. Everyone trying to sell something would like to differentiate it from other competitive offerings, to convince the buyer that it is worth paying a little more for it. The seller can reduce the clarity of specification for the buyer by such differentiation – claiming that value has been added to this particular product or service, justifying a higher price. The buyer, meanwhile, is keen to pay the lowest price for the item and would like all competitive offerings to be the same, in order to compare them simply. This is true for purchases as diverse as, say, the contract for building a new motorway bridge and buying an office chair. While the buyer is interested in the seller's ability to innovate, they are never quite sure how much they should pay for this and so would prefer it if the innovation was on offer from every supplier. The factors that influence the nature of the item – standardised commodity or differentiated offer – are many and various; in purchasing and supply it is important to recognise the propensity of an item for both characteristics and deal with it accordingly.

The financial centres of the world have grown rich and large on the basis of commodity trading. The island of Bahrain, in the Persian Gulf, for example, did so over four thousand years ago (when it was part of an ancient land called Dilmun) because of a freak of the weather and its geology. Only a few miles off the Saudi coast, the little island had fresh water supplies which travelled under the sea from the mainland, which had itself grown dry. It also had pearls in its local waters and grew dates in the parts of its land that were not desert. At the top of the gulf lay the land of Mesopotamia and the great city of Ur (in modern-day Iraq). To reach the markets of Ur, traders from outside the Gulf had to sail through the Straits of Hormuz (plagued then, as now, by pirates) and past Bahrain, where the prevailing wind changed to northerly – on the nose. Ships from Makan (Oman), laden with copper, and from the Indus valley (Pakistan), carrying lapis lazuli and spices, would reach Bahrain and sell their wares there, rather than struggle northwards against the wind. The people of Bahrain perfected the skills of sailing towards the wind and built ships designed for just this task. The towns in Bahrain grew rich as merchants bought from the incoming vessels and despatched goods northwards. The ships of the Indus valley and Makan would return home laden with pearls, dates and fresh water. Today, Bahrain no longer relies on such basic factors – and has benefited from the discovery of oil – but it is still the centre of finance in the Middle East; the culture of trade is a strong influence on national development. It still owes its presence in the modern commodity markets to its geographical location as well as its prowess in commercial dealing.

There is still a tendency for commodities to be bought and sold in a small number of centres, located in countries and cities where traders gather. To be a trading centre, the location must be seen as stable and established – as it is trust that is key to the success of its business. Traditionally, the exchanges on which the commodities are bought and sold are far from the places in which they are grown, harvested or mined. In their role as the basis for national development, commodities may represent the exploitation of natural resources or the introduction of new features. For example, the Southeast Asian country of Malaysia relied for much of the twentieth century on three commodities: tin, palm oil, and rubber. The first two were naturally present in the country but rubber was introduced to the country by the colonial British in the nineteenth century. In the 1980s, Malaysia successfully transformed itself from a largely agrarian economy to an industrial player and gained more stability than had been afforded by its reliance on the three commodities. Similar attempts to rebuild the agricultural sector in Vietnam at the end of the twentieth century by introducing coffee appear to have been less successful. Meanwhile, a collapse in the price of coffee in the early years of the current century appears to have pushed Colombian growers firmly towards another commodity – cocaine.

So, commodities are materials and services which can be specified precisely and bought largely on the basis of price and availability. They are vitally important to the nations that produce them – either naturally or as a result of economic policy – and their trade is conducted in a small number of stable centres in developed countries by people who operate in a long-established culture of dealing. As they are affected by the weather, warfare, fashions, technologies, caprice and a host of other unpredictable factors, the price of a commodity may rise or fall sharply; this has given rise over time to a set of financial measures designed to reduce – or at least, live with – the associated risks, and, in addition to dealers and merchants themselves, a variety of professional commentators, forecasters, analysts and advisers.

The standardisation of quality of a commodity is often very precise. Gold, for example, bought for industrial purposes (e.g. plating electrical contacts) is specified by its purity. Gold that is 99.99 per cent pure is called 'two nines;' the more expensive 'four nines' gold is 99.9999 per cent pure. Traders buying some four nines gold know exactly what they are getting – no differentiation is present: it is a true commodity.

Types of commodity

There are many ways of referring to types of commodity, and new ones appear from time to time. One traditional and significant differentiation is between 'hards' and 'softs'.

1 Hard commodities include metals, also divided into types:

- *base metals*, such as aluminium, aluminium alloys, lead, nickel, tin, zinc, copper;
- *precious metals*, such as gold, silver, platinum, palladium.

2 Soft commodities include such things as cocoa, cocoa mash, white sugar, cotton, orange juice.

3 Other categories are known by more straightforward generic names:

- grains and seeds (wheat, maize, barley, soybeans, soybean oil, soybean meal, potatoes, rice, palm oil);
- meat and livestock ('live cattle', lean hogs', 'pork bellies', etc.);
- energy (heating oil, gas oil, unleaded gasoline, natural gas).

The names provide the clue to the degree of processing that has gone on. For example, soybeans are sold largely as they are harvested, whereas soybean oil or meal has had value added to it by a processor. The value-adding work represents potential income for the company (or country) conducting it, and possibly a chance to differentiate the material. It also complicates the quality issue, however: soybeans sold as they are harvested may be checked fairly simply for quality (there are several grades, as with all fruit and vegetables) whereas monitoring the more developed meal product may require more complicated processes. As a developing economy grows in confidence, so its architects may be expected to want to move from simply selling harvested crops to adding more value before shipping, thus enabling that country to charge higher prices for its produce and to provide more valuable employment than that associated simply with harvesting.

As countries grow and develop so commodity markets change. However, while a developing country might decide for itself that it wants to move from selling unprocessed crops to processed materials (say, cocoa mash rather than cocoa beans), it relies upon its credibility for its opportunity in the global marketplace. For example, a country such as Tanzania has long supplied cocoa beans and in the 1970s moved to processing the beans into mash (to be shipped to Europe for making chocolate).[2] This was seen as a credible move. To move the next step, however, and make chocolate, would require an infrastructural stability that was missing from the country at that time, i.e. it would be necessary to guarantee the supply of electricity to keep the product cold. A reliable electricity supply is not an easy thing to ensure in a developing country, and a factor such as doubt over the ability to refrigerate led to a delay in Tanzania's wish to produce chocolate.[3] Once such credibility can be established, however, low production costs (labour, overheads, transportation and storage) in developing countries may provide tempting alternatives to manufacturers in developed countries and operations are transferred, at the cost of jobs in the latter.

The other major factor that lies beyond the developing country is the location of the marketplace or 'exchange' where the commodity will be traded – the actual building within which traders will gather to buy and sell the item. Before the advent of the Internet, this required people to be in close touch – probably in the same building. Trading required people to be in the same small area – the 'pit' within the market building in which traders would stand and shout at each other, using all sorts of specialised hand signals and other devices to communicate in the noise.

This system, called 'open outcry', is still used in some instances but has largely been replaced by electronic trading.[4]

Whereas the conditions that are important to the production of a commodity revolve around its geography (necessary climate, presence of mineral) and the level of a country's development (low-cost labour, agrarian economy), those governing the location of the exchange are to do with economic and political stability – relative, of course, to the period in history. This was illustrated in the example of Bahrain, and can also be seen in the great powers of later years – Venice, London, Amsterdam, Paris. As European empires exploited far-flung countries in the second half of the second millennium AD, so the commodities produced in America, Africa and Asia traded in the capitals. The location of the world's great exchanges still reflects this – with the USA and Japan major players but Europe still very significant. Just as any market town in Britain would once want to boast its own corn exchange as well as its cattle market, so every national capital is keen to host exchanges. This provides a competitive market for exchanges – to attract traders to them – and keeps their business efficient (or as efficient as any market can be).

For an exchange to work there must be sufficient liquidity in the market – enough people who wish to buy and sell and enough of the commodity available to be traded. For the staples of life (wheat, sugar, cocoa, meats, metals, vegetables, etc.) this is simply achieved – the markets of the world work to ensure that the production of such items is roughly in line with requirements. (Where markets are distorted for political reasons, major changes in supply and demand may occur, including the arrival or departure of major players in exchanges – see Box 18.1.)

For new technologies, however, the picture is not as simple. The awareness of a new item may be limited for a while and once its demand starts to soar, supply may be easily controlled, especially where barriers to entry are high in its production. For example, the demand for the DRAM component (dynamic random access memory chips) for computers grew quickly at first and they were bought

---

Box 18.1 Oil prices dive on plane bomb plot

From correspondents in New York

CRUDE prices slumped today on predictions that air traffic could suffer after British authorities said they had foiled a major bomb plot targeting US-bound passenger planes.

A statement from the Organisation of the Petroleum Exporting Countries meanwhile said that global crude supplies were adequate also soothed the market. And efforts by British energy giant BP to avoid a complete shutdown of the Prudhoe Bay oilfield, America's largest, also lent prices some relief, traders said. New York's main contract, light sweet crude for delivery in September, closed down $US2.25 at $US74.00 a barrel. In London, Brent North Sea crude for September delivery settled down $US2.00 at $US75.28 per barrel. News of the apparent foiled plot to destroy passenger jets flying to the United States from Britain drove down prices on expectations that demand for jet fuel would weaken. 'This has renewed fears, similar to those after 9/11, of seriously curtailed travel and tourism because lower consumer confidence would cut air travel and undermine oil demand,' Fimat analyst Mike Fitzpatrick said.

Box 18.1 (*continued*)

'After 9/11 prices initially rose because supply stability was the focus. Later on, oil fell because consumer confidence was expected to fall, stalling global growth,' he said, referring to the September 11, 2001 attacks. British police said 21 people had been arrested, mostly in London and the surrounding area, in connection with the alleged plot in which terrorists would smuggle explosives aboard aircraft in hand baggage and detonate them. Oppenheimer analyst Fadel Gheit said that several factors had driven down prices along with the transatlantic terror alert. 'BP's production should be shut down only by 20 per cent to 30 per cent, so it's not likely to be as bad as feared,' he said. 'A very sharp drop in temperatures in the US seems to show that demand is going to fall as well,' Mr Gheit said, adding there was market relief over the lack of US hurricanes so far this summer.

Prices shot up earlier this week, with Brent striking a record high of $US78.64, after BP said it was shutting down its vast oil field in Prudhoe Bay to repair a pipeline leak caused by corrosion. A complete shutdown would halt production totalling 400,000 barrels of oil per day, or 8.0 per cent of daily US output. But in an update today, BP said it was still producing 120,000 barrels of oil a day from Prudhoe Bay and hoped to keep some output operational. 'The company is advancing its parallel plans of shutting in production and considering viable options where BP could safely continue to operate some production,' it said. BP said it was consulting with the US Department of Transportation and Alaska's environment department to see if it could safely continue some output, rather than shutting down the whole field, while it upgrades its pipelines. The field's eastern operating area has already been closed. A decision on whether to shut in the western area 'is expected by the beginning of next week,' it said. Traders were reassured meanwhile after OPEC said in a statement that it 'remains confident that the world is still adequately supplied with oil and that no shortage will occur'. 'The fact is that some of OPEC's producers can bring additional supplies to the market very quickly, if such action is deemed necessary, subject of course to adequacy of refining capacity,' the Vienna-based cartel said. The 11-nation group reiterated that it was 'ready to do all in its power to correct any imbalance in the market'.

Source: http://goliath.ecnext.com/coms2/gi_0199-5653962/Prudhoe-Bay-Update-August-10.html

by private deals. They are still not traded as commodities – because the technical specifications change so quickly – but the liquidity is greater now and their trade is much closer to an open market.

To be a true commodity, the liquidity (availability for trade) of an item must be quantifiable (i.e. manageable lot sizes are agreed) and quality stabilised and guaranteed (usually including regulation or international agreement on specification). The basis for the location of an exchange – the commodity which they require themselves – is trust, as exemplified by the motto of the London Stock Exchange: *Dictum meum pactum* or 'My word is my bond.' Commodity exchanges deal on handshakes and trust is born of stability.

Some examples of exchanges are given in Table 18.1.

For purchasing and supply the commodity market presents a problem. While the principle of levelling all offers to a perfectly common specification (no differentiation) and then buying purely on price fits the basic interest of the purchaser, the complexity of commodity trading, the degree of long-term specialised knowledge that is required (and, it must be said, the level of education and qualification in economic theory) do not match the skill sets commonly found in Purchasing departments. It is common practice to move buyers from one type of purchasing

Table 18.1 Examples of major commodity exchanges

Exchange		URL
LME	London Metals Exchange (non-ferrous metals)	www.lme.co.uk
LBM	London Bullion Market Association (precious metals)	www.lbma.org.uk
NYMEX	New York Mercantile Exchange The world's largest: oil, energy, metals	www.nymex.com
CBT	Chicago Board of Trade (grain, rice, soy)	www.cbot.com
LIFFE	London International Financial Futures and Options Exchange Futures and options related to softs and agricultural commodities	www.liffe.co.uk

Note: These exchanges have very rich websites with large amounts of information on their status, activities, focus, history, and so on

to another fairly frequently – as seen in Chapter 9 – whereas a commodity trader may expect to spend many years in one area, building a network and a rich experience or 'nose' for the market.

This situation often results in commodities being bought not by those in the Purchasing department but by specialised economists. This is satisfactory while the item remains a true commodity but when suppliers are able to differentiate their offering, the principles of good purchasing come into play – beyond the assumptions (supply, demand, perfect information, exercise of power) of economics. An example of this is given by the case of sheet steel. For large customers (e.g. vehicle assemblers) steel is sold direct by producers; for those requiring smaller or less regular quantities, the usual route is through a steel stockholder. A visit to a steel plant will reveal immediately how the commodity has ceased to have a common specification: every car company has its own requirements, for which the steel producers are able to ask different prices. Furthermore, since the steel sheets are going to be used in pressing operations (e.g. to make the roof panel of a car), the steel producer may wish to offer further added value, such as sheets cut to length rather than coiled, or coated in oils ready for pressing, or perhaps with location holes punched in them – all so that they can be moved straight from goods receiving to the press shop at the car plant, perhaps just in time: a lean supply process, without excessive inventory. Once the steel producer begins to offer such services, the purchase is no longer for a commodity but a semi-customised product. The skills, perspectives and knowledge bases required for purchasing such a differentiated product are different from those associated with commodities traded on the open market.

Dealing with the problems of fluctuating prices

As we have seen, commodities are affected by macroeconomic and geographic forces. This may be a climate change, a bad harvest, a territorial war, a cartel and so on. As the supply of a commodity gets too high, so producers may curtail its production, to introduce scarcity, thus stoking the market and increasing prices – the most basic of economic activities. For the Middle East oil producers this may be easy – a simple agreement on how far open to 'turn the tap' – although political pressure from outside – the USA, Europe and so on – often appears to be a powerful influence. For the coffee producers, as we saw above, it is not so easy. For the purchaser, then, the problem is how to deal with the price fluctuations that result in commodity markets.

There are four principal ways of doing this:

■ private deals;

■ backward integration (i.e. owning the raw material production);

■ opportunistic buying;

■ hedging on the futures market.

Private deals

Where an organisation knows the supply market well and relationships are good, it may be possible for private deals to be struck, thus avoiding the open market pressures, for both customer and supplier. Either side might do better by using the market but the risks may be attenuated by dealing privately. This has been true traditionally in the paper and pulp industry; only about a quarter of pulp produced is traded openly, the rest being bought and sold privately. This is due to several causes – principally the nature of the raw material (trees) and its emotional position in the countries in which it is produced. In the later decades of the twentieth century, technology in growing trees and producing paper threw the long-established industry dynamics into confusion. Whereas the Scandinavians and Canadians took 30 years to grow trees, frequently passing on crops from parent to child, in the hotter climes of central America and Asia it was found to be possible to grow eucalyptus in as little as 10 years. The wood was good enough for pulping for paper and, while there were major environmental concerns about the effects on soil chemistry, the new 'super trees' became popular.

Backward integration

At the same time, some new players joined the industry, encouraging the capital equipment producers to develop massive new pulping and paper production plant. Countries such as Indonesia saw this as a valuable part of their industrialisation and, with European companies happy to exploit the potential, began to install new capacity.[5] The size of the new pulping plants meant that each of them could add as much as 2 per cent to the world supply of pulp – an increase great enough to send the price of paper plummeting. Factors such as these are enough to discourage open trading of the commodity, as prices are likely to fluctuate widely. The industry response has been to conduct private deals and to move to the second approach – backward integration: large paper producers began to buy up woodland, to grow their own trees. The environmental impacts, meanwhile, have yet to reach the level of concern at which they can influence the market's behaviour.

Backward integration may mean taking on a different industrial practice, since the separation of business activities from one another is largely influenced by the nature of those activities (financial dynamics, labour markets, resources bases, technologies, etc.). To buy into the woodlands requires the paper and pulp producers to assimilate knowledge of growing trees – not a simple, quick or cheap development. The pressures that drive this strategy are thus very profound. (A similar strategy was adopted by cider producers in the UK, who bought large shares of the cider apple orchards in the south west of the country.)

Opportunistic buying

Opportunities may arise in almost any market to get a bargain. This may be sporadic – a combination of factors provide an opportunity for an unusually low price – or seasonal – buying winter fuel in the summer may mean paying less for it. Thus, opportunistic buying may involve quick response or strategic planning. While the uncertainty over price may be removed in this way, other costs may be incurred; once again these may be sporadic or planned. For the buyer paying a low price for winter fuel in the summer, the costs of storing that fuel (coupled with potential issues such as deterioration, pilferage and so on) may be forecast and factored into the equation. The winter price of the fuel may also be expected to vary and so the buyer must use the lowest forecast – perhaps moderated by a contingency factor – to compare with the summer price plus the on-costs. This problem has been particularly prevalent recently with the sharp rises in oil and aircraft fuel prices. These price shifts can have a huge effect on a firm's market perception. It is the job of the professional buyer in this industry to try to shield companies from these adverse market effects. The extract adapted from *Business Week* articles in January 2007 given in Box 18.2 illustrates this point.

For the sporadic deal, the risks are different. The danger might be that the reason for the good price is the imminent obsolescence of the item (coupled, naturally, with a drop in its value). Despite the simplicity of this situation, bargains that turn out to be albatrosses are quite common in purchasing, providing a cautionary lesson. In high-technology industries, where products, components and technologies have short lives, obsolete stock may be a major problem. This may be redolent of inefficient, pre-just-in-time days of manufacturing, but when the space-age companies of Silicon Valley faced major troubles in the spring of 2001, with share prices falling through the floor, the principal concern in business discussions there was 'inventory'. The high-technology exemplars faced the oldest problem – being caught with product they had bought that was losing market value by the day. Traditional problems do not appear to go away simply because of technological progress.

So, when buying commodities, private deals, backwards integration and opportunistic dealing all appear to have their own problems. The system that was developed to deal with this, to enable traders to survive and prosper despite buying and selling commodities on the high seas or even still in the field or mine, thousands of miles away across the globe, was the concept of the futures market.

Box 18.2 Rising fuel prices take their toll

Guy Nickson, owner of the Wishbone restaurant in Chicago, knows the feeling. A few months ago, he began noticing small fuel surcharges creeping onto delivery invoices. 'There's $1.50 added to the delivery for napkins. I don't know what proportion of the truck our box of napkins take up, but it can't be much,' he says. But with 40 deliveries a week, the extra dollar or two here and there add up fast.

EVERYBODY'S DOING IT. Welcome to the surreal world of fuel-related surcharges. Over the last five years, most long-haul freight companies have begun adopting such fees to cushion the impact of volatile oil prices. 'It's the ultimate hedge for us,' notes Bill Zollars, CEO of Kansas-based trucking giant Yellow Roadway.

Yet now, with high oil prices, it seems anybody who can possibly tack a fuel surcharge onto an invoice does. And the record speed at which fuel costs build up is hitting manufacturers and small businesses right in the bottom line.

Most freight companies calculate fuel surcharges according to fuel indexes such as the US Energy Dept index that tracks the price of diesel fuel. Hence, a nearly 40 per cent rise in the price of diesel over the last year has added as much as 14 per cent to shipping bills.

FLAT-FEE PROBLEM. And 'we can't add it to the product, either,' notes Hildelink. Locked into long-term contracts with retailers, companies like Kohler get stuck with an out-of-control expense. Farmers, whose already razor-thin profit margins are measured in pennies per bushel, find themselves in a similar bind.

And flat-fee surcharges are showing up on everything from cab and limousine rides and airline tickets to short-haul deliveries. And unlike surcharges based on an index, which go down when prices fall, flat fees tend to stay put. Their link to actual fuel costs remains somewhat fuzzy.

'When an economy turns back on, it's normal to try to raise prices – which have been in the dumps for quite a while. And along comes an opportunity to blame it on someone else,' says Peter Berck, an economist at the University of California at Berkeley.

Source: *Business Week* articles 2 January 2007

Buying on the future market

There is not space to explain the entire concept of futures and other financial arrangements (such as derivatives) here – it would take an entire textbook on its own (see further reading at the end of this chapter). They are relevant for purchasing and supply, however, and before closing the discussion on commodities, we should explore them a little.

As we have seen, the problem with buying commodities is the risk that the price will vary between the point at which the contract is placed and the point when delivery is taken – and the process of adding value for profit can be conducted. As a simple example, the cocoa mash bought from a producer in Tanzania might take three months to reach the port of Felixstowe in the UK. As the container crosses the ship's rail, the ownership transfers from the seller to the buyer and the price on that day is paid.[6] The market price on the day the deal was agreed may have been low but may have risen by the time the shipment is received in the UK. The buyer will then have to pay more than they planned for the material and this may affect the fortunes of their company. If the reverse has occurred, it is the seller who has lost on the deal. The principle of the futures market is to moderate these risks by 'hedging'.

Hedging comes in the form of buying and selling 'futures' – financial documents that are traded in their own market – linked to the commodity in question. In order to avoid the problems of paying more than they planned, the cocoa mash customer in the example above could have bought some cocoa mash futures at the same time as agreeing to buy the cocoa mash. If the price of the futures also rose during the period of transit, the customer might then sell them at a profit when paying for the cocoa mash itself, thus offsetting the increased cost of the commodity by the profit made on the futures deal. Of course, there is no guarantee that the futures price will rise simply because the commodity price does so, and that is where the trading becomes complicated.

Figure 18.1 shows a simplified version of the relationship between commodity price and the futures price. Figure 18.2 shows a rather more typical situation.

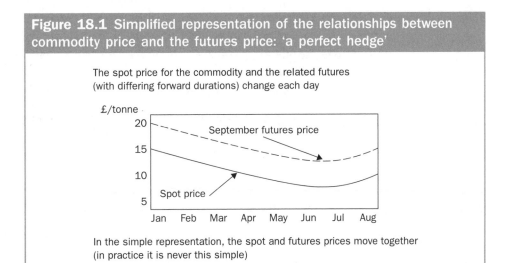

Figure 18.1 Simplified representation of the relationships between commodity price and the futures price: 'a perfect hedge'

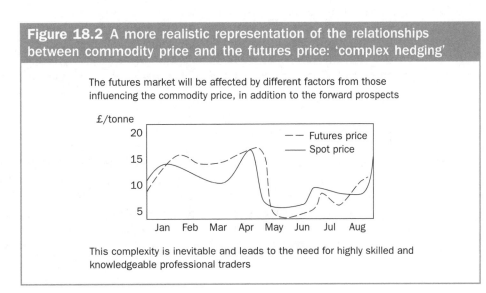

Figure 18.2 A more realistic representation of the relationships between commodity price and the futures price: 'complex hedging'

Not surprisingly, commodity trading has developed its own terminology, including special words and special meanings for normal words. Some of these are shown below:

- *Spot price*: the price that would need to be paid for the commodity for delivery on that day.
- *Contango* (literally means delaying payment): the situation in which the futures price is higher than the spot price.
- *Backwardation*: the situation in which the futures price is lower than the spot price.
- *Long*: owning commodities or futures that are not fully hedged (i.e. balanced by one another).
- *Short*: selling commodities or futures in excess of what it actually owned.
- *Arbitrage*: buying in one market and selling in another to exploit differences in prices (in the process, arbitragers help to keep markets competitive).
- *Bear*: someone who speculates (i.e. deals in their stocks of commodities and futures) expecting a fall in prices.
- *Bull*: someone who speculates expecting a rise in prices.

Box 18.3 shows hypothetical and very simple cases of dealing in commodities and futures, in order to illustrate the principle of hedging.

Box 18.3 Using hedges to reduce risk: simple examples

Example 1: the producer hedges the sale

A copper producer sells 100 tonnes of Cu from Africa to the UK. At shipping, spot price = £1,700/t. At delivery, 3 months later, market price (spot) has fallen to £1,600/t. Producer would make a loss of 100t × £100 per tonne = £10,000 (has to sell at price on delivery date).

So, at shipping, producer sells 100 tonnes worth of copper futures at £1,800/t (contango). On delivery, he buys futures at £1,700/t (fallen by the same amount) making 100t × £100/t on the deal (£10,000). The hedge is *perfect*.

Note that the same 'balancing out' would occur if prices rose, provided futures and spots kept in line with each other.

Example 2: the trader hedges the deal

A trader buys 500 tonnes of coffee in Brazil, at £800 per tonne, and arranges to deliver it in China, two months later. By this time, spot price has fallen to £700/t. Trader loses 500t × £100/t = £50,000.

So, when buying the coffee she also sells 500 tonnes worth of coffee futures at £600/t (backwardation) and buys the same quantity when selling the coffee in China, by which time the futures price has fallen to £500/t. She 'makes' 500 × £100 on this deal – £50,000, again balancing out the loss and making a perfect hedge.

Summary

We have seen that in commodity trading, purchasing and supply are undoubtedly going on but that the complexity of the process and the degree of market experience may take the activity outside conventional purchasing responsibilities. However, when producers or traders seek to differentiate their offering through adding value or changing the extent of their activity in the supply process, purchasing perspectives may indeed become important.

The term is used loosely to mean anything that is bought. Restricting the meaning to cover only items that are traded on open markets on the basis of fixed specifications and price identifies the management imperatives attached to commodities. It also recognises that an item may move in and out of commodity status, as the technology or other supply market characteristic varies. Thus, personal computers have gone through phases, since their introduction in the early 1980s, in which they were sometimes very differentiated and at others, effectively a commodity. When they all offer very similar hardware and software configurations, buyers may well choose purely on price. When one producer introduces a new development or unique feature, the commodity status is broken and the competition shifts to one of differentiation.

The advent of electronic exchanges (Chapter 17) has changed the ways in which commodity markets work – simply as a result of the increased speed of communication and provision of analysis information that computers and the Internet make possible. The spread of global activity has led to a situation in which markets operate on a complex mix of time scales, with dealers in Europe getting up early to catch Japan, and staying late to work with the USA. The impacts of global sourcing, as we have seen earlier, are similar and while the special aspects of commodities may always require the attention of specialised traders, the challenges of purchasing and supply appear to be increasingly similar to those we have seen in this chapter.

Seminar questions

1. Discuss your understanding of the definitions and operations of commodity markets as outlined in the text.

2. Using case study examples, distinguish between four various types of commodities, for example hard and soft.

3. Discuss how the commodity markets work.

4. Discuss how active and professional commodity management on the supply process can affect the firm's output.

References

Diamond, J. (2005) *Collapse: How Societies Choose to Fail or Survive*, Penguin, Harmondsworth.

Hanes, W. T. and Sanello, F. (2002) *The Opium Wars: The Addiction of One Empire and the Corruption of Another*, Sourcebooks Inc., Naperille, IL.

Milton, G. (2000) *Nathaniel's Nutmeg*, Sceptre, London.

OED (2004) *The Oxford English Dictionary*, 2nd edn, CD-Rom, Oxford University Press, Oxford.

Thompson, H. and Kennedy, D. (1996) 'The Pulp and Paper Industry: Indonesia in an International Context', *Journal of Asian Business*, Vol. 2 (2), pp. 41–55.

Further reading

Carter, C. A. (2002) *Futures and Options Markets: An Introduction to US Imports & PHIPEs*, Prentice Hall, Upper Saddle River, NJ.

Hull, D. L. (2001) *Fundamentals of Futures and Options Markets (International Edition) US Imports & PHIPEs*, Prentice Hall, Upper Saddle River, NJ.

Endnotes

1. The commodity may appear of marginal importance but still be the basis for major conflict. The terrible spice wars between Britain and the Netherlands in the eighteenth century are a prime example (for a fascinating account, see Milton (2000)). Similar disasters were associated with opium (Hanes and Sanello (2002)). International conflicts are still often linked to commodities, such as oil – clearly a factor in the twentieth and twenty-first centuries.

2. For an interesting discussion on trading see works by David Ricardo on 'Comparative Advantage' (http://internationalecon.com/v1.0/ch40/40c000.html). Another interesting text is Jared Diamond's book *Collapse* which looks at the effect of trading and globalisation.

3. Cocoa was introduced in Tanzania at the beginning of the twentieth century. It gained importance as an export crop in the 1980s. So far this century, a major global issue has been over-supply of the commodity and the collapse of the international marketing arrangements for the crop, diverting attention to more profitable crops such as coffee, cotton and cashews. Cocoa is now seen as a good small-scale foreign exchange earner ($4 million in 1992) surpassing many other non-traditional exports. *Source*: Tanzania Ministry of Agriculture and Food Security.

4. In the closing years of the twentieth century, the exchange has taken on a new lease of life in the field of electronic commerce: the electronic, virtual exchanges made possible by the Internet have brought the concept of trading and commoditisation forward from the traditional commodities markets and practices such as online auctions and are close in their nature to open outcry. See Chapter 17.

5. See Thompson and Kennedy (1996).

6. Specific deals vary on payment terms, of course; the one described is a traditional arrangement. The principle of pricing is the same, however.

Chapter 19

Services procurement

Aim of chapter

The aim of this chapter is to understand the primary issues in the procurement of services and highlight the differences between the procurement of physical goods and that of services.

Learning outcomes

At the end of this chapter, readers will:

- have a clear understanding of the differences between the purchasing of services and the purchasing of goods;
- understand the terms 'service level agreement' and 'operating level agreement';
- differentiate various types of services and understand the implications of the purchasing management process to each of these;
- have a clear understanding of how to develop a purchasing strategy for the sourcing of complex services.

Introduction

When we think of 'purchasing', we often think of buying goods and parts, i.e. manufactured items. As teachers and scholars in supply management we often talk about goods and services without differentiating between the two. In this book we decided to provide a chapter on the procurement of services, for several reasons. Firstly, we felt that this subject area is often ignored by major textbooks in the area; secondly, our industry contacts have explained that this is a very important area and that professional buyers should know about it. Finally, the purchasing of services now forms a major element of most procurement organisations' portfolios. At one time this used to be referred to as 'non-traditional' spend, i.e. these services were often not part of the general responsibility of the purchasing organisation. Purchasing professionals regarded this as bad business practice because contracts were being let for services without any professional negotiation or relationship management.

However, as purchasing takes on a much more strategic role, these non-traditional spends are now forming part of the auspices of the 'professional buyer'. Firms that have consolidated their services within the responsibility of the Purchasing department have achieved significant cost savings as well as service-level improvements. By way of an example, one large railway company interviewed as part of our research indicated that it only realised last year that it spent over £6 million on consultancy services across its business. When Purchasing consolidated this deal they were able to achieve cost savings of around 30 per cent, with a subsequent increase in the service level.

Most large firms estimate that services procurement accounts for around 35 per cent of all purchases and around 40 per cent of their total spend (including 'bought-out' goods). Services are a significant area of spending, but also represent a significant area for possible savings. This is not surprising when you consider the types of services that a typical firm purchases, ranging from professional services such as lawyers, consultants and advisers to process services such as canteen, fleet cars, travel and computing services. Service purchasers therefore have an important role to play in two respects: firstly, in making the internal processes of the organisation work, i.e. lawyers, consultants, cleaners and so on; and secondly, in facilitating the efficient operation of the supply chain itself, through the management of outsourced computer services such as invoice generation, purchase orders and payments management.

In this chapter we will develop definitions of services purchasing, discuss the basic principles and problems involved with managing services and finally introduce a framework for thinking about service purchasing strategy.

Service characteristics

Services can be defined (Kotler and Bloom, 1984) as:

> any activity or benefit that one party can offer to another that is essentially intangible and does not result in ownership. Its production may or may not be tied to a physical product.

The role of the purchasing professional in services should essentially be the same as that of buying manufactured items, namely, to gain the maximum amount of competitive advantage for the company. Naturally, this could be in the form of a price reduction, but this also includes other relationship benefits such as knowledge exchange, quality performance, timely delivery, risk and reward sharing and so on. However, within a service environment it is much more difficult to assess criteria such as quality, reliability and timeliness, as the service, by definition, is intangible.

Two words describe the service interaction: expectations and perceptions. *Expectations* refers to what the client thinks the service is going to deliver and *perceptions* refers to what the client perceives the service has delivered.

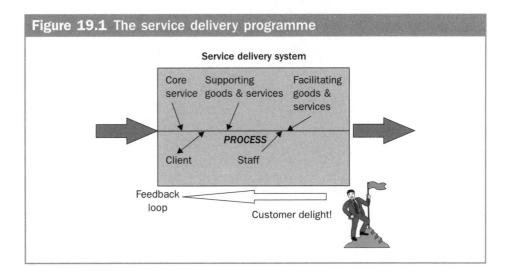

Figure 19.1 The service delivery programme

Expectations tend to be set before the service encounter (generally by marketing), and perceptions are a measure of quality during and at the end of the service experience. The means by which the service is provided is referred to as the 'service delivery system' or SDS.[1] The SDS consists of a range of elements which are shown in Figure 19.1.

The SDS illustrates a range of key issues that the Purchaser needs to be aware of when managing a service contact. The 'core service' represents the basic service that is being provided, and this needs to be clearly defined. For example, the core service of a travel agent would be providing assistance and advice on travel arrangements. The 'supporting goods and services' refers to the services that support the core process. These maybe allocating visas, delivery of tickets, providing help lines, etc. These are services that are necessary to support the day-to-day running of the business. 'Facilitating goods and services' are seen as differentiators to the business. They provide services that make the process more enjoyable but are not necessary for its efficient delivery. So, for example, there may be online booking, upgrading facilities, currency exchange and so forth. 'Clients' refer to the role that the client plays in the service encounter. So for example, some clients may want a full travel service, i.e. do nothing, where others may want to consult and chat or even do most of the booking themselves.

The client also needs to understand what the service provider can offer and to make sure it is what is needed (expectations and perceptions). It may be that the provider has various levels of service offering, which could be priced differently to allow the client or indeed the buyer to choose the specific package that would best fit their needs. 'Staff' refers to the training of the staff that interacts with the client. This is important as it is these interaction points (or touch-points)[2] that allow clients to form an understanding of the business. The service provider needs to make sure that the staff are well trained and capable of handling the types of client interaction that the client expects. Again this is a potential problem area and one that needs to be managed during the contracting stages. Finally the SDS model contains a 'feedback' loop. This aspect of the model provides information back to the provider on the client's experience of the service, and identifies opportunities for continuous improvement.

Within a purchasing context, the feedback loop feeds into what is known as the service level agreement (SLA). SLAs provide a mechanism for the buyer and supplier to measure the service being provided. They were originally developed for the computer industry when, in the late 1980s, many firms began outsourcing their computer power and departments. SLAs were set up as a payment mechanism, designed to show the reliability (or not) of the network, amount of downtime, access, etc. An SLA may be defined as:

> *A formal written agreement made between two parties: the service provider and the service recipient. It is a core concept of IT Service Management. The SLA itself defines the basis of understanding between the two parties for delivery of the service itself. The document can be quite complex, and sometimes underpins a formal contract. The contents will vary according to the nature of the service itself, but usually includes a number of core elements, or clauses. SLAs are most common for provision of IT services, particularly Internet services.*
>
> *Source*: www.wikipedia.com

Essentially, SLAs are designed to guarantee the quality of service provided to the end customer. As such, they usually contain clauses defining level of service, level of support, incentives for superior service and penalties for service failures. SLAs are now applied across a broad range of services such as travel, consultancy, legal services, cleaning and so on. In fact, they are the mechanisms that most firms use today to measure the acceptable level of service given by a provider.

The development of SLAs is a specific skill that is required for buyers who purchase services. They are not easy to produce as they are set up to measure often intangible services. Box 19.1 shows a simple example of a service level agreement.[3]

SLAs are a very important aspect of services procurement as they outline several fundamental characteristics of the relationship; in particular, what the service provider is promising to deliver, how the provider will deliver this level of service (e.g. amount of resource allocated to the project; who is responsible for delivery of the service, and how delivery will be measured). Measuring delivery is a key criterion and one which is often debated. For example, consultancy contracts tend to be awarded on a 'contingency fee' basis. The consultant's fee is contingent on them delivering what they had said they are going to deliver. This might be, for example, that they will deliver 10 per cent savings for Purchasing. But what does this mean? Is it the difference between the prices paid last time and this time? Is it a cost saving as opposed to a price saving? Is it 10 per cent in addition to what the firm's buyers could have got? Does it take account of price movements? And so on.

Our point is that it is very complicated to define a measure that meets the firm's objectives. What starts off as quite a simple task can turn out to be extremely complicated. Indeed, if these measures are not properly thought through, the provider can charge the client for its services even if the client is not convinced or happy

Box 19.1 An example of a service level agreement

Table 1 – The SLA

The *[insert service]* name is used by *[insert customer]* name to [*insert description of the service capability]*. The Internet Service Provider (ISP) guarantees that:

1 The *[service name]* will be available *[insert percentage]* of the time from *[insert normal hours of operation]* including hours and days of the week. Any individual outage in excess of *[insert time period]* or sum of outages exceeding *[insert time period]* per month will constitute a violation.

2 *[Insert percentage of service name transactions]* will exhibit *[insert value]* seconds or less response time, defined as the interval from the time the user sends a transaction to the time a visual confirmation of transaction completion is received. Missing the metric for business transactions measured over any business week will constitute a violation.

3 The IDC Customer Care team will respond to service incidents that affect multiple users (typically more than 10) within *[insert time period]*, resolve the problem within *[insert time period]*, and update status every *[insert time period]*. Missing any of these metrics on an incident will constitute a violation.

4 The IDC Customer Care team will respond to service incidents that affect individual users within *[insert time period]*, resolve the problem within *[insert time period]*, and update status every *[insert time period]*. Missing any of these metrics on an incident will constitute a violation.

5 The IDC Customer Care team will respond to non-critical inquiries within *[insert time period]*, deliver an answer within *[insert time period]*, and update status every *[insert time period]*. Missing any of these metrics on an incident will constitute a violation. A noncritical inquiry is defined as a request for information that has no impact on the service quality if not answered or acted upon promptly.

6 The external availability measurements are done by *[insert test company name]* and reported on a monthly basis to *[insert customer name]*. The internal processes are measured and reported by the ISP to the *[insert customer name]* on a monthly basis. This service includes incident reporting.

Table 2 – Monthly violations and associated penalties

- 1>5 *[Insert penalty]*. Typically a reduction in fees.

- 5>10 *[Insert penalty]*. Typically a reduction in fees plus some additional compensation and a corrective action plan.

- 10> *[Insert penalty]*. Typically a reduction in fees plus some additional compensation and a corrective action plan.

with the service that is being delivered. The SLA can be further enhanced with an operating level agreement (OLA). OLAs focus on the day-to-day management of a service delivery and tend to be extremely detailed, whereas the SLA outlines the overarching concepts involved within the delivery of the service itself.

An OLA is defined as:[4]

> An OLA *defines the interdependent relationships among the internal support groups working to support an SLA. The agreement describes the responsibilities of each internal support group toward other support groups, including the process and timeframe for delivery of their services. The objective of the OLA is to present a clear, concise and measurable description of the service provider's internal support relationships.*

The OLA provides a further level of complexity in and around the relationship and defines the roles and responsibilities of the internal resources to allow the SLA to function optimally. In other words, it is no good for a buyer to stipulate an SLA which requires input from the client and supplier and then only measure the supplier. If the client does not perform and the supplier therefore cannot perform its role, without the OLA in place the supplier would be viewed as not meeting its service requirement and would be penalised. The OLA offers protection to the supplier as well as committing resources from the buyer to make the relationship work effectively.

Service classifications

The development of SLAs and OLAs needs to be considered within the types of services that are offered to a firm. Burt and Pinkerton (1996) offer a classification of services purchasing into three distinct categories: professional, technical and operating.

Professional services refer to services provided by professional firms or individuals that tend to cover advice and management guidance. Lawyers and management consultants are excellent examples. These services have generally been purchased around a statement of work (SoW) approach, where a one-page outline of the job/task

---

Box 19.2 New computer system for NHS to improve patient care

The UK Department of Health has launched a new computer program which will provide the National Health Service (NHS) with an 'early warning' system for identifying patients with long-term conditions most at risk of admittance to hospital. The computer software is understood to use a wide range of patient data – such as the patient's age, type of illness, and recent contacts with the NHS – in order to assess which patients are most in need of care. Once prioritised, NHS care teams can then work with patients to help them maintain their health and avoid a visit to hospital. According to the UK health minister, the new system will help the NHS deliver care to people with long-term conditions.

The software has been developed for the Department of Health by the King's Fund, a charitable foundation working for better health, in partnership with researchers at New York University and Health Dialog, a care management firm specialising in analytics and chronic disease management.

Source: Telecomworldwire, 5 September 2005, New computer system for NHS to improve patient care

is drawn up and given to the professional. Whilst traditionally this has worked reasonably well, there have been a number of instances where the firm has lost a great deal of money due to unscrupulous conduct. Furthermore, these SoWs tend to have been let by managers in departments as opposed to purchasing professionals. These days, in professional purchasing organisations these services are tendered and let under an SLA, as previously discussed. Owing to the complicated nature of these services an SLA tends to be the most appropriate mechanism, despite the difficulty in defining accurate measures of performance.

Technical services refer to services provided for technical support and knowledge exchange. These may include research and development contracts, or the installation of a management information system. For example, a recent Health Services contract for the new integrated health management system linking doctors' surgeries and hospitals so that they can share patient records. See Box 19.2.

Whilst in principle this sounds like a great idea, this was a mammoth technical project and not without its difficulties. As Box 19.3 shows, this system and the

---

Box 19.3 NHS IT upgrade – managing a multi-million pound project

In 2004 it was agreed that as part of the modernisation of the NHS and its associated services a centralised information system would be necessary for the management of patient records, issuing of prescriptions and monitoring of health needs. This was a massive undertaking and would involve a consortium of consultancies and businesses working together to drive this change through. The entire project is projected to take 10 years to complete, it will network more than 30,000 GPs to nearly 3000 hospitals by 2014. It is estimated that the database will include 50 million patients with a cost of around £12.4 billion for the IT costs alone.

The National Audit Office (NAO) is responsible for making sure that Government money is spent wisely. They reported back in late 2006 saying that they felt that there was a 'lack of engagement with clinicians . . .' and that costs were beginning to rise! The NAO reported that the original £12.4bn IT bill includes £6.2bn cost of contract, which has now risen to £6.8 and is set to rise further. Predictions from a variety of sources (see bbc website) predict £20bn in spending!

In addition to the rising costs the project is also falling behind on delivery dates. The automated booking system, which is known as 'Choose to Book', is predicted to be nearly two years behind its time line. These delays could have a significant effect on the private enterprises that are underwriting the project through the Public/Private Finance Initiative. Furthermore, politicians are now becoming concerned at the increasing delays and costs and the impact that this may have on the public's perception of their leadership abilities.

This is a highly complex procurement project which has to manage a network of contacts over an extended period of time. Add to this a political dimension and possible general election and we have a highly risky procurement project which could have far reaching consequences. These can be summarised in the following quotes. Health Minister Lord Warner said: 'The project has made significant progress, but there are some areas where we could make further progress. In hindsight, there was more we could have done in consultation [with clinicians]. But I would stake my reputation that in the long term, this project will pay for itself.'

Shadow Minister for Health Stephen O'Brien said the report shed light on the delayed and 'ill-planned' NHS IT programme which the government had 'constantly tried to shield from public scrutiny'.

specification of such a system is a difficult task. Again the problem comes both from how to specify the level of service and from how to contract for delays in the delivery of the service.

These types of technical procurements of services are also very closely related to project procurement. In fact, one tends to be a subset of the other. So, for example, the project was the IT system for the NHS – the technical services to support this were contracted to the various management consultancy companies. The NHS example emphasises the complex nature of managing, specifying and obtaining damages when things go wrong with these types of services. These types of arrangements will be supported by an overarching SLA and supported by an OLA. In the NHS example, this approach allows for the allocation of resources from the NHS itself to the project as well as resources from the supplier.

Operating services refer to services that could be performed by the organisation itself but for reasons of economics or focus it has decided to outsource them. These are usually essential services that might be performed better by specialist organisations, such as catering, security, travel and agency support. The distinction between operating and professional services should be made. Professional services tend to be high-end, highly qualified individuals or firms providing professional guidance, whilst operating services tend to be commodity-based services required for the day-to-day running of the business. These types of businesses are often referred to as facilities management (FM).

Facilities management is defined as:[5]

> *The process whereby one firm (the contracting firm) enters into a fixed length contract with another (the contractor) where the contractor agrees to operate and maintain the contracting firm's information systems. The contracting firm normally agrees to provide all or a specified part of the necessary Information Systems equipment and supplies, and the contractor provides its own employees and management.*

These services are vitally important to the smooth running of the organisation and, like the previous types of service, will require the negotiation of SLAs and sometimes OLAs to support them. There can be massive problems involved in the management of facilities and also the role of purchasing in managing this process.

The next section will build on these definitions and introduce a services taxonomy model.

Purchasing services: a taxonomy-based approach

So far we have discussed some of the issues involved in managing service purchasing and have emphasised the use of service-level and operational-level agreements. We now consider Kraljic's product positioning matrix, modified to fit within the procurement service concept (see Figure 19.2). Remember that the original matrix

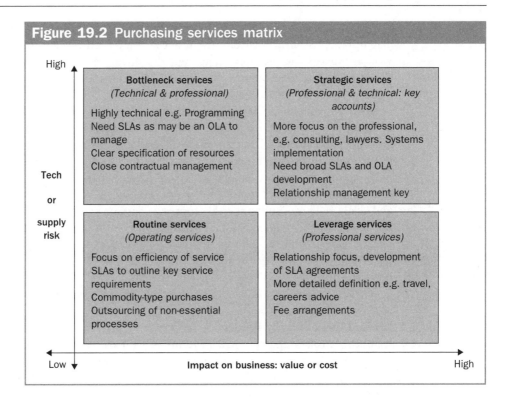

Figure 19.2 Purchasing services matrix

High

Tech

or

supply risk

Low

Bottleneck services
(Technical & professional)

Highly technical e.g. Programming
Need SLAs as may be an OLA to manage
Clear specification of resources
Close contractual management

Strategic services
(Professional & technical: key accounts)

More focus on the professional, e.g. consulting, lawyers. Systems implementation
Need broad SLAs and OLA development
Relationship management key

Routine services
(Operating services)

Focus on efficiency of service
SLAs to outline key service requirements
Commodity-type purchases
Outsourcing of non-essential processes

Leverage services
(Professional services)

Relationship focus, development of SLA agreements
More detailed definition e.g. travel, careers advice
Fee arrangements

Impact on business: value or cost — High

refers to critical, bottleneck, leverage and routine items. These can be redefined as: strategic services, bottleneck services, routine services, and leverage services. Each of these will now be discussed below.

Strategic services. These are services that are seen as having a high impact on the business. For example, consulting or legal services. Services that fall into this box are high cost and value but also high in terms of technical skills. They would be seen as 'strategically important' to the business. Previously, we defined such services as 'Professional services' due to their high value/cost. However, for the purposes of this approach, we can further divide them into 'strategic' services (both high technical and value/cost content) and 'leverage' services. Leverage services are still provided by professionals in the marketplace; however, they are less technical and more readily available, for example travel services. 'Leverage services' are discussed in more detail below.

Owing to their complex nature, strategic services will require SLA development, though the terms of definition will remain rather broad (i.e. by their nature professional services cannot be highly specified). The key for the purchasing professional here is to manage these relationships through a 'key account' type of process. For example, the firm might appoint a relationship manager to manage the 'Accenture' projects. This is important as this person can act as a key informant between and within their firm. The focus of the purchaser is managing and developing the relationship, gaining benefits from knowledge transfer and focusing on cost reduction strategies. These strategic-level services will also require OLAs to support the SLAs. The buyer must clearly specify the role that they need to play to support this service, as well as the resources that the supplier/provider is prepared to commit to the project. The OLA and SLA will then be measured on a regular basis.

Leverage services. Leverage services are service offerings that have a high value or cost, but are much more commodity focused (i.e. the skills are less technical and there is a range of service providers). Travel services, for example, would often fall into this category. Travel requires knowledge of the marketplace, routes, airlines, hotels and so on. However, whilst it requires knowledge it is not highly technical. Leverage services can be let on an SLA, which although relatively broad, can contain more definition of the type of services, call-back times, value for money and deals that are built into the contract. Some consulting contracts could also fall into this box (e.g. workshops delivering specific training). The point to emphasise here is that the title of this box is 'leverage' – therefore the buyer should be aiming to get the best deal possible for the firm, as well as more closely specifying the SLA.

Bottleneck services. These services apply predominately to what we defined as technical services, but also some highly technical professional services might fall into this category. Bottleneck services have the characteristic of being highly technical but are relatively low in terms of value or cost. For example, particular software skills that individuals might provide such as computer programming, debugging and so on. Subcontract staff could also fall into this role where they are being recruited to work on a particular project for the duration of their contract. Owing to the high technical content there may be a need for a basic OLA to be developed to allocate supporting resources to the contract. The SLA will also clearly outline the roles and obligations. An SoW may also be given to the individual or firm to outline their contractual obligations. Whilst these services might not be high cost, they have the propensity to harm the day-to-day operation of the organisation.

Routine services. These tend to be low-skill commodity-type services such as catering, security or cleaning contracts. The position of these services depends on the nature of the organisation and also on the type of service. For example, specialist security, cleaning and catering services could easily fall into any of the categories listed in the model. The deciding point for the firm is what impact they see these services having on their businesses. Indeed, sometimes firms can get this wrong! Take, for example, the recent issues with cleaning services and MRSA in hospitals, or school dinners (see Box 19.4).

The purchasing of routine services falls under our previous definition of operating services. Here the focus of the buyer should be on acquiring and maintaining an efficient service. SLAs are issued to service providers within this category; the focus is on efficiency, speed and price reduction. Any service falling into this category should be viewed on the basis of providing good 'value for money'. As per our definition of operating services, these are generally viewed as non-processes that are currently undertaken by the organisation itself; however, they can be carried out more economically (and indeed professionally) by specific service providers.

Box 19.4 New action for cleaner, safer hospitals, UK

UK Health Secretary John Reid today published plans to cut the level of hospital-acquired infections like MRSA and improve general standards of hygiene. He published a document, 'Towards Cleaner Hospitals and Lower Rates of Infection', which makes clear how the NHS and Department of Health will take forward action in these areas. John Reid said: 'Cleanliness remains a major patient concern and MRSA is a growing problem. My approach is to be open about this. Cleanliness contributes to controlling infection, but preventing infections requires more than just cleanliness. I will ensure every hospital publishes and displays its infection rates and trends, since patients have the right to know. Patients will have a choice of hospitals by the end of next year and this could become a factor in their decision. In hospital I want NHS patients to demand the highest standards of hygiene and – since human contact is a major way infection spreads in hospital – to feel happy to ask staff if they've washed their hands. I will ask local patients forums to conduct cleanliness inspections four times a year, using a checklist drawn up by infection control nurses, and the results will be made public. As bedside phones are introduced I want them to have a pre-programmed housekeeping button so patients and visitors can be put through to the hospital's cleaning service straight away. At the same time I will give matrons and nurses at ward level the power to ensure high standards are maintained. That means putting matrons in charge of cleaners. And it means putting alcohol rubs at all staff patient contact points.'

'Cleanliness is as important to the public as waiting times. Putting it at the heart of the NHS inspection regime and introducing a new target to cut MRSA will ensure that the whole NHS gives this issue the same high priority that the public does. Because MRSA rates vary from hospital to hospital I want the whole NHS to learn from the best at home and abroad. So I will fly in experts from countries with low MRSA to advise the NHS on improving infection control. But improved cleanliness alone will not alone tackle the problem of super bugs like MRSA.'

Source: Medical News Today, www.medicalnewstoday.com/sections/mrsa-superbug

Developing a strategy for services purchasing

This section aims to give the reader a brief overview of developing a strategy to manage services purchasing. Figure 19.3 represents the six distinct stages in developing a services purchasing strategy: analysis, focus, contract development/deployment, relationship strategy, implementation and feedback. Each of these stages will now be discussed in turn.

Stage 1: Analysis

The analysis stage involves the purchasing professional firstly identifying all of the services (non-traditional spend items) within the firm. This should be done via a firm-wide exercise where each budget or account centre reveals its spend on various outside services. A Pareto analysis will allow the buyer to identify high-, medium- and low-spend items. This will allow for positioning on the horizontal axis on the

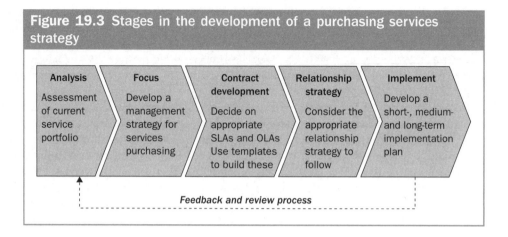

Figure 19.3 Stages in the development of a purchasing services strategy

services matrix. Secondly, the buyer will also assess the level of technical competences of the service. It is worth pointing out at this juncture that the Kraljic matrix positions services, *not* companies. This is an important distinction. For example, a supplier could provide a range of services which might stretch across one, two, three or all four segments of the model. Each service may represent a different technical competence and/or supply risk. It is the professional judgement of the buyer that dictates the positioning here. Once the analysis phase is complete we can proceed to stage 2.

Stage 2: Focus

The second stage of the model is known as 'focus'. During this stage the buyer will position all of the services into the various segments of the model. The buyer can then also link up which services belong to which supplier. If there are overlaps into the various segments, various sourcing decisions can be made either to consolidate with one supplier or to leave the supply spread over a number of suppliers in a number of segments of the model. At this point the buyer needs to understand the range of strategies that can be applied to the various service providers. Figure 19.4 illustrates this point. Services a, b and c are provided by one firm and services d, e and f are provided by another. The buyer may decide to consolidate with one or other supplier or not. If not, then varying strategies will have to be applied to each service group, i.e. different strategies with the same suppliers, depending on the service being provided.

Stage 3: Contract development

Once the buyer has completed this positioning exercise, the next stage of contract development is reached. During this stage the buyer must use the matrix to decide which SLAs and OLAs to apply and develop appropriate metrics for each. They

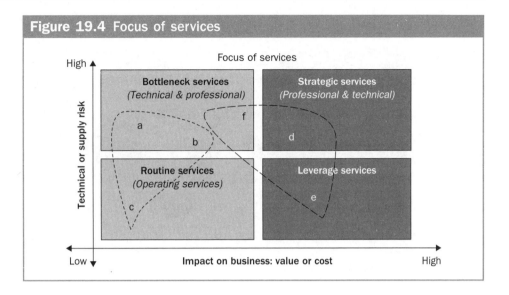

Figure 19.4 Focus of services

will work closely with management within the firm, as well as conduct detailed negotiations with the supplier. This is a crucial element of the process. During this phase the buyer will need to focus on the internal management systems, measurement systems, and reward and penalty mechanisms.

Stage 4: Relationship strategy

The development of a relationship strategy is critical. The basis of the thinking here should be on what is the *appropriate* relationship approach to deliver the benefits to the firm. For example, strategic services will require a collaborative relationship approach, whereas routine services will be much more arm's-length in nature. We refer the reader to the relationship management chapters earlier in this book for a detailed discussion of this area.

Stage 5: Implementation

The penultimate stage is 'implementation'. Implementation is concerned with the practical aspects of managing the strategy. One approach is to divide the various activities that are required to manage the strategy into two areas: time and money. For example, the strategy might involve working with a firm to focus on a range of cost-saving projects, or improvements in service levels. Figure 19.5 illustrates this idea.

The figure shows projects or tasks which might be anything from process improvement to process redesign. These projects tend to get bigger over time. The implementation chart is a mechanism to allow the buyer to focus sequentially on a range of important issues.

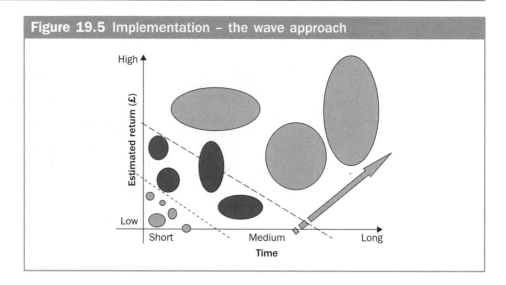

Figure 19.5 Implementation – the wave approach

Stage 6: Feedback

The final section of our model is the feedback and review process. This process takes the implementation plan and revisits the original model in an iterative manner. This process helps the buyer to develop a purchasing strategy for services procurement and to refine and develop it over time, being proactive as opposed to reactive to the external environment.

Summary

This chapter set out to give the reader a clear understanding of the complexities and intricacies of managing services procurement. Our aim in this chapter is to give the reader an overview of this area and for detailed discussions on particular topics such as service level agreements, contracting methods, and operations level agreements. The purchasing of services is an interesting and different area of procurement. Whilst it shares some similarities with the purchasing of products, there are indeed some distinctive differences. On reading this chapter, we hope the reader is more fully aware of services procurement and how to develop a strategy for the purchasing of services.

Seminar questions

1. Highlight the main differences between the purchasing of services and the purchasing of goods.

2. Define, in your own words, the terms 'service level agreement' and 'operating level agreement'.

3. Using case studies, differentiate various types of services and discuss the implications of the purchasing management process for each of these.

4. Develop a purchasing strategy for the sourcing of complex services in a company of your choice.

References

Burt, D. N. and Pinkerton, R. L. (1996) *A Purchasing Manager's Guide to Strategic Proactive Procurement*, AMACOM, New York.

Carlzon, J. (1987) *Moments of Truth*, Ballinger Publishing, Cambridge, MA.

Kotler, P. and Bloom, P. N. (1984) *Marketing Professional Services*, Prentice Hall, New Jersey.

Normann, R. (2005) *Service Management System*, 3rd edn, Wiley, New York.

Further reading

Croom, S. R. and Johnston, R. (2003) 'E-service: Enhancing Internal Customer Service Through e-procurement', *International Journal of Service Industry Management*, Vol. 14 (5), pp. 539–55.

Lings, I. N. (2000) 'Internal Marketing and Supply Chain Management', *The Journal of Services Marketing*, Vol. 14 (1), pp. 27–39.

Quinn, J. B. (1999) 'Strategic Outsourcing: Leveraging Knowledge Capabilities', *Sloan Management Review*, Vol. 40 (4), pp. 9–21.

Silvestro, R. (1999) 'Positioning Services Along the Volume-variety Diagonal: The Contingencies of Service Design, Control and Improvement', *International Journal of Operations and Production Management*, Vol. 19 (4), pp. 399–412.

Woo, K.-S. and Ennew, C. T. (2005) 'Measuring Business-to-business Professional Service Quality and its Consequences', *Journal of Business Research*, Vol. 58 (9), pp. 1178–85.

Endnotes

1. For an interesting discussion on this, please refer to Normann (2005).
2. See Jan Carlzon's 'Moments of Truth' (Carlzon, 1987) for a discussion on the importance of touch-points for managing customer interactions.
3. See www.sun.com/blueprints for a detailed discussion document of SLAs. This example is taken from this document.
4. See for a detailed discussion and definitions http://www.oit.duke.edu/enterprise/SLA-OLA/
5. www.dai-sho.com/pgsa2/pgsa-glossary.html

Part 4

FUTURE DIRECTIONS

Chapter 20

The future – a trajectory for supply management

The significant problems we face cannot be solved at the same level of thinking we were at when we created them.

Albert Einstein

Introduction

Our final chapter summarises the work we have presented and also provides the reader with some thoughts for the future. It was our aim to create a book that could be used in a variety of ways by a broad range of interest groups. We aimed to produce a text that is *scholarly*, giving a good overview of the base theories of economics and sociology that underpin supply management. Each chapter contains links and discussions on base theories that underpin its particular subject matter. We have also tried to make the book *practical* in its focus, to appeal to readers who are interested in understanding and improving their existing purchasing operations. Finally, we have tried to make this book *accessible* in its style and use of examples and treatment of the subject matter. We believe that this book offers a comprehensive coverage of the main subject areas of supply management; it incorporates a wide range of experience and subject knowledge from academia, consultancy and practice, which we hope will offer real value to our readers.

Summary and conclusion of the book

We began this book by introducing the concept of the supply wheel as a way of structuring thinking with regard to supply management. We intend to conclude by offering the chance to think about this subject area in a more abstract manner by posing some questions and thoughts on the future of supply chain management as both a discipline and potential career choice.

The book has four distinct sections, the last consisting simply of this chapter. In Part 1, we overviewed the subject area of supply management and its major academic development over the past two decades. There is now a significant body of knowledge available, from theoretical to applications-based thinking. The predominant theories seeking to explain *why* firms transact in the ways they do emanate from economics. This is not a surprise as economics is concerned with both the firm (micro) as a unit of analysis and also the wider issues of firm behaviour within the external environment (macro). Supply management thinking is underpinned by two main economic theories: transaction cost economics (TCE) and the resource-based view (RBV). These theories provide the underlying foundations for the 'discipline' of supply management to emerge and evolve.

In Part 2, we focused on '*what*' firms focus upon when thinking about strategic change. Part 2 focused specifically on the development of inter-firm relationships, with specific emphasis on sourcing configurations, supplier selection and supplier development. In Part 3, we provided a focused and structured thinking approach to supply chain management. In order to frame our thinking we returned to the concept of the supply wheel, building on the foundations presented in Part 1, and translating the theoretical perspectives in order to drive strategy and change. We saw that, if an organisation is TCE driven, it will be more cost focused; if it is more RBV driven, it will be focused on relationship development, collaboration and competence delivery.

We also focused on '*how*' firms should implement supply management solutions. This part explored some of the more specific strategies and approaches undertaken by firms in the management of supply activity. These include issues such as e-commerce, environmental and ethical issues, commodity management, public procurement and involving suppliers in new product development. All of these are current issues and problems facing supply management. In this final chapter, in addition to our brief summary of the book, we present our far-reaching view of the future.

Theory development in supply chain management

Supply management is beginning to emerge as a discipline in its own right, with theories and concepts that underpin and explain the various strategies and approaches being adopted by firms. The grounded theoretical perspective provided by TCE is being developed to explain the more complex nature of organisational evolution, from supply dyads to complex and realistic supply models such as networks. Theories such as the RBV and the relational view, which have been so influential in the strategy literature, are now being used to underpin and explain changes of thinking and practice occurring in supply management.

Social capital theory is also becoming popular in supply management research, in examining the roles and behaviours of individuals within the organisation. It helps to explain why people behave as they do. There is a close link between social capital and the concept of relational capital, which is used to understand how and why relationships operate as they do. These theories are very useful in explaining complex network interactions specifically associated with the delivery of competitive advantage from 'rents' acquired through focused used of both firm and inter-firm resources. However, there is still a great deal of theoretical development needed, for example categorising and describing groups of resources, understanding the complex interrelationships between resources and calculating the optimum mix of resources to extract the maximum amount of 'rents' from these interactions.

E. O. Wilson's work on consilience is helpful here. Wilson (1998) explains consilience as the bringing together of knowledge from a range of disciplines to create new knowledge and ways of solving problems in other disciplines, e.g. the use of mathematics and physics to help with biological and neurological problems such as gene sequencing. Supply management needs much more development of theories, unavailable from one source alone (e.g. an over-reliance on political science or neoclassical economics). Consilience is needed to bring together theories and concepts from a range of disciplines in order to create new and applicable knowledge for supply management.

Future directions in supply management

Having discussed and reviewed the development of the subject of supply it is now appropriate to consider the direction and future of the subject area. In a book such as this it is sometimes difficult to step outside the linear development of arguments and take a wider, unprejudiced, perspective on the topic. We have discussed above some theoretical issues affecting supply; we now consider some of the more practical issues for the implementation of these ideas. The question that we seek to address in the last section of this chapter is *'What will supply management look like in the future for practitioners?'*

What will supply management look like in the future for practitioners?

Trying to predict the future is always good fun and many people do it. One cannot be proved wrong until much later, of course, and this is part of the appeal. One can track specific trends but this tends to result in uninspiring conclusions. For example, it appears clear that the application of Internet technologies will increase and that the use of e-auctions will spread. It is possible to suggest that supply strategists will begin to work with value rather than price, complexity rather than simplification, and deliberate, designed and managed relationships (whether innovative and collaborative or power-ridden and adversarial) rather than haphazard dealing and delinquent negotiation tactics which quickly result in suppliers charging risk premia.

We may expect consumers to become more aware of the origins of products, so that ethical and environmental issues will become more 'front of mind' for supply strategists in sourcing. The march of global trading and the rise of the BRIC[1] economies may be expected to present major new challenges for the design and management of supply chains and networks, as well as opportunities for innovation in logistics and competition through choice of geographies. Who would have predicted 10 years ago that in 2006 IBM would move its global procurement headquarters from New York to Shenzhen?[2]

Outsourcing and the breaking up of monolithic organisations may be expected to increase and with it the need for different types of communication and information sharing. Public sector procurement strategists may become even more like their private sector counterparts, although it is unlikely that the complexity of spending public money on societal needs, and the constraints it places on government officers, will abate.

We could focus on the individual – the need for 'smart' thinking, true strategic awareness and the ability to innovate by jettisoning redundant practices to adopt new thinking; the educational and training aspects of these trends alone could fill a book.

The real challenge in describing the future is how far we can *usefully* depart from the safe approach of extrapolating present trends in a linear fashion – predictable trajectories for practices already on the drawing board. The bold approach might be to imagine radical discontinuities for the profession – casting the current debates, opportunities, challenges and arenas for competition as what Edmund Burke called 'a nursery of future revolutions'. All we can do with the future is think. And, as Einstein warns us, we need a different level of thinking to address problems that we have created for ourselves.

Taking the bold approach, but striving to produce something useful for present-day strategists, we can think differently by using an allegorical framework, populated by working situations and characters whose behaviours might be very different from today but understandable in terms of business (or social) models that we recognise in other spheres. Doing this, we can create a mental picture that provokes debate on the future of purchasing and supply chain management – focusing especially on the role of the people who work in what we like to refer to as a profession.

In workshops and seminars, this picture (drawn on a flip chart) is capable of generating hours of argument. It has been tested and developed in many seminars, conferences and boardrooms over the past few years. For practical purposes, it is incomplete; it is the role of the strategist to decide what happens next for their particular organisation – what pieces need to be added to make the picture entire. It has generated several new expressions to describe how organisations might prepare for the future. We have not included these here as they are still the confidential property of the Supply Strategists who thought them up, inspired by the debate started by the picture. Neither have we drawn the picture on these pages; instead it is for each reader to create their own version, and decide what to do about it.

The future for purchasing and supply – an allegory[3]

Imagine a large, lofty room. We are viewing it in cross-section, so it appears on the page as a simple rectangle, stood on its end. Perhaps it has a pitch roof, like a house – you decide. This is the *Purchasing Office* of the future.

Standing in the room (let's place it to the left) is a very large, shiny, smooth, black metal object. It is slim and tall, reaching almost to the ceiling. It looks very expensive; it is warm and there is a gentle humming coming from it; perhaps it has its own character and perhaps some people would even give it a nickname. From time to time it appears to be vibrating a little, but the interruption in its general calm appearance soon subsides. This is the *Black Box*.

To the right, next to the Black Box, stands a man: a Buyer. Between the Black Box and the Buyer sits a very ferocious-looking dog. The dog is constantly barking at the Buyer.

That is all there is on the floor of the room.

Half-way up the wall there is a shelf. It does not look very robust – in fact its support strut appears to be almost broken (it is not clear whether it has rotted, whether some shock has fractured it, or whether someone has deliberately sawn halfway through it). Let us call this the *Shaky Shelf*. It is a fairly large shelf, indeed it holds a desk and chair. Sitting at the desk is another man: the *Purchasing Manager*. He has rolled-up shirtsleeves and one of those old-fashioned green eye-shades. On the desk are photographs of his wife and children; there is a presentation ashtray, sporting the logo of a supplier, and a cigarette lighter in the form of an antique pistol. And there are six well-sharpened pencils, all neatly lined up on the desk like soldiers. The telephone is covered in what appear to be cobwebs; it does not ring. The Purchasing Manager is tapping away on a computer but it is unclear why – his computer screen is blank.

That is all there is in the Purchasing Office.

There are other characters in the picture but we shall return to them later. Let us explain the scene in the room first.

The Black Box does all the purchasing (it is actually not referred to as this but as 'supply'). It carries out interpretation of requirements from everyone in the organisation who requires supplies, products and services, commodities and bespoke items. It deals with designers and specifiers. It selects sources, it negotiates, it runs online auctions, accesses portals and conducts relationship management, including performance measurement of its own organisation (as a 'customer', although the term is no longer used), of suppliers, and of each unique customer–supplier relationship. It deals with all the commercial issues of what used to be called purchase orders and invoices, it sorts and solves problems, it liaises with lawyers on terms and conditions and, where necessary, liquidates damages. If the organisation is in the public sector, the Black Box deals with all the associated regulatory requirements. The Black Box works 24 hours a day, in the dark, providing its own warmth. It does not have lunch. And it doesn't accept gifts from suppliers.

It becomes apparent that the Buyer is only there to look after the Black Box, listening to its hum and ensuring it has proper ventilation, maintenance and security. He does not actually touch the Black Box but contacts specialists who will visit if anything more than dusting is required. Oh, and he feeds the dog. That is all the Buyer does. We can rename him the *Caretaker*.

The dog is there to ensure that the Caretaker never interferes with the Black Box. We can call it the *Guard Dog*.

The Purchasing Manager on the shaky shelf justifies his existence by writing explanations of how he 'adds value'. He is very good at this. There is not much to do, other than watch the Caretaker dust the Black Box. Occasionally an e-mail will arrive, giving the Purchasing Manager an opportunity to add value, although it is not clear how. If the Purchasing Manager picks up the phone, hits the computer or even breathes too hard, the Shaky Shelf trembles and appears to droop a little more, threatening the safe position of the Purchasing Manager (and possibly the Caretaker, beneath him!).

This is the internal future of the Purchasing Office. It may not be very attractive for people in Purchasing but it is good news for the organisation that needs effective supply.

Let us look upwards to the sky.

High above the room, flying through the skies, there is an aeroplane. It never lands. Instead, it flies around the world constantly. In the aeroplane is a character who represents the future of Supply. She is constantly on the phone and the Internet (through technology built into her clothing and body) communicating with Black Boxes all over the world. On behalf of her clients she is 'shopping the world'. She is the *Deal Shaper*.

The Deal Shaper is making deals to buy and sell products and services for the organisation, connecting potential customers and suppliers wherever they are located. Deals may make (or lose) billions of reals, rubles, rupees or yuan for her clients so the Deal Shaper's role is crucial in their survival. As the Deal Shaper works in many markets, she plays the role of the arbitrager – exploiting price, capacity and availability differences between exchanges. As she sees all parts of the world, she is aware of the ethical and environmental issues in the supply deals they set up and nurture and can advise the organisation on implications and risks. She is expert at spotting innovations that have potential (although she needs help with this, as we shall see).

The Deal Shaper is young, between 25 and 35. At the end of that 10-year period she will be tired but rich, ready not to retire but to move to what Charles Handy calls 'the portfolio' – dividing her time between paid activity, *pro bono* activity, charity work, learning, home and recreation. She is well qualified, with a combination of business and technical education (to the equivalent of today's Masters level) along with a good amount of traditional business 'nous' or acumen.

The Deal Shaper is not an employee but an entrepreneurial agent – self-employed and fully international, easily working for several organisations at once, in a variety of arrangements (consortia, loyalty contracts, global networks, etc.). She speaks 12 languages and is expert in handling complex numerical data in real time. The tools she uses are complicated, based on concepts such as systems modelling, fuzzy logic, complexity, soft systems theory, chaos theory, game theory, the semantic web and neural networks.

The Deal Shaper is the future of Supply. The deals she makes and the inter-organisational relationships she nurtures are the essence and energy of Supply. She is a remarkable person.

But the Deal Shaper is engaged on the business of the day. She sees all sorts of things but is not able to spend time idling, musing, reflecting – or exploring. These are the activities required to capture innovation. Since it is now broadly recognised that Supply Strategists must include innovation in their responsibilities, how does this fit into our allegory? Lower down the picture, perhaps to the right, we find the answer.

A figure clad in pith helmet and safari suit appears, parting the jungle plants with her hands so that we can see her face, grinning at us. Or perhaps we see her hacking at the undergrowth with her machete. It is difficult to tell what age she is. She is exploring dark environments, where no one has been before. She does not seek to exploit them in a drastic manner (such as clearing forests to grow soya beans or destroying wetlands to farm prawns) but to learn, to get excited, to be enlightened. She is the *Discoverer*.

The Discoverer works alone – much as the Deal Shaper does – following her nose, hanging around in shops and bars to pick up on conversations between the people who might be her customers. Or, rather, the people who might be her clients' customers, for the Discoverer is unlikely ever to run a stable business with real customers. She makes her living by realising brilliant ideas – innovations – from dark environments. Such innovations may sometimes be discontinuous, or even disruptive in Clayton Christensen's terminology (Christensen, 1997). She is in touch with several Deal Shapers – perhaps with one or two favourites. She relies on them for the work on the street; they rely on her for what is in the wind. She doesn't need to contact the Black Box, and the Deal Shaper makes sure that she is comfortably off without needing to do so (because the Deal Shaper wants that connection all to herself).

When this picture emerges in a workshop there is always a lot of discomfort in the room: not with its plausibility, which is usually agreed (albeit interpreted in a variety of ways), but with the age issue. 'What if I am over 35?' someone will say. 'Is the only place for me the Shaky Shelf? I don't have the courage to become the Discoverer at my time of life!'

The answer to this might lie in the final character – a possible role for the successful purchasing heroes who wish to remain in the picture. Whether or not they can fill this role will depend on the interpretation of the model that is used to understand it – but more of this later.

Strictly speaking, this character is not in the picture. He may be imagined sitting back on a sun-drenched terrace overlooking a beautiful blue ocean and white sandy beach under a palm tree. Perhaps he is sipping a dry martini and watching baseball on his hologram video player. This character – let us call him the *Maestro* – appears relaxed but is actually constantly in touch with many Deal Shapers, co-ordinating their activities, putting people in touch with suitable partners, forecasting and future gazing, maintaining grace and memory for the busy, shifting world of supply. Perhaps the Maestro was once a Deal Shaper, perhaps a different kind of entrepreneur. The nice thing about the Maestro character is that he could be any age, and long experience may be the critical factor in his marketability. There is a darker side to this character, however. He is in touch with governments and other organised bodies that can effect macroeconomic change. This might run as far as controlling supplies of commodities, pressurising legitimate authorities and influencing political agendas. The Maestro has considerable power.

Making sense of the allegory

The whole point of using an allegory to discuss the future is that it may be accepted as a broad view and then interpreted in a number of detailed ways – perhaps as many different ways as the number of people who view the picture. Interpretation needs models, however – sets of logical connections that we use to make sense of (we might say 'understand') what we are looking at. Of course, the selection of models is also very personal and will determine the nature of our conclusion. In the nineteenth century, for example, we might have chosen to make sense of a steam engine by applying thermodynamics (i.e. how it works) or social discourse (i.e. its utility in changing people's lives and opening up whole countries). This works for everything from envelopes to empires.

Here are our suggestions for some models that may be used to make sense of our allegory.

The *Caretaker* and the *Purchasing Manager*. Model: the welfare state. What do you do with large numbers of people made redundant by a lack of demand for their skills? Do you provide work for them through public spending, or pay them unemployment benefit? (Note: we do not seek to go any further than this in suggesting the application of our chosen models!)

The Guard Dog. Two models suggest themselves here. The first is that used in technology management – the rules for managing the maintenance of new technologies as they interfere with work patterns. (This would be a strict process control approach, perhaps mixed with some change management models.) The second is less straightforward and connects the Guard Dog to the Maestro: this is a model based on industrial espionage and we shall return to it later.

The Deal Shaper. It is tempting to model this character simply on the well-known 'trader' in commodities or derivative markets, perhaps with a sideways glance at agency theory. Indeed, this may suffice. There may be a more radical interpretation, however; perhaps a cartel model, or even a more sinister view, akin to a black market or buccaneering.

The Discoverer. The obvious model of the explorer, including paradigms such as curiosity-led research (how science and engineering work) and good old-fashioned pioneering spirit ('Because it is there!')[4] will probably suffice. To get a better handle on the character – and especially how to work with him or her – it is probably more useful to consider the model of a classic entrepreneur/inventor.

The Maestro. While the Deal Shaper is perhaps the pivotal role in the picture, it is the Maestro that should attract the most attention (if only because he will try to avoid it!). The model here appears to be that of organised crime. This character must be able to bring about very significant changes to suit his own agenda – beyond the impacts that are possible through entirely legal activity. It is probable that these will include such things as interference in developing economies (for example, the supply of rare minerals from central African states) and it is possible that such influence could lead to (or prevent) wars. This sounds extreme but the allegory must allow for very profound developments such as this.

Some of the connections between characters are indicated in the picture already. But what about second-order links? For example, when the Deal Shaper gets tired of the travelling and is rich enough to buy her own island, perhaps she will want to become a Maestro. This might happen through patronage (the old Maestro lays down his wand and becomes a disembodied spirit; the new hero picks up the sword, etc.). Or perhaps the Deal Shaper contacts her friends (Deal Shapers and Discoverers) and seeks their support as she challenges the Maestro for his throne. Or perhaps two Maestros fight and one dies, leaving a void to be filled by the fittest Deal Shaper. This is how the allegory makes us think – at a different level. Where such thoughts lead depends on who is doing the thinking.